Sale of Goods

Keith ¾ Lord
¾
28th June, 1975

At Nottingham

Sale of Goods

By

D. W. GREIG

M.A., LL.B., Barrister,
Professor of Law of
the Australian National University

LONDON
BUTTERWORTHS
1974

ENGLAND: BUTTERWORTH & CO. (PUBLISHERS) LTD.
LONDON: 88 KINGSWAY, WC2B 6AB

AUSTRALIA: BUTTERWORTHS PTY. LTD.
SYDNEY: 386 PACIFIC HIGHWAY, CHATSWOOD, NSW 2067
MELBOURNE: 343 LITTLE COLLINS STREET, 3000
BRISBANE: 240 QUEEN STREET, 4000

CANADA: BUTTERWORTH & CO. (CANADA) LTD.
TORONTO: 2265 MIDLAND AVENUE, SCARBOROUGH, M1P 4S1

NEW ZEALAND: BUTTERWORTHS OF NEW ZEALAND LTD.
WELLINGTON: 26–28 WARING TAYLOR STREET, 1

SOUTH AFRICA: BUTTERWORTH & CO. (SOUTH AFRICA) (PTY.) LTD.
DURBAN: 152–154 GALE STREET

ISBN—Casebound: 0 406 59190 3
Limp: 0 406 59191 1

Made and Printed in Great Britain at Chapel River Press, Andover, Hants

Preface

The law of sale of goods has been undergoing a series of changes. Both Parliament and the courts have been involved in this process. However, the amendments and developments have taken place in piecemeal fashion with little regard for the overall framework. Hence the present law can only be ascertained by reference to the Sale of Goods Act of 1893; to a number of pre-1893 cases which shed light on the meaning of the Act; to the post-1893 authorities which have refined or even altered the law; and to the Supply of Goods (Implied Terms) Act 1973 which has amended or affected the application of the 1893 Act. Furthermore, it is becoming increasingly difficult to explain the law of sale in the form of a commentary on the Act because many important developments in the general law of contract, though highly relevant to the sale of goods, fall outside the compass of the Act.

In the absence of a new codifying statute, the prospects for which are not encouraging, some reassessment is necessary because of the fragmentary state of the law. Hence the primary objective of this book is to synthesise the various fragments and to present the law of sale as a more unified whole. In pursuing this aim, a detailed examination has been undertaken of a large number of decisions. Use has also been made of Australian and New Zealand cases where these provide helpful illustrations of the application of the Act or offer alternative solutions to problems that have not been resolved satisfactorily by the English courts. This emphasis on the case law has a two-fold advantage. It will enable the student, whether he is studying sale of goods as part of a degree course, or for a professional examination, to see how the law has been applied in practice. And for the practitioner engaged in litigation, actual or prospective, the book will provide a comprehensive survey of those authorities which are likely to be relevant to his particular case.

The law has been stated to the end of 1973.

August, 1974   D. W. GREIG

Table of Contents

Table of Statutes

References in this Table to " Statutes " are to Halsbury's Statutes of England (Third Edition) showing the volume and page at which the annotated text of the Act will be found.

List of Cases

Introduction

Whatever may be the social implications of hire purchase as a means of acquiring goods, by far the most common method of acquiring them is the contract of sale. Even though the family car may belong to a finance company and be in the possession of the head of the household only as hirer, the family's food, its clothing, its toys and so on will normally have been obtained under a multitude of contracts of sale. And in the commercial world, it is far more likely that, however the financing of a transaction or series of transactions is arranged indirectly, the transaction itself will involve an out and out transfer of property in the goods under a contract of sale.

Unlike much of the law of contract, sale of goods has been codified, that is put in statutory form, by the Sale of Goods Act 1893.[1]. Consequently, when the law of sale is examined, the tendency is to follow the lines set out in the Act. This approach is certainly in keeping with the often quoted pronouncement of Lord HERSCHELL[2] that, in dealing with codifying legislation, "the proper course is, in the first instance, to examine the language of the statute and to ask what is its meaning", but the time has come for the sale of goods to be looked at afresh.

The second half of the nineteenth century saw the courts making valiant efforts to keep the law in touch with the needs of commerce. The Sale of Goods Act had two unfortunate effects. In the first place the Act did not in all respects accurately reproduce the pre-existing law. Secondly, the general effect of codifying the law is inevitably to render it static, and the law of sale was a branch of the law that needed to develop further if it was to answer the requirements of twentieth-century society. That this danger has not proved more serious has been due to the efforts of a number of the judges who have not been prepared to follow only the precise wording and implications of the Code. But the danger still exists as was made clear by Lord DIPLOCK in giving this recent warning:[3]

> "Unless the Sale of Goods Act 1893 is to be allowed to fossilise the law and to restrict the freedom of choice of parties to contracts for the sale of goods to make agreements which take account of advances in technology and changes in the way in which business is carried on today, the provisions set out in the various sections and sub-sections of the code ought not to be construed so narrowly as to force on parties to contracts for the sale of goods promises and consequences different from what they must reasonably have intended.

---

1 Though the "rules of the common law including the law merchant" continue to apply unless inconsistent with the Act: s. 61 (2).
2 *Bank of England* v. *Vagliano Bros.*, [1891] A.C. 107, at p. 144; [1891–4] All E.R. Rep. 93, at p. 113: Lord HERSCHELL was speaking of the Bills of Exchange Act.
3 *Ashington Piggeries Ltd.* v. *Christopher Hill, Ltd.*, [1972] A.C. 441, at p. 501; [1971] 1 All E.R. 847, at p. 882.

> They should be treated rather as illustrations of the application to simple types of contract of general principles for ascertaining the common intention of the parties as to their mutual promises and their consequences, which ought to be applied by analogy in cases arising out of contracts which do not appear to have been within the immediate contemplation of the draftsmen of the Act in 1893."

In reconsidering the law relating to the sale of goods, two main aspects will be emphasised: the property aspect, because the underlying purpose of a contract of sale is to transfer property from the seller to the buyer; and the contractual aspect, because sale is basically a contractual arrangement between two parties whereby the seller agrees to supply the buyer with the goods as described in the contract. In other words, a contract of sale has two fundamental obligations which lie at its core: to transfer title and to supply goods answering the contract description. In relation to both the proprietary and contractual aspects there exist a variety of ancillary rights and obligations but it is the major division between title and contract which will provide the framework of the ensuing discussion.

Many of the cases that are dealt with in considering what is the present law in England (and Wales) concern transactions with a foreign element, i.e. the goods are being imported to this country or are being exported overseas. English law was the law governing the particular contract for a variety of reasons which are outside the scope of the present book. The significance of the preliminary "choice of law" issue is likely to increase since the adoption of the two Hague Conventions of 1964, particularly the first, which sets out a Uniform Law on the International Sale of Goods. In contracts of sale between parties whose places of business are in the territories of different contracting States, the provisions of the Convention shall apply to regulate the rights and obligations of the buyer and seller, unless expressly or by implication the parties themselves exclude the operation of the rules laid down in the Convention in whole or in part. In adopting the Conventions as part of law in England (and Wales), Scotland and Northern Ireland, the United Kingdom Parliament laid down in s. 1 (4) of the Uniform Law on International Sales Act 1967 that, for the time being at any rate, the Uniform Law "shall apply to a contract of sale only if it has been chosen by the parties to the contract as the law of the contract". In other words, the Convention is essentially a legal regime which must, as far as a British buyer or seller is concerned, be chosen as the law governing the contract and cannot operate upon his international contracts without his express agreement. In this book, however, we shall be considering only the rules that are applied to contracts governed by the law of England.

PART ONE

The Property in the Goods

CHAPTER 1

The Nature of the Transaction

According to s. 1 (1) of the Act a sale of goods is "a contract whereby the seller transfers or agrees to transfer the property in goods to the buyer for a money consideration, called the price". This definition requires elaboration in a number of respects.

A   WHAT ARE GOODS?

These are described as *including* (i.e. it is not an exhaustive definition) "all chattels personal other than things in action and money . . . emblements, industrial growing crops, and things attached to or forming part of the land which are agreed to be severed before sale or under the contract of sale" (s. 62 (1)).

Clearly sales of real property or chattels real such as leaseholds fall outside the Act, as do choses in action like shares, bills and cheques. However, the opening words of s. 62 (1) make it clear that the interpretations of the terms covered in the sub-section do not apply if "the contract or subject matter otherwise requires". Hence a sale of coins as collectors' items could fall within the Act even if the coins in question were money in the sense of still being legal tender.[1]

Greater difficulties can arise when dealing with transactions involving minerals or growing crops. A sale of minerals can only be a sale of goods, as opposed to a sale of an interest in realty, once they are removed from the land. But if the minerals are severed and are then left as slag so that they resume an appearance of being part of the earth, a contract of sale in respect of them will *prima facie* be one for the sale of an interest in land, and not of goods.[2]

However, it is not clear how far a contract for minerals deposited in this way involving their subsequent severance and removal from the land, would create an interest in personalty and fall within the definition of goods as including "things attached to or forming part of the land which are agreed to be severed . . . under the contract of sale". Such an argument was rejected in the circumstances of *Morgan* v. *Russell & Sons*, but the High Court of Australia in *Mills v. Stokman* was careful to leave this point open.[3] The logical view would seem to be

---

1 E.g. the 1897 Jubilee £5 gold piece in *Moss* v. *Hancock*, [1899] 2 Q.B. 111: many coins achieve a rarity value because few were minted in a particular year although still in general circulation, and occasionally the intrinsic value of a coin comes to exceed its face value because of a sudden increase in the price of the metal it contains.
2 *Morgan* v. *Russell & Sons*, [1909] 1 K.B. 357; *Mills* v. *Stokman* (1966–7), 116 C.L.R. 61
3 Two members of the court (BARWICK, C.J., 116 C.L.R. at p. 71, and MENZIES, J., at p. 79) at least were careful to state that the point did not arise because there was no express contract to sever the slate dross in question.

5

that a distinction can be drawn between a contract to extract mineral and one to carry away an accumulation of waste, even that which has resumed a close connection with the ground. The latter is very much a thing attached to or forming part of the land as opposed to something which has always been part of the land. It is akin to the situation where a contractor is to be allowed to demolish a building and to remove the materials of which the building is made. In both cases the "severance" provided for in the agreement constitutes the agreement a contract for the sale of goods.

"Things attached to the land" most obviously refer to vegetation that is growing naturally on the land (*fructus naturales*), such as timber or grass. At common law a sale of *fructus naturales* was a sale of goods only if the subject matter was to be severed before or very soon after the contract was made.

> "Whereas at the time of the contract it is contemplated that the purchaser should derive a benefit from the further growth of the thing sold, from further vegetation and from the nutriment afforded by the land, the contract is to be considered as for the interest in the land; but where the process of vegetation is over, or the parties agree that the thing sold shall be immediately withdrawn from the land, the land is to be considered as a mere warehouse of the thing sold and the contract is for goods."[1]

Although this proposition was accepted as representing the post-Sale of Goods Act law by the Privy Council in *Kauri Timber Co.* v. *Commissioner of Taxes*,[2] the Act itself only requires that the "crop" in question be severed before sale or "under the contract of sale" in order to qualify as goods.[3] This expression is open to a much wider interpretation and the Court of Appeal saw no obstacle to regarding a contract for the cutting of timber over a period of 15 years as a sale of goods in *Kursell* v. *Timber Operators and Contractors, Ltd.*[4]

A contract for the purchase of an actual growing crop from a tree (e.g. apples or pears) would be a sale of goods even if they are to be severed by the buyer[5] by virtue of this aspect of the definition. However, crops which are sown and harvested in the course of a year are termed *emblements*, an expression specifically included within the definition. Goods also cover *fructus industriales* ("industrial growing crops" in the terminology of s. 62 (1)). The generally accepted view is that this expression is wider than emblements and extends to a variety of clovers and grasses that may not be "annually harvested".

B   TRANSFERRING OR AGREEING TO TRANSFER PROPERTY

This aspect of the statutory definition raises two issues. In the first place it calls attention to the distinction between an actual sale and a contract for the

---

1 Note in *Wims. Saund.*, at p. 276 (*f*): this principle originally applied to all growing crops and vegetables, but came to be limited solely to *fructus naturales*.
2 [1913] A.C. 771, at pp. 778–9.
3 Though may it also be a sale of an interest in land? See Hudson in (1958) 22 Conv. (N.S.) 137–9.
4 [1927] 1 K.B. 298.
5 If they are to be severed by the seller, it will be an agreement to sell in the future goods belonging to the seller.

future transfer of title to goods, and secondly it makes clear that it is the property in the goods that is being transferred and not some lesser right such as possession.[1]

The distinction between a sale and an agreement to transfer property in goods is of no great practical importance. The contract can operate to transfer title immediately. For example, B may have physical possession of the goods already; or the agreement may be for the sale of a specific item by which property passes at the moment of contracting under s. 18, rule 1, of the Act[2]. On the other hand, a contract of sale covers the situation where, for instance, B agrees to buy goods which S may not at that moment own but which S expects to obtain in time to perform the contract. There is no doubt concerning the validity of this transaction, but equally clearly property in the goods will not pass at the time of the original contract between B and S.

i Sale and hire purchase

However, this description of sale as a contract whereby S agrees to transfer the property is not to be taken to its logical conclusion. It does not apply to hire purchase agreements even though such agreements do involve an ultimate transfer of title to B. The normal mechanics of hire purchase involve an agreement whereby S transfers ownership in the goods to F, a finance company, from which B hires the goods for a certain period. S is paid by F immediately, while B pays to F the stipulated instalments and in return is granted an option to purchase the goods from F, often for a nominal sum, at the end of the period. It is true that under such a transaction S does not agree to transfer property to B *directly*, but even if S were financing the transaction himself, a hire purchase arrangement is not a sale of goods.[3]

ii Sale and work and materials

a *Assimilation of the two contracts*

Similarly, a contract for work and materials, though it involves a transfer of property in the materials used, is not a sale of goods. Formerly the distinction between the two types of contract was important because the contract of sale was covered by the Statute of Frauds.[4] Since the need for evidence in writing or a sufficient act of part performance to make a contract of sale enforceable was abolished in 1954,[5] this importance largely disappeared, particularly as the courts have not been reluctant to assimilate the two types of contract in other ways. For example, they have applied warranties that the materials supplied should be suitable for a particular purpose or should be of adequate quality similar to those implied into contracts of sale by s. 14 of the Sale of Goods Act.

In *Young and Marten, Ltd.* v. *McManus Childs, Ltd.*[6] the respondents' agent had specified that a particular named roof title should be used on houses they were building. The appellants who carried out the roofing work used a batch

---

1 Dealt with below, p. 15.
2 See below, p. 26.
3 *Helby* v. *Mathews*, [1895] A.C. 471; [1895–99] All E.R. Rep. 821.
4 Section 17: subsequently re-enacted as s. 4 of the Sale of Goods Act.
5 By s. 1 of the Law Reform (Enforcement of Contracts) Act.
6 [1969] 1 A.C. 454; [1968] 2 All E.R. 1169.

of the tiles which later proved to have been defective. The respondents were successfully sued by the house purchasers for the costs of re-roofing. Whether the respondents could recover this loss from the appellant sub-contractors depended upon the obligations implied into a contract for work and materials. Authority existed in the favour of implying terms as to reasonable fitness for the employer's purpose[1] and as to good quality.[2] In this particular case, as the respondents' agent, by stipulating the tile to be used, "took on himself the responsibility of selecting tiles suitable for his purpose" he had "negatived any implied warranty from his supplier that the goods were suitable for that purpose."[3] However, the appellants were liable for the supply of materials that were not of adequate quality and even though the defect in question was latent,[4] and not apparent on a reasonable examination. The requirement that the tiles should be a specific type made only by a particular manufacturer did not relieve the appellants of their obligation to use materials of normal quality.[5]

Of course the extent of the obligation may vary with the nature of the particular contract. The more akin the contract is to one of sale, "the closer should be the similarity of warranties to be implied with those arising on a sale".[6] Indeed in this type of case, there is much to be said for the view that "one who contracts to do work and supply materials ought to be under at least as high if not a higher degree of obligation with regard to the goods he supplies and the work that he does than a seller who may be a mere middleman or wholesaler".[7] On the other hand, as Lord WILBERFORCE pointed out,[8] "if the acquisition of an identifiable object is of minimal, or no interest to the 'purchaser' then, if any warranty is to be implied, it should properly relate either to the quality of the work to be done or to the use of suitable, and non-injurious, materials".

b *Differences between the two contracts*

Despite this attempt to assimilate the two types of contract, it remains true that the contract of sale is less flexible, because the courts, in their interpretation of a contract for work and materials, are not hampered by the provisions of the Sale of Goods Act. More especially, under the recent amendments to the Sale of Goods Act, a new significance has been created to the distinction in so far as the implied terms as to suitability and merchantability have been made absolute in relation to "consumer sales". This change in the law will be explained in

---

1 *Samuels* v. *Davis*, [1943] 1 K.B. 526; [1943] 2 All E.R. 3; *G. H. Myers & Co.* v. *Brent Cross Service Co.*, [1934] 1 K.B. 46; [1933] All E.R. Rep. 9.
2 *G. H. Myers & Co.* v. *Brent Cross Service Co.*, above.
3 [1969] 1 A.C. at p. 479; [1968] 2 All E.R., at p. 1180; *per* Lord WILBERFORCE. The implied warranty would similarly be negatived if the person "employing" the contractor did not make known to the latter any special factors affecting the work to be done so that he is unable to exercise his skill and judgment: *Ingham* v. *Emes*, [1955] 2Q.B. 366; [1955] 2 All E.R. 740.
4 Applying *Randall* v. *Newson* (1877), 2 Q.B.D. 102.
5 For a case where the contract placed the onus on the employer of checking the quality of the materials to be used so that there was no such warranty implied in the contract, see *Gloucestershire County Council* v. *Richardson*, [1969] 1 A.C. 480; [1968] 2 All E.R. 1181.
6 [1969] 1 A.C., at pp. 476–7; [1968] 2 All E.R., at pp. 1178–9, *per* Lord WILBERFORCE.
7 [1969] 1 A.C., at pp. 473–4; [1968] 2 All E.R., at p. 1177, *per* Lord UPJOHN.
8 [1969] 1 A.C., at p. 477; [1968] 2 All E.R., at p. 1179.

detail later.[1] For the moment, however, some comment is necessary on how to distinguish between the two types of contract.

A variety of tests have been advanced, but originally at least the distinction was much clearer. As was stated in one Australian decision: "A plaintiff cannot recover for work and labour when a chattel has been produced. We have to look at the particular contract in each case. If the result is to be the sale of a chattel, an action cannot be maintained for work and labour."[2] Hence in the case in which that statement was made, as the undertaking was to make a particular apparatus and it was clear that "when the work and labour were brought to an end, the result was a chattel",[3] the contract was one for the sale of goods. Such a rule was of easy application. In *Grafton* v. *Armitage*,[4] a contract under which a party was to devise plans for a manufacturing process was held to be for work and labour; there was no question of making anything "that could properly become the subject of an action for goods sold and delivered".[5] On the other hand, as COLTMAN, J., pointed out in that case, the "claim of a tailor or shoemaker is for the price of goods when delivered, and not for the work or labour bestowed by him in the fabrication of them".[6] Similarly, in the important case of *Lee v Griffin*,[7] an action, brought by a dentist to recover for two sets of false teeth which he had made and supplied, was held to be on a contract of sale. The judges (CROMPTON, HILL and BLACKBURN, J.J.) were all emphatic that when "the contract is such that a chattel is ultimately to be delivered . . . the cause of actions is goods sold and delivered".[8]

This relatively simple test can also be applied to situations in which a manufacturer has to make and then install a piece of machinery or other furniture, although the position is complicated by the fact that, unless property passes under the contract before installation, the equipment may cease to be "goods" once it is "affixed to the realty". Hence, while the purchase of the apparatus in *Lyons* v. *Hughes* was obviously the sale of a chattel, the supply and installation of a lift in a particular building would not be a sale of goods.[9] It will often be a question of degree whether the installation is sufficiently important to render the contract a single whole (so that property would only pass on completion) and therefore for work and materials, or whether the contract may be regarded as a sale of a chattel plus installation. In Australia it has been held that a contract for the supply and installation of a revolving cocktail cabinet to be fitted on to a pivot let into floor and ceiling was for work and materials.[10]

---

1 See below, p. 225 *et seq.*, where the Supply of Goods (Implied Terms) Act, 1973, is discussed.
2 *Lyons* v. *Hughes* (1875), 1 V.L.R. (L) 1, at p. 4, *per* BARRY, J.
3 *Ibid.*
4 (1845), 2 C.B. 336.
5 2 C.B., at pp. 340–1, *per* TINDALL, C.J.
6 2 C.B., at p. 341.
7 (1861), 30 L.J.Q.B. 252; [1861–73] All E.R. Rep. 191.
8 30 L.J.Q.B., at p. 253; [1861–73] All E.R. Rep., at p. 192.
9 *Sydney Hydraulic and General Engineering Co.* v. *Blackwood & Son* (1908), 8 S.R. N.S.W. 10.
10 *Brooks Robinson Pty., Ltd.* v. *Rothfield*, [1951] V.L.R. 405; and, less convincing, the contract for lecture theatre seats in *Aristoc Industries Pty., Ltd.* v. *R. A. Wenham (Builders) Pty. Ltd.*, [1965] N.S.W.R. 581.

However, where the method of installation is comparatively simple, as would be the case with fitted carpets[1] or a domestic heater[2] the contract will be one of sale.

Unfortunately, the law is not so readily analysed on the basis of the relatively neat and apparently comprehensive solution achieved in *Lee* v. *Griffin*. Even before that case, it was held in *Clay* v. *Yates*[3] that a contract for the printing of 500 copies of a treatise was for work and materials. The correctness of the decision was doubted by the members of the court in *Lee* v. *Griffin* who preferred to treat it as *sui generis*. There were dicta in the case, however, which were later to influence the Court of Appeal in *Robinson* v. *Graves*.[4] The judges in *Clay* v. *Yates* introduced the proposition, expressed by POLLOCK, C.B., as follows: "in the case of a work of art . . . where the application of skill and labour is of the highest description, and the material is of no importance as compared with the labour, the price may be recovered as work, labour and materials".[5] In *Robinson* v. *Graves* this pronouncement was seized upon as authority for holding that a commission for the painting of a portrait was a contract for work and materials. The *Lee* v. *Griffin* approach was modified and the law restated by GREER, L.J.:[6]

> "If you find, as they did in *Lee* v. *Griffin*, that the substance of the contract was the production of something to be sold by the dentist to the dentist's customer, then that is a sale of goods. But if the substance of the contract, on the other hand, is that skill and labour have to be exercised for the production of the article and that it is only ancillary to that that there will pass from the artist to his client or customer some materials in addition to the skill involved in the production of the portrait, that does not make . . . a contract for the sale of goods."

It was admitted, however, that where, as in *Isaacs* v. *Hardy*,[7] "a picture dealer whose sole object was to acquire something which he might sell in his business engaged an artist to paint and deliver . . . a picture of a given subject at an agreed price" the contract would be a sale.[8]

It can hardly be claimed that *Robinson* v. *Graves* is entirely satisfactory. It is not enough to suggest that, for a contract involving the simple transfer of property in a chattel to be regarded as for work and materials, all that is necessary is for the skill to outweigh greatly in value the cost of the raw material. This test alone would not be a convincing ground upon which to distinguish the work of an artist from the shoemaker who makes shoes to personal order. Nor does it seem logical to distinguish between an artist painting a portrait on commission for an individual whose interest is primarily in the subject matter of the picture (though he also acquires a saleable item), and an artist working on a commission from a dealer whose immediate object is to sell the finished product.

---

1 *Philip Head & Sons, Ltd.* v. *Showfronts, Ltd.*, [1970] 1 Lloyd's Rep. 140.
2 *Collins Trading Co. Pty. Ltd.* v. *Maher*, [1969] V.R. 20.
3 (1856), 1 H. & N. 73.
4 [1935] 1 K.B. 579; [1935] All E.R. Rep. 935.
5 1 H. & N., at p. 78.
6 [1935] 1 K.B. 579, at pp. 587–8; [1935] All E.R. Rep., at p. 939.
7 (1884), Cab. & El. 287.
8 [1935] 1 K.B., at p. 594; [1935] All E.R. Rep., at p. 942.

C THE PRICE

i Sale and Exchange

As the transfer of goods to the buyer is expressly stated by s. 1 to be "for a money consideration, called the price", a transfer in exchange for other goods is not a sale. Accordingly, with the rapid growth in the use of trading stamps over the past 15 years, it was felt necessary to introduce certain safeguards, similar to those contained in ss. 12 and 14 (2) of the Sale of Goods Act, for a person acquiring goods in return for such stamps.[1]

However, where the contract involves a part exchange, that is where the "price" is goods plus a money payment, it will normally be one of sale. In *Forsyth* v. *Jervis*,[2] the plaintiff agreed to provide the defendant with a gun worth 45 guineas to be paid for by delivery of the defendant's gun and payment of an additional 15 guineas. The plaintiff performed his part of the bargain, but the defendant failed to hand over the gun or pay any money. In an action to recover the 45 guineas, it was objected that only 15 guineas was due. This plea was rejected. As the contract was for the sale of goods to be in part paid for by the delivery of goods of a stipulated value, upon refusal of the buyer to pay for them in that way, the seller was entitled to recover the entire price in money. Similarly, today, in the case of a sale of a motor car, there will often be a part exchange allowance of the buyer's old vehicle against the price of another vehicle, whether new or second hand. Unless the transaction is financed under a hire-purchase arrangement, the contract to buy the replacement vehicle will be one of sale.[3]

The position of the car that has been traded in is less clear As long as a specific value is ascribed to the vehicle,[4] there would seem to be no reason why the transaction should not be regarded as a "sale within a sale". In one New Zealand case,[5] it was held that, where the two vehicles were valued at the same price, the transaction was governed by the Sale of Goods Act. Additional support for the proposition may be found in the case of *South Australian Insurance Co.* v. *Randell*.[6] Farmers deposited corn with the respondent, a miller. As he was allowed to use it in the course of his business, he mixed it with his own stock,

---

1 Trading Stamps Act 1964, s. 4 as amended by the Supply of Goods (Implied Terms) Act 1973, s. 16; s. 3 of the 1964 Act creates a right to redeem trading stamps for cash. The assumption that an acquisition of goods in exchange for stamps is not a sale under the Sale of Goods Act is supported by *O'Dea* v. *Merchants' Trade-Expansion Group, Ltd.* (1938), 37 N.S.W. Ind. Arb. R.
2 (1816), 1 Stark. 437; *Sheldon* v. *Cox* (1824), 3 B. & C. 420 (horse for mare and 40 guineas plus 5 more guineas if the horse suited). By the time of *Aldridge* v. *Johnson* (1875), 7 E. & B. 885, the point was so well established as not to be worth arguing.
3 *G. J. Dawson (Clapham) Ltd.* v. *H. & G. Dutfield*, [1936] 2 All E.R. 232.
4 In many cases, even if a specific price is not expressly achieved, the value will be apparent. In *Bull* v. *Parker* (1842), 2 Dowl N.S. 345, no money price had been given to the new saddle and bridle being bought; the consideration was the buyer's old saddle and bridle plus £2. It was accepted, however, that a new saddle and bridle cost £4 but that there was no obstacle to the seller recovering the £4 in full for failure by a buyer to perform his part of the bargain.
5 *Davey* v. *Paine Bros. (Motors), Ltd.*, [1954] N.Z.L.R. 1122.
6 (1869), L.R. 3 P.C. 101.

and either ground it or sold it. The farmers were to be paid in cash or could ask for a like quantity of the same quality corn as they had deposited. The actual dispute was whether the corn was the miller's property (and so covered automatically by a policy of insurance), or was only held on behalf of the farmers. All that was necessary for the decision, therefore, was to hold that property had passed and that the transaction was not at any time a bailment. However, the Judicial Committee gave this explanation:[1]

> "whenever there is a delivery of property or a contract for an equivalent in money or some other valuable commodity, and not for the return of the identical subject in its original or an altered form, there is a transfer of property for value—it is a sale and not a bailment."

This pronouncement is open to two different interpretations. In the first place, it could be said that a contract which provides for a transfer of property on a sale or barter basis, the choice between the two to be made subsequently, is nevertheless a contract of sale. On the other hand, it could be said that where a value is put on goods, it is a sale whether the consideration is paid in money or in kind.[2]

ii Ascertaining the price

Normally the ascertainment of the price will create no problems: when goods are bought the price is usually stipulated expressly. However, as s. 8 (1) of the Act states, not only may the price be "fixed by the contract", it may also "be left to be fixed in manner thereby agreed, or may be determined by the course of dealing between the parties". Section 8 (2) goes on to provide that "where the price is not determined in accordance with the foregoing provisions the buyer must pay a reasonable price". What constitutes a reasonable price "is a question of fact dependent on the circumstances of each particular case". In other words, where nothing is said on the matter, it is inferred that the parties intended that the buyer should pay a reasonable value, and this rule existed prior to 1893 whether the contract was executed[3] or executory[4].

a *Contracts to make a contract*

Difficulty can arise where the parties have attempted to lay down some method of fixing the price, but have failed to do so with sufficient precision. Is it still possible to infer an intention that a reasonable price should be paid for the goods?[5] The issue can only be resolved by a process of construction to ascertain the parties' intention. In the notorious case of *May and Butcher, Ltd.* v. *R.*,[6] the

---

1 At p. 108.
2 *Koppel* v. *Koppel*, [1966] 2 All E.R. 182, where the "price" was principally the sale of the "buyer's" own household goods in order that she could come to live in the seller's house and look after his children.
3 *Acebal* v. *Levy* (1834), 10 Bing. 376, at p. 382.
4 *Hoadly* v. *McLaine* (1834), 10 Bing. 482, where it was referred to as "no new doctrine" (at p. 487).
5 As Macleod, *Sale and Hire Purchase*, p. 21, succinctly comments, "s. 8 assumes that a contract has been made; but it must be borne in mind that the determination of the price is often an important factor in deciding *whether* a contract has been concluded".
6 [1934] 2 K.B. 17n.; [1929] All E.R. Rep. 679.

parties had agreed that the appellants should purchase tentage that should become available for disposal at a price to be agreed upon by the parties themselves. It was also "understood that all disputes with reference to or arising out of" the agreement would be submitted to arbitration. In the absence of any subsequent agreement as to price, the House of Lords held that the arrangement between the parties did not constitute an effective contract. Nor was it possible, because the parties had reserved to themselves the power to decide upon the price, to infer any intention that a reasonable price should be payable. Accordingly there was no contract and it was not possible to rely upon the arbitration clause which only provided a means of resolving disputes once a contract had been finalised.

The importance of construing the contract to discover the intention of the parties is brought out by the Australian case of *Wenning* v. *Robinson*.[1] The defendant sought to have a contract for the purchase of the plaintiff's business declared unenforceable on the ground that, as it included a provision "plus stock at valuation", the price was not stated with sufficient certainty. The court held that, although the parties probably envisaged that they would agree on the valuation between themselves at the time of the transfer, what they intended was a "fair valuation", that is, a reasonable price. As the parties had not agreed upon the valuation, a reasonable price could be inferred.

Although there is no difference between an executory and an executed contract in the direct application of s. 8 to situations where the contract makes no provision as to price or as to how it should be ascertained, there is a difference in practice when it comes to trying to construe an ambiguous or defective arrangement relating to price. In *Foley* v. *Classique Coaches, Ltd.*,[2] the defendants had purchased a piece of land from the plaintiff and, as part of the arrangement between the parties, had entered into a secondary contract whereby they agreed to buy all the petrol they required from the plaintiff's pumps on the adjoining land at a price "to be agreed by the parties in writing and from time to time". It was also agreed that in the event of a dispute the matter should be submitted to arbitration. For three years this arrangement operated to the parties' mutual satisfaction, but the defendants then discovered that they could obtain petrol at a price lower than that for which the plaintiff was willing to sell. Were the defendants entitled to claim that in the absence of any further agreement on the price of petrol, they were entitled to ignore their part of the arrangement entirely? In practical terms, it was difficult to accept an argument based upon the proposition that the parties had for a lengthy period been operating under a contract that was too uncertain to be enforced. The contract had been acted upon by the parties in a clear manifestation of their intentions. Their subsequent disagreement arose out of an existing contract which provided arbitration as the means for resolving disputes. Hence, if the parties could not agree a price, there was a method prescribed for resolving the issue.

Foley v. *Classique Coaches Ltd.* was also symptomatic of a change in judicial

---

1 [1964–5] N.S.W.R. 614.
2 [1934] 2 K.B. 1; [1934] All E.R. Rep. 88.

attitudes that can be traced to statements made by members of the House of Lords in *Hillas & Co., Ltd.* v. *Arcos, Ltd.*[1] Certainly the more recent trend has been to uphold the efficacy of arrangements that might, if the attitude represented by *May and Butcher* v. *R.* had been adopted, have failed for uncertainty or inadequacy. Because the courts are "always loath to hold a clause invalid for uncertainty if a reasonable meaning can be given to it",[2] they will only hold a contract ineffective if there is neither machinery, nor formula, by which to resolve the omission.[3] Where there is a formula provided for in the contract, the courts will apply that formula. Section 8 of the Sale of Goods Act (provided it is not ousted by the terms of the contract itself) is one example of such a formula. Alternatively the formula may be provided by the past dealings of the parties (as in *Hillas* v. *Arcos*), or by the contract itself. In *Brown* v. *Gould*,[4] for example, a tenant had an option to renew his lease "at a rent to be fixed having regard to the market value of the premises at the time of exercising this option taking into account to the advantage of the tenant any increased value of such premises attributable to structural improvements made by the tenant during the currency of this present lease". Clearly such an arrangement was intended to have legal effect and it had been in reliance upon this option that the tenant had spent more than £30,000 in rebuilding the premises. MEGARRY, J., had no hesitation in upholding the validity of the option.

But even though the parties have provided no *formula* with which to resolve the issue, if *machinery* is provided, such as submission to arbitration of any matter of dispute arising out of the contract, the tendency will be for a court to hold that the agreement is not defective. However, in the final analysis the strongest evidence of the efficacy of a contract that is subsequently alleged to be "void for uncertainty" remains that it has been acted upon by the parties. In *Mack and Edwards (Sales), Ltd.* v. *McPhail Bros.*,[5] the parties still continued to dispute the price of the goods long after they had been purchased by the defendant retailer and resold to his customers. The Court of Appeal pointed out that, as the parties had not settled the price, there had been no concluded bargain between them. Hence, in the words of Lord DENNING, M.R., if "the contract had been wholly executory and the goods not delivered, there would be no contract. But when the goods had been delivered there was in law a necessary implication from the conduct of the parties that a reasonable price was to be paid".

---

1 [1932] All E.R. Rep. 494, at p. 499; 38 Com. Cas. 23, at p. 29, *per* Lord TOMLIN; [1932] All E.R. Rep., at pp. 503–4; 38 Com. Cas., at pp. 36–7, *per* Lord WRIGHT.
2 *Greater London Council* v. *Connolly* [1970] 2 Q.B. 100, at p. 110; [1970] 1 All E.R. 870, at p. 876, *per* Lord PEARSON; and see also *per* Lord DENNING, M.R., [1970] 2 Q.B., at p. 108; [1970] 1 All E.R., at p. 874.
3 As in *King's Motors (Oxford), Ltd.* v. *Lax*, [1969] 3 All E.R. 665.
4 [1972] Ch. 53; [1971] 2 All E.R. 1505; or more obviously *Acebal* v. *Levy* (1834), 10 Bing. 376, in which a sale was held effective where the price was stated as that current for the commodity in question at the port of shipment.
5 (1968), 112 Sol. Jo. 211; though cf. the altogether different situation that arose in *Re Nudgee Bakery Pty., Ltd.'s Agreement*, [1971] Qd. R. 24.

b *By valuation*

As an alternative means of resolving an initial failure to agree on a price, the parties may provide in their contract that the matter should be settled by the valuation of a third party. By s. 9 (1) if there is such an agreement and the third party "cannot or does not make such valuation, the agreement is avoided", although "if the goods or any part thereof have been delivered to and appropriated by the buyer he must pay a reasonable price therefore". However, where the third party is "prevented from making the valuation by the fault of the seller or buyer, the party not in fault may maintain an action for damages against the party in fault" (s. 9 (2)).

If a valuer is appointed, his valuation is binding unless he acted dishonestly. Similarly he will not be liable in damages at the suit of the disappointed party on the grounds of negligence, failure to act reasonably, or mistake. As was stated in *Tharsis Sulphur and Copper Co.* v. *Loftus*,[1] "the safe rule when parties agree to be bound by the decision of a third party on any matter is that they take him in such a case for better or worse and if he discharges his duty faithfully and honestly they must be satisfied". Hence in *Boynton* v. *Richardson*,[2] where a firm of valuers had been employed under a contract for the sale of growing timber to value the timber for the purpose of establishing a proper purchase price, it was held that no action would lie in negligence in respect of their valuation.

D THE CONCEPT OF PROPERTY

Historically the contract of sale was more in the nature of an assignment; it was a contract whereby the seller agreed to transfer to the buyer his interest in the goods. As in most cases he had actual possession of the goods, he could transfer at least a possessory title. There being no documentary evidence (as there would be in the case of land), the fact of possession would be strong evidence of ownership. But the common law courts were reluctant to encourage actions brought by buyers who subsequently discovered that the goods had belonged not to their seller but to a third party. Unless a specific undertaking had been given by the seller that he was the owner, the buyer was left without a remedy.

To an extent his position was not as unsatisfactory as it may appear. Until comparatively modern times the majority of transactions were conducted in fairs and markets. The Law Merchant had early recognised the need to protect these "commercial transactions". Hence with the reception of the law merchant by the common law it was accepted that in the case of a sale in market overt a *bona fide* buyer took a good title.[3]

With the increasing migration of commerce from the country to the cities,

---

1 (1872), L.R. 8 C.P. 1, at pp. 7–8, per KEATING, J.; cited with approval in *Finnegan* v. *Allen*, [1943] 1 K.B. 425, at p. 433.

2 [1924] W.N. 262; also approved by the Court of Appeal in *Finnegan* v. *Allen* (above). As the duty of the quasi-arbitrator is to hold the scales evenly between the parties, he owes no duty to either of them under *Hedley Byrne & Co., Ltd.* v. *Heller*, [1964] A.C. 465; [1963] 2 All E.R. 575: see *Arenson* v. *Arenson*, [1973] Ch. 346; [1973] 2 All E.R. 235.

3 For the market overt rule, see below, pp. 102–5.

from the market place to the High Street, some of the judges began to recognise the need to extend the protection of buyers who were obliged to rely upon the good faith of their seller to guarantee title.[1] However, it was not until 1864 that *Eicholz* v. *Bannister*[2] established that an undertaking of title was raised by implication from the fact of the sale itself. As ERLE, C.J., stated:[3]

> ". . . in almost all the transactions of sale in common life, the seller by the very act of selling holds out to the buyer that he is the owner of the article he offers for sale. The sale of a chattel is the strongest act of dominion that is incidental to ownership. A purchaser under ordinary circumstances would naturally be led to the conclusion that, by offering an article for sale, the seller affirms that he has a title to sell, and that the buyer may enjoy that for which he parts with his money."

Once it is accepted that a sale imports the notion of transfer of ownership, the underlying nature of the transaction changes. Unless it is stipulated that the transferor is assigning some lesser interest, the transfer of property becomes fundamental to the concept of sale. Hence, when Chalmers codified this part of the law not only did he include an "implied condition on the part of the seller that, in the case of a sale, he has a right to sell the goods, and that, in the case of an agreement to sell, he will have a right to sell the goods at the time when the property is to pass" (s. 12 (1)),[4] but he defined the contract as one "whereby the seller transfers or agrees to transfer the property in goods to the buyer" (s. 1 (1)). And by "property" he specified "the general property and not merely a special property" (s. 62 (1)), that is ownership or dominion, and not just some possessory right. This change in the law was recognised by ATKIN, L.J.'s dictum in *Rowland* v. *Divall*[5] that there can be

> "no sale at all of goods which the seller has no right to sell. The whole objetc of a sale is to transfer property from one person to another."

Under the amended version of s. 12, introduced by the Supply of Goods (Implied Terms) Act 1973, it is now recognised (by s. 12 (2)) that there can be a contract of sale in which "there appears from the contract or is to be inferred from the circumstances of the contract an intention that the seller should transfer only such title as he cr a third person may have". In this exceptional situation, s. 12 (2) goes on to imply certain warranties into the contract for the protection of the buyer,[6] but the principal obligation in all cases to which s. 12 (2) does not apply is the seller's undertaking (in s. 12 (1)) that he has a right to sell the goods, or will have such a right at the time property is to pass. Furthermore, by the new s. 55 (3) in a contract of sale of goods:

> "Any term of that or any other contract exempting from all or any of the provisions of s. 12 of this Act shall be void."

The obligations contained in s. 12 are thus clearly recognised as fundamental to the contract of sale.

---

1 E.g. the members of the Court of Exchequer in *Allen* v. *Hopkins* (1844), 13 M. & W. 94; but cf. the reaction of PARKE, B., in *Morley* v. *Attenborough* (1849), 3 Exch. 500, at pp. 511–2.
2 17 C.B. N.S. 708.   3 At p. 723.
4 See below, p. 167.   5 [1923] 2 K.B. 500, at pp. 506–7.   6 See below, p. 173.

CHAPTER 2

Transfer of Property to the Buyer

Sections 16–20 of the Act are grouped under the heading "Transfer of Property as between Seller and Buyer". It has been surmised that this wording might signify that the property rights transferred are only effective as between seller and buyer. This suggestion gains some support from the heading of the following group of Sections, "Transfer of Title", which might be taken to refer to rights effective against third parties. However, the most likely explanation of the admittedly rather unfortunate choice of terms is that the two headings are in no way interrelated. The expression "Transfer of Property as between Seller and Buyer" was chosen because ss. 16–20 deal solely with the relationship of seller and buyer *inter se*. The following sections, as we shall see, cover a variety of situations in which a buyer takes a good title even though the seller was not the owner and was not entitled to sell the goods in question. As the phrase "takes a good title" is a standard, though perhaps rather a loose, way of referring to situations where what amounts to a new title is created in place of the former owner's title, it is hardly surprising that the word "title" was used in the heading.

The point of time at which the seller ceases to be owner of the goods and ownership passes to the buyer is dependent in the first place on the category of goods being sold. The Act distinguishes between *specific* or *ascertained* goods on the one hand and *unascertained* or *future* goods on the other.

A. THE PASSING OF PROPERTY IN UNASCERTAINED OR
FUTURE GOODS

Unascertained goods are not defined by the Act, but the expression would seem to cover a number of possibilities. The most obvious type of goods to which the expression refers is a part of a much larger quantity, for example, a dozen cartons of frozen peas from a refrigerated store containing many more such cartons; or ten gallons of petrol from a tank containing several thousand gallons; or even a car to be supplied from the dealer's stock of vehicles of the model in question. However, unascertained goods also include most cases[1] of *future* goods, which are defined by s. 5 (1) as "goods to be manufactured or acquired by the seller after the making of the contract of sale". Hence, a contract for the purchase

---

1 The principal exception, i.e. where future goods are also specific, is mentioned below, p. 34.

17

by a customer of the latest Jaguar car which the dealer has to order from the manufacturer will be a sale of future, unascertained goods.

i Property cannot pass until goods ascertained

Quite clearly there can be no immediate transfer of property in goods that are not yet identified. As BOVILL, C. J., said in *Heilbutt* v. *Hickson*,[1] "where goods are not ascertained or may not exist at the time of the contract, from the nature of the transaction, no property in the goods can pass to the purchaser by virtue of the contract itself". It is not possible to point to any of the large quantity of cases of frozen peas in the refrigerator as being those of the buyer; nor, at the time of the contract, has any one car in the dealer's stock been singled out as the buyer's; while the latest Jaguar car to be ordered from the manufacturer may not yet have been completed.

This principle is set out in s. 16 of the Act which provides that, where there is a contract for the sale of unascertained goods, "no property in the goods is transferred unless and until the goods are ascertained". In *Laurie and Morewood* v. *Dudin & Sons*,[2] for example, the defendants held 618 quarters of maize in their warehouse. 200 quarters were sold and a delivery order was subsequently lodged with them by the plantiff buyers in respect of this quantity. When the original sellers directed the defendants to withhold delivery under the order, it was held that the plaintiffs' claim failed because, as the 200 quarters had never been separated from bulk, no property in the goods could have passed to them. Similarly, in *Healy* v. *Howlett*,[3] the plaintiff sent 190 boxes of mackerel from Ireland by rail and ship to his customers in England. Twenty of the boxes were for the defendants, but the boxes were not earmarked until they reached Holyhead. Clearly, therefore, the goods had been unascertained when dispatched, because at that stage, as AVORY, J., pointed out,[4] nobody could "possibly tell which twenty out of the 190 belonged to the defendants and which boxes belonged to the other purchasers".

ii Passing of property dependent upon intention of the parties

It follows therefore that property can only be transferred once the goods become ascertained. Whether it will pass at that moment is dependent upon the intention of the parties (s. 17 (1)), and for the purpose of ascertaining that intention "regard shall be had to the terms of the contract, the conduct of the parties, and the circumstances of the case" (s. 17 (2)). Section 18 then goes on to provide a number of rules to be applied for ascertaining the intention of the parties if that intention cannot be deduced in accordance with s. 17 (2). Of these rules, only Rule 5 relates to unascertained goods. Rule 5 (1) reads:

> "Where there is a contract for the sale of unascertained or future goods by description, and goods of that description and in a deliverable state are un-conditionally appropriated to the contract, either by the seller with the assent

---

1 (1872), L.R. 7 C.P. 438, at p. 449.
2 [1926] 1 K.B. 223; [1925] All E.R. Rep. 414.
3 [1917] 1 K.B. 337.
4 At p. 346.

of the buyer, or by the buyer with the assent of the seller, the property in the goods thereupon passes to the buyer. Such assent may be express or implied, and may be given either before or after the appropriation is made."

To a large extent s. 17 (2) and Rule 5 (1) are interrelated and not successive factors. It is true that an express statement of the parties' intention will operate to the exclusion of Rule 5 (1), but when one comes to consider the tenor of the contract, the conduct of the parties and the surrounding circumstances, this examination will be conducted in the light of Rule 5 (1). In practical terms, Rule 5 (1) is treated as creating a presumption that will be applied unless the circumstances suggest otherwise.

iii How are goods "ascertained"

The Act itself at no stage expressly states how unascertained goods are "ascertained", but Rule 5 (1) comes nearest to suggesting how this occurs. However, whether the "ascertaining" of goods is synonymous with "unconditionally appropriating" them with the assent of the other party in the terms of 5 (1) depends upon how one interprets the decision in *Wait and James* v. *Midland Bank*.[1]. S, the plaintiffs, had sold a quantity of wheat from bulk. B took delivery of part of this purchase, but deposited the delivery orders in respect of the remaining 850 quarters with the defendant Bank by way of pledge. S sold off the wheat in the warehouse until only 850 quarters remained. When B became insolvent, it was held that property in the 850 quarters had vested in B when the goods became "ascertained" by a process of exhaustion. Hence, the Bank's security over the goods was valid against the plaintiffs as unpaid sellers.

At no stage was any reference made to s. 18 Rule 5 of the Act. It was argued solely on the basis that unless the goods had been ascertained, no property passed, and that once the goods were ascertained property did pass. ROCHE, J., acknowledged that the normal method of ascertaining goods from bulk was to weigh them out, but in this case, as the rules of the local corn trade association covered the situation that arose if there was any excess or deficiency in the quantity delivered, there was nothing to prevent the parties adopting any method which was satisfactory to them.

However a method of ascertaining goods which is satisfactory to both parties is not very much different from an unconditional appropriation by one party with the assent of the other. In this case the seller had by implication assented to the method of ascertainment (for why else would he have retained approximately the amount necessary to satisfy the buyer's order?). It is not as easy to say that the buyer had assented to the process of exhaustion prior to his insolvency because there was no evidence that he was aware of what the seller had been doing. Nevertheless, *Wait and James* v. *Midland Bank* appears to support the proposition that, if there is a sale of a stipulated amount from a greater quantity which is itself designated (as in this case where the wheat was the cargo of a particular ship), the process of exhaustion is a reasonable method

---

1 (1926), 31 Com. Cas. 172.

(and therefore presumably acceptable to both parties) of ascertaining the goods and of passing property to the buyer. And once that proposition is accepted it is but a small (and, in the interests of a logical application of the Act, a necessary) step to regard the decision as falling within the ambit of s. 18 Rule 5.

iv The buyer's assent to the appropriation

Although Rule 5 (1) stipulates that there should be this assent, the fact that the assent may be implied has avoided many of the difficulties that could have arisen in applying the Rule. For example, if the seller notifies the buyer that an appropriation has been effected and the buyer does not reply, his assent will be assumed. In *Pignataro* v. *Gilroy*[1], there was a contract for the sale of 140 unascertained bags of rice. Immediately he received B's cheque, S sent him a delivery order and informed him where the bags were located. Fifteen of them were at S's place of business, but B did not ask for them until nearly four weeks later when it was discovered that they had been stolen. As the theft had occurred without fault on S's part, he could only be liable for the loss if he still had the property in the goods. It was held that property had passed to B because he had by implication assented to S's appropriation of the goods.

Assent to the appropriation can also be inferred from the contract itself. If an order for goods is made by post and it is expected that the goods will be similarly dispatched, it is reasonable to imply the buyer's assent to the appropriation made by the seller when he posts the goods in question.[2] Or, if an order is placed with a shop, the goods to be sent to the home or place of business of the buyer, assent will normally be presumed to the shopkeeper's subsequent appropriation of the goods.[3] *A fortiori*, where the buyer sends containers into which the goods are to be loaded for dispatch to him, the seller's act of loading even part gf the goods will amount to appropriation of that part with the buyer's implied assent.

In *Aldridge* v. *Johnson*,[4] B, the plaintiff, had agreed that S should have 32 bullocks at £6 each and that he would take in exchange 100 quarters of barley at £2.3s. per quarter and pay the £23 difference in cash. It was also agreed that B should send sacks to S and that S should fill them and place them free of charge on trucks at the railway station to be sent to the plaintiff. B sent enough sacks for only part of the barley, and these S filled. Being unable to arrange transport, S emptied the barley back into bulk. S became bankrupt and the defendant took possession of the barley as trustee. It was held that B was entitled to part of the barley because property in that part had passed as soon as it had been placed in his sacks. He had clearly assented to this process and the court had no doubt that an appropriation occurred with the loading of the sacks.

---

1 [1919] 1 K.B. 459.
2 *Badische Anilin und Soda Fabrik* v. *Basle Chemical Works*, [1898] A.C. 200.
3 *Furby* v. *Hoey*, [1947] 1 All E.R. 236.
4 (1857), 7 E. & B. 885; see also *Langton* v. *Higgins* (1859), 4 H. & N. 402 (peppermint oil into the buyer's bottles).

v When does property pass?

It has already been stated that property cannot pass until the goods have been "identified" or "ascertained" in some way. What is less clear is the precise moment of time when property passes once they are ascertained. If the appropriation of the goods takes place with the prior assent of the buyer (e.g. if it is implied from the contract itself) then property will normally pass at the moment the appropriation is made. The fact that the buyer had provided the sacks in *Aldridge* v. *Johnson* clearly demonstrated his assent to the method of appropriation adopted by the seller. It was irrelevant that the seller had still to place the sacks on trucks at the railway yard. The seller had made a selection from which he could not resile.

Many of the difficulties can be explained, even if they are not easily resolved, by the need to balance the apparent intention of the seller with the need for some evidence of assent on the part of the buyer. Where the packing and making ready of the goods for collection, or conveyance, is a task over which the buyer has no control, then the need for his assent to what the seller has actually done is that much the greater. In the New Zealand case of *Donaghy's Rope and Twine Co.* v. *Wright, Stephenson and Co.*,[1] S manufactured 26 tons of twine to B's order and stored it in a separate stack. About half of this quantity was delivered. S notified B that the remainder was being held in store, and B replied requesting that S should continue to hold it on his behalf free of charge. It was held that property did not pass until this reply which constituted B's assent to what S had done.

It may not be altogether an academic question whether there can be an act of appropriation to which there is as yet no assent so that property will not yet have passed, or whether the absence of assent vitiates the act of appropriation itself. If it is possible to have an unconditional appropriation to which there is as yet no assent, the seller, once he has appropriated the goods, can no longer (in theory at any rate) change his mind and select other goods in satisfaction of the buyer's order.

The premise at least upon which this proposition is based seems to find support from the decision in *Carlos Federspiel & Co. S.A.* v. *Charles Twigg & Co., Ltd.*[2] S was to manufacture and ship cycles to B under the terms of a f.o.b. contract. The cycles were packed in crates and addressed to B. Before the crates could be shipped S became insolvent. In deciding that property had not yet passed to B, PEARSON J., indulged in a survey of the authorities relevant to rule 5. His Lordship correctly pointed out that a "mere setting apart or selection by the seller of the goods which he expects to use in performance of the contract is not enough" but continued by stating that to "constitute an appropriation of the goods to the contract, the parties must have had, or be reasonably supposed to have had, an intention to attach the contract irrevocably to those goods, so

---

1 (1906), 25 N.Z.L.R. 641. It may be that where goods are made to meet B's special requirements and there is no provision for examination and approval of the finished product by B, there is an implication that B has assented to any appropriation that S might make: see *B. & H. Constructions* v. *Campbell*, [1963] N.S.W.R. 333.
2 [1957] 1 Lloyd's Rep. 240.

that those goods and no others are the subject of the sale and become the property of the buyer".[1] This second part of his Lordship's pronouncement is open to two possible interpretations. In the first place it may mean that goods may be unconditionally appropriated prior to becoming the property of the buyer; or, secondly it could mean that the goods become the property of the buyer by being unconditionally appropriated. This ambiguity permeates his Lordship's judgment, but in the concluding paragraph of his analysis of Rule 5 PEARSON, J., seemed to be favouring the former possibility:[2]

> "usually, but not necessarily, the appropriating act is the last act to be performed by the seller. For instance if delivery is to be taken at the seller's premises and the seller has appropriated the goods when he has made the goods ready and identified them and placed them in position to be taken by the buyer and has so informed the buyer, and if the buyer agrees to come and take them, that is assent to the appropriation. But if there is a further act, an important and decisive act, to be done by the seller, then there is *prima facie* evidence that probably the property does not pass until the final act is done".

In other words, goods may be appropriated to a contract although it is only at a later stage that some further event brings about the passing of property.

In many situations the subsequent event will be the assent of the buyer (and thus the situation will fall within Rule 5 (1)). However, where the subsequent event is under the control of the seller property will not normally pass until that stage is reached. In *Federspiel* v. *Twigg* itself, the subsequent event was the shipping of the goods.[3] Furthermore, this decision does appear to establish that there can be an initial appropriation before the time property passes, but does it necessarily follow that the seller is in any sense bound by such an act? In the Australian case of *Christie* v. *Foster Brewing Co.*,[4] S, the defendant company, was charged with having in its possession for sale bottles of beer to which were affixed labels containing a false description. The beer had been specially brewed by S to the order of a particular customer who had supplied the labels. It had been bottled and the labels had been affixed, although the bottles had not been packed ready for delivery. The magistrates had held that, as property in the beer had passed, no offence had been committed. This finding was, however, over-ruled *inter alia* on the grounds that "the company had not by affixing the labels irrevocably appropriated the goods"[5] to the

---

1 At p. 256.
2 At pp. 255–6.
3 Though it is doubtful whether a situation of this type (i.e. a f.o.b. contract) is covered by Rule 5 (1) at all. It is the common understanding of the mercantile world (presumably covered by s. 17 (1)) that property under such a contract does not pass until the moment when the goods are loaded: *Colley* v. *Overseas Exporters*, [1921] 3 K.B. 302; [1921] All E.R. Rep. 596 (S was unable to sue for the price as he would have been able to do had B nominated an effective ship and thus enabled S to load the goods); *Stock* v. *Inglis* (1885), 10 App. Cas. 263, at pp. 271, *per* Lord BLACKBURN.
4 (1892), 18 V.L.R. 292.
5 At pp. 297–8. The Supreme Court of Victoria also held that, if there had been an appropriation, B had not assented to it, a particularly stringent approach to the assent requirement that is peculiar to the State of Victoria: see for example *Warnock* v. *Blyth* (1873), 4 A.J.R. 47, 180; *Clarke & Co. Pty., Ltd.*, v. *Owen*, [1915] V.L.R. 23.

contract. Hence the goods to which the false labels were affixed were still in S's possession for sale. In so far as this conclusion does go beyond the premise that there can be an appropriation prior to the passing of property to the buyer, it may give slight support for the further proposition that, in appropriate circumstances, the seller can be held to that appropriation.

vi Delivery to a carrier

This analysis is complicated by the existence of a second sub-paragraph to Rule 5 which lays down that where

> "in pursuance of the contract, the seller delivers the goods to the buyer or to a carrier or other bailee . . . (whether named by the buyer or not) for the purpose of transmission to the buyer, and does not reserve the right of disposal, he is deemed to have unconditionally appropriated the goods to the contract".

The difficulty with this provision is that there is no ready explanation of what significance should be attached to it. It obviously would not apply to a situation where property passed before the goods are put into the hands of a carrier (as in *Aldridge* v. *Johnson*[1]). Nor is it applicable to c.i.f. contracts in which, in most cases, the transfer of property occurs at the moment when the shipping documents are delivered to the buyer.[2]

It is certainly true that if property has not passed already, delivery of the goods to the buyer will normally effect a transfer of property. And, if the goods are delivered to a carrier who is B's agent to collect or receive them, the same principle will apply. In *Wardar's (Import and Export) Co., Ltd.* v. *W. Norwood & Sons, Ltd.*,[3] a carrier was sent by B to collect 600 cartons of kidneys that were being held for S in a cold store. When the carrier arrived, he discovered that 600 cartons had been stacked on the pavement ready to be loaded. It was held by the Court of Appeal that, as soon as the store official received the delivery note and indicated to the carrier that the cartons on the pavement were for him to collect, property passed. There was constructive delivery of the goods to him as B's agent.

However, sub-rule (2) uses the expression that the seller is "*deemed* to have unconditionally appropriated the goods to the contract" by delivering the goods to a carrier. One would have supposed that the word "deemed" would have been chosen to apply to a situation where delivery would not normally constitute an unconditional appropriation. However, this interpretation has not been adopted by the courts. In *Healy* v. *Howlett & Sons*,[4] in which the seller had delivered a large number of boxes of mackerel to a railway company for dispatch to several of his customers, it was held that the risk of deterioration

---

1　(1857), 7 E. & B. 885, see above, p. 20.
2　As Bowen, L.J., said in *Sanders* v. *Maclean* (1883), 11 Q.B.D. 327, at p. 341, property in the goods passes by "endorsement and delivery of the bill of lading, whenever it is the intention of the parties that the property should pass, just as under similar circumstances the property would pass by an actual delivery of the goods". Hence S is entitled to sue for the price under a c.i.f. contract as soon as he tenders the bill of lading to B: *E. Clemens Horst & Co.* v. *Biddell Bros.*, [1912] A.C. 18; [1911–13] All E.R. Rep. 93.
3　[1968] 2 Q.B. 663; [1968] 2 All E.R. 602.
4　[1917] 1 K.B. 337.

did not pass at that time because the goods had not then been appropriated to the several contracts. In RIDLEY, J.'s opinion, the "essence of the authorities which decide that appropriation of goods to the contract by delivery to the carrier at the beginning of the transit may be sufficient to pass the property is that it should be known to whom the goods are appropriated".[1]

The same approach is to be seen in the courts' attitude to cases in which they have held that the carrier is in fact the seller's agent.[2] The most likely circumstance to raise the inference that the carrier is the seller's agent, and not the buyer's, is where the seller is responsible for delivering the goods to the buyer's address. The carrier is the seller's agent to carry out this obligation and property will normally pass on delivery to the buyer's premises.

Under the pre-1893 law, delivery to a carrier was only *prima facie*, and in appropriate circumstances, an unconditional appropriation. This eminently reasonable principle has been preserved by disregarding the strict wording of sub-rule (2). In the circumstances, it is perhaps to be regretted that the provision should have been included in the Act. At best it is ignored;[3] at worst it can create confusion in the judicial mind.

Instructive in this context is the Victorian case of *Harrison* v. *Lia*.[4] Milk was collected from S, the defendant, by a carrier provided by B, a milk depot, at S's expense and on S's behalf. S handed a can of milk to the carrier but before it reached its destination a test was carried out which revealed that the milk was adulterated. S could only be convicted of selling adulterated milk if he had actually "sold" the milk, i.e. if property had already passed to the buyer when the can was in transit. The court held that the carrier was S's agent so that property had not yet passed.

It is certainly true that, on the approach generally adopted to Rule 5 (2), that sub-rule would be excluded by the fact that the carrier was S's agent, but was not Rule 5 (1) satisfied? The judge stated that "where the seller appropriates goods to the contract and entrusts them to his own agent for delivery to the purchaser, under an agreement with the buyer for delivery by the seller at this destination, the property, unless something more appears, does not pass".[5] This principle should not however be applied too readily. If the buyer's assent can be implied to the appropriation (as it clearly can in *Harrison* v. *Lia*), there is no reason why Rule 5 (1) should not apply. The only alternative interpretation would be that the contract showed sufficient contrary intention to oust the rules contained in s. 18 altogether. However, the mere fact that the carrier is the seller's agent does not seem to be sufficient evidence of contrary intention to avoid the application of Rule 5 (1), as well as of Rule 5 (2), in all cases.

It is true that members of the House of Lords in *Badische Anilin und Soda Fabrik* v. *Basle Chemical Works*[6] seemed to be of the opinion that the time

---

1 At p. 345.
2 That this is an exceptional situation is clear from s. 32 (1), dealt with below, p. 113.
3 In *Healy* v. *Howlett & Sons* (above), no reference at all was made by the court to r. 5 (2).
4 [1951] V.L.R. 470.
5 At p. 475.
6 [1898] A.C. 200, at pp. 203–4; 207, 209.

when property passed depended upon whose agent the carrier was. However, these observations should not lead too readily to an assumption that this is the only criterion. Lord HERSCHELL, for example, suggested that the test might be that the carrier should be both an agent of the buyer (or seller) and a person for whom the buyer (or seller) was responsible.[1] It might have been permissible to regard the carrier in *Harrison* v. *Lia* as the seller's agent for some purposes only. As he was provided by B, there seems little to be said for the view that property had not passed under Rule 5 (1) irrespective of whether it also passed under Rule 5 (2). The seller was hardly responsible for all the carrier's activities while the goods were in the latter's hands.

Finally, it should be observed that the "carrier" in the *Badische Anilin* case was, at the outset, the Swiss Post Office. It has been surmised[2] that the effect of this case, taken in conjunction with s. 32 (1) whereby *prima facie* at least a carrier is regarded as having been selected by the seller on the buyer's behalf, is to pass the property in goods supplied by mail order to the buyer from the moment of posting. In other words, the risk of loss would fall on the buyer. To a large extent this danger may be more apparent than real, because the majority of such arrangements are "sale or return" contracts and subject to a different rule.[3] But in any case it is doubtful to what extent the post office should be regarded as a normal carrier, and as capable of being an agent for either party.

vii Conditional appropriation

The situation referred to in Rule 5 (2) where the seller reserves a right of disposal is dealt with below in the context of s. 19. However, both Rule 5 (1) and Rule 5 (2) are based upon the concept of an "unconditional appropriation". Not only can S reserve a right of disposal in order to prevent property passing, but, logically, it would seem possible for him to appropriate goods *conditionally*.

The decisions usually referred to in this connection deal with circumstances in which the courts have taken the view that the appropriation was conditional on payment. In *Godts* v. *Rose*[4] the sale was of oil from a larger quantity held by a wharfinger to be "delivered and paid for in fourteen days". The jury apparently accepted the statement made in re-examination by a broker that under the terms of such a contract the seller could deliver at any time within 14 days and require immediate payment. They found that the plaintiff's clerk did not intend to part with a notice of transfer in respect of the oil without being paid. Even though the buyer obtained possession of the notice and thereby delivery of the goods, it was held that property did not pass because appropriation under the notice was conditional upon a payment which had not been made.

---

1 At p. 207.
2 By Atiyah, *The Sale of Goods*, 4th Ed., p. 160.
3 See below, p. 39.
4 (1854), 17 C.B. 229. As ATKIN, J., said in *Stein, Forbes & Co.* v. *County Tailoring Co.* (1916), 86 L.J.Q.B. 448, at pp. 448–9, "I doubt whether goods are appropriated unconditionally if the seller does not mean the buyer to have them unless he pays for them."

If one looks again at *Federspiel* v. *Twigg*,[1] however, it becomes apparent that it is possible to have an appropriation which is not effective to pass property. In other words, it remains conditional until some other event has the effect of transferring the property in the goods. That event could be the assent of the buyer, or it could be some subsequent step to be taken by the seller himself, the "important and decisive act" to which PEARSON, J., referred in that case.[2] In *National Coal Board* v. *Gamble*,[3] the question arose as to the exact moment when property passed in respect of a lorry load of coal being taken by a carrier to the premises of the buyer. The lorry had been loaded from a hopper and it then proceeded to a weighbridge where the Board's servant issued a ticket giving the weight of the load. A majority of the Court[4] took the view that until the weight had been certified, property did not pass. In other words, though the goods had been appropriated to the contract this appropriation remained conditional upon the subsequent assent of both parties (i.e. the weighbridge operator on the seller's behalf, and the driver on behalf of the buyer). The seller would have been within his rights to have refused to allow the vehicle to depart with, and the carrier could similarly have declined to take, the excess load.

B. THE PASSING OF PROPERTY IN SPECIFIC GOODS

When the goods which are the subject matter of the contract are "ascertained" by the contract itself, they are termed "specific" goods. In the words of s. 62 (1), such goods are "goods identified and agreed upon at the time a contract of sale is made".

Because there is no inherent factor which automatically delays the passing of property (i.e. there is no need for the goods to become "identified" by appropriation), it is obviously possible for property to pass at any time from the moment the contract is made. Subject to the overriding prescription of s. 17 (1) that, where there is a contract for the sale of specific goods, "the property in them is transferred to the buyer at such time as the parties to the contract intend it to be transferred", s. 18 goes on to lay down a number of rules for ascertaining their intentions. However, the primary principle appears in Rule 1:

> "Where there is an unconditional contract for the sale of specific goods, in a deliverable state, the property in the goods passes to the buyer when the contract is made, and it is immaterial whether the time of payment or the time of delivery, or both, be postponed."

If one looks at Rules 2 and 3 it will be seen that they are in effect complementary to the application of Rule 1. Rule 2 makes clear that where goods are not in a

---

1 [1957] 1 Lloyd's Rep. 240; above, p. 21.
2 At p. 256.
3 [1959] 1 Q.B. 11; [1958] 3 All E.R. 203. The N.C.B. had been charged with aiding and abetting the carriers in committing an offence in respect of the overloaded lorry. It was held that the Board could properly be convicted as the weighbridge operator could have refused to issue a ticket in respect of the vehicle's weight.
4 Lord GODDARD, C. J., and DEVLIN, J.; SLADE, J., dissented.

deliverable state, the passing of property is delayed until they are and the buyer is aware of the fact, while Rule 3 provides that if the seller has to weigh or measure, etc., the goods in order to ascertain the price, then property does not pass until he has taken this step. In contrast, Rule 4 deals with the quite separate type of transaction where the goods are taken "on sale or return": in such a case, as there may or may not be an actual sale of the goods in question, Rule 1 can have no direct application.

Whatever the strict application of Rule 1 might involve, the attitude of the courts has led to some change of emphasis. As a consequence the present position can perhaps more helpfully be rendered as follows:

(i) property cannot pass to the buyer until the contract is finalised—although until such issues as payment and delivery are settled the contract may not be considered as finalised;

(ii) but it will only pass then if

  (a) there is no contrary intention—in considering this aspect of the problem the fact that the time of payment or delivery is postponed may nevertheless give rise to an inference under s. 17 (1) that property is not to pass until that time;

  (b) the contract is unconditional;

  (c) the goods are specific; and

  (d) they are in a deliverable state.

i The contract must be finalised

a *Offer and acceptance*

It goes without saying that there can be no transfer of property until a contract is actually made. However, it may not always be easy to state with precision when that stage is reached. The concept of offer and acceptance as well as the principle embodied in Rule 1 are both more appropriate to a simple purchase of a relatively inexpensive item arranged between two individuals than they are to a commercial transaction of some complexity, or even in many instances to a sale in a shop or showroom.

When the parties are involved in a lengthy correspondence it would be impossible at the time to label any particular letter as "the" offer and it is rather artificial to do so at a later date. Furthermore, a communication setting out the goods and the price might be viewed by the courts as an inadequate basis upon which the other party could finalise the contract by an acceptance.

In the well known case of *Clifton* v. *Palumbo*,[1] the parties had been negotiating for the sale of an estate. It was held that, because of the size and diversity of the estate, a letter in which the vendor stated that he was "prepared to offer" the estate to the purchaser for £600,000 did not constitute an offer, but was only a further step in the negotiations. As Lord GREENE pointed out,[2] in words equally appropriate to any commercial dealings, when parties

---

1 [1944] 2 All ER 497.
2 At pp. 498–9.

"are beginning to negotiate a transaction of this magnitude it is common experience—and indeed, it is only business—to find that the first thing they begin to think about, is the price, because it is quite useless making elaborate investigations and conducting complicated negotiations if it is going to turn out in the end that their views as to price do not agree."

Once some agreement was reached on the price, however, the question arose as to where the parties stood. The Master of the Rolls continued:[1]

"There is nothing in the world to prevent an owner . . . contracting to sell . . . to a purchaser, who is prepared to spend so large a sum of money, on terms, written out on a half sheet of note-paper, of the most informal description, and even, if he likes, on unfavourable conditions; but I think it is legitimate, in approaching the construction of a document of this kind . . . to bear in mind that the probability of parties entering into so large a transaction, and finally binding themselves to a contract of this description . . . is remote."

b *Invitations to treat*

The difficulty of ascertaining the moment when the contract is made is also raised in the most simple and obvious of transactions, a sale in a shop. If the buyer asks the price of a particular item or commodity, the seller's reply to this question is not likely to be construed as an offer which the buyer is thereupon entitled to convert into a contract by an order for the goods in question.[2] It would, however, only require a slight variation in what the buyer said in such a situation to convert the seller's reply into an offer. For example, if the buyer had asked if the seller could supply one ton of coal for immediate delivery and what would be the price, the seller's affirmative response together with a firm price being given would almost certainly be construed as an offer.

While this type of distinction can at least be said to coincide with the apparent intention of the parties, the attitude of the courts towards goods displayed and priced in shops is less satisfactory. *Pharmaceutical Society of Great Britain* v. *Boots Cash Chemists (Southern), Ltd.*[3] is generally taken to have settled any doubts by laying down that "it is a well established principle that the mere exposure of goods for sale by a shopkeeper indicates to the public that he is willing to treat but does not amount to an offer to sell",[4] and that same rule is equally applicable to a self-service store where the offer is made by the customer presenting the goods at the pay-out counter.[5] This view of the law was accepted and acted upon by a Divisional Court in *Fisher* v. *Bell*[6] in which it was held that the

---

1 At p. 499. For a similar comment on the application of the postal acceptance rule see the joint judgment of DIXON, C.J., and FULLAGAR, J., in *Tallerman & Co. Pty., Ltd.* v. *Nathan's Merchandise (Victoria) Pty., Ltd.* (1957), 98 C.L.R. 93, at p. 112:
   "in such a case as the present, where solicitors are conducting a highly contentious correspondence, one would have thought that actual communication would be regarded as essential to the conclusion of agreement on anything."
2 See *Kelly* v. *Caledonian Coal Co.* (1898), 19 N.S.W.L.R. 1, at p. 6, *per* DARLEY, C.J.
3 [1952] 2 Q.B. 795; [1952] 2 All E.R. 456.
4 [1952] 2 Q.B. 795, at p. 801; [1952] 2 All E.R. 456, at p. 458.
5 There seems little good reason why the goods on display could not be regarded as the offer, and the acceptance could be regarded as taking place at the cash desk to the retailer's agent to receive communication of such acceptance.
6 [1961] 1 Q.B. 394; [1960] 3 All E.R. 731.

display of a flick-knife, with a price-tag adjoining it, in a shop window did not constitute an "offer of sale" within s. 1 of the Restriction of Offensive Weapons Act 1959.

It cannot be claimed that this attitude has a great deal to commend it. By treating the shop display as an invitation to treat, the law is certainly at variance with the expectations of the average customer. This contrast was admitted by Lord PARKER, C.J., in *Fisher* v. *Bell*:[1]

> "Most lay people would be inclined to the view (as indeed, I was when I first read these papers), that if a knife were displayed in a window like that with a price attached to it, it was nonsense to say that it was not offering it for sale. The knife is there inviting people to buy it, and in ordinary language it is for sale; but any statute must be looked at in the light of the general law of the country, for Parliament must be taken to know the general law. It is clear that, according to the ordinary law of contract, the display of an article with a price on it in a shop window is merely an invitation to treat."

c *The Trade Descriptions Act* 1968

The reaction of the normal customer, who, when he tries to buy an article at a marked price, is told that in fact the price is higher, is to feel that he has been cheated. That this reaction is not unreasonable has been recognised by Parliament in s. 11 (2) of the Trade Descriptions Act, 1968:

> "If any person offering to supply any goods gives, by whatever means, any indication likely to be taken as an indication that the goods are being offered at a price less than that at which they are in fact being offered he shall, subject to the provisions of this Act, be guilty of an offence."

It will immediately be apparent that, by using the most obvious form of wording, the draftsman was still left with the problem of dealing with the difficulty encountered in *Fisher* v. *Bell*. Accordingly, s. 6 was included to avoid such an interpretation:[2]

> "A person exposing goods for supply or having goods in his possession for supply shall be deemed to offer to supply them."

Although s. 11 (2) would thus *appear* to create a criminal offence of wide application to make up for what could be regarded as a defect in the normal rules of contract law, the protection afforded to the consumer is severely curtailed by s. 24 (1) of the Act, or more specifically by the interpretation placed upon that provision by the House of Lords in *Tesco Supermarkets, Ltd.* v. *Nattrass*.[3] Section 24 (1) provides that it shall be a defence for a person charged with an offence under the Act to prove:

> "(*a*) that the commission of the offence was due to a mistake or to reliance

---

1 [1961] 1 Q.B. 394, at p. 399; [1960] 3 All E.R. 731, at pp. 732–3.
2 Referring to s. 6, ASHWORTH, J., commented in *Doble* v. *David Greig Ltd.*, [1972] 2 All E.R. 195, at p. 198, "those words are important, because they serve to correct what might otherwise be the impression that the mere displaying of goods on a counter was not an offer to supply".
3 [1972] A.C. 153; [1971] 2 All E.R. 127.

on information supplied to him or to the act or default of another person, an accident or some other cause beyond his control; and
(*b*) that he took all reasonable precautions and exercised all due diligence to avoid the commission of such an offence by himself or any person under his control."

It is reasonable enough to provide the trader with a defence of mistake if, inadvertently, a price tag became dislodged so that it appeared to refer to other, more expensive goods, providing of course he could show that he had exercised due diligence to avoid such errors and in checking regularly to correct such errors if they did occur. It might, for example, be reasonable to carry out such an inspection at the end of a day's trading. A trader would presumably be able to plead the defence in respect of a price tag that he could prove had become transposed in the course of the day in which the alleged offence is claimed to have taken place.

Perhaps the main obstacle to the operation of the Act is, however, the problem of identifying who should be prosecuted. If M is in charge of S's shop in which there is a price tag which has fallen into the wrong place and which it is A's task to check daily, who could be successfully prosecuted if the error is not picked up and a complaint[1] is made by a customer who sought to purchase the incorrectly priced item? However, the answer to this question will be dealt with later when the general framework of the Trade Descriptions Act is discussed.[2] For the moment it should be noticed that "another person" for the purpose of establishing a defence under s. 24 can be a person in S's employment and for whose activities within the scope of that person's normal authority S would in contract be liable.

d *Agreement on means of payment*

Section 18 Rule 1 presupposes that a contract of sale is no more than an agreement on the goods to be sold and the price to be paid. Even if one reaches this stage in the transaction, however, common sense suggests that the seller is as interested in the means of payment as he is in the amount to be paid. It is arguable therefore that, unless there is evidence to the contrary in the course of negotiations, a contract of sale is a cash transaction and the contract is finalised with agreement on the price only if the price is to be paid in cash. Where the transaction *may* be on credit, then no contract can be said to be formed until agreement is reached on the terms of the credit. A sale on credit would of course include a transaction in which the price is to be paid by cheque.

There is a surprising dearth of authority for, or even against, this view although the point was considered in the well-known case of *Ingram* v. *Little*.[3] The sellers had agreed a price for their car with B who thereupon attempted to pay by cheque. When the sellers at first refused to take the cheque, B persuaded them to accept it by convincing them that he was X. The sellers attempt to recover

---

1 By s. 26 enforcement of the Act is placed in the hands of the local weights and measures authority: see Weights and Measures Act 1963, ss. 34 *et seq.*
2 See below, p. 264.
3 [1961] 1 Q.B. 31; [1960] 3 All E.R. 332.

the car from a third party would have been doomed from the outset if it could have been said that the contract under which they had sold the car had been finalised at the moment when the price had been agreed, because at that stage B's identity had been irrelevant. Both SELLERS, L.J., and PEARCE, L.J., preferred the conclusion of SLADE, J., at first instance that no contract had been formed at that moment. To SELLERS, L.J., "the price of anything which is sold is a price in cash unless anything else is said to the contrary",[1] and for PEARCE, L.J., when B pulled out the cheque book, from a "practical point of view" the negotiations had reached "an impasse". It had been argued that a contract had come into existence as soon as the price was agreed. Whatever the theoretical merits of this approach, in PEARCE, L.J.'s opinion, "the judge's more realistic approach was right. Payment and delivery still needed to be discussed and the parties would be expecting to discuss them. Immediately they did discuss them it became plain that they were not *ad idem* and that no contract had yet been created".[2]

ii Factors negativing the application of Rule 1

a *Evidence of a contrary intention*

The application of any of the rules contained in s. 18 is, as has already been discussed in relation to Rule 5, dependent upon there being no evidence of a contrary intention. Despite the wording of Rule 1 that "it is immaterial" to the passing of property "whether the time of payment or the time of delivery or both be postponed", there is an increasing reluctance to hold that property passes to a buyer who has yet to pay for the goods or to take delivery of them. In *R. V. Ward, Ltd* v. *Bignall*,[3] B agreed a price of £850 for S's two cars. B paid £25 and went to his bank to obtain the balance in cash. While he was away he had second thoughts about the transaction and tried to persuade S to accept a lower price, or to allow him (B) to take only one of the vehicles. In the course of giving judgment, SELLERS, L.J., touched upon the question of whether property in the cars had at any time passed to B, and concluded that it had not. The fact that the buyer after inspection

> "agreed to buy the two vehicles ... and paid £25 in cash at the time goes but little way to establishing that the parties intended the vehicles then and there to become the buyer's property. There was not even a payment by cheque. The buyer went to his bank to get cash and that was to be handed over ... He had not even seen the log books or inquired of their existence. No mention was made of the removal of the vehicles or of their insurance ..."[4]

Or, as DIPLOCK, L.J., put it,[5]

> "the governing rule is s. 17, and in modern times very little is needed to

---

1 [1961] 1 Q.B. 31, at p. 49; [1960] 3 All E.R. 332, at p. 335.
2 [1961] 1 Q.B., at p. 58; [1960] 3 All E.R., at p. 342.
3 [1967] 1 Q.B. 534; [1967] 2 All E.R. 449.
4 [1967] 1 Q.B. at p. 541; [1967] 2 All E.R., at p. 451.
5 [1967] 1 Q.B., at p. 545 [1967]; 2 All E.R., at p. 453. Hence in a supermarket or "cash and carry" type of shop the intention is that "property shall not pass until the price is paid": *Lacis* v. *Cashmarts,* [1969] 2 Q.B. 400, at p. 407.

give rise to the inference that the property in specific goods is to pass only on delivery or payment."

It would seem, therefore, that a case like *Tarling* v. *Baxter*[1] though supported by the unanimous weight of pre-1893 authority, can no longer be regarded as a reliable guide. In that case, B agreed on January 4 to pay £145 for a stack of hay belonging to S. Payment was to be made on the following February 4 but the stack was to be allowed to remain on S's brother's land until May 1. The hay was destroyed by fire without fault on the part of either party on January 20. It was held that, the goods being specific and there being nothing remaining for S to do, property passed at the time of the contract so that B was liable for the price. If such a transaction were placed in the context of a present-day consumer sale, the reaction of the average buyer would certainly be that he should be under no obligation to pay for goods he had not yet received, and there seems no strong reason why the law should not coincide with this expectation.

The parties can of course make express provision governing the time when property is to pass. All that is necessary, if the expression of intention is clear, is to show that such expression forms part of the contract. Whereas an absence of agreement over the means of payment or delivery may lead a court to conclude that no contract has been finalised, there is no room for similar doubts if the sale is by auction. The contract is concluded and, unless the auctioneer's conditions of sale (adequately displayed to form part of the contract) stipulate otherwise, property will pass at the fall of the hammer. In *Dennant* v *Skinner and Collom*,[2] S, an auctioneer, only allowed B to take possession of a number of vehicles, knocked down to him at the auction, on the strength of a written statement by B that ownership was not to pass until B's cheque was cleared. Because the contract had already been concluded by the time B gave this undertaking, it was held that the contract had therefore been unconditional and that Rule 1 operated to pass the property in the vehicles to B.

Even if a written document does form part of the contract, it will be a question of construction for the court whether the words used by the parties as to the passing of property or the risk of loss in fact have the effect of displacing Rule 1. In *Re Anchor Line (Henderson Bros), Ltd.*,[3] B had assumed possession of a berth in a dock basin formerly occupied by S. At the berth was a crane belonging to S which B was anxious to use. An agreement was entered into whereby B took over the crane "for a deferred purchase price" of £4,000. Annual payments were to be made in respect of interest and depreciation, but the latter sums were to be deducted from the £4,000 on "completion of the purchase". Until that time, B was to have "entire charge of and responsibility for the crane in every respect". Before the price was finally paid, B went into liquidation and the rights to the crane depended upon whether property in the crane had passed to B at the time of the contract. The transaction was similar to a sale in

---

1 (1827), 6 B. & C. 360. A better solution to the problem of the passing of property on sale of a haystack is that there is a custom in the trade that property is to pass at the time of the contract: *Lord Eldon* v. *Hedley Bros.*, [1935] 2 K.B. 1.
2 [1948] 2 K.B. 164; [1948] 2 All E.R. 29.
3 [1937] Ch. 1; [1936] 2 All E.R. 941.

which the price was to be paid by instalments. However, the Court of Appeal held that the payments in respect of depreciation until "completion of the purchase" and the fact that the parties felt it necessary to make special provision to impose responsibility for the crane on B, together constituted evidence of an intention inconsistent with the application of Rule 1.[1].

b *The contract is not 'unconditional'*

The weight of academic opinion[2] favours the view that the adjective "unconditional" in Rule 1 signifies a contract which does not contain a condition precedent that suspends performance of the contract or the passing of property. Certainly it would render Rule 1 inapplicable in any circumstances if "unconditional" were interpreted to mean "incorporating" or "including" no conditions because ss. 12–15 of the Act itself imply into contracts of sale a series of conditions. Where the inconsistency and ambiguity has arisen is that Chalmers, in drafting the Act, adopted a long established use of the expression "unconditional" in Rule 1, but distorted the previous law by using the term "condition" in ss. 12–15.

Under the pre-1893 law there were a number of warranties, corresponding to the terms contained in ss. 12–15 of the Act, that were implied into contracts of sale. Whether breach of one of these warranties entitled a buyer to reject the goods, or limited him to a remedy in damages, depended upon whether the buyer could show that performance by the seller of the undertaking contained in the warranty constituted a condition precedent to the buyer's obligation to perform his side of the bargain. In the case of goods which were not specific or were not in a deliverable state, the buyer's obligation was to accept the goods and to pay for them. With specific goods which were in a deliverable state, property passed and the buyer was obliged to pay the price. A breach of a warranty relating to the goods could no longer give the buyer a right to reject once property had passed because there had been no total failure of consideration.

However, it was still possible for the buyer to establish that the seller had by implication given an undertaking that, even if property had passed, the buyer would nevertheless be entitled to set aside the contract.[3] It would be equally possible for the buyer or seller to show that it was implicit in their dealings that performance by the other party of some particular obligation was a *sine qua non* to the passing of property, or to the operation of the contract. For example, property could not be said to pass if the goods did not answer the contract description. A failure to satisfy the obligation to supply goods answering that description would constitute a breach of a condition precedent

---

1 And see *Minister of Supply and Development* v. *Servicemen's Co-Operative Joinery Manufacturers, Ltd.* (1951), 82 C.L.R. 621 (S sold to B certain machinery on premises let by S to B. The price was not paid and S retook possession of the machinery by resuming possession of the premises. It was held that the term "net cash before delivery" had the effect of ousting Rule 1: until the price was paid B took possession of the goods as bailee and not as a buyer).

2 Atiyah, *The Sale of Goods*, 4th Ed., pp. 144–5; *Chitty on Contracts*, 23rd Ed., Vol 2, p. 709; Fridman, *Sale of Goods*, pp. 71 *et seq.*; Sutton, *Sale of Goods in Australia and New Zealand*, pp. 154 *et seq.*

3 As in *Bannerman* v. *White* (1861), 10 C.B.N.S. 844.

to the buyer's obligations and to the passing of property. In that sense, a sale of specific goods was always (and, for that matter, still is) "conditional", though property will *prima facie* pass at the time the contract is made if the goods are of the type described.

More detailed analysis of the significance of the "description" of the goods will be left until performance of the contract is dealt with[1] but its role in relation to the passing of property can be illustrated by reference to the case of *Varley* v. *Whipp*.[2] S told B that he had a second-hand reaping machine for sale that had been new the previous year and had only been used to cut fifty or sixty acres. B agreed to buy the machine and to pay the cost of carriage if S would put it on the railway. At that time S did not in fact own the machine, but he purchased it in order to fulfil his contract with B. When B received the machine he discovered that it was a very old one and had been mended. B informed S that it was no use as he did not care about old machinery, and subsequently he returned it to S. Although the goods were specific in the sense that they were "identified and agreed upon" at the time of the contract, Rule 1 could not operate because the goods belonged to a third party and not to S. Nevertheless, CHANNELL, J.,[3] seems to have treated the case as if S had been the owner at the time of the contract. Not only did he comment that this was not "an unconditional contract for the sale of specific goods",[4] but he gave a number of examples where the failure of the goods to answer the particular description given by the seller prevented property passing even on a normal sale of specific goods.[5] In other words the passing of property even on a sale of specific goods will normally be "conditional" upon the goods answering their description.

c *That the goods are not "specific"*

Although the goods in *Varley* v. *Whipp* were specified, they were "future" goods because the seller was not at the time of the contract the owner of them. Accordingly property could not have passed at that moment whatever the intentions of the parties may have been. In fact, the tendency has been for the courts in the past to interpret the need for the goods to be specific strictly in relation to Rule 1. In *Kursell* v. *Timber Operators and Contractors Ltd.*,[6] for example, it was held that a contract for the sale of all timber of certain dimensions growing in a particular forest in Latvia on a named date was not a sale of specific goods. In this case, of course, there was no question of property passing on the date of the contract because a later date had been agreed between the parties. However, it was not possible to argue that property in trees of the specified size had passed on that later date because the trees were never "specific". As SCRUTTON, L.J., pointed out,[7]

---

1 See below, p. 117.   2 [1900] 1 Q.B. 513.
3 With whom BUCKNILL, J., presumably agreed, as he was "of the same opinion", at p. 517.
4 At p. 517.
5 At p. 516. Similarly property in a sale of unascertained goods will not pass if goods not answering the description are appropriated to the contract: see *Thornley* v. *Tuckvill (Butchers) Ltd.*, [1964] Crim. L.R. 127.
6 [1927] 1 K.B. 298.
7 At p. 311.

"specific goods are defined as goods identified and agreed upon at the time the contract of sale is made. It appears to me that these goods were neither identified nor agreed upon. Not every tree in the forest passed, but only those complying with a certain measurement not then made."

d *Goods not in a deliverable state*

1 *The application of Rule* 2. In addition to holding that property had not passed in *Kursell* v. *Timber Operators* because the timber was not specific, the Court of Appeal also held that the timber could not be regarded as in a deliverable state. There were a number of reasons for this decision. In the first place, until the timber was cut, it could not be "goods", even though the contract was a sale of goods by virtue of s. 62 (1). Accordingly, until that point in time, property could not pass to a buyer.[1] But, in any case, as the contract referred to agreement by the parties' representatives on which trees should be cut, it was at least arguable that the goods could not be regarded as in a deliverable state until the trees had been cut in accordance with this arrangement.[2]

The requirement that the goods should be in a deliverable state is in fact spelt out by s. 18 Rule 2:

"Where there is a contract for the sale of specific goods and the seller is bound to do something to the goods, for the purpose of putting them into a deliverable state, the property does not pass until such thing be done, and the buyer has notice thereof."

The Act refers only to the seller putting the goods in a deliverable state. *Kursell* v. *Timber Operators and Contractors, Ltd.* suggests that the same principle may be applicable even when it is the buyer who has to "do something to the goods". Certainly SCRUTTON, L.J., made the comment[3] that he did not think that the timber was in "a deliverable state until the buyer has severed it". For that principle to apply, the inference must be drawn from the terms of the contract and the circumstances of the case. It is only when it is for the seller to put the goods in a deliverable state that the Act draws that inference.

Although the point may be largely academic, it is possible to regard the fact that goods are not in a deliverable state either, or both, as evidence of a contrary intention to oust the application of Rule 1, or/and as falling within the specific application of Rule 2. In other words, Rule 2 (and Rule 3 as well) is more in the nature of an exception to Rule 1 than a rule of similar status to Rules 1, 4 and 5.

In *Underwood, Ltd.* v. *Burgh Castle Brick and Cement Syndicate*,[4] S agreed to sell to B a machine weighing 30 tons that was bolted to and embedded in a concrete floor. Under the terms of the contract S was to dismantle the machine and to place it free on rail in London. While the machine was being loaded on a railway truck it was damaged. S was only entitled to sue for the price if property

---

1 And this would be so even if the parties *intended* property to pass at the time of the contract: *Morison* v. *Lockhart*, 1912 2 S.L.T. 189, at p. 193, *per* Lord JOHNSTON, cited with approval by the Court in *Kursell's* case.
2 The judgments are not altogether clear on this point, see *per* Lord HANWORTH, M.R., [1927] 1 K.B., at p. 308, and *per* SCRUTTON, L.J., at p. 312.
3 At p. 312.
4 [1922] 1 K.B. 343; [1921] All E.R. Rep. 515.

had already passed before the time of the accident. BANKES, L.J., with whom ATKIN, L.J. agreed, held that because of the risk and expense involved in dismantling and moving the engine, the proper inference to be drawn was that property was not to pass until the engine was safely placed on rail in London. In other words, the rules contained in s. 18 were irrelevant. However, all three members of the court were agreed that, even if that inference could not be drawn, Rule 2 clearly applied. As SCRUTTON, L.J. observed,[1] it was

> "impossible to apply the definition in s. 62 ... of a 'deliverable state' as 'a state in which the buyer is bound to take delivery of the goods' to this case, where the buyers find an engine so firmly attached that it takes two days before it can be got loose, and in such a state that it cannot be put on rail, where they stipulated to have it, until a further two weeks' work has been done upon it."

The same principle was applied in the very different circumstances that occurred in the more recent case of *Philip Head & Sons, Ltd.* v. *Showfronts, Ltd.*[2] The plaintiff undertook to provide and to lay carpet in a suite of offices, which included a large showroom. The carpet to cover the showroom floor, which had been stitched together for the purpose, was delivered to the premises but, before it could be put in place, it was stolen. The plaintiffs sued to recover the price on the ground that the goods had been ascertained and appropriated to the contract under Rule 5 (1) of s. 18 and that property had therefore passed. MOCATTA, J., held that this argument failed. He referred to the pre-Act case of *Seath* v. *Moore*[3] in which Lord BLACKBURN had pointed out that, whether goods were specific or had been ascertained, property could not pass until the seller had done all that was necessary to put the subject matter of the sale in the state "in which it is to be finally delivered to the purchaser". In this case, even though the contract had been for unascertained and not specific goods, it still remained for the seller to fit the carpet once it had been "ascertained" and, until he did lay it, the goods were not in a deliverable state.

The Rule incorporates as its final words the expression "and the buyer has notice thereof". It seems reasonable enough that if, for example, the seller is to repair or alter the goods the buyer should be made aware of the fact that the repair or alteration has been completed before property passes. Of course, it should be borne in mind that, as the increasing tendency is for the courts to disregard Rule 1 on the basis of the parties supposed contrary intention, the significance of Rule 2 is correspondingly diminished. The fact that goods have to be repaired or altered before delivery is more likely to lead a court to conclude that property is not to pass until delivery.

2 *The application of Rule* 3. If the seller agrees to supply the buyer with a specific mass of a particular commodity at a stipulated price per unit (whether it be by weight, volume, etc.) it would clearly be possible for property to pass at the moment of contract. However the courts have always taken the view that, if the task of fixing the price in accordance with the formula agreed by the

---

1 [1922] 1 K.B. 343, at p. 346.
2 [1970] 1 Lloyds Rep. 140.
3 (1886), 11 App. Cas. 350, at p. 370.

parties is left to the seller, then property does not pass until he performs that task. Hence Rule 3 of s. 18 states:

"Where there is a contract for the sale of specific goods in a deliverable state, but the seller is bound to weigh, measure, test, or do some other act or thing with reference to the goods for the purpose of ascertaining the price, the property does not pass until such act or thing be done, and the buyer has notice thereof."

Although this provision refers to goods already being in a "deliverable state" in origin Rule 3 was probably not distinguished from the principle contained in Rule 2. In other words, goods did not become "in a deliverable state" until the seller had done all that he was supposed to do, including weighing them or measuring them, under the terms of the contract. In *Hanson* v. *Meyer*,[1] S sold an entire bulk of starch at a specified price per hundredweight. The bailee, who was instructed to weigh and deliver the goods, had only done so with respect to part of the goods when B became bankrupt. S thereupon countermanded the delivery order. It was held that property in the part that had not been weighed did not pass. While suggesting that ascertainment of the exact price was first necessary, it is clear[2] that the main ground for Lord ELLENBOROUGH'S decision was that if anything remained "to be done on the part of the seller, as between him and the buyer, before the commodity purchased is to be delivered, a complete present right of property has not attached in the buyer".[3]

The suggestion in *Hanson* v. *Meyer* that the exact ascertainment of the price was necessary before property could pass would be equally applicable to the situation where the obligation to weigh the goods fell on the buyer. It was certainly true that, at common law, where the price was fixed specifically by the contract and the buyer was only to weigh the goods for his own satisfaction,[4] property would already have passed. However, it is less certain what the position would be today in a situation where a unit price is given and the exact price can only be ascertained once the goods are weighed or measured in a contract under which that task is entrusted to the purchaser after he has taken possession of the goods. The courts could either take the view, expressed in *Hanson* v. *Meyer*, that property would not normally pass until the price is accurately determined; or regard the transfer of possession as amounting to evidence of an intention that property should also pass.

The case usually cited in this connection, *Nanka-Bruce* v. *Commonwealth Trust*,[5] is not entirely satisfactory. The sale was of 160 bags of cocoa at so many

---

1 (1805), 6 East 614.
2 From Lord ELLENBOROUGH, C.J.'s observation in *Rugg* v. *Minett* (1809), 11 East 210, at p. 217, that:
    "according to the case of *Hanson* v. *Meyer* . . . everything having been done by the sellers, which lay upon them to perform, in order to put the goods in a deliverable state in the place from whence they were to be taken by the buyers, the goods remained there at the risk of the latter."
3 6 East, at p. 627.
4 *Hammond* v. *Anderson*, (1803), 1 B. & P.N.R. 69; *Swanwick* v. *Sothern* (1839), 9 Ad. & El. 895.
5 [1926] A.C. 77.

shillings[1] per 60 lbs. The normal course of dealings was for S to put the goods on board a train and for a consignment note to be given to B. B would then resell the goods and transfer the consignment note to the third party, T. The cocoa would then be weighed by T when the consignment was eventually received. On the occasion in question, S attempted to have his contract with B set aside and to claim that property had not passed to B or, therefore, to T until the weighing took place. The courts of the Gold Coast had held that the transaction between S and B had been a completed sale. Indeed it is hard to imagine how the weighing of the goods by the third party could have any suspensive effect on the passing of property between seller and buyer under a contract following which the buyer was known to be going to resell the goods to that third party. In addition, as the Judicial Committee said,[2] to

> "effect such suspension ... would require a clear contract between vendor and vendee to that effect. In this case there was no contract whatsoever to carry into effect the weighing which was simply a means to satisfy the purchaser that he had what he had bargained for and that the full price claimed per the contract was therefore due."

It can be seen therefore that no clear authority exists for the proposition that, where the weighing or measuring is the buyer's responsibility, property will already have passed. No provision governing the point is included in s. 18 because the time at which property will pass in such a situation would depend almost entirely upon the circumstances of the case. Where the precise ascertainment of the price is a matter of importance to the parties, then there is no reason why its ascertainment by the buyer cannot have the same suspensive effect as when it is ascertained through the act of the seller. On the other hand, where the accuracy of the price is a factor of little significance it is unlikely that a court would consider the act of weighing or measuring by the buyer as being in any way suspensive of the passing of property. Indeed so rarely has s. 18 Rule 3 been called in aid that one must conclude that weighing or measuring by the seller is usually a matter of no importance in deciding when the property is to pass in accordance with the parties intentions under s. 17.

Rule 3, like Rule 2, concludes with the words "and the buyer has notice thereof", and the same considerations are relevant here as under Rule 2.[3] It is also true to say that notice to the buyer is somewhat anomalous in that it is only the assent of the other party (usually the buyer) that is required when goods are appropriated to the contract under Rule 5 (1). Where unascertained goods are part of bulk, weighing or measuring the goods is the normal means of appropriating them. If it is done with the buyer's assent, it can still take place without his having any knowledge of the precise time when that occurs. Under Rule 3, the contract itself should constitute the buyer's consent, but there is the additional (and, at common law, unnecessary) requirement that the buyer should be aware that the weighing or measuring has occurred.

---

1 Given as 59s. per load of 60 lb. in [1926] A.C. 77, but as 50s. per 60 lb. in 94 L.J.P.C. 169.
2 [1926] A.C., at p. 79.
3 See above, p. 36.

C. GOODS SUPPLIED ON APPROVAL

Rule 4 covers the passing of property in situations where "goods are delivered to the buyer on approval or 'on sale or return' or other similar terms". Despite the potentially wide ambit of the provision, it must be taken in the context of the Act as a whole. That is to say, the rule is only applicable to the case of an agreement between the parties that one of them should have possession of the goods for a trial period pending a sale. Hence if there is no such prior agreement, Rule 4 would not be applied to pass property in unsolicited goods that had been delivered "on approval". However, the two situations are analogous, and comparisons will be made in relation to the passing of property and to the risk of loss or damage to the goods.

i The relationship between the parties prior to the passing of property

It will be noticed that Rule 4 deals only with the passing of property: the Act is silent as to the general nature of the relationship between the parties. Hence some comment is necessary on the position in which the parties are placed prior to the moment at which property passes.

Where goods are supplied on the basis that the person taking possession of the goods is to try them out, it is possible that that person becomes a bailee of the goods until he decides to buy them, or he may become a buyer from the outset with a power to return the goods and bring the contract to an end at a later stage if he so wishes. It is a question of construction of the terms of the contract in the light of the circumstances of the case to decide which of these alternatives is intended by the parties. However, although the Act refers to the person who takes goods on approval as a "buyer" the better view is that, in a situation covered by Rule 4, he is only a bailee of the goods with an option to purchase them. Accordingly, until he exercises that option[1] he is not a buyer in possession of goods who is able to pass a good title to a third party under s. 25 of the Sale of Goods Act.[2]

a *Can S revoke within the trial period*

It is a moot point whether B's possession as bailee is contractual or whether it is at will. An offer, unsupported by consideration, may be revoked at any time.[3] But is the standing offer contained in the option open to the bailee in a sale "on approval", included in such a category? It is certainly different from a promise to keep an offer open for a specified period where there is no question of the offeror taking possession of the goods on trial during that time. But does this difference have legal significance?

---

1 Though an attempt by B to transfer the goods to a third party will amount to an exercise of the option if Rule 4 applies: see below, p. 44.

2 *Percy Edwards, Ltd.* v. *Vaughan* (1910), 26 T.L.R. 545, at p. 546, *per* COZENS-HARDY, M.R.; as opposed to a buyer under a conditional contract who can pass title: *Marten* v. *Whale*, [1917] 2 K.B. 480. See below, p. 82.

3 *Dickinson* v. *Dodds* (1876), 2 Ch.D. 463; the proposition was said to be "clearly established by a century of decisions" by ISAACS, J. in *Goldsborough Mort & Co., Ltd.* v. *Quinn* (1910), 10 C.L.R. 674, at p. 690.

1 *The need for consideration*. The rule that a party may resile from a promise to keep an offer open for a specified period is not one that would commend itself to the layman,[1] and it may be that its ambit should not be unnecessarily extended. In *Ellis* v. *Mortimer*,[2] S agreed to let B have a horse for 30 days on trial and to sell it to him for 30 guineas if B liked it. B took the horse but after a fortnight he told S that, though he liked the horse, he did not like the price. Thereupon S demanded the return of the animal. This B did not do for another ten days. S refused to take the horse back and sued B for the 30 guineas. The decision that S was not entitled to the price of the horse because no sale had taken place is clearly correct. However, while one member of the court expressed the opinion that a claim in *trover* would have lain, the majority view was that B was nevertheless entitled to complete the trial as it was still possible he might change his mind about buying the animal.

Part of the difficulty with this case stems from the general uncertainty that surrounds the law of bailment. Whether one takes the classification suggested by HOLT, C.J., in *Coggs* v. *Bernard*,[3] or the simple division between gratuitous bailees and bailees for reward,[4] the viewpoint of the law is principally that of the bailor and his rights. There are references to bailments for a term and to bailments at will. A contract of hire will normally fall within the former category, although a loan is usually determinable at the will of the bailor. The trial of the horse in *Ellis* v. *Mortimer* was certainly for a specified period, but is it not necessary that there should be consideration to make this term binding as against the bailor whether it is regarded as part of a standing offer or as an aspect of bailment? The answer is probably that only a minimal benefit to the bailor or detriment to the bailee is necessary to provide the necessary consideration. In *Bainbridge* v. *Firmstone*,[5] the bailor sued in *assumpsit* on the bailee's promise to return some valuable boilers after he had weighed them. It was held that, however valueless the temporary possession of the boilers for the purpose of weighing them might appear to be, it constituted sufficient consideration to support the action. It would seem permissible to argue, therefore, and this view seems to have been that adopted by the majority in *Ellis* v. *Mortimer*, that the trial by the potential purchaser (i.e. that he is prepared to take the trouble of so seriously considering the seller's proposition) is consideration sufficient to keep open the offer for, and to bind the seller to, the trial period.[6]

---

1 Much of the difficulty in *Dickinson* v. *Dodds* (above) stemmed from the fact that the plaintiff at least believed such a promise to be binding.

2 (1805), 1 B. & P. N.R. 257.

3 (1703), 2 Ld. Raym. 909.

4 A distinction which is itself largely anachronistic in the light of the Court of Appeal's conclusion in *Houghland* v. *R.R. Low (Luxury Coaches), Ltd.*, [1962] 1 Q.B. 694; [1962] 2 All E.R. 159 that the bailee's duty is to take reasonable care of the chattel in all the circumstances of the case, and that whether the bailee is paid or not for his services is only one aspect to be considered. See also below, p. 43.

5 (1838), 8 Ad. & El. 743.

6 It may be that in all cases of voluntary bailment (i.e. where bailor and bailee agree that the bailee is to take possession of the bailor's goods) the law could find consideration on the part of the bailor in allowing the bailee possession of the goods and on the part of the bailee in assuming the obligation to look after the goods. Whether the bailment was for a specific period or was determinable at the will of either party would then be only a term in the contract.

2 *Rejection of the seller's offer.* The facts of *Ellis* v. *Mortimer* raise another issue. The minority opinion that *trover* might have lain against the defendant was probably based on the assumption that the parties had in fact determined the bailment. The true principle however would seem to be far from clear. There was an even more striking division of opinion in *Bradley & Cohn, Ltd.* v. *Ramsay & Co.*[1] S's agent allowed B to have some opals on approval, the price named being £750. B decided that they were not worth that amount of money and offered £300. This offer was communicated to S, but before S's rejection reached the agent for communication to B, B sold the opals to the defendant. A judgment for the price of the stones was obtained against B who was then adjudicated bankrupt. Both PHILLIMORE, J., and the Court of Appeal held that the effect of the judgment against B was to affirm the contract of sale to him and a transfer of property to the defendant. However, there was a divergence of opinion over the effect of B's refusal to pay £750 and his offer of £300. PHILLIMORE, J., took a view that the rejection of S's terms put an end to the "on approval" transaction. KENNEDY, L.J., with whom COZENS-HARDY, M.R., "expressed his entire concurrence", was of the opinion that, although "in certain cases a mere statement in answer to an offer to sell at a certain price that the goods would be bought at a lower price may and ought to be considered as a refusal of the original offer", in the present case "the relationship as originally created continued to exist".[2] In contrast, BUCKLEY, L.J., while agreeing that it was possible under a contract of sale on approval for the potential buyer to make an offer of a lower price without rejecting the original offer, held that in the present circumstances the outright rejection of the price brought the initial arrangement to an end. From that moment the goods remained in B's possession on the basis that he should retain them until it was learnt from S whether he was prepared to accept the lower price or what he wanted to be done with the goods.

3 *Counter-offers.* The dilemma in this type of situation is closely related to the rule that a counter-offer by the offeree operates as a rejection of (and therefore as terminating) the original offer, but that a request for information does not have this effect. The leading, and it would seem the first, case on this point, was *Hyde* v. *Wrench.*[3] S wrote to his agent, noting B's refusal to pay £1,200 for S's farm, but saying that he (S) would "make one more offer, which I shall not alter from": the price was to be £1,000 and S stated that he would "expect a reply by return". This letter was communicated to B's agent who immediately called on S and made an offer of £950. S expressed a wish to consider the matter and more than two weeks later he wrote declining the offer. B's agent thereupon wrote purporting to accept the offer to sell for £1,000. It will immediately be apparent that, as Lord LANGDALE, M.R., held, under these circumstances, there would be "no valid binding contract between the parties".[4] Even if one takes the view that expecting a reply by return does not make an immediate

---

1 (1912), 106 L.T. 771.
2 At p. 774.
3 (1840), 3 Beav. 334.
4 At p. 337.

reply essential, it certainly suggests that the offer would have lapsed long before the date of the letter, written two and a half weeks later, in which B's agent "accepted" that offer. As Lord LANGDALE acknowledged, if S's offer to sell for £1,000 "had been *at once* unconditionally accepted, this would undoubtedly have been a perfect binding contract". It is true that Lord LANGDALE went on to say that B made an offer of his own and "thereby rejected the offer previously made",[1] but this view seems perfectly justifiable in the circumstances of S's offer which "expected" an immediate response.

The idea that a counter-offer automatically terminates the original offer does not appear to be supported by any earlier authority,[2] and its existence as a rule on the basis of *Hyde* v. *Wrench* is dependent primarily upon the wording of the head-note to that case. A more satisfactory approach would be to apply the test whether, in the circumstances or from its terms, the counter-offer necessarily involved an outright rejection of the offer.

The other case usually cited in this connection, *Stevenson, Jacques & Co.* v. *McLean*,[3] is also unsatisfactory because the jury found that the relationship between the parties was one of buyer and seller, whereas the course of their correspondence gave the impression that the parties themselves both regarded the buyer as acting more in the capacity of an agent. S, wishing to sell warrants he held for a quantity of iron he had previously purchased from B, asked B if he could obtain an offer for them. There ensued a correspondence until at one stage B had in his hands a letter stating that S was not inclined to make a firm offer and a subsequent letter to the effect that S would sell for 40s. nett cash per ton, the offer to remain open until Monday. B telegraphed S "Please wire me whether you would accept forty for delivery over two months, or if not, longest limit you would give." Later that day B telegraphed notifying S that he had obtained the terms earlier suggested by S, but by then S had already sold the goods elsewhere. It was argued on S's behalf that B's first telegraphed message amounted to a counter-offer which had the effect of terminating S's original offer. This argument was rejected by LUSH, J., who held that B had sent the message "only as an inquiry, expecting an answer for his guidance and this is the sense in which the defendant ought to have regarded it".[4] However, LUSH, J., appeared to accept the broad proposition for which *Hyde* v. *Wrench* is usually cited, because he commented that if the form of the telegram had been "I offer forty for delivery over two months", it would have been governed by that decision.

In *Stevenson* v. *McLean*, the seller did stipulate a period for which the offer was to operate, and it would seem to be reasonable to take the view that in the absence of an express, or clearly implied, rejection by B, or of a retraction by S

---

1 At p. 337.
2 No case was cited by Lord LANGDALE, and the defendant's counsel referred only to *Holland* v. *Eyre* (1825), 2 Sim. & St. 194 which was authority solely for the proposition that "to constitute an agreement, the answer . . . must be a simple acceptance of the terms proposed, without the introduction of a new and different term", *per* LEACH, V. C., at p. 195.
3 (1880), 42 L.T. 897.
4 At p. 898.

himself, the offer should remain open for that time. If one returns to the facts of *Ellis* v. *Mortimer*,[1] it will be apparent that the buyer was expressing his dissatisfaction with the price, but not necessarily at that stage rejecting an offer which still had two weeks or more to run. In contrast, in *Bradley & Cohn, Ltd.* v. *Ramsay & Co.*,[2] the potential buyer's statement to the seller's agent was the clearest intimation that he was not prepared to pay a price which he considered absurd: the counter offer included an express rejection of the terms of the original offer. The buyer remained in possession of the goods but clearly it could not be on the terms of that offer.

b *Risk of loss or damage*

The second area of difficulty that arises prior to the passing of property in accordance with Rule 4 is the responsibility for loss or damage to the goods. The general rule laid down by s. 20, which is discussed later,[3] is that the risk passes with the property, so that, logically, until a sale under Rule 4 takes place, the risk is still on the seller. In the pre-1893 case of *Elphick* v. *Barnes*[4] in which a horse, handed over on approval for eight days, died on the third day without the fault of either party, it was held that the buyer was still entitled to signify within the period prescribed that he did not want to complete the transaction. As Rule 4 only applies to the case where property has yet to pass (as opposed to a sale in which the buyer has a trial period during which he has a power to rescind the contract), the potential buyer is no more than a bailee who is not liable for damage to the goods in the absence of negligence.

The standard of care to which he is subject depends upon the circumstances. As the goods were placed in his hands with his agreement, he is certainly obtaining the benefit of the opportunity to approve or reject them at his leisure. It would be necessary therefore to regard him as something more than a gratuitous bailee.[5] Although the current trend of judicial opinion is against the traditional distinction between gratuitous bailees (who are liable only for gross negligence) and bailees for reward (who *are* liable for negligence), and in favour of a sufficient standard of care in the circumstances of the case, the status of the bailee is still a relevant factor in establishing that standard.[6] As he is a "voluntary" bailee, however, the burden is placed on him of showing that the goods had been damaged or lost without fault on his part.[7]

---

1 (1805), 1 B. & P.N.R. 257.
2 (1912), 106 L.T. 771.
3 Below, p. 215.
4 (1880), 5 C.P.D. 321, in which DENMAN, J., applied *Head* v. *Tattersall* (1871), L.R. 7 Exch. 7, and explained an earlier and apparently contrary dictum of COLERIDGE, J., in *Moss* v. *Sweet* (1851), 16 Q.B. 493, at p. 495.
5 A carrier who transports passengers and their baggage may not charge specifically for the baggage, but that activity is to his business advantage, and he could hardly be regarded as a gratuitous bailee of the baggage: *Houghland* v. *R.R. Low (Luxury Coaches) Ltd.*, [1962] 1 Q.B. 694, [1962] 2 All E.R. 159; see also *Makower, McBeath & Co. Pty. Ltd.* v. *Dalgety & Co., Ltd.*, [1921] V.L.R. 365; but cf. *Giblin* v. *McMullen* (1868), L.R. 2 P.C. 317.
6 *Houghland* v. *R.R. Low (Luxury Coaches), Ltd.*, [1962] 1 Q.B., at p. 698; [1962] 2 All E.R., at p. 161.
7 *Houghland* v. *R.R. Low (Luxury Coaches) Ltd.*, (above); *Hunt and Winterbotham (West of England), Ltd.* v. *B.R.S. (Parcels), Ltd.*, [1962] 1 Q.B. 617; [1962] 1 All E.R. 111.

If there is no prior contract at all, and goods are sent to B "on approval" without his consent, the common law position is that he will not be liable for not returning them unless he caused damage to the goods wilfully.[1]

ii When property passes

When goods are delivered on sale or return or similar terms, property passes to the buyer according to Rule 4

> "(*a*) When he signifies his approval or acceptance to the seller or does any other act adopting the transaction"; *or*
>
> "(*b*) If he does not signify his approval or acceptance to the seller but retains the goods without giving notice of rejection, then, if a time has been fixed for the return of the goods, on the expiration of such time, and, if no time has been fixed, on the expiration of a reasonable time. What is a reasonable time is a question of fact."

a *Signifying approval or adopting the transaction*

Obviously enough, as soon as the potential buyer informs the seller that he wishes to buy them, property passes, and this will be the case even if the trial period specified has not yet run. However, the buyer's assent may equally be implied from his conduct so that if he does any act in relation to the goods that is consistent only with his having become owner of them, then that is an act "adopting the transaction" and property will pass.

The situation that has faced the courts most frequently has arisen in the jewellery trade where B has induced S to part with goods on approval or on sale or return and has then pledged them with a third party. It was argued originally that a person taking goods on sale or return could hardly adopt a transaction by doing some act other than selling them. However this analogy with a type of agency relationship was rejected by the Court of Appeal in *Kirkham* v. *Attenborough*.[2] In the view of Lord ESHER, M.R.,[3] "any act which is consistent only with his being the owner is sufficient" to show that B has adopted the transaction. In this case, pledging the goods had placed it out of B's power to return them without repaying the sum advanced: B should not have pledged them unless he meant to treat himself as purchaser. Accordingly B was able to create rights in the pledgee that were good as against S.

Similar considerations apply where S alleges that B has made excessive use of the goods. If B does more than is necessary to give the goods a fair trial he is in effect treating them as his own and he will presumably no longer be allowed to return them to S. While this proposition is a plausible deduction from cases[4] where B has to decide whether goods already purchased are suitable for their purpose, it was apparently rejected in the context of Rule 4 by the Court of

---

1 *Howard* v. *Harris* (1884), 1 Cas. & El. 253; cp. *Newman* v. *Bourne and Hollingsworth* (1915), 31 T.L.R. 209.
2 [1897] 1 Q.B. 201; applied in *London Jewellers, Ltd.* v. *Attenborough*, [1934] 2 K.B. 206; and in the rather different circumstances of *Genn* v. *Winkel* (1912), 107 L.T. 434.
3 [1897] 1 Q.B., at p. 203.
4 *Street* v. *Blay* (1831), 2 B. & Ad. 456, at pp. 463–4; *Okell* v. *Smith* (1815), 1 Stark. 107.

Appeal in *Poole* v. *Smith's Car Sales (Balham), Ltd.*[1] In that case, a car, handed over to B "on sale or return", was returned to S nearly three months later in poor condition and having been driven 1,600 miles. The Court held that property had passed under para. (*b*) of Rule 4;[2] only WILMER, L.J., specifically mentioned para. (*a*), but he did not think it "of any relevance", because B had not done any "act adopting the transaction".[3]

Unfortunately counsel's argument on this point was not reported, so it is not possible to decide whether S was arguing that excessive use could amount to an act adopting the transaction. Despite the possible negative reaction of the Court to this contention, in principle it remains perfectly reasonable to regard use greater than is consistent with the purpose of a trial as tantamount to an assertion of ownership by the buyer.

It is also possible for a person who receives unsolicited goods to signify his approval of them and thereby accept the sender's offer to sell. Similarly, too, he can adopt the transaction by making use of the goods, or by attempting to sell them or otherwise dispose of them. However, s. 1 of the Unsolicited Goods and Services Act 1971, enables the recipient of such goods, who has had possession of them for six months and who has not unreasonably refused to permit the sender to retake possession, or who serves a notice on the sender in accordance with s. 1 (2) and (3), to "use, deal with or dispose of them as if they were an unconditional gift to him, and any right of the sender to the goods shall be extinguished"; provided "the recipient has no reasonable cause to believe that they were sent with a view to their being acquired for the purposes of a trade or business and has neither agreed to acquire nor agreed to return them".

b *Retention of the goods*

1 *The retention must be by the buyer or because of his acts.* It is readily apparent if the buyer has retained the goods, and it is no excuse for him to say that he gave instructions for their return.[4] Similarly the buyer cannot escape from the contract if he has put it out of his power to return the goods within the time prescribed or within a reasonable time, for example, by having put the goods into the hands of a third party on sale or return terms no longer consistent with his arrangement with the seller.[5]

Some difficulty may be experienced in cases where the goods are seized by a third party exercising a power to distrain on the buyer's goods. If goods are sent to a buyer on a sale or return basis, he must have had the opportunity of exercising a choice in the matter. Hence where goods were seized by B's assignees in bankruptcy on the day the goods arrived, the property remained in S.[6] Similarly, where B had goods on sale or for return within a week, and

---

1 [1962] 2 All E.R. 482.
2 See below, p. 46.
3 [1962] 2 All E.R. 482, at pp. 487–8.
4 *Blankensee* v. *Blaiberg* (1895), 2 T.L.R. 36, *Poole* v. *Smith's Car Sales (Balham), Ltd.*, [1962] 2 All E.R. 482, see below, p. 46.
5 *Genn* v. *Winkel* (1912), 107 L.T. 434.
6 *Gibson* v. *Bray* (1817), 8 Taunt. 76.

they were seized on behalf of two of B's creditors within two days, it was not possible to say that B had retained the goods within the meaning of Rule 4 (*b*).[1] On the other hand, if B does retain the goods until the time fixed or a reasonable time has expired, a seizure of the goods thereafter will be effective because property will already have passed to B.[2]

2 *Retention beyond a fixed period.* The "sale or return" or "on approval" transaction places the seller in a position of some disadvantage. If the potential buyer turns out to be dishonest, the seller will normally have no security and no right of recovery against a third party into whose hands the goods have come. It can be surmised therefore that the time limit would be applied strictly against the buyer, so that if he does not give clear expression to his intention not to proceed with the sale, property will pass. In *Marsh* v. *Hughes-Hallett*,[3] after protracted correspondence, B wired his agreement on 22nd January to S's suggestion that he (B) should try S's horse for a week for 5 guineas, but, if satisfied, B was to pay a total of £65 to cover the use and purchase price of the animal. On January 29, B wrote saying that he had not had the opportunity of thoroughly testing the horse and requesting an extention of the time limit. S replied to the effect that, as the trial period had elapsed, he considered the horse sold, and this view was upheld by the court.[4]

3 *Retention beyond a reasonable time.* Where no time is specified in the arrangement between the two parties, the potential buyer is not allowed to retain the goods for an indefinite period: if he retains the goods without giving notice of rejection property will pass to him "on the expiration of a reasonable time". This part of Rule 4 is based on the decision in *Moss* v. *Sweet*[5] in which the jury had expressed concurrence with the explanation given in evidence that the meaning of delivery "on sale or return" was that goods are taken as sold unless returned, at the buyer's option, within a reasonable time. The members of the Court of Queen's Bench endorsed this finding as coinciding with their experience and view of the law.

In the only modern case dealing with the point, *Poole* v. *Smith's Car Sales (Balham), Ltd.*,[6] S entrusted two cars to B at the end of August "on sale or return". B sold one of the cars, but, as the other had not been returned by October, S made repeated attempts by telephone to obtain the return of the vehicle. Eventually, on November 7, he wrote to B stating that if the car was not returned by November 10, the car would be deemed to have been sold to B. It was not returned, according to S's evidence, until about two weeks after November 10. By that time the vehicle was in a bad condition and S refused to accept it. The Court of Appeal held that a reasonable time had clearly elapsed for two reasons. First, there was evidence that one of B's directors had given

---

1 *Re Ferrier: Ex p. The Trustee* v. *Donald*, [1944] Ch. 295.
2 *Neate* v. *Ball* (1801), 2 East 117; *Livesay* v. *Hood* (1809), 2 Camp. 83.
3 (1900), 16 T.L.R. 376.
4 Presumably an earlier communication would at least have had the effect of suspending the running of time if S made no immediate refusal: *Hughes* v. *Metropolitan Rail Co.* (1877), 2 App. Cas. 439.
5 (1851), 16 Q.B. 493.
6 [1962] 2 All E.R. 482.

instructions, which had apparently been ignored, for the return of the car early in October because there was no prospect of the vehicle being sold. And secondly, the Court was prepared to take judicial notice of the fact that there is a decline in the demand, and therefore in the value, of second-hand cars in the autumn which made an earlier sale a matter of importance.

4 *Rejection of the goods.* Retention of the goods will only pass property under Rule 4 (*b*) if the buyer has not given notice of rejection within the stipulated time or within a reasonable time if none is stipulated. There is thus no obligation on the buyer to return the goods in order to prevent property passing although he would clearly be liable in detinue if he withheld the goods after giving notice of rejection.[1]

The question of the extent of the power to reject is largely ignored by academic writers.[2] MacLeod[3] suggests that, while a buyer's right under a normal contract of sale is limited by the contract, that of a potential buyer under a "sale or return" transaction is "unrestricted". Benjamin[4] is less emphatic: having said that B can reject "for any reason", the rider is added "if he *bona fide* does not approve" of the goods.

The only authority directly on the point is *Berry & Son* v. *Star Brush Co.*,[5] in which B asked S to supply on approval a machine manufactured in Germany. B agreed to pay the carriage from Germany and the price if he decided to keep the machine; and the carriage from and back to Germany plus the cost of having the machine cleaned if he did not wish to keep it. B rejected the machine within the time stipulated, explaining that, although it was "satisfactory in every way", he feared trouble with his employees if he introduced the machine permanently. It is true that the Court of Appeal upheld B's right of rejection for a reason other than a defect in the goods, but it went on to comment that the rejection had been *bona fide* because it was a legitimate reason for refusing a machine that might create trouble with the work force.

If one takes the view that B must have a *bona fide* reason for rejecting goods then it is not possible to say that he has an "unrestricted right". Furthermore it is difficult to accept the inference in MacLeod's statement that the power to reject may not be limited by the terms of the arrangement between S and B. If, as will be discussed shortly, it is possible for Rule 4 to be ousted by evidence of a contrary intention, there seems no good reason why the parties' intentions should not also be paramount in a situation which Rule 4 leaves undefined.[6] Particularly where B takes goods on approval (as opposed to "on sale or return"), it would be logical to accept the proposition that the area of his discretion to reject can be limited by the terms of the contract to specific aspects of the goods. There would appear to be a difference between a case where B takes a horse or

---

1 If he subsequently dealt with the goods as if he were the owner it would presumably be open to S to adopt the transaction: *Bradley & Cohn, Ltd.* v. *Ramsay & Co.* (1912), 106 L.T. 771.
2 There is no mention in Atiyah, or Sutton, *op. cit.*
3 *Op. cit.* 177: Fridman is apparently of the same opinion, *op. cit.*, p. 79.
4 *Op. cit.*, 8th Ed., p. 318.
5 (1915), 31 T.L.R. 603.
6 And see *Ornstein* v. *Alexandra Furnishing Co.* (1895), 12 T.L.R. 128.

a second-hand car on trial to see "if he likes it", and a business transaction where B is allowed to use an expensive item of new equipment (and not just a demonstration model) to discover whether it answers certain specifications laid down by B.

c *Evidence of a contrary intention*

It has already been pointed out that, in a straightforward "sale or return" transaction governed by Rule 4, the seller is very much at the mercy of his potential buyer. To an extent, it is not unreasonable for the law to adopt this standpoint because S at least is able to exercise his judgment in deciding whether to entrust the goods to B. What is less justifiable is the freedom allowed by the common law to S to protect himself, ultimately at the expense of a transferee or pledgee from B. Rule 4, like the other rules in s. 18, is only applicable if there is no evidence of a contrary intention. The courts have allowed S wide freedom in this regard.

In *Weiner* v. *Gill*,[1] S delivered jewellery to B on the terms of a memorandum which stated: "On approbation. On sale for cash only or return ... Goods had on approbation or on sale or return remain the property of S ... until such goods are settled for or charged." B, believing X had a buyer, handed the goods to X who pledged them with G. It was held that the statutory rule did not apply because the parties had agreed to a different time when property should pass. Hence S was entitled to recover the goods from G. A similar construction was placed upon the statement made by the seller in *Kempler* v. *Bravington*[2] that he reserved "the right to charge any of the undermentioned goods which shall not have been returned within seven days. The goods specified ... remain my property until charged by me, you in meantime being responsible for loss or damage".

Perhaps the most extreme example of a case where the seller's apparent intentions were allowed to defeat the rights of a third party was *Percy Edwards, Ltd.* v. *Vaughan*.[3] On October 12, B was allowed to take an expensive pearl necklace on sale or return so that he could show it to his fiancée. He promised to return it or the cash on or by October 18. It was held that the intention of the parties was that property should not pass except on payment of cash on or before October 18. Accordingly B did not obtain property in the necklace in order to create rights in his pledgee by his act of pawning it on October 16.

The position of the third party is further prejudiced by the fact that B under a sale or return transaction is a bailee of the goods until property passes. As will be discussed later,[4] a buyer in possession of goods can pass a good title to a third party under s. 25 (2) of the Act even though the buyer may not yet have acquired the property in the goods. However, it was laid down in the Court

---

1 [1906] 2 K.B. 574.
2 (1925), 133 L.T. 680.
3 (1910), 26 T.L.R. 349, on appeal, 545. And the parties can also vary the terms and therefore the effect of their initial agreement by subsequent arrangement: *W. Truman Ltd.* v. *Attenborough* (1910), 26 T.L.R. 601.
4 Below, p. 80.

of Appeal by Cozens-Hardy, M.R., in *Percy Edwards, Ltd.* v. *Vaughan*[1] that a "transaction on sale or return was not a case where a person was in possession under an agreement to buy within s. 25 of the Sale of Goods Act 1893".

It has already been pointed out that, though the sale or return arrangement is closely analogous to an agency agreement, the consequences are very different. This point is brought out most clearly by the decision in *Weiner* v. *Harris*,[2] a case which also illustrates how the very nature of the transaction itself is dependent upon the apparent intentions of the parties. At one time S and B had conducted their operations on the basis of the same undertaking that had been given in *Weiner* v. *Gill*.[3] Later, new terms were adopted in which B acknowledged that:

> "I have had from you on sale or return the goods entered up to this date in the book . . . which is in your possession, and which I have examined, and I admit that I have to account to you for such goods. The goods referred to in that book mentioned are your property, and to remain so until sold or paid for, they being only left with me for the purpose of sale or return, and not to be kept as my own stock. The goods I receive from you are to be entered at cost price, and my remuneration for selling them is agreed at one half the profit . . . It is clearly understood that you have no interest in my business and I have none in yours, and that no arrangement of any kind is existing or to exist between us . . ."

Some of the goods he received from S on sale or return B pledged with the defendant. The Court of Appeal held that the mere fact that the goods were said to be taken on sale or return was not in any way conclusive of the real nature of the contract: regard must be had to the transaction as a whole to see whether that was its real meaning and effect. In this case it was impossible to say that the parties ever intended or contemplated that B should be the purchaser of the goods because the "price" he had to pay to S was dependent upon the price for which B was able to sell them. Furthermore the fact that B was to be paid part of the profit suggested that he was not a buyer of the goods but rather S's agent to sell them. In other words, the true nature of the transaction was one of agency not of sale and return. Hence B was clearly an agent to sell S's goods, that is a mercantile agent within the meaning of the Factors Act 1889 who was able effectively to pledge those goods with the defendant.

---

1 26 T.L.R., at p. 546.
2 [1910] 1 K.B. 285.
3 See above, p. 48.

CHAPTER 3

Transfer of Title by a Non-owner

It has already been explained that a contract of sale is essentially a contract involving the transfer of property from the seller to the buyer. A buyer who discovers that the seller was not the owner, and whose possession is disturbed by the true owner, is entitled to a remedy in damages against the seller. However, although a non-owner cannct *pass* title to the goods he sells, it is nevertheless possible, in some circumstances, for the buyer to *obtain* title to those goods. These circumstances are dealt with by ss. 21–25 of the Act.

A AGENCY

Subject to those provisions, s. 21 lays down the normal rule that "the buyer acquires no better title to the goods than the seller had", but the section also expresses one general exception, namely the situation where a person sells the goods "under the authority or with the consent of the owner". This is reinforced by s. 61 (2) which provides that the "rules of common law, including the law merchant, save in so far as they are inconsistent with the express provisions of this Act, and in particular the rules relating to the law of principal and agent . . . shall continue to apply to contracts for the sale of goods". Accordingly any ambiguity arising from the use of such a general expression as "under the authority or with the consent of the owner" is avoided because s. 61 (2) clearly covers cases of ostensible authority.

It is not possible to dismiss the agency relationship as being entirely outside the scope of a book on sale because many of the exceptions to the *nemo dat quod non habet* rule contained in ss. 21–25 are related to agency. For example, as will be explained, it is often difficult to distinguish between estoppel creating an authority to sell and an estoppel creating title; the courts have also sought to use a concept of ostensible ownership in contradistinction to ostensible authority; and the law relating to factors (mercantile agents) is largely a statutory application or extension of the concept of ostensible, or apparent, authority.

i Actual authority

A sale by an agent (S) on behalf of the owner of goods (O) within the scope of S's actual authority will obviously pass title to the buyer (B). And this will be the case even if B was not aware that S was acting, not on his own behalf, but on behalf of some undisclosed principal. The difficulties that arise in connection with the doctrine of the undisclosed principal concern O's position in relation to the contract entered into by S and B, but do not affect the validity and effectiveness of the transaction as far as the transfer of any property is concerned.

When one talks of actual authority, one is not referring solely to the express powers granted by the arrangement between the seller and his agent. As DIPLOCK, L.J., pointed out in *Freeman and Lockyer* v. *Buckhurst Park Properties (Mangal), Ltd.* :[1]

> " 'Actual Authority' is a legal relationship between principal and agent created by a consensual agreement to which they alone are parties. Its scope is to be ascertained by applying ordinary principles of construction of contracts, including any proper implications from the express words used, the usages of the trade, or the course of business between the parties."

Hence, if a board of directors appoint one of its members as managing director, they "thereby impliedly authorise him to do all such things as fall within the usual scope of that office".[2] Similarly, a shop assistant would have implied power to sell the goods stocked in the shop on behalf of the proprietor of the shop.

ii Ostensible authority: agency by estoppel

Although it has been said that actual and "ostensible" or "apparent" authority "are quite independent of one another",[3] such a statement must be treated with caution. An agent's actual authority normally includes the range of his ostensible authority. Difficulty will only arise when the seller has placed some limitation upon the agent's freedom to exercise his ostensible authority. In the case of an assistant in a dress shop, it may be that she is instructed not to sell dresses to a value greater than £25 without the express approval of the manager of the shop. A sale of a £30 dress would thus be outside the scope of her actual authority, although it would be an effective transaction because the buyer would be entitled to rely upon her ostensible authority.

Ostensible authority is a form of estoppel[4] and is based upon a general representation[5] made by the principal that his agent is endowed with the powers

---

1 [1964] 2 Q.B. 480, at p. 502; [1964] 1 All E.R. 630, at p. 644.
2 *Per* Lord DENNING, M.R., in *Hely-Hutchinson* v. *Brayhead, Ltd.*, [1968] 1 Q.B. 573, at p. 583; [1967] 3 All E.R. 98, at p. 102.
3 *Per* DIPLOCK, L.J., in *Freeman and Lockyer* v. *Buckhurst Park Properties (Mangal), Ltd.*, *loc. cit.*; and also the comment by SLADE, J., in *Rama Corporation, Ltd.* v. *Proved Tin and General Investments, Ltd.*, [1952] 1 All E.R. 554, at p. 556, that ostensible or apparent authority "negatives the existence of actual authority".
4 *Rama Corporation, Ltd.* v. *Proved Tin and General Investments, Ltd.*, *loco. cit.*
5 The representation in such cases is of course usually by conduct, and that conduct can involve an omission, i.e. a failure by the principal to prevent the agent acting with the appearance of being an agent: "representation by conduct may include omission to interfere where interference could reasonably be expected", *per* BANKES, L.J., in *Soanes* v. *London and South-Western Rail. Co.* (1919), 88 L.J.K.B. 524, at p. 527; [1918–19] All E.R. Rep. 852, at p. 854.

that normally attach to a person in the agent's position.[1] However, it is equally possible for the estoppel to arise out of some specific representation made by the principal. An assistant in a dress shop would not normally have authority to purchase stock for the business. But if the proprietor had by his conduct held the assistant out as possessing such a power (e.g. by on previous occasions sending her to fashion shows as a buyer on his behalf), he would be estopped from denying her authority to act in a similar situation to someone who was aware of the earlier conduct.

This dual nature of estoppel in enabling a buyer to act in reliance either upon the seller's general representation that his agent has the normal powers attached to a particular position or upon a specific representation that his agent has authority to exercise a specific power of sale is well illustrated by the Australian case of *Robinson* v. *Tyson*.[2] B had entered into a contract to purchase 3,000 head of cattle from S, the manager of O's cattle station. When O heard of the transaction he refused to deliver the cattle, claiming that S had acted without authority. It was held that it was not within the usual authority of a station manager to exercise a power of sale over the property. For B to succeed therefore he had to be able to show that O was estopped from denying S's specific power of sale. It could be demonstrated that S had made similar sales on previous occasions (though probably only with the approval of O's nephew acting on O's behalf during the latter's absence overseas), but what was fatal to B's case was that he had not been aware of these sales so that they could not possibly raise an estoppel against O *vis-à-vis* B.

iii Ratification

It is of course always open to a seller whose goods have been sold by another person without authority to adopt the transaction. The difficulty in the present context is that the doctrine of ratification is restricted to situations where the person concerned purported to act as an agent and named or clearly identified O as the person for whom he was acting. Where a person sells goods belonging to O without authority and without claiming to act on O's behalf, O cannot ratify the transaction.[3]

iv Agency of necessity

The master of a ship may exercise a power of sale over his ship or its cargo in cases of emergency. This agency of necessity is severely restricted in modern conditions by the fact that it is only available if the master is unable to contact the owners on whose behalf he is purporting to act.[4] A similar power has been attributed by the courts to carriers by land,[5] though perhaps rather illogically, not to other bailees.[6]

---

1 *Freeman and Lockyer* v. *Buckhurst Park Proprieties (Mangal), Ltd.*, [1964] 2 Q.B., at pp. 503–4, [1964] 1 All E.R., at p. 644; *per* DIPLOCK, L.J.
2 (1888), 9 N.S.W.L.R. 297.
3 *Keighley, Maxsted & Co.* v. *Durant*, [1901] A.C. 240; [1900–3] All E.R. Rep. 40.
4 *Acatos* v. *Burns* (1878), 47 L.J.Q.B. 566.
5 *Sims & Co.* v. *Midland Rail. Co.*, [1913] 1 K.B. 103; *Springer* v. *Great Western Rail. Co.*, [1921] 1 K.B. 257; [1920] All E.R. Rep. 361.
6 *Sachs* v. *Miklos* [1948] 2 K.B. 23; [1948] 1 All E.R. 67.

B ESTOPPEL

As has already been discussed, if the owner of goods represents that another is his agent to dispose of them, he will be estopped subsequently from denying that other person's authority to sell the goods in question. This principle is preserved by s. 61 (2) quite apart from s. 21. However, estoppel is of more general application. Section 21 (1), having laid down the general rule of *nemo dat*, expressly adds "unless the owner of the goods is by his conduct precluded from denying the seller's authority to sell". Not only can such a broad provision cover the case where S sells apparently on behalf of O, the owner (ostensible authority), but it also extends to the situation in which O allows S to sell the goods as if they actually belonged to S (ostensible ownership). The very imprecision of s. 21 (1) has been no incentive to the courts to rationalise its application, and it must be admitted that the decisions in this area have left the law in a state of some uncertainty.

i Conduct giving rise to an estoppel

The idea of "ostensible ownership" was a principle which the courts created to cover the situation in which O allowed S to appear to all the world as owner of the goods, or held out S as the owner specifically to B. Merely permitting S to have possession of goods would not estop O from denying S's authority to sell because there are many reasons why S might be in possession of O's goods, the most obvious being that O has lent or hired the goods to S. Alternatively S might have obtained possession of them by stealing them or even finding them.

For B to acquire title to the goods in such a situation he would have to show that O had made some representation that the goods belonged to S. In the early case of *Pickard* v. *Sears*,[1] after S had levied execution on O's property while it was in the hands of another person, O had made no objection to the subsequent sale and had even, on occasion, consulted with the execution creditors' attorney. The Court of King's Bench held that the trial judge had erred in refusing to allow the jury to consider whether O had concurred in the sale. More recently, in *Eastern Distributors, Ltd.* v. *Goldring*[2] the appearance of ownership was created by O signing an application, directed to B, a finance company, to take on hire purchase a car which he (O) in fact owned but which the application formed stated belonged to S, a dealer.

It is often stated that the appearance of ownership can also be created by some more general representation by O. If O provides S not only with possession of the goods, but also with some *indicium* of title, O is in effect holding out S as owner to anyone with whom S has dealings on the strength of that *indicium*. While this principle may appear unexceptionable in theory, in practice the courts have been less prepared to act upon it. The principal case supporting it was *Commonwealth Trust* v. *Akotey*[3] in which S had received a consignment of cocoa from O. He sold the cocoa to B and handed the delivery notes to B's agent

---

1 (1837), 6 Ad. & El. 469.
2 [1957] 2 Q.B. 600; [1957] 2 All E.R. 525.
3 [1926] A.C. 72.

The latter was thereby able to effect a redelivery of the goods to B. Property in the goods at no time passed to S because O and S had never agreed a price for the cocoa. B could only claim to be entitled to the goods as against O if it could be shown that O was estopped from denying S's ownership. The Privy Council held in B's favour because to "permit goods to go into the possession of another, with all the insignia of possession thereof and of apparent title, and to leave it open to go behind that possession . . . and upset a purchase of the goods made for full value and in good faith, would bring confusion into mercantile transactions".[1]

If this decision were correct, it would seem to follow that any generally recognised "document of title" could be regarded as an *indicium* of title. Such documents are defined by s. 1 (4) of the Factors Act 1889, to include "any bill of lading, dock warrant, warehouse-keeper's certificate, and warrant or order for the delivery of goods, and any other document used in the ordinary course of business as proof of the possession or control of goods, or authorising or purporting to authorise, either by endorsement or by delivery, the possessor of the document to transfer or receive goods thereby represented".[2] A mercantile agent (or factor as he can be called) can pass title by a transfer of such a document[3] in a transaction effected in the normal course of his business, even though he does not have actual possession of the goods. It may be possible to argue that a person who is not a mercantile agent is able to pass title if he is armed with such a document *from the owner* and if he also has actual possession or control of the goods in question.

However the decision in the *Akotey* case has come in for a good deal of criticism, most notably on the ground that it is inconsistent with *Mercantile Bank of India, Ltd.* v. *Central Bank of India, Ltd.*[4] However, it does not appear impossible to distinguish the two decisions. In the latter case, A had advanced money to X on the security of railway warrants covering a consignment of goods. A returned the warrants to X as was customary in such circumstances to allow X to obtain delivery of the goods. Instead X pledged the warrants with B. The Judicial Committee held that A's prior interest could not be defeated. It was impossible to say that A made any representation to B that X had authority,

---

1 At p. 76.
2 Though a motor vehicle's "log book" is neither a "document of title" within s. 1 (4) nor an *indicium* of title which, when coupled with possession of the vehicle itself, can create an estoppel under s. 21 (1) of the Sale of Goods Act: *Central Newbury Car Auctions* v. *Unity Finance*, [1957] 1 Q.B. 371; [1956] 3 All E.R. 905.
3 With the exception of a bill of lading which is for most purposes equivalent to a negotiable instrument and therefore capable of creating rights in a holder in due course (i.e. a *bona fide* purchaser for value) whatever the position of his transferor may have been.
4 [1938] A.C. 287; [1938] 1 All E.R. 52. One of the criticisms voiced of *Akotey's* case was the statement of Lord SUMNER in *R. E. Jones, Ltd.* v. *Waring and Gillow, Ltd.*, [1926] A.C. 670, at p. 693, that the Privy Council had ignored comments made in *Farquharson Bros. & Co.* v. *King & Co.*, [1902] A.C. 325, at pp. 335, 342, and by Lord PARMOOR in *London Joint Stock Bank, Ltd.* v. *Macmillan and Arthur*, [1918] A.C. 777, at p. 836. The significance of this criticism is weakened if one takes account of the facts that *Farquharson Bros. & Co.* v. *King & Co.* was expressly distinguished in *Akotey's* case and that Lord Parmoor was actually one of the members of the Judicial Committee in *Akotey's* case.

or was entitled, to obtain an advance on the goods for himself. There would appear to be no reason for saying that A committed any breach of any duty owing either to B or to anyone else. Furthermore the possession of the warrants no more conveyed a representation that X was entitled to dispose of the property than the actual possession of the goods themselves would have done. *Akotey's* case can hardly apply to this situation. However it might have been applicable if the warrants had contained a representation by A, upon which B had relied, that X was entitled to deal with the goods in question.

ii The representation must be made by the owner to the buyer

Despite the authority of *Akotey's* case, the trend has undoubtedly been to limit the application of the doctrine of estoppel either to cases where the owner has made a specific representation by word or conduct to the buyer, or where he has through negligence enabled the seller to represent (apparently on the owner's behalf or with his approval) that the goods belong to the seller.

a *Specific representation*

The best known authority on this point is *Henderson & Co.* v. *Williams*[1] in which O was induced by S's fraud to instruct W (a warehousemen) to transfer the goods to S's order. S then sold the goods to B who had been specifically informed by W that he held the goods on S's account. The decision of the Court of Appeal in the case that W could not contest B's title as he was estopped from denying S's authority to sell as owner is clear enough. However, Lord HALSBURY went on to state that in his opinion O was the real defendant in the case. S had been invested with a "full power of disposition", and it was "impossible to argue that this was not a holding out, by the true owner of the goods, of [S] as capable of giving a good title".[2] This proposition is justifiable in the circumstances because O had given W instructions the content of which W was entitled to relay to B.

A similar approach may be discerned in *Eastern Distributors, Ltd.* v. *Goldring*[3] O wished to obtain a second vehicle in addition to the van he already owned. He agreed with S, a car dealer, that S should pretend to B, the plaintiff finance company, that the van belonged to S and that O wished to purchase both the van and a car on hire purchase. S would then transfer the van and the car to B and would credit O with the proceeds of the sale of the van as deposit money in respect of the two hire purchase transactions. In furtherance of this scheme, O signed the proposal forms and memoranda of agreement in respect of the two vehicles and these documents were then forwarded to B for acceptance. B accepted the proposal with respect to the van, but not that relating to the car. S clearly had no authority from O to go through with the hire purchase transaction on the van unless the agreement on the car was also effected. Nevertheless he finalised the arrangements with regard to the van, although he subsequently informed O that the whole transaction had been cancelled. O then sold the van to the defendant who had no knowledge of O's dealings with S. The Court of

---

1 [1895] 1 Q.B. 521.
2 At p. 525.
3 [1957] 2 Q.B. 600; [1957] 2 All E.R. 525.

Appeal held that B was entitled to succeed because S had been armed by O with documents which enabled him to represent to B that he (S) was the owner of the van and had the right to sell it. The result was that, in the words of s. 21, O was precluded from denying S's authority to sell, and consequently B acquired the title to the goods. The decision that, as between B and O, B was entitled to the goods is unexceptionable.[1] However, the suggestion that the reason was because S had been armed with documents which enabled him to represent himself as owner is too wide, in the light of *Mercantile Credit Co. Ltd.* v. *Hamblin*,[2] which will be discussed shortly. The reason why O was estopped from denying B's title was that he had armed S with a document directed at, or intended for, B which specifically represented that S was the owner of the vehicle in question.

b *No specific representation: the question of negligence*

It will be recalled that in *Mercantile Bank of India Ltd.* v. *Central Bank of India Ltd.*,[3] it was held that the railway warrants, which the first pledgees had returned to the pledger to enable him to obtain delivery of the goods on their behalf, contained no representation by them that the pledgor was entitled to dispose of the property, nor could it be said that they were in breach of any duty owed to the second pledgee, or indeed to anyone else, in handing over the warrants.

This conclusion was based squarely upon the decision of the House of Lords in *Farquharson Bros. & Co.* v. *King & Co.*[4] O had instructed W (a dock company) to accept all orders signed by S. S gave W a number of orders to transfer some of O's timber to the order of a fictitious name. S then sold the timber to B by adopting the fictitious name. It was held that O was in no way precluded from denying S's authority to sell under the assumed name because it had never held out such a person as being the owner of the goods or entitled to dispose of them.

Both these cases seem to accept by implication that it is not impossible for a representation made by the owner to be general rather than directed at the particular buyer. Understood in this light they are not irreconcilable with *Commonwealth Trust Ltd.* v. *Akotey*.[5] However, the trend has been for liability upon such general statements (usually made in documentary form) to depend upon the existence of a duty of care.[6]

Probably the first broad statement of principle setting out the circumstances in which an estoppel could operate was the pronouncement of Lord DENMAN, C.J., in *Pickard* v. *Sears*[7] that "where one by his words or conduct wilfully causes another to believe the existence of a certain state of things, and induces him to

---

1 For discussion of the nature of a title created by estoppel, see below, p. 58.
2 [1965] 2 Q.B. 242; [1964] 3 All E.R. 592; see further below, p. 57.
3 [1938] A.C. 287, [1938] 1 All E.R. 52, above, p. 54.
4 [1902] A.C. 325; [1900–3] All E.R. Rep. 120.
5 [1926] A.C. 72.
6 E.g., Lord WRIGHT's statement in *Mercantile Bank of India, Ltd.* v. *Central Bank of India, Ltd.*, [1938] A.C. 287, at p. 304, that the duty may be owed to the general public of whom the buyer is one and that his "identity may be ascertainable only by the event, in the sense that he has turned out to be the member of the general public actually reached and affected by the conduct".
7 (1837), 6 Ad. & El. 469, at p. 474.

act on that belief, so as to alter his own previous position, the former is [pre]cluded from averring against the latter a different state of things existing at the same time". The meaning of "wilfully" in this context was probably not altogether clear,[1] so the court in *Freeman* v. *Cooke*[2] laid down what was regarded as authoritative guidance on the point:

> "By the term 'wilfully' . . . in that rule we must understand, if not that the party represents that to be true which he knows to be untrue, at least, that he means his representation to be acted upon, and that it is acted upon accordingly; and if whatever a man's real intention may be, he so conducts himself that a reasonable man would take the representation to be true, and believe that it was meant that he should act upon it, and did act upon it as true, the party making the representation would be equally precluded from contesting its truth; and conduct by negligence or omission, where there is a duty cast upon a person, by usage of trade or otherwise, to disclose the truth, may often have the same effect".

The repeated reference in the cases to the need to establish a duty of care, or to the concept of a "reasonable man", has had the effect of equating the owner's obligations with the notion of negligence. A man owes no duty of care towards others to ensure the safety of his own belongings. Possession of goods alone does not create ostensible authority or amount to ostensible ownership. If, by carelessness, a man loses his goods or they are stolen, he owes no duty of care to someone who subsequently acquires those goods in good faith.[3] Similarly the first pledgees in *Mercantile Bank of India, Ltd.* v. *Central Bank of India, Ltd.*,[4] in handing over the railway warrants in order for the pledgor to obtain delivery of the consignment of goods, owed no duty of care to anyone with whom the pledgor subsequently deposited the warrants by way of security.

The idea that estoppel in some way depends upon negligence was considered by the Court of Appeal in *Mercantile Credit Co., Ltd.* v. *Hamblin*.[5] In this case O, wishing to raise money on the security of her car, approached S, a car dealer of her acquaintance. At S's suggestion, O signed a number of documents which S said he would complete on her instructions once he ascertained the terms upon which he could obtain a loan. In return, S gave O a blank cheque he had signed for her to complete with the amount of the loan. Among the forms signed by O was an application directed to B, the finance company, for the hire purchase of a car to be sold by S to B. S dishonestly completed the form to make it appear that he was the owner of O's car and that he was selling it to B and that O was offering to hire the car from B on hire purchase terms. B accepted this arrangement and paid S for the car. S kept the money and subsequently B attempted to enforce the hire purchase transaction against O. In the main judgment, PEARSON, L.J., based the representor's duty in negligence:[6]

---

1 See the very wide extension to the principle given by the court in *Gregg* v. *Wells* (1839), 10 Ad. & El. 90, at pp. 97–8.
2 (1848), 2 Ex. Ch. 654, at p. 663.
3 *Swan* v. *North British Australasian Co.* (1863), 2 H. & C. 175, at p. 181; *Farquharson Bros. & Co.* v. *King & Co.*, [1902] A.C. 325, at pp. 332–3, 335–6.
4 [1938] A.C. 287; [1938] 1 All E.R. 52.
5 [1965] 2 Q.B. 242; [1964] 3 All E.R. 592.
6 [1965] 2 Q.B. 242, at p. 271; [1964] 3 All E.R. 592, at p. 602.

> "In order to establish an estoppel by negligence the plaintiffs [B] have to show (i) that the defendant [O] owed to them a duty to be careful, (ii) that in breach of that duty she was negligent, (iii) that her negligence was the proximate or real cause of [the plaintiff's loss]."

The Court was of opinion that, because O must have been aware that the documents would be presented to someone, she owed a duty of care to such a person. However, in this case she had not broken that duty. She knew S as a prosperous and apparently reliable local business man so that she had no reason to believe anyone would be deceived.[1]

While one may accept that S was in a way held out to be O's agent, his authority was apparently that of an owner of goods transferring goods to B as part of a hire purchase arrangement that would constitute O the hirer. As will be discussed shortly,[2] the crux of the case should have been whether O had held out S as owner of the goods in relation to B. In deciding this issue the question of negligence should not be relevant. Indeed, it is difficult to avoid the conclusion that the concept of a duty of care is an unnecessary, and often a confusing, factor to employ in a type of situation in which it has no obviously useful part to play.

iii The nature of a title by estoppel

A factor which created uncertainty in the development of estoppel as an exception to the *nemo dat* rule was the apparent difficulty the courts found in deciding whether B, if he obtained a title to goods because O had represented that S was the true owner, had a title that was transferable. Doubt arose because, in situations not directly involving title, an estoppel would normally only bind the parties to the representation. However, it would have been a most unsatisfactory state of affairs if B had been unable to sell the goods he had thus acquired on the grounds that the effect of the estoppel ceased as soon as the goods passed to a third party, and that his transferee would have been without a defence to an action brought by O.

The simplest solution would have been for the courts to have stated clearly that, once O was estopped from denying the title he had allowed B to acquire from S,[3] B took a title which, for the purposes of subsequent use or disposition, was no longer dependent upon the estoppel. In other words, once a title was created, it could not be defeated.

---

1 PEARSON, L.J., also held that O's carelessness was not the proximate cause of B's loss which could be attributed solely to S's fraud. However this argument seems circuitous. The duty of care and its breach could only exist or occur through S in whose hands O had placed the document. If S had not been known to O she would clearly have been in breach of a duty owed to B, and S's fraud would have been the causal link between her actions and B's loss. She would not of course have been liable had S lost the document and it had been filled in by someone else: in those circumstances the causal link would have been broken.

2 Below, pp. 62–3.

3 There will obviously be situations similar to that which arose in *Henderson* v. *Williams* (above, p. 55), but in which the estoppel will only operate against O's bailee. In such cases, O will not be deprived of title, nor will B obtain title; but B will be able to sue the bailee as if he (B) were owner, and the bailee will be estopped from setting up O's title: *Gosling* v. *Birnie* (1831), 7 Bing. 339; *Knight* v. *Wiffen* (1870), L.R. 5 Q.B. 660.

Although the position of B's transferee was not in issue in the early cases, it was a consideration which had an influence on the trend of authority. To reach a conclusion that would not prejudice the position of a transferee should it be directly raised, while at the same time appearing to preserve the "privity of estoppel" notion, the courts made use of at least two principles, based upon estoppel, but allegedly differing from it and from each other.

In the first place, the doctrine of ostensible authority was relied upon. Much of the law on this subject was dealt with in successive Factors Acts which will be considered below.[1] However, it will be recalled from what has been said already that, where S sells O's goods to B in a transaction which falls within the usual authority possessed by a person of the class to which S belongs, the fact that S has not been given that authority is irrelevant if B was unaware of the want of authority. Secondly, the principle of apparent ownership was invented to cover situations in which O allowed S to appear as owner to all the world or held out S as the owner specifically to B.[2] However, that the law was in something of a confused state when Chalmers came to draft the Sale of Goods Act is demonstrated by the fact that s. 21 (1) was obviously included to cover a variety of disparate situations[3] which he presumably felt unable to cast in the form of distinct and coherent rules.

Section 21 (1) provides in effect that a sale by a non-owner does give the buyer a better title than the seller had if the true owner is by his conduct precluded from denying the seller's authority to sell. It may be that this provision is broad enough to establish that "title by estoppel", even if originally arising as a rule of evidence, is now firmly part of the substantive law. Once this development is recognised, of course, there would be no need to worry about the effect of the estoppel even if the goods were in the hands of a third party.

However, when the issue was raised before the Court of Appeal in *Eastern Distributors, Ltd.* v. *Goldring*,[4] the court came down firmly in favour of the proposition that s. 21 was based upon the apparent authority of the seller, and not upon any notion of ostensible ownership. It will be recalled that O, the owner of a van, and S embarked upon a scheme for raising the deposit for the hire purchase of a second vehicle by pretending that both vehicles belonged to S. B, the finance company, was only prepared to accept the proposal in respect of the first vehicle which in fact belonged to O. Without O's authority and knowledge, S had finalised the hire purchase transaction. O had sold the vehicle to an innocent party. The case centred therefore not on whether B's transferee took a good title, but whether O still had a title to pass to a person who was not a party to the estoppel.

The judgment of the Court was given by Devlin, J. It seemed to accept that, if B's case rested on estoppel, B could not claim to succeed on the basis of title

---

1 Page 64.
2 *Boyson* v. *Coles* (1817), 6 M. & S. 14, at p. 24; *Pickard* v. *Sears* (1837), 6 Ad. & El. 469; *Gregg* v. *Wells* (1839), 10 Ad. & El. 90.
3 See the cases cited in the footnote to the last clause of s. 21 (1) in early editions of Chalmers' *Sale of Goods Act*, e.g. 6th Ed. (1905), p. 56, n. 5.
4 [1957] 2 Q.B. 600; [1957] 2 All E.R. 525; the facts of which were given above, p. 55.

because B had received no title: the crucial question was whether the defendant, because he acquired the van from O, was bound by an estoppel which prevented O from pleading the truth of the matter. But an estoppel would only bind a representor and his privies and the better view was that a purchaser for value without notice was not a privy to the estoppel and would not be bound by it.

However, the common law had admitted a number of exceptions to the *nemo dat* rule. Hence "the courts of common law allowed a good title to a buyer who bought in good faith from a man who apparently had been given by the true owner the right to dispose of the goods".[1] Such a buyer did not merely acquire a title by estoppel, based upon the implied representation by the owner that there was a right of disposition and vulnerable at the suit of anyone who was not bound by that representation. He acquired in the same way as the transferee of a negotiable instrument or the buyer in market overt a good title against all the world.

This apparent right of disposal was equally applicable to cases where the person in possession was apparently the owner or where he was apparently authorised to deal with the goods. Although "apparent ownership or authority has generally taken the form of arming the agent with some *indicia* which made it appear that he was either the owner or had the right to sell . . . the principle applies to any form of representation or holding out of apparent ownership or the right to sell".[2] It was a principle which was embodied in s. 21 of the Sale of Goods Act. That section expressed the old rule "that apparent authority to sell is an exception to the maxim *nemo dat quod no habet*; and it is plain from the wording that if the owner of the goods is precluded from denying authority, the buyer will in fact acquire a better title than the seller".[3]

It was the Court's view, however, that this rule, though sometimes referred to as "common law estoppel", ought not to be regarded as part of the law of estoppel. At any rate, it certainly differed from what was sometimes referred to as "equitable estoppel" in that the effect of its application was to transfer a real title and not merely a metaphorical title by estoppel. However, whatever the limits of the doctrine, it clearly applied to the present case. "[S] was armed by [O] with documents which enabled him to represent to the plaintiffs that he was the owner of the [van] and had the right to sell it. The result is that [O] is, in the words of s. 21, precluded from denying [S]'s authority to sell, and consequently the plaintiffs acquired the title to the goods which [O] himself had and [O] had no title left to pass to the defendant".[4]

The decision reached in the plaintiff's favour was unexceptionable, and, although it hardly seemed necessary to classify s. 21 as a rule of apparent authority, such an approach might at least have the beneficial effect of freeing judges from their earlier neurosis that a "title by estoppel" as such is not transferable. Once the estoppel operates to prevent the owner denying the seller's

---

1 [1957] 2 Q.B. 600, at p. 607; [1957] 2 All E.R. 525, at p. 529.
2 [1957] 2 Q.B. 600, at p. 610; [1957] 2 All E.R. 525, at p. 531.
3 [1957] 2 Q.B. 600, at p. 611; [1957] 2 All E.R. 525, at p. 532.
4 *Ibid.*

authority to sell on behalf of the owner or as owner, an effective title is passed, and not one based upon estoppel.[1]

If it was the intention of the members of the Court to eradicate some of the difficulties arising out of s. 21 by advancing this general principle of apparent authority, it cannot be claimed that they have had any great success, whether from a substantive viewpoint or considered solely as a question of semantics. For example, in *Stoneleigh Finance Ltd.* v. *Phillips*,[2] DAVIES, L.J., referred to an "ostensible title to sell" in connection with *Eastern Distributors* v. *Goldring* and then stated that a certain party had been held out to the plaintiffs "as being owners of the goods and as, accordingly, having title to sell". On the other hand, RUSSELL, L.J. in *Snook* v. *London and West Riding Investments, Ltd.*[3] baldly stated that the plaintiff in the case was "estopped by his own conduct from denying the defendants' title, and this title by estoppel is a true title", citing *Eastern Distributors* v. *Goldring* and *Stoneleigh Finance* v. *Phillips*.

The difficulties, whether substantive or semantic, of applying the principle propounded in the *Eastern Distributors* case may be demonstrated by reference to the circumstances of *Motor Credits (Hire Finance), Ltd.* v. *Pacific Motor Auctions Pty., Ltd.*[4] The plaintiffs, O, became owners of a number of cars in the possession of, and displayed for sale by, a firm called Motordom, S, under a "floor plan agreement" in which O in return advanced a substantial percentage of each car's value. These cars were, however, retained by S and sold by it in the same way as it sold other cars which it had received in the course of business and which it had not transferred to the plaintiffs. When the vehicles covered by the plan were sold, S accounted to O for the purchase money received. S got into difficulties. When the news reached O, they revoked S's authority to sell cars covered by the plan. S nevertheless purported to sell to the defendants, B, some 29 cars for £16,510, the amount of the debt that S owed to B. The cheque made out to S was handed over to S's manager who immediately endorsed it in favour of B and handed it back to B's accountant.

As we shall see,[5] B could not claim that the sale by S was by a mercantile agent in possession and therefore binding upon O because the sale had not been carried out in the normal course of business. In fact, as an agent can hardly sell his principal's goods in settlement of his own debt, it could hardly be contended that any issue of ostensible authority was involved at all. B's case depended therefore upon whether O had held out S as the owner of the cars other than by leaving them in its possession. On the facts of the case the only representations that had been made were those of S's manager to the effect that the cars were S's

---

1 See also *Mercantile Credit Co., Ltd.* v. *Hamblin*, [1965] 2 Q.B. 242, at p. 270; [1964] 3 All E.R. 592, at p. 601, *per* PEARSON, L.J.; *Lloyds and Scottish Finance, Ltd.* v. *Williamson*, [1965] 1 All E.R. 641, at p. 645.
2 [1965] 2 Q.B. 537, at p. 571; [1965] 1 All E.R. 513, at p. 523.
3 [1967] 2 Q.B. 786, at pp. 803–4; [1967] 1 All E.R. 518, at p. 529; with DIPLOCK, L.J., agreeing on this point. This pronouncement is in fact an echo of his similar statement in *Stoneleigh Finance, Ltd.* v. *Phillips*, [1965] 2 Q.B., at pp. 577–8; [1965] 1 All E.R., at p. 527.
4 (1963), 109 C.L.R. 87; reversed on other grounds (discussed below, pp. 78–9), [1965] A.C. 867; [1965] 2 All E.R. 105.
5 Below p. 72.

absolute and unencumbered property. Clearly O's position could not be affected by these statements.

In dealing with *Eastern Distributors, Ltd.* v. *Goldring*, OWEN, J., was content to distinguish it on the ground that the plaintiffs were not privy to the manager's representations; but TAYLOR, J., expressed the view that that case had been "primarily one of ostensible ownership and not one of ostensible agency".[1] Such an opinion is remarkable in view of the considerable pains taken by DEVLIN, J., to create a widely-embracing formula of apparent authority upon which to base various applications of s. 21. Furthermore, it is even possible to justify the decision in that case on the basis of agency. O, the owner of the van, had entrusted it to S with a limited authority to sell (i.e. limited by the fact that the sale was ancillary to the hire purchase arrangement with respect to the car). However, by giving S not only possession of the car, but also documents presenting S as owner, in a proposed sale to B, O was estopped from denying S's authority to effect a sale to the plaintiffs. There was no need therefore for the Court of Appeal to have relied upon s. 21 at all.

Semantics apart, however, to identify s. 21 too closely with some form of agency in the guise of ostensible authority, unnecessarily limits the potential ambit of the section and therefore of the concept of a title by estoppel. The danger of this approach is well illustrated by *Mercantile Credit Co., Ltd.* v. *Hamblin*.[2] In that case, O had signed forms with which S, by completing them, had been able to appear as owner in entering into a hire purchase transaction with B apparently on O's behalf. In the principal judgment, PEARSON, L.J., restricted the issues so that they could be considered within the narrow framework of S's ostensible authority. In the first place, unless some estoppel operated against O, the presentation of the forms to B was not her act: the "crucial question" therefore was whether, as against B, O was estopped from denying S's authority to complete the forms and present them on her behalf.[3] However, as there was no actual authority, B could only succeed by showing an ostensible authority based on negligence.[4] In the circumstances, PEARSON, L.J. was prepared to hold that O owed a duty of care in putting into circulation the signed proposal forms, but had not broken that duty because S had been a person of apparent reliability.[5]

---

1 109 C.L.R., at p. 97. The passage in the judgment which explains this conclusion (at pp. 98–9) is confusing. It correctly states that S's manager's statement about the ownership of the cars did not bind O, but it was erroneous to suggest that knowledge of the existence of a "floor plan" arrangement made it clear to B that S was dealing with vehicles that did not belong to it. As far as B knew, S sold many cars that were not covered by the "floor plan", and they also had the manager's assurance that the cars in question did not belong to O under the plan. The reason why the estoppel point failed is that possession alone is not sufficient to give a power to sell as owner or agent unless there is some additional evidence of title or authority. In this case, the High Court held that no such evidence (estoppel; sale in course of business) existed.

2 [1965] 2 Q.B. 242; [1964] 3 All E.R. 592; see above, p. 57.

3 [1965] 2 Q.B. 242, at p. 268; [1964] 3 All E.R. 592, at p. 600.

4 [1965] 2 Q.B. 242, at p. 271; [1964] 3 All E.R. 592, at p. 602.

5 [1965] 2 Q.B. 242, at pp. 274–5; [1964] 3 All E.R. 592, at pp. 604–5.

Counsel's reliance upon *Eastern Distributors, Ltd.* v. *Goldring*[1] was rejected because in that case O had agreed with S that the forms should be presented to B: there had been "a clear case of ostensible authority by holding-out".[2] With respect *Eastern Distributors* is not so readily distinguished. As has already been pointed out,[3] it was clearly a correct decision on the basis of ostensible authority alone, whether within or outside the scope of s. 21. However, it could equally well have been decided on the basis of ostensible ownership. O had provided S with *indicia* of title which made him appear to B as if he were the owner. Similarly in *Mercantile Credit Co., Ltd.* v. *Hamblin*, O had armed S with documents which enabled him to appear as owner by the simple procedure of completing them. As he had ostensible authority to do so, the appearance of ownership was complete and B's action should have succeeded against O. It is difficult to see how the question of negligence was relevant to O's relationship with B: either S had the appearance of authority or he had not. The existence of documents directed to B, signed by O, and in S's hands created the appearance of authority vested in S to complete the transaction. And this transaction was based entirely upon the understanding between O, S and B that S was the owner.

C. MERCANTILE AGENTS

The Sale of Goods Act makes no specific provision covering the powers of mercantile agents (or factors as they are sometimes called). However, s. 21 (2) (*a*) lays down that nothing in the Act is to affect the "provisions of the Factors Acts, or any enactment enabling the apparent owner of goods to dispose of them as if he were the true owner thereof".

The principle that a transaction entered into by an agent within the scope of his ostensible authority was binding developed as a matter of "commercial convenience". The transaction of business would have been severely restricted if the parties could not act on the assumption that the apparent situation was the real situation, and were obliged to check an agent's actual authority with his principal before finalising an agreement. Hence it was also early recognised that a mercantile agent, whether he sold in his own name or specifically as agent, could in normal circumstances pass a good title to a buyer even if the actual sale went outside the authority granted to the agent by his principal.

This development took place because the courts of common law were prepared to afford recognition to this practice of the commercial community. However, there remained a judicial reluctance to extend the area of recognition. Inevitably, there followed a conflict between the conservatism of the judiciary who were determined to protect property (the basic maxim of the common law was *nemo dat quod non habet*), and the determination of the commercial community to protect transactions.

---

1 [1957] 2 Q.B. 600; [1957] 2 All E.R. 525.
2 [1965] 2 Q.B. 242, at p. 276; [1964] 3 All E.R. 592, at p. 605, *per* PEARSON, L.J.
3 See above, pp. 59–61.

The difference in approach may be illustrated by the case of *Sanders* v. *Maclean*[1] in which objection had been taken to the tender of two copies of a bill of lading without the third. In fact the Court of Appeal[2] accepted that such a tender was good on the ground that to require presentment of all three together would frustrate the whole purpose of mercantile custom that bills of lading should be drawn up in triplicate. As BOWEN, L.J., pointed out,[3] the

> "only possible object of requiring the presentation of the third . . . must be to prevent the chance, more or less remote, of fraud on the part of the shipper or some previous owner of the goods. But the practice of merchants . . . is not based upon the supposition of possible frauds. The object of mercantile usages is to prevent the risk of insolvency, not of fraud. . . . Credit, not distrust, is the basis of commercial dealings; mercantile genius consists principally in knowing whom to trust."

In the context of mercantile agents, this conflict between the lawyers on the one hand and the bankers and merchants on the other resolved itself into a battle between the judges in the courts and the legislators in Parliament. The first of the Factors Acts was passed in 1823 to remedy the stand taken by the common law that though it was prepared to recognise a mercantile agent's (i.e. a factor's) ostensible power of sale, it was not prepared to uphold this authority as extending to a power to pledge the goods, even though such agents frequently did resort to pledges as a means of raising finance until a beneficial sale could be arranged.[4] A series of Factors Acts followed designed principally to rectify the restrictive interpretations that the courts consistently placed upon the existing legislation.[5] The Factors Acts were placed in their final form by the Act of 1889, although some parallel provisions were also included in the 1893 Sale of Goods Act.

A mercantile agent's power to deal with the goods is now set out in s. 2 (1) of the 1889 Act:

> "Where a mercantile agent is, with the consent of the owner, in possession of goods or of the documents of title to goods, any sale, pledge, or other disposition of the goods, made by him when acting in the ordinary course of business of a mercantile agent, shall, subject to the provisions of this Act, be as valid as if he were expressly authorised by the owner of the goods to make the same; provided that the person taking under the disposition acts in good faith, and has not at the time of the disposition notice that the person making the disposition has not authority to make the same".

i Who is a mercantile agent

A mercantile agent is defined by s. 1 (1) of the Factors Act as

---

1 (1883), 11 Q.B.D. 327.
2 Reversing the decision of POLLOCK, B., at first instance.
3 At p. 343.
4 See the judgment of WILLES, J., in *Fuentes* v. *Montis* (1868), L.R. 3 C.P. 268, at pp. 277–8.
5 The restrictive interpretation adopted in *Fuentes* v. *Montis* by WILLES, J. (above) and by the Court of Exchequer Chamber (4 C.P. 93) had to be dealt with in the Act of 1877 which provided *inter alia* that a secret revocation of authority should be inoperative; see now s. 2 (2) of the Act of 1889.

"a mercantile agent having in the customary course of his business as such agent authority either to sell goods, or to consign goods for the purposes of sale, or to buy goods, or to raise money on the security of goods".

It cannot be said that this definition is elegantly drafted, but it does emphasise that a mercantile agent must normally be in business as a buyer or seller of goods, or otherwise as a broker for pledging and raising money on the security of goods. The description applies only to those "persons whose employment corresponds to that of some known kind of commercial agent". But it "does not include a mere servant or caretaker, or one who has possession of goods for carriage, safe custody, or otherwise, as an independent contracting party".[1]

Somewhat inconsistently, however, the use of the expression "in the customary course of his business as such agent" has not prevented the courts from classifying as a mercantile agent a person who is for the first time entrusted with goods for sale in respect of a single transaction or series of transactions. In *Heyman* v. *Flewker*,[2] from which the above statement of the law is taken, O had entrusted five pictures to S with instructions that S should sell them on a commission basis. S was an insurance agent who occasionally performed other services for commission, but it was no part of his ordinary business to sell goods. S pledged the goods with B. This transaction would only give B rights against O if it could be established that S was acting as a mercantile agent. The Court saw "no sufficient reason for limiting the general language of the act, . . . 'ordinary course of business', by construction to business usually carried on by the defaulting agent". It was enough that "the character of the employment in the particular instance is the same as that of others who do carry on business generally".[3] In this case S had been entrusted with the goods in the capacity of an agent within the meaning of the Act. As was stated in one Australian case,[4] "there is nothing to prevent a man . . . becoming *instanter* such agent . . . by virtue of the terms of the transaction in which particular goods are entrusted to him".

ii Mercantile agent in possession

According to s. 1 (2) of the Factors Act, a person "shall be deemed to be in possession of goods or of the documents of title to goods, where the goods or documents are in his actual custody or are held by any other person subject to his control or for him or on his behalf". Hence if goods are transferred in the books of a warehouseman to the order of a mercantile agent (S), the latter has possession of them in order to transfer title by a sale to a third party (B) even though the third party might have no knowledge of the entry in the books and therefore be unable to rely upon any estoppel that might preclude the owner (O) from pleading his title to the goods.

Not only does the mercantile agent have to be in possession of goods, but it has long been established that the goods also have to be entrusted to him in his

---

1 *Per* WILLES, J., giving the judgment of the Court in *Heyman* v. *Flewker* (1863), 13 C.B. N.S. 519, at p. 527.
2 (1863), 13 C.B. N.S. 519.
3 At p. 527.
4 *Mortgage Loan and Finance Co.* v. *Richards* (1932), 32 S.R. (N.S.W.) 50, at pp. 58–9; and see also *Weiner* v. *Harris*, [1910] 1 K.B. 285, above p. 49.

capacity as a mercantile agent. In *Cole* v. *North Western Bank*,[1] S carried on in Liverpool the business of a sheep's wool broker and warehouse keeper. In the latter capacity he frequently received from O, London merchants, bills of lading for both goats' and sheep's wool arriving at Liverpool. It was for S to arrange for the collection of the wool from the dock and to warehouse the wool on O's behalf. He would then report the safe storage of the wool to O who often gave S authority to sell specific batches of sheep's wool. On this occasion S pledged the whole consignment of wool that had arrived with B to secure an advance. S then absconded with the money. It was clear that S had not been a mercantile agent in respect of goats' wool in which he had never dealt. Nor, it was held, could he be considered as such an agent in respect of the sheep's wool. He was in possession of the goods as a bailee in the course of a business unconnected with his being a broker. As BLACKBURN, J., pointed out,[2] if a furnished house were let to an auctioneer, he is entrusted with the furniture as tenant, and it could never be the law that, by carrying the furniture to his auction room and there selling it, he could confer a valid title on the buyer.

This principle has been given extended application. It has been held that a mercantile agent who acquires possession of goods as hirer under a hire-purchase agreement, and not in the normal course of business as a mercantile agent, is not in possession of the goods within the meaning of the Act. In *Staffs Motor Guarantee, Ltd.* v. *British Wagon, Ltd.*[3] for example, S, a dealer, owned a lorry the title of which he transferred to O, the defendant company, and which O hired back to him under a hire purchase agreement. During the time this arrangement was made, S retained possession of the vehicle, but he subsequently sold it to B, the plaintiff finance company. When S failed to keep up payments to O, O repossessed the vehicle. In an action brought by B against O, it was held, *inter alia*, that when S purported to transfer title to B he no longer had possession as a mercantile agent. Accordingly he was unable to pass a valid title under s. 2 (1) of the Factors Act. Although the decision in this case on s. 25 (1) of the Sale of Goods Act, which relates to the power of a seller who continues in possession of the goods to pass title, has been overruled,[4] the present trend of authority favours the continued acceptance of the principle that a change in the nature of the mercantile agent's possession of goods can affect his power to deal with them as such agent.[5]

---

1 (1875), L.R. 10 C.P. 354.
2 At p. 369; but cf. the situation that arose in *Lowther* v. *Harris*, [1927] 1 K.B. 393; [1926] All E.R. Rep. 352.
3 [1934] 2 K.B. 305; [1934] All E.R. Rep. 322; applying the explanation of CHANNELL, J., in *Oppenheimer* v. *Frazer and Wyatt*, [1907] 1 K.B. 519, at p. 527, of how the different wording of the 1889 Factor Acts compared with the earlier Acts had not altered the law on this point.
4 See below, p. 78.
5 See *Astley Industrial Trust, Ltd.* v. *Miller*, [1968] 2 All E.R. 36; *Worcester Works Finance, Ltd.* v. *Cooden Engineering Co., Ltd.*, [1972] 1 Q.B. 210, at p. 220, [1971] 3 All E.R. 708, at pp. 713–4, *per* MEGAW, L.J.; certainly the Judicial Committee's different approach to s. 25 (1) of the Sale of Goods Act in *Pacific Motor Auctions Pty., Ltd.* v. *Motor Credits (Hire Finance), Ltd.*, [1965] A.C. 867, at p. 884; [1965] 2 All E.R. 105, at p. 112; was solely attributable to the use of the expression "continues . . . in possession" in that section.

The law is perhaps not so clear where the goods are entrusted to a mercantile agent for purposes of display only. In one Australian case, *Universal Guarantee Pty, Ltd.* v. *Metters, Ltd.*[1] S, a dealer in electrical appliances, had at his premises a refrigerator belonging to O, the defendant, "for display or return". One of S's employees fraudulently completed a hire-purchase application in the name of another person. This application was accepted by B, the plaintiff finance company, who advanced the balance of the purchase price although they had no knowledge of the whereabouts of the appliance in question. O subsequently seized the goods, and B commenced this action alleging that property in the refrigerator had passed to them. As no representative of B had seen the appliance on display at S's premises, it was clear that there had been no holding out of S as O's agent as far as B was concerned. Nor, it was held, could it be claimed that S was a mercantile agent in possession of the goods, because he had no power of sale over them. He was bailee for purposes of display only.

It would appear that this case protects the proprietary rights of the owner or "principal" to too great a degree. In the course of his judgment in *Pearson* v. *Rose and Young, Ltd.*[2] DENNING, L.J., accepted that if the owner of goods left them with a person who was both a dealer and a repairer in order for the goods to be repaired, that person would not be in possession as a mercantile agent. The possession would have to be "for a purpose which is in some way or other connected with his business as a mercantile agent. It may not actually be for sale. It may be for display or to get offers, or merely to put in his showroom". If goods are, by agreement, displayed in an agent's showroom[3] it is obviously reasonable that the actual owner should be bound by a transaction entered into in respect of those goods by the agent. Normally the buyer of such goods would be able to rely upon the ostensible authority of the agent quite apart from the mercantile agent provisions of the Factors Act. A sale would be effective irrespective of any limitation upon the agent's authority of which the buyer was unaware. The mercantile agent provisions reinforce this ostensible authority and extend it to cover transactions other than sale. It would be an unsatisfactory situation if, in such other transactions, the authority of the agent could be limited by restrictions placed upon the agent's authority by the owner of which the pledgee or other transferee was unaware. Providing the agent has possession for the purposes of soliciting offers, or orders in respect of the goods or others identical with them, the mercantile agent provisions should be applicable.

A person will not become a mercantile agent and take possession as a mercantile agent if he undertakes to arrange a sale as an act of friendship. In *Budberg* v. *Jerwood and Ward*[4], O, the plaintiff, a Russian emigrée, entrusted her necklace to S, a Russian lawyer in London. S was to obtain offers for the necklace but,

---

1 [1966] W.A.R. 74.
2 [1951] 1 K.B. 275, at p. 288; [1950] 2 All E.R. 1027, at p. 1032.
3 If the showroom where the goods are displayed is in the possession of the owner, then the agent can hardly be said to be in possession: *Brown* v. *Bedford Pantechnicon* (1889), 5 T.L.R. 449; although he may later become a mercantile agent in possession if he is allowed to take possession of the goods with the owner's consent: *Lowther* v. *Harris*, [1927] 1 K.B. 393; [1926] All E.R. Rep. 352.
4 (1934), 51 T.L.R. 99.

without informing O, he sold it to B, the defendants, and pocketed the proceeds. When O discovered what had occurred she commenced this action. B's contention was that S had been a mercantile agent and that O was therefore bound by the transaction. This argument was rejected by MACNAGHTEN, J. It was true that a person could be constituted a mercantile agent by being employed to sell goods in respect of a single transaction, but in this case there had been no business relationship between O and S. It was apparent that S had acted merely as a friend, a circumstance that was inconsistent with the suggestion that he had acted as a mercantile agent. The result would have been different of course if S had regularly sold jewellery as a business venture, because then he would have appeared to be acting as a mercantile agent even though in the actual transaction he was selling, without commission or profit, as an act of friendship.

Once it is accepted that a person can obtain possession of goods in order to deal with them in a way that is normally associated with the activities of a mercantile agent without *ipso facto* becoming a mercantile agent,[1] the question arises whether, if he subsequently becomes a mercantile agent, he can deal with the goods within s. 2 (1) of the Factors Act. There is a broad statement by LUSH, J., in *Heap* v. *Motorists' Advisory Agency, Ltd.*[2] which appears to answer the matter in the negative:

> "In order to see whether that section applies one must consider first whether the owner parted with the possession of the chattel to a mercantile agent. If at the time the owner parted with the possession the recipient was not a mercantile agent, if the owner did not part with the possession to a man who was filling that capacity, then . . . the section does not apply . . . The fact that he afterwards becomes a dealer and sells it as a mercantile agent does not bring the case within the section, because the owner . . . did not put it into the power of a mercantile agent to sell and make an apparently good title to the chattel".

In this case O allowed S to have O's car so that S could try to sell it to X. S later told O that he had sold the car to X. There was no such person as X and S subsequently arranged for the sale of the car to B. By the time this sale took place S had taken employment as a salesman with a firm of motor car dealers. Amongst the reasons advanced by LUSH, J., in favour of his decision that O was entitled to succeed in his action against B was therefore that, by becoming a mercantile agent, S did not in some way convert his possession into possession as such an agent. However, it cannot be claimed that this view of the law has much to commend it. If the nature of S's possession is consistent with the activities of a mercantile agent (i.e. he is supposed genuinely or otherwise to be disposing of the goods on O's behalf), then the fact that S is a mercantile agent or becomes one should enable S to pass a good title as such agent. If S's posses-

---

1 A person obtaining possession on a sale or return basis cannot pass title as a mercantile agent: *Jerome* v. *Bentley & Co.*, [1952] 2 All E.R. 114; unless of course the transaction is held to be one of agency and not of sale or return: *Weiner* v. *Harris*, [1910] 1 K.B. 285 [1908–10] All E.R. Rep. 405; see above p. 49.
2 [1923] 1 K.B. 577, at p. 588; [1922] All E.R. Rep. 251, at p. 256.

tion is not in a capacity similar to that of a mercantile agent, then it does not matter whether he is or becomes such agent: he will not be able to pass title[1].

iii Possession with the owner's consent

The requirement that the agent should have possession with the owner's consent was included in the 1889 Act in place of the previous "where a mercantile agent is *entrusted as such*" with possession of goods or documents of title. The unanimous view is that the altered wording signifies no change in the law[2]. Section 2, however, goes on to provide that a determination of the owner's consent is ineffective unless the person taking under the disposition has notice of this fact at the time thereof (s. 2 (2)); that where the agent has possession of goods or of any documents of title with the owner's consent, and thereby is able to obtain possession of any other documents of title to the goods, the latter possession is also deemed to be with the owner's consent (s. 2 (3)); and that the consent of the owner to the possession of goods or documents of title will be presumed in the absence of evidence to the contrary (s. 2 (4)).

It goes without saying that when the ownership to goods is divided, the necessary consent will have to be given by all those persons constituting "the owner", unless of course one individual has apparent authority to act on behalf of them all.[3]

iv There must be a sale or other disposition

It has already been explained[4] that one important issue dealt with by an earlier Factors Act had been the power of a mercantile agent to deal with the goods other than by way of sale. Until the point was clarified by statute, the courts regarded any pledge by a mercantile agent, in possession of goods to sell them, as outside the scope of his apparent authority. At the same time that legislation laid down that a pledge by such an agent was effective, the opportunity was taken to settle a number of points stemming from this power.

By s. 3 of the 1889 Act, a pledge of documents of title is deemed to be a pledge of the goods to which the documents relate. The extent of the pledgee's interest is limited to the consideration he provides in return for the security at the time of the pledge (ss. 4, 5). However, the "consideration necessary for the validity of a sale, pledge, or other disposition, of goods, . . . may be either a payment in cash, or the delivery or transfer of other goods, or of a document of title to goods, or of a negotiable security, or any other valuable consideration" (s. 5).

The expression "any other disposition" is of the most general application. In the context of a different statutory provision,[5] STIRLING, J., once commented[6]

---

1 Take for example, LUSH, J.'s illustration in *Heap's* case, *ibid.*, of the man who obtained possession of O's car by borrowing it on the pretext of an urgent mission to fulfil: whether he is or becomes a mercantile agent is irrelevant as he is not entrusted with the vehicle in that capacity.
2 See the explanation of the law given by CHANNELL, J., in *Oppenheimer* v. *Frazer and Wyatt*, [1907] 1 K.B. 519, at p. 527.
3 *Lloyds Bank, Ltd.* v. *Bank of America*, [1938] 2 K.B. 147; [1938] 2 All E.R. 63.
4 Above, p. 64.   5 Fines and Recoveries Act, 1833, s. 77.
6 *Carter* v. *Carter*, [1896] 1 Ch. 62, at p. 67.

that the terms "dispose" and "disposition" were "ordinary English words of wide meaning, and where not limited by the context those words are sufficient to extend to all acts by which a new interest (legal or equitable) in the property is effectually created". This dictum was recently applied by the Court of Appeal[1] to a transaction where the cheque given by the buyer of a car was dishonoured and the seller retook possession of the vehicle. As MEGAW, L.J. explained, there was no doubt that the effect of the repossession was that the interest in property in the car reverted to the seller. "It was not, in law, a mere transfer of possession. It was a transfer of the goods under a disposition in the true sense of the word."[2]

v In the ordinary course of business

Not only must a mercantile agent be in possession of goods in that capacity, he must also sell or otherwise dispose of them in such capacity, i.e. in the ordinary course of business.

In *Oppenheimer* v. *Attenborough & Son*,[3] S, a diamond broker, had represented to O, the plaintiff, that he (S) could sell diamonds to one of two named firms. O entrusted some diamonds to the broker who, instead of approaching the firms, pledged the diamonds with B, the defendants. The case would have been straightforward but for the fact that a custom of the trade was proved that a diamond broker, employed to sell diamonds, had no authority to pledge them in order to obtain advances of money for his principal. O argued that "acting in the course of business of a mercantile agent" should be interpreted as meaning "in the course of business of a mercantile agent in such a trade as that in which he carries on business". It was the Court of Appeal's view, however, that the "ordinary course of business" referred to the transaction of business "within business hours, at a proper place of business, and in other respects in the ordinary way in which a mercantile agent would act, so that there is nothing to lead the pledgee to suppose that anything is being done wrong".[4]

In one sense the Court was drawing an unreal distinction because a disposition *within* a trade in a manner contrary to the custom of the particular trade would be a fact leading the buyer or pledgee to suppose that something wrong was being done. On the other hand, a disposition *not* within the trade might well be considered as falling outside the ordinary course of business of a diamond broker. The illogicality of the distinction drawn by the Court of Appeal can be illustrated by the position of an auctioneer who, as counsel pointed out, is patently an agent entrusted with goods for sale. Unless his position is read subject to the custom of his profession, the effect of the Act would be to give him a power to pledge goods. Lord ALVERSTONE, C.J., met this contention by suggesting "that there may be particular agents, such as auctioneers, with regard to whom a pledge by them of goods entrusted to them would be such a departure from the

---

1 In *Worcester Works Finance, Ltd.* v. *Cooden Engineering Co., Ltd.*, [1972] 1 Q.B. 210; [1971] 3 All E.R. 708; see further below, p. 79.
2 [1972] 1 Q.B. 210, at p. 220; [1971] 3 All E.R. 708, at p. 714.
3 [1908] 1 K.B. 221; [1904–7] All E.R. Rep. 1016.
4 *Per* BUCKLEY, L.J., [1908] 1 K.B. 221, at pp. 230–1; [1904–7] All E.R. Rep. 1016, at p. 1020.

ordinary course of their business as to put the pledgee upon notice".[1] But does this statement amount to anything more than a recognition that, where an agent's normal course of business is to sell to the public, any limitation on the extent of the ordinary course of the business must be sufficiently notorious amongst the public at large? Where the ordinary course of an agent's business is restricted (as would be the case with the diamond merchant), the limitation need only be customary in the trade, and known by persons operating in the trade.

The justification for the course adopted by the Court of Appeal is that, while a person is deemed a mercantile agent if he has in the course of *his* business as such agent a power to sell, etc. goods, once he is a mercantile agent his power of disposition under s. 2 (1) is that of *a* mercantile agent in the ordinary course of business. The fallacy of this argument is, of course, that the application of s. 2 (1) is based upon the supposition that there is such a being as a "standard" or "normal" mercantile agent. It is obvious that there is no "standard" mercantile agent in the business world: mercantile agents operate within frameworks of a variety of different trade customs and usages. Hence if there is to be a "standard" mercantile agent, his existence must depend upon the Act. However, s. 1 (1) made no attempt to establish such a creature: in fact, it defined a mercantile agent as "a mercantile agent having in the customary course of his business as such agent an authority to sell", etc.

The criticism that may be directed against the decision in *Oppenheimer* v. *Attenborough* is partly borne out by the later Court of Appeal decision in *Newtons of Wembley, Ltd.* v. *Williams.*[2] The person who disposed of the goods in this case was a buyer whose title to a car was defective because the contract upon which it was based had been set aside. Under s. 25 (2) of the Sale of Goods Act,[3] any disposition by a buyer in possession has the same effect as a similar disposition by a mercantile agent in possession of goods with the consent of the owner. The sale in this case had been effected for cash in a street market for second-hand cars that had grown up in a particular area of central London. The sale took place, therefore, outside normal business hours and not at a proper place of business. If there is such a creature as a "standard" mercantile agent, he would not hawk his goods at a street corner. The sale could only be justified, as indeed it was by the Court of Appeal, on the ground that account could be taken of what, in a particular trade, was a proper place of business. In the used car trade, this method of buying and selling at that particular place was a recognised way of doing business. A mercantile agent, and therefore the buyer in possession, could thereby give a good title.

What constitutes "in other respects in the ordinary way in which a mercantile agent would act", within BUCKLEY, L.J.'s dictum in *Oppenheimer* v. *Attenborough & Son*[4] may be illustrated by reference to a number of cases arising out of the motor trade.

---

1 [1908] 1 K.B. 221, at p. 226; [1904–7] All E.R. Rep. 1016, at p. 1018.
2 [1965] 1 Q.B. 560; [1964] 3 All E.R. 532.
3 See below, p. 80 *et seq.*, esp. at pp. 86–7.
4 [1908] 1 K.B. 221, at p. 230–1; [1904–7] All E.R. Rep. 1016, at p. 1020, quoted above, p. 70.

The *raison d'etre* of the requirement according to that dictum was that there should be nothing suspicious in the course of the transaction that might lead the buyer or pledgee to suppose that anything was wrong. This suspicion need not amount to an absence of good faith, which forms a separate requirement within s. 2 (1). In *Motor Credits Ltd.* v. *Pacific Motor Auctions Pty., Ltd.*[1] it will be recalled, S had sold part of his stock of vehicles to O, but had remained in possession of them under a "floor plan" arrangement. Subsequently he had sold some of these vehicles to B in return for a cheque. However, instead of accounting to O, S's manager had endorsed the cheque and returned it to B's accountant to cover the amount of a debt owed by S to B. There was nothing to impugn B's good faith in that B believed that the cars belonged to S. However, he could not rely upon S's ostensible authority as a mercantile agent because it was quite outside any authority he was likely to have from a principal (if there were one) that he could sell the principal's goods in settlement of his own debt. Accordingly, the High Court of Australia concluded, such a sale was not in the ordinary course of business of a mercantile agent.

However, the Court of Appeal has taken a much more restrictive view of what falls within the normal course of business of a dealer within the motor-car trade. In *Pearson* v. *Rose and Young, Ltd.*[2] O, the plaintiff, left his car with S, a dealer, to see what offers would be made for it. S intended to sell the car as soon as possible and misappropriate the proceeds. In the course of a discussion between S and O, O handed the registration book to S. S thereupon induced O to leave on a bogus errand. O had no intention of leaving the registration book with S but, being distracted, forgot temporarily that he had in fact left it behind. S was thus able to sell the car with the registration book. The Court of Appeal pointed out that, although S's possession of the car was nevertheless sufficient to satisfy the Act despite the fact he had obtained it by means of larceny by a trick, he had not obtained possession of the registration book in his capacity as a mercantile agent because O had never intended to give S such possession. The Court held that a sale without the registration book was not a sale in the ordinary course of business so that the buyer from S did not take a good title.

This decision was taken a stage further in *Stadium Finance, Ltd.* v. *Robbins,*[3] in which the dealer, S, had been given possession of O's car in order that he should find a buyer. O kept the ignition key, clearly intending to control the sale himself. Inadvertently he left the registration book in the locked glove compartment. It was held by the Court of Appeal that, as S had not been given possession of the registration book and ignition key, a subsequent sale could not be in the ordinary course of business, even though he obtained a duplicate key and was therefore able to hand a key and the registration book to the hirer. Hence the hire purchase company, to which S had purported to transfer the car under the agreement with the hirer, failed in its action against O who had retaken possession of the car.

---

1 (1963), 109 C.L.R. 87; see above, p. 61.
2 [1951] 1 K.B. 275; [1950] 2 All E.R. 1027.
3 [1962] 2 Q.B. 664; [1962] 2 All E.R. 633.

These decisions raise two issues. First, would the withholding of the ignition key alone have been sufficient to take the sale outside the ordinary course of business in the *Stadium Finance* case? Secondly, and more fundamentally, are the two cases correctly decided or should the opportunity be taken to reconsider them?

As far as the first question is concerned both ORMEROD,[1] and DANCKWERTS, L.JJ.,[2] seemed to regard the keys and the registration book as equally important. On the other hand, WILLMER, L.J., treated the key as important principally because of the access it gave to the registration book in the glove compartment. "The mere fact that, in the absence of a key, the car could not go would not be sufficient, standing by itself, to justify the conclusion that the car was never in the possession" of the dealer as a mercantile agent. However, in the special circumstances of this case, the "absence of the key is important . . . because

> (i) its absence was symbolic of the owner's intention to retain a *jus disponendi*, and
> (ii) the key was needed in order to open the glove compartment and give delivery of the registration book".[3]

The first reason advanced by WILLMER, L.J., raises the other issue, namely of deciding whether this line of authority is correct. As far as the key is concerned, it would obviously be outside the ordinary course of business for a dealer to sell a car without one, but so long as he provides an ignition key that fits the vehicle in question, the sale is in the ordinary course of business. The initial withholding of the key relates to the capacity in which the car was entrusted to the dealer. Hence the title given by the dealer depends upon whether the dealer was entrusted with the car as a mercantile agent. As has already been stated, however, it would largely defeat the intention of the factors legislation for an owner to be allowed to plead such a reservation of the right of disposition.

The position of the log book would seem to be somewhat different. In the second-hand trade, the log book has taken on the aura of being something akin to a document of title.[4] As far as new vehicles are concerned, however, it is customary for the log book to be sent off so that the vehicle can be taxed and the buyer's name registered with the records office. Hence, in *Astley Industrial Trust, Ltd.* v. *Miller*, CHAPMAN, J., held[5] *obiter* that a sale of a new car could be in the normal course of business if it was supplied without a log book which was being withheld for submission to the appropriate taxing authority.

The doubt that this opinion raises is whether the sale of a second-hand vehicle can be within the normal course of business if a persuasive reason for the absence

---

1 [1962] 2 All E.R. 633, at p. 636; [1962] 2 Q.B. 664, at p. 671: ". . . the car must be taken to be one which was defective in two important qualities. There was no registration book and there was no ignition key . . . I fail to see how the sale of a car deficient in these two important respects can be in the ordinary course of business of a mercantile agent."
2 [1962] 2 Q.B. 664, at p. 677; [1962] 2 All E.R. 633, at p. 640.
3 [1962] 2 Q.B. 664, at p. 674; [1962] 2 All E.R. 633, at p. 638.
4 Though it clearly is not so, see above, p. 54, n. 2.
5 [1968] 2 All E.R. 36, at pp. 42–4.

of the log book is given by the dealer to his customer. On this point there is no means of forecasting which way a court might decide.

In the final analysis it appears illogical for the courts to set themselves against recognising the log book as having some of the attributes of a document of title, yet creating for it some special status in relation to the concept of "ordinary course of business" of a second-hand car dealer. The degree of illogicality is increased by their acceptance of the proposition that a sale of the car with the log book is still not in the ordinary course of business if the log book is obtained without the owner's consent. A distinction should surely be drawn between possession of the goods to be sold (i.e. the car itself) which must be obtained in the capacity of a mercantile agent, and their subsequent disposition which requires the log book to qualify as a sale within the ordinary course of business. The test for establishing the first is primarily subjective (what were the owner's intentions?); the test in relation to the second should be purely objective (does the sale, from the buyer's standpoint, appear to be in the ordinary course of business?).

vi In good faith and without notice

By the proviso to s. 2 (1), a disposition by a mercantile agent in the ordinary course of business will not be effective unless "the person taking under the disposition acts in good faith, and has not at the time of the disposition notice that the person making the disposition has not authority to make the same".

It is obvious enough that a person cannot act in good faith if he has knowledge of a lack of authority on the part of the agent. While it is probable that by notice the proviso means actual notice and not constructive notice,[1] nevertheless the circumstances of the sale might be so suspicious that they raise the doubt that the buyer or pledgee had not received the goods in good faith. The most obvious illustration of a circumstance that should arouse suspicion would be a purchase at a price much less than the value of the goods in question. In *Heap* v. *Motorists' Advisory Agency*,[2] LUSH, J., held that a sale of a car, which the plaintiff wished to sell at £210, to the defendants for £110 was a fact which suggested that the price was so low that it should have put the defendants on their guard: hence they were unable to show that they had bought in good faith.

In many cases the circumstances giving rise to the implication that the buyer has not acted in good faith will also tend to show that the transaction in question was not in the seller's ordinary course of business as a mercantile agent. In *Mehta* v. *Sutton*,[3] for example, B's Paris agent had been approached by S who said that he had pawned some pearls which he wished to sell. In fact S had obtained them from O, a dealer in precious stones, by fraudulently representing that he (S) had a buyer for the pearls. The pearls were redeemed and transferred

---

1 There are a number of emphatic judicial statements that the doctrine of constructive notice plays no part in commercial transactions: e.g. *per* LINDLEY, L.J., in *Manchester Trust* v. *Furness*, [1895] 2 Q.B. 539, at p. 545, citing Lord HERSCHELL in *London Joint Stock Bank* v. *Simmons*, [1892] A.C. 201, at pp. 217–8; also *Greer* v. *Downs Supply Co.*, [1927] 2 K.B. 28; [1926] All E.R. Rep. 675.
2 [1923] 1 K.B. 577; [1922] All E.R. Rep. 251.
3 (1913), 109 L.T. 529.

to the agent on B's behalf. They were subsequently sent to B in England. When O discovered what had happened to the pearls, he commenced this action. BRAY, J., in the Commercial Court, held that, even if the transaction had been governed by English law, the Factors Act would not have protected B. It was proved that a Paris pearl broker had no authority to sell, but only to report back to his principal who alone could approve the proposed transaction by invoicing the goods to the buyer. In this case, the likelihood of S being the owner of such valuable pearls was remote: B's agent could not claim to have acted in good faith by deliberately refraining from making further enquiries about S. In fact the judge disbelieved the agent's denial that he suspected S of being a pearl broker. The reason for this denial was obvious. Such a departure from the ordinary course of business of a Paris pearl broker would have been the strongest evidence of a lack of good faith on the part of O's agent.[1]

In this context it is worth reconsidering the situation that arises, in relation to the log book, in the sale of a second-hand vehicle. It will be recalled that some doubt was expressed on whether the owner's consent was relevant to the mercantile agent's possession of the log book which was in no sense part of the "goods" which are disposed of in the ordinary course of business.[2] Whether or not one regards the presence of a log book as being essential to a sale of a second-hand car in the ordinary course of business, its absence would undoubtedly give rise to doubts about the good faith of the transaction. As MORRIS, L.J., pointed out in *Central Newbury Car Auctions, Ltd.* v. *Unity Finance, Ltd.*,[3] the "absence of a registration book when a car is being sold will naturally give rise to much enquiry". It would certainly be more rational to treat the presence or absence of a log book as relevant to the good faith of the transaction rather than to the question of whether the transaction takes place in the ordinary course of business. A plausible explanation of the absence of a log book is much more readily tested in the context of good faith than in relation to what is a normal course of business.

D. THE SELLER OR BUYER IN POSSESSION

Historically, the position of a seller remaining in possession of goods after a sale had been effected or of a buyer taking possession before property had passed, was closely connected with the position of a mercantile agent. This connection

---

1 The reason for the agent's reluctance to make enquiries about S was that he had in fact carried on a highly dubious business on his own account of redeeming pledges at a profit by way of a high discount or rate of interest. The charging of an exceptional rate of interest would probably be taken as evidence of a pledgee's suspicions of the pledgor's title and therefore of a lack of good faith on the part of the pledgee: see *Janesich* v. *George Attenborough & Son* (1910), 102 L.T. 605, at p. 606, *per* HAMILTON, J.

2 DENNING, L.J.'s statement to the contrary in *Pearson* v. *Rose and Young, Ltd.*, [1951] 1 K.B. 275, at p. 289; [1950] 2 All E.R. 1027, at p. 1033; notwithstanding: see *Stadium Finance, Ltd.* v. *Robbins*, [1962] 2 Q.B. 664, at pp. 670–1, 676; [1962] 2 All E.R. 633, at pp. 636, 639; *Astley Industrial Trust, Ltd.* v. *Miller*, [1968] 2 All E.R. 36, at p. 43.

3 [1957] 1 Q.B. 371, at p. 398; [1956] 3 All E.R. 905, at p. 920; and see DENNING, L.J.'s comments in relation to the good faith requirement of a sale in market overt in *Bishopsgate Motor Finance Corporation, Ltd.* v. *Transport Brakes, Ltd.*, [1949] 1 K.B. 322, at p. 338; [1949] 1 All E.R. 37, at p. 46. For sales in market overt, see below, p. 102.

may be illustrated by the decision in *Johnson* v. *Credit Lyonnais Co.*[1] S, a broker in the tobacco trade, also dealt in tobacco as an importing merchant. He received a consignment of tobacco at the Port of London, warehoused it, and received the dock warrants. He then sold the tobacco to the plaintiff, but the latter, not wishing to pay duty on the tobacco until he needed the tobacco, left it in bond. Thus remaining in control of the tobacco by virtue of the dock warrant that had been issued in his name, S pledged the tobacco with the defendants.

It was held that the decisions in the plaintiff's favour in his claims against the defendants were correct. The Factors Acts could not assist the defendants because S had not been " 'intrusted' with these goods, or with the documents of title relating to them, as agent to sell or consign, or indeed as agent in any sense, but stood only in the position of a paid vendor remaining in possession of the thing sold till it suited the convenience of the buyer to accept delivery".[2] Nor could there be an estoppel because the juries' findings had negatived negligence on the plaintiff's part, and there was no reason for disturbing either verdict. Quite apart from the plaintiff's assertion that he had no idea that there had been any dock warrants in existence, it had become such a normal practice in the tobacco trade for purchasers to leave goods in the hands of importers that what the plaintiff had done could hardly be considered negligent *vis-à-vis* other persons with a knowledge of the trade.[3]

As soon as the decisions at first instance in the two cases brought by the plaintiff became public, Parliament passed the 1877 Factors Act to give a seller remaining in possession a power of disposition, and also to enable a buyer, allowed to have possession of documents of title but not yet the owner of the goods, to pass a good title.[4] The power to pass title of a seller or buyer in possession of documents of title was further extended by the Factors Act of 1889, and substantially similar provisions were included in the 1893 Sale of Goods Act.

i Seller remaining in possession

By s. 8 of the Factors Act:

> "Where a person, having sold goods, continues, or is, in possession of the goods or of the documents of title to the goods, the delivery or transfer by that person, or by a mercantile agent acting for him, of the goods or documents of title under any sale, pledge, or other disposition thereof, [or under any agreement for sale, pledge, or other disposition thereof,] to any person receiving the same in good faith and without notice of the previous sale, shall have the same effect as if the person making the delivery or transfer was expressly authorised by the owner of the goods to make the same."

---

1 (1877), 3 C.P.D. 32.
2 At p. 36, *per* COCKBURN, C.J.
3 This aspect of the decision was applied by the Judicial Committee in *Mercantile Bank of India, Ltd.* v. *Central Bank of India, Ltd.*, [1938] A.C. 287; [1938] 1 All E.R. 52, see above, p. 54.
4 Such a buyer was not an agent entrusted with the goods for sale because he held the goods or documents of title in his own right; i.e. as "potential" owner: *Jenkyns* v. *Usborne* (1844), 7 Man. & G. 678.

a *Comparison with s. 25 (1) of the Sale of Goods Act*

The corresponding provision in the Sale of Goods Act, s. 25 (1), omits the words in brackets. There are a number of pronouncements by academic writers[1] that this section is "narrower" than that appearing in the Factors Act. This view seems to be based upon the reasoning of SCRUTTON, L.J., in *Marten* v. *Whale*[2] that as the two provisions were not identical they had to be read together. The conclusion of such writers does not follow from the premise. Schmitthoff, for example, states that because the Sale of Goods Act provision is narrower the Factors Act provision is not repealed. With respect, the main reason for the non-repeal is that s. 21 (2) of the 1893 Act lays down that "nothing in this Act shall affect . . . the provisions of the Factors Acts." SCRUTTON, L.J. was saying no more than that, because of the difference in wording, both provisions had to be considered: if the wording had been identical it would have been immaterial which provision had been taken into account. This statement, however, does not mean that, at a later stage, it may not be possible to decide that the two provisions have the same *effect*. The wording of the Sale of Goods Act provision may be "narrower" but it is not certain that it is "narrower" in effect. Indeed, there is no reason why a delivery of goods by a seller remaining in possession to a second buyer in good faith should not be equally effective under an agreement to sell. The reference to "other disposition" in the phrase "under any sale, pledge or other disposition" would seem to be wide enough to cover an agreement in those rare cases where the agreement has not become a sale (i.e. been fully executed) by delivery.[3]

The point may be largely academic in England where both s. 8 and s. 25 (1) co-exist on the Statute Book, but in the Australian States of Victoria and New South Wales, for example, the only provision is the "narrower" one so that it could be a matter of some importance whether the omission of the words "or under any agreement for sale, pledge or other disposition thereof" has any practical significance.

Many of the interpretative issues raised by s. 25 are similar or identical to those that have already been considered in relation to mercantile agents. The generally accepted view is that the section, having its origins in the Factors legislation, should be interpreted in the same way.[4] In addition a number of phrases are specifically given the same meanings as those laid down in the Factors Act.[5]

b *The seller's possession*

Where the two Acts do diverge is in their treatment of the seller's possession as compared with the possession of a mercantile agent. It will be recalled that

---

1 Schmitthoff, *The Sale of Goods*, 2nd Ed. p. 111; Sutton, *The Law of Sale of Goods in Australia and New Zealand*, p. 257.   2 [1917] 2 K.B. 480, at p. 486.
3 It will of course always become a sale by a transfer of title.
4 *City Fur Manufacturing Co., Ltd.* v. *Fureenbond (Brokers) London, Ltd.*, [1937] 1 All E.R. 799 (possession).
5 Section 25 itself (3), states that "mercantile agent" "has the same meaning as in the Factors Acts"; similarly s. 62 (1) in dealing with "documents of title to goods".

under s. 2 (1) of the Factors Act, a mercantile agent had to be in possession of goods with the consent of the owner; and that it had been established that a change in the nature of his possession (e.g. from possession as mercantile agent to possession as hirer under a hire-purchase transaction) destroyed his power to pass title. Section 25 (1) of the Sale of Goods Act, however, refers to a person who "having sold goods continues, or is, in possession of the goods, or of the documents of title". Despite the obvious difference in wording, the courts proceeded to act as if there were no such difference.

In *Staffs Motor Guarantee, Ltd.* v. *British Wagon Co., Ltd.*,[1] S sold a lorry to B1, the defendant finance company. B1 agreed to hire it back to S on hire purchase. The lorry remained in S's possession throughout. S subsequently resold the vehicle to B2, the plaintiff finance company. When S failed to keep up his payments to B1, B1 took possession of the vehicle. MacKinnon, J., held that B'2s claim faced the same difficulty under s. 25 (1) as it had under s. 2 (1), i.e. that S's

> "possession of the lorry at the time when the plaintiffs made their bargain with him was not the possession of a seller who had not yet delivered the article sold to the buyer, but was the possession of the bailee under the hire-purchase agreement . . . into which he had entered with the defendants".[2]

Although this interpretation was accepted by the Court of Appeal in *Eastern Distributors, Ltd.* v. *Goldring*[3] and by the High Court of Australia in *Motor Credits (Hire Finance), Ltd.* v. *Pacific Motor Auctions Pty., Ltd.*,[4] the High Court was reversed and the earlier decisions disapproved, on this point when the latter case went on appeal to the Privy Council.[5]

The facts of this decision have already been considered in some detail.[6] It will be recalled that S sold a number of cars in his showrooms to B1 under an arrangement whereby S would remain in possession of the vehicles and sell them under a general authority from B1. Once a particular car was sold, it was then for S to account to B1 for the proceeds of sale. Because of doubts about S's financial

---

1 [1934] 2 K.B. 305; [1934] All E.R. Rep. 322; dealt with from the standpoint of s. 2 (1) of the Factors Act above, p. 66.
2 [1934] 2 K.B., at p. 314; [1934] All E.R. Rep., at p. 325. In reaching this decision, MacKinnon, J., relied upon the New Zealand case of *Mitchell* v. *Jones* (1905), 24 N.Z.L.R. 932, in which S sold *and delivered* a horse to B1, but received it back on hire; S sold the animal to B2. The situation was not therefore analogous to the English case, but MacKinnon, J., relied upon the statement by Stout, C.J., 24 N.Z.L.R., at p. 935, that in that case "the person who sold goods gave up possession of them, and gave delivery of them to the buyer. The relationship, therefore, of buyer and seller between them was at an end. It is true that the seller got possession of the goods again, but not as seller. He got the goods the second time as the bailee of the buyer, and as the bailee he had no warrant . . . to sell the goods again, nor could he make a good title to them to even a *bona fide* purchaser". See also *per* Williams, J., at p. 936, and Edwards, J., at p. 937. The members of the court were of the opinion that a seller "is" in possession of goods as opposed to "continues" in possession if he sells goods not in his possession, and afterwards obtains possession before delivery to B1. In such circumstances a second sale would be effective to pass title on delivery to B2.
3 [1957] 2 Q.B. 600; [1957] 2 All E.R. 525.
4 (1963), 109 C.L.R. 87.
5 *Sub nom. Pacific Motor Auctions Pty., Ltd.* v. *Motor Credits, Ltd.*, [1965] A.C. 867; [1965] 2 All E.R. 105.
6 See above, p. 61.

position, B1 withdrew S's authority to sell on B1's behalf, but S nevertheless went ahead and sold a number of the cars to B2. The High Court held that the equivalent provision in the New South Wales Act to s. 25 (1) had no application because the character of S's possession had changed: S had sold as hirer and not as a seller in possession. The Privy Council, however, decided that the expression, "where a person having sold goods continues in possession of the goods", was inconsistent with such an interpretation. The "continues ... in possession" was "intended to refer to the continuity of physical possession regardless of any private transaction[5] between the seller and purchaser which might alter the legal title under which the possession was held". The view previously held would require that the section be read as "continues in possession *as seller*", but there was no justification for implying such a qualification. It followed from the interpretation now adopted that "when a person sells a car to a finance house in order to take it back on hire-purchase the finance house must take physical delivery if it is to avoid the risk of an innocent purchaser acquiring title to it".[1]

Any doubts that may have existed whether the domestic English courts would apply this change in interpretation have been resolved by the Court of Appeal in *Worcester Works Finance, Ltd.* v. *Cooden Engineering Co., Ltd.*[2] B2, the defendants, sold a car to S whose cheque for the price was subsequently dishonoured. S transferred title but not possession of the vehicle to B1, the plaintiff finance company, which was to hire it to B2 under a hire purchase agreement. B2 did not receive the car from S, but S paid B2's instalments to cover up his activities. Because the cheque was dishonoured, B2 retook possession of the vehicle from S, with S's consent. S stopped paying the instalments on the car and, when B1 discovered the whereabouts of the vehicle, they (B1) brought this action against B2. It has already been explained[3] that the Court of Appeal accepted that the taking of possession of the car with S's agreement constituted a disposition of the goods on S's part. Counsel for B1 argued that, although S had been in possession of the goods immediately after the sale to B1, S had become a trespasser with his failure to hand over the goods to B2 and his subsequent concealment of what was happening. In other words, there had been a change in the nature of S's possession of the goods. This change, however, the Court held to be irrelevant: it was sufficient if the seller remained continuously in physical possession of the goods for him to be in a position to pass title to the second purchaser.

c *The delivery or transfer*

It should be noticed that, in addition to a "disposition" of the goods by the seller remaining in possession, there must also be a delivery or transfer of the goods or documents of title to the second buyer. Although this aspect of s. 25 (1) has received little attention, it cannot be said that the wording of the section is altogether clear.

---

1 [1965] A.C. 867, at p. 888; [1965] 2 All E.R. 105, at p. 114.
2 [1972] 1 Q.B. 210; [1971] 3 All E.R. 708.
3 Above, p. 70.

In *Nicholson* v. *Harper*,[1] the court was faced with the following circumstances. The plaintiffs, B1, had purchased 250 dozen bottles of port from S. These bottles were stored at the premises of S's bailee, who subsequently became B2, when S signed a memorandum of lien in B2's favour as security for a loan. When a receiving order was made against S, B2 advertised the port for sale by auction, but B1 claimed to be entitled to the bottles. NORTH, J., held in B1's favour. As there had been no delivery of the goods or transfer of documents of title to the goods since the sale (the goods having been throughout in B2's possession), B2 was not entitled to the protection of s. 25 (1), the requirements of which had not been satisfied.

This decision involves a transposition of the words employed in s. 25 (1). It does not require a "delivery of goods" or "a transfer of documents of title", but a "delivery or transfer . . . of the goods or documents of title". For the purposes of s. 25 (1) of the Sale of Goods Act, or s. 8 of the Factors Act, B2 was, until the lien was granted, a bailee of the goods on S's behalf. Clearly, therefore, until that moment, S was in possession of the goods as they were held by another person "subject to his control or for him or on his behalf".[2] The effect of the memorandum creating the lien in B2's favour was to transfer possession of the goods because, from that moment, B2 no longer held the goods solely on S's behalf. And even if that act did not constitute a transfer of the goods, it was certainly a transfer of possession, i.e. a "delivery" of the goods within the meaning given to that expression by s. 62 (1) of the Sale of Goods Act.[3]

ii Buyer obtaining possession

Much of what has been said in relation to s. 25 (1) is also directly relevant to s. 25 (2), although some differences in wording have created a number of distinctive features in the application of sub-s. (2). Section 25 (2) reads (the words in brackets appearing in the parallel s. 9 of the Factors Act):

> "Where a person having bought or agreed to buy goods obtains, with the consent of the seller, possession of the goods or the documents of title to the goods, the delivery or transfer by that person, or by a mercantile agent acting for him, of the goods or the documents of title, under any sale, pledge, or other disposition thereof, [or under any agreement for sale, pledge, or other disposition thereof,] to any person receiving the same in good faith and without notice of any lien or other right of the original seller in respect of the goods, shall have the same effect as if the person making the delivery or transfer were a mercantile agent in possession of the goods or documents of title with the consent of the owner."

a S. 25 (2) *applies primarily to an agreement to sell*

Section 25 (1) applied only in cases of an actual sale because otherwise, under an agreement to sell, S would still retain property and be able to pass title to a second buyer. Correspondingly, s. 25 (2) should deal with the case of a buyer who has agreed to buy goods because, if he had already bought the goods, i.e.

---

1 [1895] 2 Ch. 415; [1895–9] All E.R. Rep. 882.
2 Factors Act, s. 1 (2).   3 But see further, below, p. 111.

property had already passed to him, he would be able to pass a good title irrespective of s. 25 (2). However, s. 25 (2) is expressed to extend to cases where the buyer has actually "bought" the goods in question. The reason for this is twofold. In the first place, where the seller reserves a right of disposal, property will only pass when the conditions imposed by the seller are fulfilled. This is expressly laid down by s. 19 (1) and (2):

> "(1) Where there is a contract for the sale of specific goods or where goods are subsequently appropriated to the contract, the seller may, by the terms of the contract or appropriation, reserve the right of disposal of the goods until certain conditions are fulfilled. In such case, notwithstanding the delivery of the goods to the buyer, or to a carrier or other bailee for the purpose of transmission to the buyer, the property in the goods does not pass to the buyer until the conditions imposed by the seller are fulfilled.
>
> (2) Where goods are shipped, and by the bill of lading the goods are deliverable to the order of the seller or his agent, the seller is *prima facie* deemed to reserve the right of disposal."

Secondly, the wording also covers the situation where the buyer, having agreed to buy goods in advance of payment, obtains possession of the documents of title: a sale by him would, because of s. 25 (2), operate to defeat the original seller's lien as an unpaid seller. The drafting is slipshod, and it is therefore necessary to place reasonable limits on its application. For example, it would be unreasonable to apply s. 25 (2) in such a way that a buyer, who has acquired both property in and possession of the goods without paying for them, would be prevented from passing property to a third party who takes in bad faith, i.e. is aware of the fact that the seller has not yet been paid.[1]

1 *Options to purchase.* Whatever doubts there might be on its application in cases of an actual sale as opposed to an agreement to sell, it has been decided that the section cannot relate to someone who has only an option to purchase but is not bound to purchase the goods in question, as under a hire purchase agreement or the like.[2] Whether a contract is one of sale or of hire is of course a question of construction. In the words of Lord HERSCHELL, "the parties cannot, by calling it a hiring, or by any mere juggling with words, escape from the consequences of the contract into which they entered".[3] Similarly, as we have seen, s. 25 (2) cannot apply to someone who has taken goods on sale or return,[4] though it will be a matter of construction whether the person taking the goods does so on sale or return or on some other basis.[5]

---

1 See Atiyah, *op cit.*, 2nd Ed., p. 139; J. C. Smith (1963), 7 J.S.P.T.L., p. 226; Atiyah, *op. cit.* 3rd Ed., pp. 157–9; 4th Ed. p. 200.
2 *Helby* v. *Matthews*, [1895] A.C. 471; [1895–9] All E.R. Rep. 821; distinguishing *Lee* v. *Butler*, [1893] 2 Q.B. 318; [1891–4] All E.R. Rep. 1200.
3 *Helby* v. *Matthews*, [1895] A.C., at p. 475; [1895–9] All E.R. Rep., at p. 823. See *Hull Ropes Co., Ltd.* v. *Adams* (1895), 65 L.J.Q.B. 114; and the Australian case of *Commonwealth Furniture Supply* v. *Waterman* (1916), 18 W.A.L.R. 36.
4 *Edwards, Ltd.* v. *Vaughan* (1910), 26 T.L.R. 545. Of course, a sale by B who has taken goods on sale or return or on approval is an "act adopting the transaction" under s. 18, rule 4 (a), which operates to pass the property to B and thence to X, the purchaser from B. However, rule 4 can be excluded by the original contract as in *Weiner* v. *Gill*, [1906] 2 K.B. 574; [1904–7] All E.R. Rep. 773; see above, pp. 48–9.
5 *Weiner* v. *Harris*, [1910] 1 K.B. 285, see above, p. 49.

As it is possible for a contract of sale to be conditional under s. 1 (2) of the Sale of Goods Act, a person taking under a conditional contract can still be a person who has agreed to buy goods within s. 25 (2). In *Lee* v. *Butler*,[1] the condition was the payment of the price by instalments; in *Marten* v. *Whale*,[2] the sale of a car was conditional upon the purchase by the owner of the vehicle of a piece of land belonging to the buyer of the car. In both situations it was held that the buyer in possession of the goods could pass title to a purchaser.

2 *Conditional sales and hire purchase.* However, this position has been modified by statute in the form of the Hire Purchase legislation. A conditional sale for the purpose of the Hire Purchase Act 1965 is defined by s. 1 (1) of that Act as meaning:

> "an agreement for the sale of goods under which the purchase price or part of it is payable by instalments, and the property in the goods is to remain in the seller (notwithstanding that the buyer is to be in possession of the goods) until such conditions as to the payment of instalments or otherwise as may be specified in the agreement are fulfilled".

If the total purchase price does not exceed £2,000[3] and the agreement to buy the goods is not made by or on behalf of a body corporate,[4] such a conditional sale agreement is treated as a hire purchase transaction and is made subject to the hire purchase legislation. Hence, although it was the absence of an option to refuse to complete the transaction which distinguished the conditional sale from a hire purchase at common law, s. 27 of the 1965 Act expressly gives the buyer under a conditional sale agreement the right to terminate the agreement at any time before the final payment falls due. In fact this right exists whether or not property has passed to the buyer unless the buyer has transferred the property "to a person who does not become the buyer under the agreement".[5] And, in case there is any doubt about the effect the creation of such an option might have, s. 54 expressly provides that for the purposes of s. 9 of the Factors Act and of s. 25 (2) of the Sale of Goods Act

> "the buyer under a conditional sale agreement shall be deemed not to be a person who has bought or agreed to buy goods".

The effect of the 1965 Hire Purchase Act is thus to add more than one complicating factor. The distinction between an agreement to buy and a

---

1 [1893] 2 Q.B. 318; [1891–4] All E.R. Rep. 1200.
2 [1917] 2 K.B. 480.
3 Hire Purchase Act, 1965, s. 2 (2): power is granted by s. 3 to amend the Act to increase this amount by Order in Council: s. 3. By s. 58 (1) the "total purchase price" means "the total sum payable by the buyer" (exclusive of any sum payable as a penalty, compensation etc. for breach of the agreement), and includes, by s. 58 (2), any sum paid by way of deposit or other initial payment under the agreement.
4 Section 4.
5 Section 27 (2); a "buyer" by s. 58 (1) is defined "in relation to a conditional sale agreement" as "the person who agrees to purchase goods under the agreement and includes a person to whom the rights or liabilities of that person under the agreement have passed by assignment or by operation of law".

hire-purchase transaction based on the existence of an option to purchase is still vital to the application of s. 25 (2) if:

(i) the sale is conditional on some factor other than the payment of the price by instalments; or
(ii) if the sale is conditional and involves payment by instalments[1] but

    (*a*) the buyer is a corporate body; or
    (*b*) the "total purchase price" exceeds £2,000.

Where the transaction falls within the ambit of the Act (i.e. it is a conditional sale of goods the total purchase price of which is less than £2,000 to a person other than a corporate body and the method of purchase is by instalments), the buyer, though in possession, cannot pass a good title under s. 25 (2) of the Sale of Goods Act and s. 9 of the Factors Act. However, this restriction would not prevent the buyer giving a good title in a situation falling within one of the other exceptions to the *nemo dat* rule. In addition the Hire Purchase Act 1964, Part III, created an entirely new exception to the rule in relation to the sale of motor vehicles by the hirer under a hire purchase agreement or buyer under a conditional sale agreement, but these provisions will be dealt with later.[2]

b *The possession must be with the seller's consent*

Unlike s. 25 (1) which contains no limitation upon the nature of the possession retained by the seller, s. 25 (2) provides that the buyer can only pass a good title if he has acquired possession of the goods or documents of title with the seller's consent.

In considering whether S, the seller, has consented to B's, the buyer's, possession, it is obviously necessary to consider whether S *intended* that B should have possession of the goods. Once this intention exists, it matters not that it has been brought about by fraud on B's part. In *Du Jardin* v. *Beadman Bros., Ltd.*,[3] B agreed to buy a Standard car from S, the defendant. B gave S a cheque in payment, and left another vehicle, a Hillman, as security for the cheque. S therefore allowed B to take the Standard away with him. Later the same day, and without S's knowledge, B also removed the Hillman. Three days afterwards B sold the Standard to the plaintiff. B's cheque proved to be worthless and he was subsequently convicted of obtaining the Standard by false pretences. This car was returned to S by the police, but the plaintiff brought this action claiming that he was entitled to the vehicle having bought it from B. It was clear that B

---

1 The definition of a conditional sale agreement in s. 1 (1) as set out above involves two elements:

    (i) the purchase price or part of it being payable by instalments; and
    (ii) the property in the goods remaining in the seller "until such conditions as to payment of instalments or *otherwise as may be specified in the agreement* are fulfilled".

The words in italics suggest that a conditional sale under this provision could be conditional because of something other than the payment of price by instalments, although payment by instalments is essential to the application of the Act.

2 Below, p. 99.

3 [1952] 2 Q.B. 712; [1952] 2 All E.R. 160.

had agreed to buy the car, so the only question to be decided was whether he had obtained possession with S's consent. SELLERS, J., held, employing the same approach as that adopted in relation to s. 2 of the Factors Act,[1] that if B had obtained possession of the goods with S's consent, it did not matter that S's state of mind had been affected by B's fraud.[2] Accordingly B had been able to pass title to the plaintiff under s. 25 (2).

It will be recalled that until recently the view was that a seller had to be in possession as seller in order to pass title under s. 25 (1). Does the buyer under s. 25 (2) have to obtain possession as buyer in order to pass title, or would a temporary loan of the goods prior to the time when the transaction is to take effect be sufficient to give him a power to pass title?

This issue does not appear to have been considered in any English case. In *Marten* v. *Whale*,[3] B had agreed to purchase a car from S as part of a transaction involving the sale by him to S of a piece of land. Soon after this contract was made S allowed B to have the vehicle on loan. B sold the car to a third party. Subsequently S's solicitors refused to approve certain restrictions on the land and the whole transaction between S and B fell through. It was held that the third party took a good title from B who was a person who had agreed to buy goods: it was not disputed that B had obtained possession with the owner's consent.[4]

Similarly, in the Australian case of *Langmead* v. *Thyer Rubber Co., Ltd.*[5] S entered into negotiations to sell a car to B. As the vehicle needed painting, B was given a choice between buying it for £190 as it was, or buying it after S had painted it for a higher price. S, throughout, insisted that the payment should be in cash. B agreed to buy for £190 and said he would call in a day or so to pay for and collect the car. When B came, he brought a cheque which S refused to accept. It was then agreed that B should take the car to have it painted while arrangements were made for cash payment. In fact B took the car away and sold it. The South Australian Full Court held that B was a person who had agreed to buy the car and had possession of it with S's consent. Hence B had been able to pass a good title to his purchaser.

However, some doubt was expressed on how far s. 25 (2) could be extended.[6] Would it apply to a situation where possession was given to the buyer for a purpose entirely unrelated to the buyer/seller relationship? For instance, S agrees to sell his car to B, a dealer, for £500 to be deducted from the price of a new car to be supplied when one becomes available. Before then S takes his car to B's garage for a routine service. B is not in possession as a mercantile agent,

---

1 Applying *Folkes* v. *King*, [1923] 1 K.B. 282; [1922] All E.R. Rep. 658; and *Pearson* v. *Rose and Young Ltd.*, [1951] 1 K.B. 275; [1950] 2 All E.R. 1027; see above, p. 69.
2 Unless the fraud induces a mistake of identity sufficient to destroy the contract altogether: see *Folkes* v. *King*, [1923] 1 K.B. 282, at p. 305; [1922] All E.R. Rep. 658, at p. 665; per SCRUTTON, L.J., and see below, pp. 92–5.
3 [1917] 2 K.B. 480.
4 See *per* SWINFEN EADY, L.J. at pp. 483–4; *per* SCRUTTON, L.J., at p. 487.
5 [1947] S.A.S.R. 29; see also *Reed* v. *Motors, Ltd.*, [1926] S.A.S.R. 128, at p. 134.
6 [1947] S.A.S.R., at p. 34.

so a sale to X would not pass title under s. 2 of the Factors Act.[1] However, he is a person who has agreed to purchase the car in question, and he is in possession with S's consent. In theory, at any rate, s. 9 of the Factors Act, or s. 25 (2) of the Sale of Goods Act, applies. One doubts, however, whether too literal an application of s. 9/s. 25 (2) would be adopted in such circumstances.

c *The effect of a sale by a buyer in possession*

If one takes s. 25 (2) too literally, one is led to conclude that a sale by S, a non-owner, to B, if he is also able to give B possession of the goods, would enable B to pass title on a sale to a third party. It has already been explained that a contract by S to sell goods that do not at that time belong to him is a valid, indeed a common, transaction.[2] B would clearly be a person who has agreed to buy goods. And, if S can obtain possession of the goods from the owner so as to pass possession to B, B will have possession with the consent of the seller. It is reasonable enough to apply s. 25 (2) in this way to provide subsequent purchasers in a chain of transactions with a valid title even if the initial sale is void, or has been avoided before they had agreed to buy the goods in question.[3] It is far from reasonable for an owner to be deprived of goods which for example, he merely lends or hires to S, but which S has agreed to sell to B and which B, as soon as he obtains possession, sells and delivers to an innocent third party. Taken to its logical conclusion such an application of s. 25 (2) would lead to the situation where a sale by a person who has bought and obtained possession of the goods from a thief is effective to give title to, or rather create title in, the purchaser.

To avoid these possibilities it would be necessary for the courts to place some limit on the application of s. 25 (2) and it is possible that the concluding words of the sub-section provide a means of escape. In contrast to the final words of s. 25 (1) which provide that a sale by a seller in possession is, in appropriate circumstances, to "have the same effect as if the person making the delivery or transfer were expressly authorised by the owner of the goods to make the same", s. 25 (2) states that a sale by a buyer in possession is to have the same effect "as if the person making the delivery or transfer were a mercantile agent in possession of the goods or documents of title with the consent of the owner".

It cannot be claimed that it is at all obvious what is meant by these words. It is perhaps possible to start with the proposition that a buyer in possession with the seller's consent is to have powers no wider than those of a mercantile agent in possession with the owner's consent. Accordingly, if the buyer happens to be a mercantile agent no difficulties arise. If he is not in possession as a mercantile agent, if he is only bailee of a car while carrying out repairs on it, the mere fact that he has also agreed to purchase the vehicle will not extend his powers in order to transfer title. If he is in possession in connection with the sale, however, he would be able to pass title under s. 2 of the Factors Act and also, as he has agreed to purchase the car, under s. 25 (2)/s. 9 as well.

---

1 See above, p. 66.
2 See above, pp. 17–18.
3 See below, p. 91.

If the buyer is not a mercantile agent, "all that s. 9 can be said clearly to do is to place [him] . . . in the position of a mercantile agent when he has in fact in his possession the goods of somebody else, and it does no more than clothe him with that fictitious or notional position".[1] In the case from which that quotation is taken, *Newtons of Wembley, Ltd.* v. *Williams*, S, the plaintiffs, sold a car to B in return for a cheque. B was given possession of the car and its log book. He had himself registered as owner. The cheque was dishonoured and S took effective steps to disaffirm the contract but was unable to find the car. Later B sold the car to X by a contract which was negotiated in Warren Street, London, where there was a regular trade in second-hand cars. X eventually sold the vehicle to the defendant. The Court of Appeal held that the sale had been conducted in what would have been the normal course of business for a dealer in second-hand cars had B in fact been such a dealer. Accordingly, as X had bought in good faith, he took a good title which he could subsequently transfer to the defendant.

Both DAVIES L.J., who heard this case at first instance,[2] and the members of the Court of Appeal were prepared to attach the requirement that the sale should be in the ordinary course of business[3] to a situation where the buyer in possession was not himself a mercantile agent. The approach was only possible because of the very unusual circumstances in which a private buyer actually sold "through the trade". What if he had sold from a private address by advertising in the ordinary local press? The impression one gets from the judgments is that in such a situation the transaction would be ineffective to pass title, but this is surely to make nonsense of s. 25 (2) as a whole. It has not been argued in other cases involving s. 25 (2) that the buyer in possession had to create an atmosphere of a business operation in order for the sale to be effective.[4]

In this respect, *Newtons of Wembley, Ltd.* v. *Williams* cannot be supported on any logical grounds. It was an attempt by the courts to cover a transaction by applying s. 25 (2) instead of s. 23. The latter section, which will be dealt with shortly,[5] provides that a person who has a voidable title which has not yet been avoided at the time of a sale is able to pass a good title to an innocent purchaser of the goods. The difficulty existed because it had been established by the Court of Appeal in *Car and Universal Finance Co., Ltd.* v. *Caldwell*[6] that a contract of sale could be rescinded in certain circumstances by a seller without communicating this fact to the buyer, and, more importantly in the present context, without the seller repossessing the goods that were the subject matter of the contract of sale.

---

1 *Per* SELLERS, L.J., in *Newtons of Wembley, Ltd.* v. *Williams*, [1965] 1 Q.B. 560, at p. 574; [1964] 3 All E.R. 532, at p. 537.
2 [1964] 2 All E.R. 135.
3 Contained in the definition of a mercantile agent in s. 1 (1) of the Factors Act (see above, p. 64).
4 Although in fact the buyer in possession in *Marten* v. *Whale*, [1917] 2 K.B. 480, had displayed the vehicle at a garage prior to selling it, this fact was not thought necessary for the application of s. 25 (2).
5 Below, pp. 91 *et seq.*
6 [1965] 1 Q.B., at p. 535; [1964] 1 All E.R. 290.

In *Newtons of Wembley, Ltd.* v. *Williams*, the Court of Appeal was prepared to use the equating in s. 25 (2) of a sale by a buyer in possession with the seller's consent with a sale by a mercantile agent in possession with the owner's consent as a justification for applying the "in the ordinary course of business" requirement in the definition of a mercantile agent as nearly as possible to a sale by a private buyer. Indeed, the Court also made use of another provision of the Factors Act. By s. 2 (2) the consent of the owner to a mercantile agent's possession of the goods is deemed to continue even if such consent is withdrawn. The Court held that the fact that the seller's consent had been withdrawn by the act of determining the contract with the buyer was ineffective to prevent the buyer being able to transfer title under s. 25 (2)/s. 9.
same", s. 25 (2) states that a sale by a buyer in possession is to have the same

This approach appears to be a misapplication of the words used in s. 25 (2). However, it does at least provide an alternative interpretation to the suggestion that the section enables a buyer in possession from a seller who has no title, to pass a better title than either he or the seller had. This absurd consequence can be avoided by imposing, on the basis of s. 25 (2), the dual requirement that, as a buyer, he should be in possession with the seller's consent and that, in his notional guise of a mercantile agent, he should be in possession with the owner's consent. If the seller has acquired possession of the goods by stealing them, or by hiring or borrowing them, it is not unreasonable to demand that a purchaser from the buyer show that both requirements are satisfied before the true owner's rights are defeated. It would be a strange situation indeed if s. 25 (2) required that a buyer should be treated as a mercantile agent if in possession with the seller's consent, but to refuse to take into account that he did not have the consent of the true owner of the goods as would have been necessary if he were in fact a mercantile agent.

d *The documents of title*
Under s. 3 of the Factors Act, a "pledge of the documents of title to goods shall be deemed to be a pledge of the goods". However, the scope of this provision is not altogether clear. Sections 2–7 of the Act are given the heading "Dispositions by Mercantile Agents", whereas ss. 8–10 are headed "Dispositions by Sellers and Buyers of Goods". It was concluded by the House of Lords on an appeal from Scotland in *Inglis* v. *Robertson*[1] that therefore s. 3 had no application to s. 9/s. 25 (2). However, this decision would not necessarily be followed because, as *Newtons of Wembley, Ltd.* v. *Williams*[2] illustrates, the Court of Appeal has taken the view that the reference to the disposition having the same effect as if the buyer were a mercantile agent in s. 9 is sufficient to bring in other provisions dealing with the powers of a mercantile agent contained elsewhere in the Factors Act. In fact it is difficult to read s. 9/s. 25 (2) without concluding that for most purposes a transfer of the documents of title is tantamount to a delivery of the goods.
This reading of s. 9/s. 25 (2) is reinforced by s. 10 of the Factors Act and the

---

1 [1898] A.C. 616.
2 [1965] 1 Q.B. 560; [1964] 3 All E.R. 532; see also *Cahn* v. *Pockett's Bristol Channel Steam Packet Co., Ltd.*, [1899] 1 Q.B. 643, discussed, below, p. 89.

proviso to s. 47 of the Sale of Goods Act. These two provisions are substantially the same in effect: s. 47 will be dealt with later;[1] s. 10 reads:

> "Where a document of title to goods has been lawfully transferred to a person as a buyer or owner of the goods, and that person transfers the document to a person who takes the document in good faith and for valuable consideration, the last-mentioned transfer shall have the same effect for defeating any vendor's lien or right of stoppage *in transitu* as the transfer of a bill of lading has for defeating the right of stoppage *in transitu*".

As will be discussed later,[2] an unpaid vendor is in certain circumstances allowed to exercise a lien over the goods, or, if they are in transit prior to delivery to the buyer or his agent, a right to give notice to the carrier to retain the goods on his (the seller's) behalf. These rights of the seller are defeated on transfer of a bill of lading or any other document of title to a person taking in good faith and for valuable consideration. The position as regards the bill of lading was described by BOWEN, L.J., in *Sanders* v. *Maclean* in the following terms:[3]

> "A cargo at sea while in the hands of the carrier is necessarily incapable of physical delivery. During this period of transit and voyage, the bill of lading by the law merchant is universally recognised as its symbol, and the endorsement and delivery of the bill of lading operates as a symbolical delivery of the cargo. Property in the goods passed by such endorsement and delivery of the bill of lading, whenever it is the intention of the parties that the property should pass, just as under similar circumstances the property would pass by an actual delivery of the goods".

As between the original unpaid seller and a buyer who has not obtained property in the goods except through the bill of lading, however, a transfer by that buyer of the bill of lading will only defeat the seller's rights against the goods if the transfer is for valuable consideration.[4] The bill of lading is for most purposes[5] a negotiable instrument which is unimpeachable in the hands of the holder in due course (the *bona fide* purchaser for value).[6]

The normal method of transferring a bill of lading is by endorsement and delivery. For the purposes of the Factors Act, however, s. 11 states that "the transfer of a document may be by endorsement, or, where the document is by custom or by its express terms transferable by delivery, or makes the goods deliverable to the bearer, then by delivery". This is certainly a curious provision because it seems to suggest that a document of title can be effective by endorsement alone. Almost universally a negotiable instrument, and therefore a document of title which has much in common with a negotiable instrument, is transferred either by endorsement plus delivery or, where appropriate, by delivery alone. Despite the fact that the wording of s. 11 is derived from the

---

1 Below, p. 308.
2 Pp. 292 *et seq.*
3 (1883), 11 Q.B.D. 327, at p. 341.
4 A rule emanating from *Lickbarrow* v. *Mason* (1794), 5 Term Rep. 683.
5 But not if, for example, the bill had been stolen: see *per* Lord CAMPBELL, C.J., in *Gurney* v. *Behrend* (1854), 3 E. & B. 622, at p. 634; [1843–60] All E.R. 520, at p. 524.
6 See *The Argentina* (1867), L.R. 1 A. & E. 370.

earlier Factors Act of 1877, one is tempted to regard it as a case of misdrafting.[1] Nevertheless, even this explanation is difficult to reconcile with Chalmers' own use of quite explicit, yet contrary, terminology in drafting s. 31 of the Bills of Exchange Act.[2]

The relationship between unpaid seller and buyer in this context is also dealt with in s. 19 (3) of the Sale of Goods Act:[3]

> "Where the seller of goods draws on the buyer for the price, and transmits the bill of exchange and bill of lading to the buyer together to secure acceptance or payment of the bill of exchange, the buyer is bound to return the bill of lading if he does not honour the bill of exchange, and if he wrongfully retains the bill of lading the property in the goods does not pass to him".

What are the consequences if the buyer fails to honour the bill of exchange, but wrongfully retains the bill of lading and then transfers it to a third party who takes "in good faith and for valuable consideration"?

This situation was dealt with by the Court of Appeal in *Cahn* v. *Pockett's Bristol Channel Steam Packet Co., Ltd.*[4] S agreed to sell B a quantity of copper which was shipped on board the defendant's vessel. S sent B the bill of lading together with a draft for the price for B to accept. B was in fact insolvent: he did not accept the draft, but he delivered the bill of lading to X in performance of a contract he had made earlier. X took in good faith and paid B the price of the goods. S purported to stop the goods in transit. X sued the carriers for failing to deliver the goods on production of the bill of lading. The Court held that, although s. 19 (3) was conclusive on the relationship between S and B (property clearly did not pass), this provision was not the determining factor on the relationship between S and X. At first instance MATHEW, J., had held[5] that S's consent to B's possession of the bill of lading had been conditional only and that such consent was not covered by s. 25 (2). With this conclusion the Court of Appeal disagreed. The consent had existed at the outset and by s. 2 (2) of the Factors Act that consent was deemed to continue. Whether one applied s. 9/s. 25 (2) or s. 10/s. 47, it was clear that X took a good title under the bill of lading.

It will be noticed that there is an ambiguity about s. 9/s. 25 (2) that does not exist in s. 10/s. 47. Under s. 25 (2), where the buyer obtains "possession of *the* goods or *the* documents of title to the goods, the delivery or transfer by that person . . . of *the* goods or documents of title" is, in the circumstances prescribed, to have the same effect as a similar disposition by a mercantile agent. It will be noticed that there is no *the* before the second "documents of title", so that it is uncertain whether the documents, which are transferred by the buyer, have to be the same ones that were issued by the seller to the buyer. In contrast, s. 47 makes it quite clear that "the document" transferred by the

---

1 Similarly, in s. 1 (4) of the Factors Act a document of title is defined in terms of documents used as "authorising or purporting to authorise, either by endorsement or delivery, the possessor of the document to transfer or receive goods thereby represented".

2 By sub-s. (2) a "bill payable to bearer is negotiated by delivery"; by sub-s. (3), a bill "payable to order is negotiated by the endorsement of the holder completed by delivery".

3 This provision is based upon *Shepherd* v. *Harrison* (1871), L.R. 5 H.L. 116, at pp. 130, 132.

4 [1899] 1 Q.B. 643.   5 [1898] 2 Q.B. 61.

buyer must be the same one that he received from the seller. In *D. F. Mount, Ltd.* v. *Jay and Jay (Provisions) Co., Ltd.*,[1] SALMON, J., adopted the view that, under s. 25 (2), a buyer could deliver to his transferee different documents from those he had received from the seller, and suggested that, in this respect, the language of s. 25 (2) was "less rigorous than that of the proviso to section 47".[2]

This interpretation has been criticised on the ground that it creates an unsatisfactory distinction between the two sets of provisions, and it has also been pointed out that the omission of the word "the" was almost certainly in the erroneous belief that its absence made no difference.[3] The 1877 Factors Act, s. 4, which s. 9/s. 25 (2) was designed to expand and replace, covered the situation where "the vendee" obtained "possession of the documents of title . . . from the vendor" and gave effect to "any sale, pledge, or other disposition of such goods or documents" by the vendee. In s. 9/s. 25 (2) the word "the" was selected to replace "such" and presumably without the intention of altering the substance of that part of the provision. However, it is apparent that by using "the" before "goods or documents of title", the absence of the emphasis carried by "such" does lead to a totally different reading of the section. It is difficult to avoid the conclusion that, solely as a matter of applying the natural meaning of the words concerned, SALMON, J.'s view is correct.

e *Transfer or delivery*

As under s. 25 (1), so under s. 25 (2), there must be a delivery or transfer of the goods or documents of title to the third party under the sale, pledge or other disposition before that third party is protected as against the original seller. The doubts expressed in relation to *Nicholson* v. *Harper*[4] are equally applicable in the present context.

A rather different problem arose in the somewhat curious circumstances of *Kitto* v. *Bilbie, Hobson & Co.*[5] S had hired an engine to B under some sort of hire-purchase arrangement.[6] By deed, B sold, assigned and transferred to X all his stock in trade for the benefit of his creditors. X later took possession of these goods by having a padlock put on the door of B's premises. Subsequently S broke into the premises and removed the engine. WILLIAMS, J., held that the assignment was never intended by B to apply to the engine which did not belong to him; and that X had only taken possession of those goods on B's premises that were covered by the assignment, so that s. 9 of the Factors Act did not apply to the engine to pass title to X. One can agree with this decision on the basis that, as a matter of construction, the deed did not apply to goods which B had in his possession but did not own. It is also possible to accept, as following from

---

1 [1960] 1 Q.B. 159; [1959] 3 All E.R. 307.
2 [1960] 1 Q.B., at pp. 168–9; [1959] 3 All E.R., at p. 311.
3 By Borrie, in (1960), 23 M.L.R. 100.
4 [1895] 2 Ch. 415; 1895–99 All E.R. Rep. 882; see above, p. 80.
5 (1895), 72 L.T. 266.
6 *Helby* v. *Matthews* (see above, p. 81) had not yet gone to the House of Lords and was not reported in 72 L.T. until p. 841. In any case the arrangement did not include any express option on B's part to discontinue payments except upon forfeiture of all payments already made, so that, according to *Lee* v. *Butler*, [1893] 2 Q.B. 318, s. 25 (2) could apply.

the first, the second ground that there was no intention to deliver into X's possession goods not covered by the assignment.[1] However, it patently does not follow that, had the assignment appeared to cover goods which B had agreed to buy, s. 25 (2) would still not have applied. X would have obtained possession of the goods and there is no reason why the assignment of S's goods could not be classified as an "other disposition" within s. 25 (2).[2]

E DISPOSITION BY A PERSON HAVING A VOIDABLE TITLE

Quite apart from s. 25 of the Sale of Goods Act which was based upon ss. 8 and 9 of the Factors Act, the common law had for long protected the interest obtained by a third party under a disposition for value by a person (usually a buyer) whose title rested on a voidable contract which had not yet been rescinded by the original transferor (usually the seller). As COCKBURN, L.J., said in giving the judgment of the Court of Queen's Bench in *Moyce* v. *Newington*[3] decided in 1878:

> "We must now take it to be settled . . . that though a seller is induced to sell by the fraud of the buyer, and though it is competent to the seller by reason of such fraud to avoid the contract, yet, till he does some act to avoid it, the property remains in the buyer, and that, if he in the meantime has parted with the thing sold to an innocent purchaser, the title of the latter cannot be defeated by the original seller."

This principle was in fact put in statutory form by s. 23 of the Sale of Goods Act, although the transferor under the second contract is referred to as the seller:

> "When the seller of goods has a voidable title thereto, but his title has not been avoided at the time of the sale, the buyer acquires a good title to the goods, provided he buys them in good faith and without notice of the seller's defect of title."

For the sake of the present discussion, however, the parties will be referred to as S, the original seller; B the person holding under a voidable title (i.e. the "seller" referred to in s. 23); and X who acquires the goods under a disposition

---

1 A "delivery" means the "voluntary transfer of possession from one person to another" (s. 62 (1)).

2 In so far as this case suggests that such an assignment is not a disposition within s. 25, it is surely inconsistent with *Worcester Works Finance, Ltd.* v. *Cooden Engineering Co., Ltd.*, [1972] 1 Q.B. 210; [1971] 3 All E.R. 708. In Halsbury, 3rd Ed., Vol. 19, p. 565, para. 565, *Kitto* v. *Bilbie, Hobson & Co.* (1895), 72 L.T. 266, is cited for the proposition that if "the hirer includes in an assignment for the benefit of his creditors a chattel of which he is in possession under a hire purchase agreement, the trustee acquires no title as against the owner of the chattel". This is true of a *Helby* v. *Matthews*, [1895] A.C. 471, H.P. transaction, but the authority is certainly not *Kitto* v. *Bilbie, Hobson & Co.* to which s. 25 (2) could have applied on the basis of *Lee* v. *Butler*, [1893] 2 Q.B. 318, if the assignment had purported to cover the engine in question and the learned judge had not taken such a narrow view of the term "disposition" in s. 25. Even with goods held under a normal H.P. arrangement which includes an option on B's part to discontinue the transaction, it may still be possible for the trustee to acquire rights against S on the basis that B is the reported owner of goods in his possession in his trade or business by S's consent and with S's permission: see Bankruptcy Act 1914, s. 38.

3 (1878), 48 L.J.Q.B. 125, at p. 127.

from B (X being referred to as the "buyer" in s. 23). The reason for adopting this nomenclature is because of the close parallel that exists between s. 23 and s. 25 (2) which has just been dealt with.

i The contract between S and B

In nearly all cases the transaction between S and B will be one of sale, although it is possible for a voidable title to be created in other ways (e.g. by an exchange of goods).

A "voidable title" is a shorthand expression for a title dependent upon a voidable contract. It is therefore essential to determine what constitutes a voidable contract, and more particularly to distinguish it from a contract which is deemed to be void *ab initio*.

The crux of the matter is the question of consent. If the fraud on B's part (or it may be the duress or undue influence he has exercised over S) is such as to negative any consent by S to the transaction, the law treats the contract as a nullity, as never having come into existence at all. On the other hand, where B's fraudulent activities induce S to consent to the transaction in question, though he would not have done so had he been aware of the true circumstances, S is entitled, within a reasonable time of learning the true state of affairs, to set the contract aside. Where the main difficulty arises, of course, is in distinguishing between a mistake, occasioned by B's fraud, on S's part in entering into the contract which vitiates S's consent, and an error which merely entitles S at a later stage to set aside the contract. A disposition by B to X before S purports to rescind would be effective in the latter circumstances, but would be of no effect in the former.

The court's dilemma has been particularly acute in relation to those cases generally described as dealing with "mistake as to identity". Where B has represented himself as a different person, the courts are faced with the difficult choice of treating the contract as being between S and Z, the person with whom he (S) supposed he was dealing, or between S and B, the person with whom S was actually dealing.

In the well-known case of *Phillips* v. *Brooks, Ltd,*[1] B, whose name was in fact North, entered S's shop and asked to see some pearls and rings. He chose some pearls and a ring, and wrote out a cheque in payment for both, saying as he did so that he was Sir George Bullough. S checked the address given by B and found that it was listed against Sir George Bullough in a directory. Thus reassured, he allowed B to leave with the ring. B pledged the ring with X. The cheque was subsequently dishonoured and S sought to recover the ring or its value from X. HORRIDGE, J., held that the "proper inference" to be drawn in such a situation was that, although S "believed the person to whom he was handing the ring was Sir George Bullough, he in fact contracted to sell and deliver it to the person who came into his shop, and who was not Sir George Bullough, but a man of the name of North, who obtained the sale and delivery by means of the false pretence that he was Sir George Bullough".[2] It followed that B had obtained a

---

1 [1919] 2 K.B. 243; [1918–19] All E.R. Rep. 246.
2 [1919] 2 K.B., at p. 246; [1918–19] All E.R. Rep., at p. 247.

good title under the contract even though it was a contract which was voidable at S's option. However, before S had been able to set the contract aside, B had pledged the ring with X: the contract could not therefore be set aside in a way that would defeat the interest thus acquired by X.

Of course, it is possible for the inference that the seller intended to contract with whom he was negotiating, whether in person or by correspondence,[1] to be rebutted. If the presumption is rebutted the consequence will be that no contract at all will come into existence for an offer addressed to Z and to Z alone, cannot be accepted by B even by pretending to be Z. And if there is no contract, B will not be able to pass a good title to the innocent third party; nor will S have to take any steps to set aside a contract which was void *ab initio*.

In *Ingram* v. *Little*,[2] B, calling himself Hutchinson, answered S's advertisement of a car for sale. After much bargaining a price was agreed, whereupon B pulled out a cheque book. S1 immediately informed him that the deal was off: they had expected cash and were not prepared to accept anything other than cash. At this stage B claimed to be a P. G. M. Hutchinson, a business man of substance who lived at Stanstead House, Stanstead Road, Caterham. S2 checked this information in a telephone directory at the local post office. Thus reassured—there was a person with that name at that address—they accepted the cheque and allowed B to take away the car. B was not who he said he was: he sold the car to X and then disappeared. It was held by the Court of Appeal that S's claim for damages succeeded. Had they not made it so clear that payment by cheque from anyone other than P. G. M. Hutchinson was not acceptable "it might have been held that an offer in such circumstances was to the party present, whatever his true identity would be".[3] SELLERS, L.J., then distinguished *Phillips* v. *Brooks, Ltd.*: that case was "not an authority to establish that where an offer or acceptance is addressed to a person (although under a mistake as to his identity) who is present in person, then it must in all circumstances be treated as if actually addressed to him. I would regard the issue as a question of fact in each case depending on what was said and done and applying the elementary principles of offer and acceptance".[4] As PEARCE, L.J., said,[5] "clearly, though difficult, it is not impossible to rebut the *prima facie* presumption that the offer can be accepted [only] by the person to whom it is physically addressed". In this case no contract had come into existence between S and the person who had called at their home because their offer to sell in return for payment by cheque had been made to P. G. M. Hutchinson alone. As there was no contract, X could not rely upon s. 23 of the Sale of Goods Act.

It goes without saying that if S can establish that his contract with B was no contract at all, X is placed in an invidious position because of circumstances totally unknown to him. And indeed the dividing line between a contract that is and one that is not "void for mistake" is so narrow, yet the consequences

---

1 As in *Cundy* v. *Lindsay* (1878), 3 App Cas. 459; [1874–80] All E.R. Rep. 1149.
2 [1961] 1 Q.B. 31; [1960] 3 All E.R. 332.
3 [1961] 1 Q.B. 31, at p. 51; [1960] 3 All E.R. 332, at p. 337.
4 [1961] 1 Q.B. 31, at p. 51; [1960] 3 All E.R. 332, at pp. 337–8.
5 [1961] 1 Q.B. 31, at p. 57; [1960] 3 All E.R. 332, at p. 341.

from X's point of view so disastrous, that the question is bound to be raised whether the distinction should be made at all. In reality, S deals with Z rather than B because he believes (and B presumably thinks he will believe) that Z is a man of substance whose credit is good. In fact, if S actually receives payment, he will not mind whether he contracted with B or Z. The fault may lie not with the principle of law but with the circumstances in which it is applied.

The misgivings of the judges over the present position are illustrated by the latest in this line of authority, *Lewis* v. *Averay*.[1] As in *Ingram* v. *Little*, B prepared his ground well. He had begun by speaking about the film industry. At a later stage he had informed S that he was "Richard Green" a well-known film actor, and, when it came to persuading S to accept a cheque, B had produced a pass to Pinewood Studios which bore the name "R. A. Green" and B's photograph. Despite the similarity with the facts of *Ingram* v. *Little*, the Court of Appeal was unanimous in holding that a contract was formed between S and B, so that a purchaser from B of what had formerly been S's car obtained a good title.

It is possible to reconcile this decision with established principles, though rather difficult to distinguish the application of those principles from their application in *Ingram* v. *Little*. PHILLIMORE, L.J., thought the facts of the two cases were distinguishable and was not prepared to hold that the presumption that a person intends to contract with the party with whom he was dealing had been rebutted. MEGAW, L.J., reached a similar conclusion by placing a different interpretation on the circumstances of the present case: at the time when S offered to sell the car, he had not regarded the identity of B as a matter of vital importance, so, presumably, he could not be said to have intended to contract with anyone other than B.

However, underlying the views expressed by the members of the Court was a general dissatisfaction with the decision in *Ingram* v. *Little*, a sentiment which was most openly expressed by the Master of the Rolls. While paying lip-service to the presumption held to be rebutted in the earlier case, Lord DENNING made it clear that he regarded it more as a rule of law:[2]

> "When two parties have come to a contract—or rather what appears, on the face of it, to be a contract—the fact that one party is mistaken as to the identity of the other does not mean that there is no contract, or that the contract is a nullity and void from the beginning. It only means that the contract is voidable . . ."

This pronouncement is tantamount to a rejection of *Ingram* v. *Little*, although that case is no more than a reasonable extension of *Cundy* v. *Lindsay*[3] in which the House of Lords held that the similar, though probably weaker, presumption that an offeror intends to contract with the person with whom he is corresponding had been rebutted in the circumstances. Certainly *Lewis* v. *Averay* serves notice that some of the judges are reluctant to see s. 23 ousted by the over-refined distinction between a contract that is voidable because of fraud and one

---

1 [1972] 1 Q.B. 198; [1971] 3 All E.R. 907.
2 [1972] 1 Q.B. 198, at p. 207; [1971] 3 All E.R. 907, at p. 911.
3 (1878), 3 App. Cas. 459; [1874–80] All E.R. Rep. 1149.

that never came into existence at all because the effect of the fraud was to lead S
to believe he was dealing with someone other than B.[1]

ii Conduct sufficient to avoid the contract

As far as the relationship between S and B is concerned, the established view
was that S could only rescind the contract by giving notice to B or by repossessing
the goods. However, these requirements seemed to create a difficulty if S had
to deal with a buyer who was acting fraudulently and whose main object would
be to escape subsequent detection. This difficulty presented itself to the Court of
Appeal in *Car and Universal Finance Co., Ltd. v. Caldwell.*[2]

One evening, S sold a car to B and accepted a cheque for a substantial part
of the price. When the cheque was presented the next morning, it was dishonoured. S immediately went to the police and also asked the A.A. if they could
trace the vehicle. The car was discovered a week later in the possession of X1,
who had acquired the car from B but had at once sold it to X2, a finance company from whom he, X1, was hiring it under a hire purchase agreement. The
decision of Lord DENNING, M.R., sitting as a judge of first instance,[3] in S's
favour was affirmed by the Court of Appeal on the ground that, where B had
acted fraudulently, the rule requiring notification by S of his rescission of the
contract did not have to be strictly adhered to. As SELLERS, L.J., explained:[4]

> "Where a contracting party could be communicated with, and modern
> facilities make communication practically world-wide and almost immediate,
> it would be unlikely that a party could be held to have disaffirmed a contract
> unless he went so far as to communicate his decision to do so . . . But in
> circumstances such as the present case the other contracting party, a fraudu-
> lent rogue who would know that the vendor would want his car back as soon
> as he knew of the fraud, would not expect to be communicated with as a
> matter of right or requirement and would deliberately, as here, do all he could
> to evade any such communication being made to him. In such exceptional
> contractual circumstances, it does not seem to me appropriate to hold that a
> party so acting can claim any right to have a decision to rescind communicated
> to him before the contract is terminated. To hold that he could would involve
> that the defrauding party, if skilful enough to keep out of the way, could
> deprive the other party to the contract of his right to rescind, a right to
> which he was entitled and which he would wish to exercise as the defrauding
> party would well know or at least confidently suspect."

---

1 Of course subtle shades of distinction between the various decisions abound. For
example, while *Phillips* v. *Brooks, Ltd.* and *Cundy* v. *Lindsay* involved people who sold
goods as part of their normal business, *Ingram* v. *Little* and *Lewis* v. *Averay* dealt with
private transactions which were conducted very much on a personal basis. Alternatively,
one could take the view that only in *Cundy* v. *Lindsay* did the identity of the buyer,
as buyer, appear at all relevant. The imagined buyer in that case was the sort of person
the seller would normally deal with; in the other cases the purchaser could have been
anyone provided the seller believed he would be paid for his goods.
2 [1965] 1 Q.B. 525; [1964] 1 All E.R. 290.
3 [1963] 2 All E.R. 547.
4 [1965] 1 Q.B. 525, at pp. 550–1; [1964] 1 All E.R. 290, at p. 293.

It would follow therefore that all S has to do is

> "to establish clearly and unequivocally that he terminates the contract and is no longer bound by it. If he cannot communicate his decision he may still satisfy a judge or jury that he had made a final and irrevocable decision and ended the contract".

This conclusion raises a number of fundamental issues. In the first place, it was contrary to authority to decide that informing the police was sufficient to rescind the contract. In *Moyce* v. *Newington*,[1] B paid for 49 sheep he had bought from S with a worthless cheque. Although a warrant was issued against B, the Court of Queen's Bench had no doubt that a later sale by B to X had the effect of passing title to X. As the Court observed:[2]

> "The question which in some cases might be a very material one, as well as one of some nicety, namely, what on the part of the defrauded seller, *short of retaking possession of the thing sold,* will amount to an avoidance of the contract, does not arise in the present instance. The defendant [S] not knowing what had become of his sheep, or where to find Wale, his buyer, had done and could do nothing *beyond giving notice to the police,* up to the time when the sheep were bought by the plaintiff. We must take it as incontestable that . . . no question could be raised as to the title of the plaintiff."

Although *Caldwell's* case has been followed on this point by the Court of Appeal in *Newtons of Wembley, Ltd.* v. *Williams,*[3] it is worth noting that in Scotland there is emphatic authority that an intimation to the police in such circumstances is of no "materiality to found a plea of rescission" of a contract.[4]

In the second place, the Court in *Caldwell's* case, when dealing with the contract between S and B, refused to take into account the position of the innocent third party. As SELLERS, L.J., said,[5] the "position has to be viewed . . . between the two contracting parties . . . That another innocent party or parties may suffer does not in my view of the matter justify imposing on a defrauded seller an impossible task". However, as Lord UPJOHN admitted,[6] this type of problem can only arise between the original seller and a party who subsequently buys the goods. If the courts are prepared to violate basic principles in this situation, it seems more satisfactory that the violation should be in favour of the third party rather than in favour of the seller who was gullible enough to accept a worthless cheque. Indeed the violation in favour of S is far greater than any distortion that may have been necessary to protect X. It is reasonable enough to accept the Court of Appeal's arguments as they affected the relationship between S and B, but it surely would not be too much of a gloss on the existing law to hold that a contract for the sale of goods which could in turn be sold to a third

---

1 (1878), 4 Q.B.D. 32; 48 L.J.Q.B. 125.
2 4 Q.B.D., at pp. 35–6; 48 L.J.Q.B., at p. 127 (emphasis supplied).
3 [1965] 1 Q.B. 560; [1964] 3 All E.R. 532.
4 *Macleod* v. *Kerr*, 1965 S.L.T. 358, at p. 363, *per* Lord CLYDE; *ibid., per* Lord CARMONT; at p. 364, *per* Lord GUTHRIE.
5 [1965] 1 Q.B. 525, at p. 551; [1964] 1 All E.R. 290, at pp. 293–4.
6 [1965] 1 Q.B. 525, at p. 555; [1964] 1 All E.R. 290, at p. 296.

party can only be rescinded by the original seller repossessing the goods before any third party rights are created in those goods.

A solution to some of a third party's difficulties was in fact provided by the subsequent court of Appeal decision in *Newtons of Wembley, Ltd.* v. *Williams*,[1] which relied upon s. 25 (2) as a way out of the limitation placed upon the scope of s. 23. It is therefore to the relationship between s. 23 and s. 25 that attention must now be turned.

iii The relationship between s. 23 and s. 25 (2)

a *The disposition by B to X*

It will be recalled that s. 25 (2) enables a buyer in possession of goods to pass title or other interest by "any sale, pledge, or other disposition"[2] in the circumstances prescribed. On the other hand, s. 23 is limited to a sale by a person (usually a buyer) having a voidable contract. However, it has already been pointed out that s. 23 is based upon a common law principle of more general application. Hence, even since 1893, the courts have found no difficulty in applying the principle to protect a pledgee who has advanced money on the security of goods to which the pledgor had only a voidable title.[3]

It is also stated in s. 25 (2) that the buyer should be in possession of the goods or documents of title at the time of the contract with the third party, and should also deliver or transfer those goods to the third party in order for the sub-section to operate.[4] No such restrictions apply in the case of s. 23. As long as B has a voidable title a disposition to X will be effective whether B has possession of the goods, and whether or not there is a delivery or transfer of them to X.

b *The seller's consent*

As *Car and Universal Finance Co., Ltd.* v. *Caldwell* illustrates, the courts have been prepared to allow a clear manifestation of intent by S to disaffirm the contract with B as sufficient to terminate that contract and also to put an end to B's title to the goods. Accordingly any transaction entered into by B with X after that time will be ineffective to transfer any interest to X under s. 23.

However, as has already been explained, s. 25 (2) is in essence s. 9 of the Factors Act, and under both provisions a disposition by a buyer in possession, followed by a delivery to X, of the goods or documents of title "shall have the same effect as if the person making the delivery . . . were a mercantile agent in possession of the goods or documents of title with the consent of the owner". And this reference to the position of a mercantile agent has been taken by the courts as a basis for bringing in other provisions of the Factors Act, including s. 2 (2) which states that, if any disposition by a mercantile agent would have been valid if the owner's consent to his possession of the goods had continued, the disposition "shall be valid notwithstanding the determination of the consent".

---

1 [1965] 1 Q.B. 560; [1964] 3 All E.R. 532.
2 See above, p. 80.
3 *Whitehorn Bros.* v. *Davison*, [1911] 1 K.B. 463; [1908] All E.R. Rep. 885; *Phillips v. Brooks, Ltd.*, [1919] 2 K.B. 243; [1918–19] All E.R. Rep. 246, above, p. 92.
4 See above, p. 90.

In *Newtons of Wembley Ltd.* v. *Williams*[1] it was accepted that, by informing the police and the Hire Purchase Information Bureau, and by conducting an extensive search for the fraudulent buyer, S had done all he could to rescind the contract. *Caldwell's* case was regarded as decisive on this point. However, as we have seen, the Court of Appeal went on to hold that by s. 25 (2) of the Sale of Goods Act, reinforced by s. 2 (2) of the Factors Act, B's sale to X was effective to pass title to him.

c *The requirement of good faith*

A sale under a voidable title within s. 23 is only effective to a person who buys the goods "in good faith and without notice of the seller's defect of title". On the other hand, s. 25 (2) requires that the person concerned should receive the goods or documents of title "in good faith and without notice of any lien or other right of the original seller in respect of the goods".

In *Car and Universal Finance Co., Ltd.* v. *Caldwell*,[2] it will be recalled, B had disposed of the car to X1 who, it was held, had notice from which to infer that B had not come by the vehicle honestly. This fact would clearly have prevented X1 obtaining title under s. 23 had the contract between S and B not been rescinded before the transaction between B and X1. This conclusion is inescapable because, at first instance,[3] Lord DENNING, M.R., had held that in the sale by X1 to X2, X1 had acted as X2's agent so that any claim X2 might have was vitiated by the knowledge acquired by his agent.[4]

However, it is by no means certain that evidence showing a lack of good faith under s. 25 (2) will automatically be regarded as evidence of an absence of good faith under s. 23. The Sale of Goods Act, s. 62 (2) states that a "thing is deemed to be done 'in good faith' within the meaning of this Act when it is in fact done honestly, whether it be done negligently or not". This definition should apply equally to both sections, but authority does exist for the proposition that a different burden of proof is applicable.

In *Heap* v. *Motorists' Advisory Agency, Ltd.*,[5] LUSH, J., discussed the difference between s. 23 and s. 2 of the Factors Act in this respect. In *Whitehorn Bros.* v. *Davison*,[6] it had been held that, under s. 23, the onus of proving bad faith lay with the original seller who was trying to assert his title. In *Heap's* case, LUSH, J., explained the contrast in the following passage:[7]

> "That . . . was quite a different case from this, because there the title that the seller [B] would have . . . was a good title. It was a voidable title, but that voidable title had not been avoided at the time when the purchaser [X] bought. The section gave him a good title that he would retain unless it could be shown that he had not bought in good faith or without notice . . . Under

---

1 [1965] 1 Q.B. 560; [1964] 3 All E.R. 532; see above, p. 95.
2 [1965] 1 Q.B. 525, at p. 530; [1964] 1 All E.R. 290.
3 [1965] 1 Q.B. 525; [1963] 2 All E.R. 547.
4 Lord DENNING, M.R., was reversed on this point by the Court of Appeal, but it does not alter the fact that X's bad faith would have prevented his relying on s. 23.
5 [1923] 1 K.B. 577; [1922] All E.R. Rep. 251.
6 [1911] 1 K.B. 463; [1908–10] All E.R. Rep. 885.
7 [1923] 1 K.B. at p. 590; [1922] All E.R. Rep., at p. 257.

s. 2 of the Factors Act, however, the buyer [X] gets no title apart from the section. He is allowed to get what I may call a statutory title provided he complies with the terms of the section. In order to acquire a title which he would not otherwise have, the buyer has to prove all these things that I have mentioned: that the owner consented to the mercantile agent having possession, that the agent acted in the ordinary course of business, and also . . . that the buyer acted in good faith and without notice."

In this case, the vehicle bought by X had been at a price considerably under value, and it was certainly a factor which led LUSH, J., to conclude that X was unable to establish his good faith in the transaction.[1]

This approach can be contrasted with a case under s 23 which has already been mentioned, *Lewis* v. *Averay*.[2] S had sold a car to B for £450. Five days later, B sold the car to X for £200. Even if one accepts the first price as too high for the model in question, the second price was demonstrably too low. A more reasonable figure would have been around £330.[3] Furthermore, it could be argued that a person in X's position, who had advertised for a car in a trade journal, presumably had a good idea of what his £200 was likely to buy. However, no attempt appears to have been made to question X's good faith, presumably because the onus would have been on S to establish X's bad faith.

In the light of the close relationship that has been created between s. 23 and s. 25 (2) in their application, this difference in the burden of proof may assume great significance. Had S in *Lewis* v. *Averay* carried out the procedures accepted in *Caldwell's* case for rescinding the contract before B sold the car to X, s. 23 would no longer have been applicable. X would have been required to establish his good faith and to explain away the fact that he obtained a much better vehicle than he might reasonably have expected for his £200.

F SALE OF A MOTOR VEHICLE

The decision in *Helby* v. *Matthews*,[4] placed the purchaser from a person having an option to purchase under a hire purchase agreement outside the protection afforded by s. 25 (2) of the Sale of Goods Act. Nor could such a purchaser plead that the owner of the goods was estopped from pleading his rights on the ground that the latter had invested the hirer with apparent ownership of the goods in question.[5]

As hire purchase transactions became an increasingly common aspect of life and particularly with the spread of car "ownership", the risks involved in buying second-hand goods also increased. Motor vehicles obviously created the

---

1 See also the discussion in *Newtons of Wembley, Ltd.* v. *Williams* at first instance, [1964]
2 All E.R. 135, at pp. 139–40, on the price of the car.
2 [1972] 1 Q.B. 198; [1971] 3 All E.R. 907.
3 The damages awarded by the County Court Judge of £100 as the value of the vehicle
at the date of the award, together with £230 for detention of the vehicle, would together
total its approximate value at the time X acquired it.
4 [1895] A.C. 471; [1895–9] All E.R. Rep. 821; see above, p. 81.
5 See above, p. 53.

greatest problems because they could be acquired on hire purchase one day and be "sold" by the hirer the next day in a different part of the country. Although the motor car trade established a register of vehicles subject to hire purchase arrangements, it was used fairly extensively within the trade but infrequently amongst private buyers of second-hand vehicles. It would have been possible to have introduced some form of compulsory registration of beneficial ownership of vehicles as part of the normal registration system, but the 1964 Hire Purchase Act settled for a new exception to the *nemo dat* rule.

Part III of the Act in which this objective was achieved has been widely criticised for the complexity of its drafting. However, the principal object of the Act was to protect the private purchaser of goods subject to a hire purchase or conditional sale agreement. The method employed by the Act is as follows:

Section 27, according to sub-s. (1), is to "have effect where a motor vehicle has been let under a hire-purchase agreement, or has been agreed to be sold under a conditional sale agreement, and, at a time before the property in the vehicle has become vested in the hirer or buyer, he disposes of the vehicle to another person". Accordingly:

(1) Where the disposition is to a private purchaser "and he is a purchaser cf the motor vehicle in good faith and without notice of the hire purchase agreement or conditional sale agreement,[1] that disposition shall have effect as if the title of the owner or seller to the vehicle had been vested in the hirer or buyer immediately before that disposition" (s. 27 (2)).

(2) Where there is a disposition by the hirer etc. to a trade or finance purchaser,[2] followed by a sale to a private purchaser who takes in good faith and without notice, "the disposition of the vehicle to the first private purchaser shall have effect as if the title of the owner or seller to the vehicle had been vested in the hirer", immediately before he disposed of it to the trade purchaser (s. 27 (3)). In other words, the private purchaser will acquire title, although title will not have been vested at any time in the trade or finance purchaser.

(3) Where the trade or finance purchaser lets the goods to the "private purchaser" under a hire purchase or conditional sale agreement, the final disposition by the trade or finance purchaser under the agreement to the "private purchaser"

---

1 Some conditional sale agreements are not covered by the hire purchase legislation (see sub-s. 2 (2), 4, H.P.A. 1965) except in relation to this particular exception to the *nemo dat* rule: hence they could also be subject to the principle in *Lee* v. *Butler*, [1893] 2 Q.B. 318; [1891–4] All E.R. Rep. 1200; see above, p. 82. In addition s. 25 (5) provides that s. 27 (1)–(4) is to have effect "without prejudice to the provisions of the Factors Acts . . . or of any other enactment enabling the apparent owner of goods to dispose of them as if he were the true owner of the goods".

2 Defined by s. 29 (2) as meaning:
  "a purchaser who, at the time of the disposition made to him, carries on a business which consists, wholly or partly—
    (a) of purchasing motor vehicles for the purpose of offering or exposing them for sale, or
    (b) of providing finance by purchasing motor vehicles for the purpose of letting them under hire-purchase agreements or agreeing to sell them under conditional sale agreements".

A "private purchaser" is someone "who, at the time of the disposition made to him, does not carry on any such business".

takes effect along the lines of s. 27 (3): as long as the private purchaser took in good faith at the inception of the agreement, it does not matter whether he remains in good faith until he exercises his option under the agreement (s. 27 (4)).

(4) The situation where a hirer lets goods to a private purchaser is not specifically covered by the Act, although in an era when an increasing number of dealers hold stock which they have sold to, and then hired from, a finance company, the omission is perhaps surprising. It would appear that s. 27 (2) applies automatically. The only slight doubt that could arise concerns the position where the private purchaser, although in good faith at the outset of the hire purchase arrangement, receives knowledge of the true situation before the time arrives for him to exercise his option. However, the terms "disposes of" and "disposition" are defined so widely by s. 29 (1) that they include both the "letting under a hire purchase agreement" as well as the subsequent transfer of property in pursuance of such an agreement. Accordingly, the private purchaser can be regarded as taking in good faith under a disposition from the inception of the hire-purchase arrangement.

(5) In order to facilitate the application of s. 27 to situations involving a series of transactions and of different parties, s. 28 lays down a number of "presumptions relating to dealings with motor vehicles". These presumptions operate (s. 28 (1)) in relation to s. 27 once it is proved (a) that the vehicle had been let under a hire purchase agreement or sold under a conditional sale agreement, and (b) that a person has been a private purchaser of the vehicle in good faith and without notice.

First, by s. 28 (2) unless the contrary is proved, it is presumed that the disposition of the vehicle to a person who is a private purchaser in good faith was made by the actual hirer under the initial hire-purchase (or conditional sale) agreement. If it can be proved that the disposition was not made by the hirer, then it is presumed that the original hirer did dispose of the goods to a private purchaser who took in good faith and that the person whose title is in issue in the proceedings "is or was a person claiming under the person to whom the hirer . . . disposed of the vehicle" (s. 28 (3)). However, if both these presumptions can be disproved, then s. 28 (4) provides that if the original purchaser from the hirer was a trade or finance purchaser then it shall be presumed that the first private purchaser took in good faith and that the person whose title is in issue "is or was a person claiming under the original purchaser".

(6) However, it should be borne in mind that, although an exception to the *nemo dat* rule, Part III of the 1964 Hire Purchase Act is of restricted application. In most cases, it will have the effect of enabling the *bona fide* private purchaser from a hirer to take a good title. But the apparently wide ambit of s. 27 (2), which, as we have seen, lays down that such a disposition is to take effect as if the title of the owner had been vested in the hirer immediately before the disposition, is limited by s. 29 (5) which defines that title as:

> "such title (if any) to the vehicle as, immediately before that disposition, was vested in the person who then was the owner in relation to the hire purchase agreement, or the seller in relation to the conditional sale agreement, as the case may be".

In other words, if the car had, say, been stolen at some time so that the owner under the hire purchase agreement was not in fact the true owner of the vehicle, a disposition by the hirer to a *bona fide* private purchaser could only pass such title as the hire purchase owner possessed.

(7) Finally, it should be pointed out that the overall effect of Part III is to give title if, and only if, the first private purchaser is in good faith. A subsequent private purchaser in good faith takes no title if the first private purchaser was in bad faith; and a subsequent private purchaser in bad faith still takes title if the first private purchaser bought in good faith.

Part III is indeed a curious piece of legislation.

G SALE IN MARKET OVERT

The Sale of Goods Act, in s. 22 (1), retained the historical rule that:

> "Where goods are sold in market overt, according to the usage of the market, the buyer acquires a good title to the goods, provided he buys them in good faith and without notice of any defect or want of title on the part of the seller."

The retention of this rule and judicial attitudes towards it both demonstrate the continuing dilemma of having to choose between property and transactions. Section 22 (1) is in a sense a compromise between abolition (thus protecting property) and acceptance of a general rule protecting a buyer if he could prove that he bought in good faith by retail at trade premises or by public auction[1] (thus protecting a much wider range of transactions). As far as the judiciary are concerned, their approach in modern times seems to have vacillated between an inclination to allow limited extensions to cover private transactions in open market, and a refusal to apply the rule to situations which do not fall within this general category.

The rationale of the rule, which dates at least from early Mediaeval times, was that, if something was stolen, the deprived owner could by the exercise of diligence recover the goods if they went on display for sale at a local market. Both the existence of a market overt and the circumstances of the sale were governed by the overriding requirement that the transaction should take place in public.[2] However, whereas the "public saleroom" of 1574 was the market place, the saleroom of 1974 is more likely to be the shop in the high street or the car showroom. In *Lee* v. *Bayes*,[3] B had purchased a horse, which had been stolen from O, at a public auction held at a repository for the sale of horses. It was contended on behalf of one of the defendants that, the sale having taken place in an open and public place for the sale of such animals, the transaction was covered by the market overt rule. In answer to counsel's statement that the "authorities do not very clearly define what is market overt", JERVIS, C.J., retorted[4] that it was "an open, public and legally constituted market" which

---

1 Law Reform Committee, 12th Report, Cmnd. 2958, para. 33.
2 See *Clayton* v. *Le Roy*, [1911] 2 K.B. 1031, at p. 1039, *per* SCRUTTON, J.
3 (1856), 18 C.B. 599.
4 At p. 601.

this repository was not. And in reply to counsel's further suggestion that it should be regarded as a market overt because it was a place to which any of the public might resort for the purpose of buying, CRESSWELL, J., rejoined[1] that such a definition might apply to any shop, but that only shops in the city of London constituted market overt.[2]

The emphasis in the definition advanced by JERVIS, C.J., and repeated by many of the text-book writers,[3] should be in the "legally constituted" aspect. As has already been mentioned, by custom shops within the confines of the City of London fall within the rule; otherwise there must be a "regularly constituted market"[4] by Charter, prescription, or even, in more modern times, under statutory powers.[5]

Once it is established that the place of the sale is a market overt and that the whole transaction is effected there,[6] the open and public aspect of the circumstances becomes vital. In the recent case of *Reid* v. *Metropolitan Police Commissioner*,[7] a pair of Adam candelabra were stolen from O's home in Chelsea. Two months later they appeared at a market held every Friday from 7 a.m. in Southwark. Dealers made a habit of getting there early in the morning to obtain the best bargains. B, who was a dealer, found the candelabra in different pieces in boxes on a stall which S was in the process of erecting. Without making any enquiries about S or where he obtained these goods, B agreed to buy them for £200. At the time the transaction was effected, the sun had not risen and it was still only half light. Although the trial judge had held in B's favour because the sale had been in market overt and during the normal market hours, the Court of Appeal reversed this decision. Taking the principle, dating from Coke's time, that the goods should be openly on sale where those who stood or passed by could see them, the Court thought it equally applicable to time as well as place. It must be in daytime when all who passed could see the goods and what better test could there be than that also enunciated by Coke, i.e. the sale must occur between sunrise and sunset.

It cannot be claimed that this decision has much in its favour except for the very obvious fact that the Court was more concerned to protect property than the transaction in question. It may be that the members of the Court felt that the buyer had deliberately refrained from enquiring where the goods had come from

---

1 18 C.B., at p. 601.
2 See *The Case of Market Overt* (1596), 5 Co. Rep. 83b.
3 E.g. Benjamin, *op. cit.*, 8th Ed., p. 17; Atiyah, *op. cit.*, p. 194; Macleod, *op. cit.*, p. 236.
4 *Per* JERVIS, C.J., 18 C.B., at p. 603.
5 *Bishopsgate Motor Finance Corporation, Ltd.* v. *Transport Brakes, Ltd.*, [1949] 2 K.B. 322; [1949] 1 All E.R. 37; and see *Ward* v. *Stephens* (1886), 12 V.L.R. 378.
6 Hence a sale by sample is not covered by the rule: *Crane* v. *London Dock Co.* (1864), 5 B. & S. 313; as Lord ELLENBOROUGH said in *Tewkesbury (Bailiffs of)* v. *Diston* (1805), 6 East 438, at p. 451,

> "the policy of the law which binds the property of another by sale in market overt requires that every part of the transaction, as well the contract of sale as the delivery, shall take place in market overt, otherwise it shall not bind the property of third persons".

See also *Ardath Tobacco Co., Ltd.* v. *Ocker* (1930), 47 T.L.R. 177.
7 [1973] Q.B. 551; [1973] 2 All E.R. 97.

and that, despite the trial judge's holding to the contrary, the buyer was not in a position positively to establish his good faith. Be that as it may, strict application of the sunrise and sunset rule in the age of electricity seems even more anachronistic than the continued existence of the rule itself.

A sale in market overt is effective to pass title only if it takes place, in the words of s. 22 (1), "according to the usage of the market". Hence in the normal shop in the City of London, the sale must be *by* the shopkeeper and not *to* him.[1] However, there was always a good deal of uncertainty about the extent to which custom could affect the type of transaction falling within the rule,[2] and there were a number of cases which accepted the proposition that if the custom of the shopkeeper's trade covered the buying, as well as the selling of goods, a purchase by him could be protected by the market overt rule.[3] This development placed the emphasis on the custom rather than on the public display of the goods considered so important in Elizabethan times,[4] the latter aspect of the rule being satisfied if the place where the transaction took place could be seen by the public. In the light of the emphasis placed in *Reid* v. *Metropolitan Police Commissioner*[5] on the requirement of the public display of the goods, however, it is doubtful whether the extension of the rule to include sales to a shopkeeper, even in the ordinary course of his business, would be applied today.

In contrast, a sale in an established market will fall within the market overt rule even if the seller is not a trader, providing the sale is according to the usage of the market. In *Bishopsgate Motor Finance Corporation, Ltd.* v. *Transport Brakes, Ltd.*,[6] S, having possession of O's car, took it to Maidstone market and put it in the hands of an auctioneer. In the course of the day two unsuccessful attempts were made to auction the vehicle, but S did manage to sell it to B by private treaty. The Court of Appeal held that the market in Maidstone was a market overt for the purposes of the rule either because of a Charter of 1746 as amended in 1824 and 1933 by Acts of Parliament, or, if the subsequent Acts had the effect of extinguishing the Charter, by virtue of the Acts themselves.[7] The trial judge had accepted the practice of selling vehicles privately in the market after they had been passed in at the public auction as being sufficiently well established to fall within the "usage of the market", and with this conclusion the Court of Appeal was prepared to agree. The conditions of a sale in market overt being satisfied, title had passed to B at the time of the transaction.

This decision brings out another aspect of the usage of the market requirement

---

1 *Hargreave* v. *Spink*, [1892] 1 Q.B. 25; *Ardath Tobacco Co., Ltd.* v. *Ocker* (1930), 47 T.L.R. 177.
2 See *Clayton* v. *Le Roy*, [1911] 2 K.B. 1031, at pp. 1039–42, *per* SCRUTTON, J.
3 *Lyons* v. *De Pass* (1840), 11 A. & E. 326; providing of course the goods purchased were covered by the custom of the buyer's particular trade: see *Taylor* v. *Chambers* (1604), Cro. Jac. 68.
4 *Case of Market Overt* (1596), 5 Co. Rep. 83b.
5 [1973] Q.B. 551; [1973] 2 All E.R. 97.
6 [1949] 1 K.B. 322; [1949] 1 All E.R. 37.
7 Rejecting the argument that a market overt could not rest upon statute.

and that is that the goods in question must fall within the class of goods usually bought and sold in the market in question. Cars were regularly brought for auction in Maidstone and sold privately if the bidding failed to reach the reserve price. On the other hand, one would not expect to purchase clothes at Smithfield meat market. And a similar principle applies to transactions effected in shops in the City of London. To use the classic illustration given by Coke, one would not expect to find gold plate for sale in a scrivener's shop.[1]

The market overt rule does have other idiosyncrasies. It does not affect goods belonging to the Crown.[2] Nor does it apply to transactions effected in fairs and markets in Wales.[3] At one time the rule covered sales in shops in Bristol,[4] though it is now confined to the City of London. Finally, although a sale in market overt gives the *bona fide* buyer a good title and one that can be transmitted by disposition to a third party, if title to the goods should at a later date become vested in the original seller in market overt, there is some authority that the original owner's title revives.[5]

Under s. 28 (1) of the Theft Act 1968, where goods have been stolen, and a person has been convicted of any offence with reference to the theft, the court has a discretion to order restitution of the goods. And s. 28 (3) deals with the case of a purchaser of stolen goods in good faith by allowing the court to order payment for the goods out of any money in the convicted person's possession at the time he was apprehended. Of course, it is unlikely that a convicted person would have been carrying money sufficient to pay for expensive items like candelabra or motor cars. If there had been a sale in market overt of such items, the court might be reluctant to exercise its discretion to the prejudice of the innocent purchaser.

vi Miscellaneous

By s. 21 (2), (*b*) of the Sale of Goods Act, nothing contained in the Act is to affect the "validity of any contract of sale under any special common law or statutory power of sale or under the order of a court of competent jurisdiction".

This saving provision made clear that there would continue to exist a wide variety of powers of sale, most often created by statute or open to a court of law. These powers have in many cases been extended since 1893. All that needs be said in the present context is that many bailees of goods (pawnbrokers, repairers, innkeepers) have powers to sell goods in certain circumstances. A landlord who has validly exercised a power to distrain goods for non-payment of rent may sell those goods. And a bailiff acting under a court order may exercise a similar

---

1 *Case of Market Overt* (above); and see also *Taylor* v. *Chambers* (1604), Cro. Jac. 68.
2 *Case of Market Overt* (above).
3 Laws in Wales Act 1542, s. 47.
4 See *Clifton* v. *Chancellor* (1600), Moore, K. B. 624; cited, without comment on this point, *Hartrop* v. *Hoare* (1743), 3 Atk. 44, at p. 48.
5 This qualification is given by both Coke (2 Inst. 713) and Blackstone (2 Bl. Com. 450), although reason suggests that it should be confined to cases where the seller had been in bad faith.

power. Indeed, the effect of a writ of execution is specifically dealt with by s. 26 (1) of the Act:

> "A writ of . . . execution against goods shall bind the property in the goods of the execution debtor as from the moment when the writ is delivered to the sheriff to be executed . . .
>
> "Provided that no such writ shall prejudice the title to such goods acquired by any person in good faith and for valuable consideration, unless such person had at the time when he acquired his title notice that such writ . . . had been delivered to and remained unexecuted in the hands of the sheriff."

PART TWO

The Contractual Aspect

The Contractual Aspect

Prior to 1893, the emphasis on the contractual side of the law relating to the sale of goods was on the performance of the contract and on the remedies available to the parties if the contract was not performed to their satisfaction. To an extent this approach was bound up with the method of pleading. For example, if the buyer was sued for non-acceptance of the goods or refused to pay the full price, he could either plead a breach of warranty as constituting a breach by the seller of a condition precedent to his obligation to accept and pay for the goods, or rely on the breach of warranty as entitling him to a reduction in price.

The Sale of Goods Act, by laying down that certain conditions were, in the absence of contrary intention, automatically part of a contract of sale shifted the emphasis in dealing with the contract of sale (whether as judge or commentator) from the remedies available to the terms of the contract. The objective to be attained was of course the same (to decide what were the rights and obligations of the parties in case of a breach), but the Act constituted a shift in attitudes. It is believed that this shift has created difficulties not least in relation to the concept of the fundamental obligation. Formerly the position of the buyer who claimed that his seller had "fundamentally" failed to perform the contract was, as a matter of pleading, no different from the buyer who was seeking to justify his non-acceptance of the goods for failure by the seller to perform a condition precedent, based upon the quality of the goods, to his (the buyer's) obligations. Since 1893, however, the concept of a fundamental obligation has been viewed as an extraordinary plea available to a buyer who is unable to rely upon the protection afforded by the terms implied into contracts of sale by the Act.

This dichotomy is also to be seen in recent legislation. The Misrepresentation Act 1967 concentrates on remedies to the disregard of formal classification, while the Supply of Goods (Implied Terms) Act 1973 operates within the framework of the 1893 Act. The original common law has thus had built upon it a number of strata of statutory provisions so that the ultimate answer to the apparently simple question—has the buyer a remedy?—can only be provided after what might be termed a major excavation of the site.

In contrast to current academic tradition the course of the present investigation will be to concentrate on the law of sale from its remedies aspect. Not only is it felt that this will preserve a sense of historical continuity (which can provide a better understanding of the law), but it is believed that the practical consequence of recent legislation (whatever its philosophical basis) will be to restore the emphasis on the remedies standpoint of the law.

Accordingly, this survey will commence with a chapter on performance of the contract; it will then deal with the basis of the remedies available (usually to the buyer) under the contract; Chapter 6 covers a number of factors which affect contractual liability; and the last two chapters deal with the remedies available to the parties.

CHAPTER 4

Performance of the Contract

Performance of the contract involves a delivery of the goods by the seller and their acceptance, plus payment of the price, by the buyer. As s. 27 of the Sale of Goods Act states:

> "It is the duty of the seller to deliver the goods, and of the buyer to accept and pay for them, in accordance with the terms of the contract of sale".

A. DELIVERY

Although s. 27 is drafted in terms of delivery as the principal obligation of the seller, the common law of sale is not in fact as straightforward as this provision would seem to suggest.

Under Scots law, for example, the transfer of ownership will normally take place at the moment of delivery. However, as we have seen, it is often the case under English law that the time when property passes is totally divorced from the transfer of possession by delivery. Property might well pass before, or even after, the act of delivery. The existence of s. 12 of the Sale of Goods Act makes it clear that, in the majority of cases, the obligations of the buyer are dependent upon delivery by the seller of the goods in question together with, at some stage in the transaction, the ownership of those goods.[1]

It is also implicit in the nature of the transaction that the delivery should be of the goods prescribed by the contract, and not of other goods which do not answer the contract description. Although this aspect of the law will be dealt with later at some length,[2] it must be remembered in the present context that delivery as performance of the seller's obligations is dependent upon the goods being those that, according to the terms of the contract, the buyer actually ordered.

i The actual delivery

The meaning of "delivery" is not easy to describe with accuracy. The definition contained in s. 62 (1) that it is a "voluntary transfer of possession from one person to another" is hardly informative, not least because one is then thrown back to the equally difficult task of having to define possession.

---

1 See below, p. 167.
2 See below, p. 117.

III

However, for present purposes, possession can most simply be described as denoting both actual or prospective physical control, and constructive possession, that is, the legal right to obtain possession which is gained once goods are held on the buyer's behalf.

a *Actual or prospective physical control*

Delivery of physical possession to the buyer needs no real comment, beyond making a point that may cause some surprise to the layman, namely that delivery is given *prima facie* by the seller doing no more than making the goods available for collection. In the words of s. 29 (1):

> "Whether it is for the buyer to take possession of the goods or for the seller to send them to the buyer is a question depending in each case on the contract, express or implied, between the parties. Apart from any such contract, express or implied, the place of delivery is the seller's place of business, if he have one, and if not, his residence: Provided that, if the contract be for the sale of specific goods, which to the knowledge of the parties when the contract is made are in some other place, then that place is the place of delivery."

By making the goods available, the seller is enabling the buyer to complete the act of delivery by taking possession of the goods. However, where the goods are not under the immediate control of the seller, the seller can, by giving the buyer the means of access to the place where the goods are housed (a key to where the goods are stored is the example usually given[1]), effect a transfer of possession because it is the buyer who then has prospective control of the goods.

b *Constructive possession*

Where actual physical possession is assumed on the buyer's behalf or where the person having such possession acknowledges (attorns) to the buyer that he holds on the buyer's behalf, the buyer is regarded as having constructive possession of the goods because he is entitled to insist that physical control of the goods is handed over to him. The buyer will also obtain constructive possession of the goods if he acquires a document of title which for most purposes represents the goods and symbolises his rights in the goods. In the words of s. 29 (3):

> "Where the goods at the time of sale are in the possession of a third person, there is no delivery by seller to buyer unless and until such third person acknowledges to the buyer that he holds the goods on his behalf; provided that nothing in this section shall affect the operation of the issue or transfer of any document of title to goods."

In the last resort, of course, all depends upon the terms of the contract and the circumstances of the case. It is possible that the seller may constitute himself agent of the buyer to hold the goods by attorning to the latter.[2] On the other

---

1 The key must give access: see *Wrightson* v. *McArthur and Hutchisons*, [1921] 2 K.B. 807, at pp. 817–18. If B were given the key to a room in premises to which S alone had access, there would be no transfer of possession: *Milgate* v. *Kebble* (1841), 3 Man. & G. 100.

2 Though this does not operate as a delivery to the buyer for all purposes: see s. 41 (2) discussed below, p. 294.

hand, although delivery to a carrier is deemed to be delivery to the buyer, it is possible to establish that, on the facts, the carrier was actually the seller's agent.[1]

ii Where delivery is to a carrier

a When equivalent to delivery to the buyer

The rule laid down in s. 32 (1) that delivery to a carrier is delivery to the buyer is only presumptive: it is open to the parties to make express provision, for example, by requiring that the seller deliver the goods to the buyer's premises.

In *Galbraith and Grant, Ltd.* v. *Block*,[2] S, a wine merchant, had agreed to sell a case of champagne and to deliver it to B's premises. The case was conveyed by a carrier engaged by S for this purpose. The carrier claimed to have delivered it at a side entrance and alleged that someone on the premises had signed the delivery sheet in B's name. The County Court Judge had clearly been correct in holding that no delivery occurred when the goods were put into the carrier's hands because, on the terms of the contract, S's obligation was to deliver at B's premises, and, on the facts, the carrier was clearly his agent and not B's. However a new trial was ordered in order to decide whether there had been a delivery to a person apparently authorised to receive the goods. The principle was stated by the Divisional Court as follows:[3]

> "A vendor who is told to deliver goods at the purchaser's premises discharges his obligations if he delivers them there without negligence to a person apparently having authority to receive them. He cannot know what authority the actual recipient has. His duty is to deliver the goods at the proper place, and, of course, to take all proper care to see that no unauthorised person receives them. He is under no obligation to do more. If the purchaser has been unfortunate enough to have had access to his premises obtained by some apparently respectable person who takes his goods and signs for them in his absence, the loss must fall on him, and not on the innocent carrier or vendor".

A distinction also exists in relation to certain contracts in which the seller undertakes to arrange for the shipment of goods. Under the normal c.i.f. contract, the buyer pays a composite price to the seller to cover the *cost* of the goods, their *insurance*, and the *freight* charges in respect of their carriage. Although the risk of damage or loss passes at the moment the goods cross the ship's rail,[4] the seller's obligation to deliver is not performed until he tenders the shipping documents (i.e. the bill of lading issued by the carrier, the insurance policy, and the seller's invoice for the goods) to the buyer. With the tender of the documents, the buyer's obligation to pay for the goods arises; and with delivery of the documents property in the goods is transferred. Thus, delivery to the carrier is clearly not a delivery to the buyer under a c.i.f. contract.

However, s. 32 (1) does apply to f.o.b. contracts. Under such a contract the

---

1 See above, p. 24.
2 [1922] 2 K.B. 155; [1922] All E.R. Rep. 443.
3 [1922] 2 K.B., at p. 157; [1922] All E.R. Rep., at p. 444; see also *Barrett* v. *Deere* (1828), Mood & M. 200.
4 See KENNEDY, L.J.'s dissenting judgment in *Biddell Bros.* v. *E. Clemens Horst Co.*, [1911] 1 K.B. 934, at p. 956; upheld on appeal *sub nom. E. Clemens Horst Co.* v. *Biddell Bros.*, [1912] A.C. 18, at pp. 22, 23.

seller's obligation is to place the goods *free on board* ship, usually a vessel nominated by the buyer. In this situation, the risk passes at the moment of loading, and delivery is effected once the goods are on board.[1]

b *Seller's duty in selecting carrier*

If the contract falls within the general presumption of s. 32 (1) whereby the carrier is *prima facie* deemed to be the agent of the buyer, but the carrier is nevertheless one chosen by the seller, s. 32 (2) provides the buyer with some protection:

> "Unless otherwise authorised by the buyer, the seller must make such contract with the carrier on behalf of the buyer as may be reasonable having regard to the nature of the goods and the other circumstances of the case. If the seller omit so to do, and the goods are lost or damaged in course of transit, the buyer may decline to treat the delivery to the carrier as a delivery to himself, or may hold the seller responsible in damages."

It would follow from this principle that the seller should select a suitable carrier and make sure the goods are safely entrusted to that carrier.[2] Furthermore, in employing the carrier, the seller should obtain the most reasonable terms obtainable in the circumstances on the buyer's behalf. For example, if the carrier sought to impose a maximum limit on his liability unless the true value of the goods was declared and an additional charge paid, the seller would have implied authority, and would be under a duty, to declare and pay for any additional value of the goods in order to protect the buyer.[3]

In *Thomas Young & Sons, Ltd.* v. *Hobson & Partners*,[4] B (the defendants) had agreed to buy a number of electric engines some of which were still in a ship that S (the plaintiffs) was breaking up. It was agreed that S was to have them loaded on six wagons for dispatch by rail from Sunderland to Leighton Buzzard. The goods were damaged in transit because S had not secured them in the wagons. B refused to accept the goods because, as they had been sent "at owner's risk", he would have had no remedy against the carrier. The Court of Appeal held that B was entitled to refuse to take delivery of the goods:

> "In the present case the plaintiffs had agreed to put the goods in box wagons, and the question is whether it was reasonable to send goods of this nature unsecured at owners' risk when they could have been sent at the same cost at company's risk, subject to inspection by the railway officials, who could, in a case like this, have required that the the engines be properly secured by means of battens. We cannot think that such a requirement would have placed an unreasonable burden on the plaintiffs, and in all the circumstances we are of the opinion that . . . the defendants succeeded in showing that the plaintiffs had failed in their duty under s. 32 (2) . . . to make such a contract . . . as was

---

1 Property would not pass of course if the goods were still unascertained as in *Healy* v. *Howlett and Sons*, [1917] 1 K.B. 337; see above, p. 18.
2 *Buckman* v. *Levi* (1813), 3 Camp. 414.
3 *Clarke* v. *Hutchins* (1811), 14 East 475; unless the seller could rely upon a previous course of dealings to the contrary with the buyer in question: *Cothay* v. *Tute* (1811), 3 Camp. 129.
4 (1949), 65 T.L.R. 365.

reasonable having regard to the nature of the goods and the other circumstances of the case, and that the defendants were accordingly entitled to decline to treat the delivery to the railway company as delivery to them."[1]

c *Insurance of the goods*

1 *Sea Transit and s. 32 (3)*. Under a number of contracts involving the sea transit of goods, the obligations of the seller do not extend to insuring the goods. When the Sale of Goods Act was drafted, it was felt that the seller should be required to notify the buyer of the facts and circumstances that would enable him to arrange adequate insurance of the goods. According to s. 32 (3):

> "Unless otherwise agreed, where goods are sent by the seller to the buyer by a route involving sea transit, under circumstances in which it is usual to insure, the seller must give such notice to the buyer as may enable him to insure them during their sea transit, and, if the seller fails to do so, the goods shall be deemed to be at his risk during such sea transit."

However, the question must be raised whether the wording employed in the sub-section achieves what was its apparent object.

In *Wimble* v. *Rosenberg*, S sold 200 bags of rice "f.o.b. Antwerp . . . cash against bills of lading". On August 9, B sent S instructions to ship the rice to Odessa, and to select a ship and pay the freight on his (B's) behalf. The rice was shipped on August 24; the vessel sailed the following day, but early on August 26 she ran aground and became a total loss. B received no information about the shipment until S presented the bills of lading for payment on August 29. B claimed that, as S had failed to comply with the requirements of s. 32 (3), he was not obliged to pay for the goods. At first instance[2] BAILHACHE, J., held that, not only did s. 32 (3) not apply to c.i.f. and "ex-ship"[3] contracts, but it also could not be said to cover normal f.o.b. contracts in which the ship is nominated by, or on behalf of, the buyer. In the Court of Appeal,[4] VAUGHAN WILLIAMS, L.J. and BUCKLEY, L.J., expressed the view that s. 32 (3) applied to f.o.b. contracts because under such a contract the seller was in fact *sending* goods to the buyer whoever nominated the ship in which they were carried. However, the decision in S's favour was upheld because the third member of the Court, HAMILTON, L.J., held that the sub-section did not apply to f.o.b. contracts, while BUCKLEY, L.J., held that, though s. 32 (3) did apply, B had available sufficient information, even without the name of the ship and its date of departure, to have insured the goods.

This degree of uncertainty is not altogether resolved by the later case of *Northern Steel and Hardware Co., Ltd.* v. *John Batt & Co. (London), Ltd.*[5] In the only judgment reported (SCRUTTON, L.J., and NEVILLE, J., were said to have concurred), Lord READING, C.J., held that it was not open to the present

---

1 At p. 366, *per* TUCKER, L. J., giving the judgment of the Court.
2 [1913] 1 K.B. 279.
3 This is a contract for the delivery of the goods to a normal unloading place in the port nominated: see *Comptoir d'Achat etc. Belge S.A.* v. *Luis de Ridder Limitada,* [1949] A.C. 293; [1944] 1 All E.R. 269.
4 [1913] 3 K.B. 743.
5 (1917), 33 T.L.R. 516.

Court to differ from the majority opinion in *Wimble* v. *Rosenberg* that s. 32 (3) applied to f.o.b. contracts, although he did express sympathy with the cogent reasons given by HAMILTON, L.J., for dissenting on the issue.

In view of the hesitation with which the application of s. 32 (3) to f.o.b. contracts was supported, some further comment would seem necessary on the background to the provision. The inspiration came from Scots law, although apparently none of the pre-1893 cases related to f.o.b. contracts, but to incidents of coastal traffic which fell within none of the main categories of sale contracts involving maritime transit.[1] Although this explanation may be sufficient to counter the argument that, if s. 32 (3) does not apply to f.o.b. contracts, it would have no field of application at all, it is not necessarily an answer to the view that s. 32 (3) seems to have no useful role in relation to such contracts.

Once the principle is accepted, however, there is still the problem of deciding in what circumstances the buyer can take advantage of it. In *Wimble* v. *Rosenberg*, BUCKLEY, L.J., held that the contract itself gave the buyer all the knowledge that was necessary to enable him to insure the goods. He knew the cargo and the port of loading, and he himself was entitled to name the ship and the port of destination. Simply because he requested the seller to arrange for a ship to carry the goods, he could not impose an additional obligation on the seller that was not incurred by virtue of the contract. If this line of argument is adopted, it is difficult to escape the further conclusion, that under a f.o.b. contract, unless the seller expressly undertakes to arrange for shipment of the goods, s. 32 (3) has no part to play. Indeed, it was this *reductio ad absurdum* which reinforced HAMILTON, L.J., in his belief that s. 32 (3) could not apply to the normal f.o.b. contract under which the buyer's obligation was to name a ship.

Whatever view one takes of s. 32 (3) in its application to f.o.b. contracts, it is at least clear that its significance is minimal. Even if it does apply to such contracts, the likelihood is that it will have little effect on the legal relationship between the parties. Only in the exceptional situation where the contract of sale imposes the obligation to select the vessel to carry the goods on the seller, and the choice whether to insure or not on the buyer, will the seller be in possession of information which may affect the ability of the buyer to obtain satisfactory insurance cover of the risk. In such circumstances, a notice in accordance with s. 32 (3) would be necessary.

2 *Where the seller is to insure.* Clearly s. 32 (3) is of no relevance to c.i.f. contracts under which the seller is to ship and insure the goods. Under such a contract, the obligation to insure merges with the seller's general obligation contained in s. 32 (2) to obtain the most reasonable terms from the buyer's point of view with the carriers as is possible in the circumstances.

In the case of *Plaimar, Ltd.* v. *Waters Trading Co., Ltd.*,[2] S was to ship a consignment of clove oil from Zanzibar to Fremantle under a c.i.f. contract made in November, 1941. B argued that neither the bill of lading nor the insurance policy provided adequate protection during the period of transhipment at Singapore through which the goods had to pass, and where transfer of the

---

1 See *Wimble* v. *Rosenberg*, [1913] 3 K.B. 743, at pp. 762–3, *per* HAMILTON, L.J.
2 (1945), 72 C.L.R. 304.

goods to another vessel had to take place. The High Court of Australia held that S could not be held accountable for the loss of the goods outside the limited protection provided by the policy because no extended cover was available at the time in question.[1] Nor could S have been expected to obtain a more favourable bill of lading. All that B was entitled to was "that measure of protection which the seller can reasonably procure according to the usage and practice obtaining in the trade and with reference to the available routes".[2]

3 *Carriage by land.* Although the rule introduced by s. 32 (3) has no application to the land carriage of goods (unless it forms part of the contract expressly, or by implication from the custom of the trade or course of dealings between the parties), the underlying principle of s. 32 (2) will usually extend to give the buyer a degree of protection. The practice of paying a higher freight charge on goods above a certain value is in effect equivalent to the payment of a premium in respect of loss above the limit imposed on his liability by the carrier.[3] In other words, the carrier becomes the insurer of the goods. It is a moot point whether, if the seller is unable to obtain "carrier's risk" terms, he would be under an obligation to insure the goods separately or to notify the buyer of the difficulty. Much will depend upon commercial practice in the particular trade[4] and, of course, on the terms upon which carriers are likely to handle the goods in question.

iii Delivery of the wrong goods

Delivery of the wrong goods may take either or both of two forms. Either the goods will be of a different type, or, although of the correct type, the quantity supplied will be too much or too little. Logically, delivery of the wrong goods altogether would seem to be a more serious failing on the part of the seller than delivery of a lesser or greater amount of the correct goods. However, in its drafting, the 1893 Act chose to treat the obligation, in a contract for the sale of goods by description, to supply goods answering that description as an "implied condition" (s. 13 (1));[5] while the delivery of the wrong quantity, or delivery of the goods contracted for, mixed with those of a different description, specifically entitles the buyer to reject the entire consignment if he so wishes (s. 30).

a *Goods of a different description*

1 *Historical background.* Prior to 1893 there were a number of warranties that, in the absence of a contrary intention, were implied into contracts for the sale of goods. It was understood, for example, that in certain circumstances the

---

1 The limitation of liability to 15 days in transhipment clauses caused so much difficulty as Japan extended its operations through South-East Asia, that, in August, 1942, a special unlimited cover was made available under the War Risks Reinsurance Scheme.
2 72 C.L.R., at p. 316.
3 *Clarke* v. *Hutchins* (1811), 14 East 475; and see *Von Traubenberg* v. *Davies, Turner & Co. Ltd.*, [1951] 2 Lloyd's Rep. 462, dealing with the obligations of a forwarding agent.
4 See *W.L.R. Traders (London), Ltd.* v. *British and Northern Shipping Agency, Ltd.*, [1955] 1 Lloyd's Rep. 554, in which *Von Traubenberg* v. *Davies, Turner & Co., Ltd.* (above) was distinguished.
5 Originally, s. 13, but renumbered s. 13 (1) by the Supply of Goods (Implied Terms) Act 1973, s. 2.

goods should be suitable for a particular purpose or should be of merchantable quality. If a warranty (i.e. a promise about the subject-matter of the contract) were broken, the buyer as injured party could repudiate the contract if he was able to show that compliance with the warranty was a condition precedent to his own liabilities under the contract. Because of the importance of the suitability of goods, or their merchantability, to a buyer, breach of one of these implied undertakings by the seller would usually constitute a breach of a condition precedent to the buyer's liability to accept and pay for the goods. Taken in isolation, therefore, s. 14, sub-ss. (1) and (2), of the 1893 Act were a fairly accurate reproduction of the previous law.[1]

However, distortion of the common law position did occur in the reproduction in s. 13 of the seller's more fundamental obligation to deliver the goods contracted for. This obligation was certainly a condition precedent to the buyer's liabilities, but it was of a different nature to those contained in s. 14. It was in no sense based upon any "implied warranty", a point most forcibly made by Lord ABINGER in his well-known dictum in *Chanter* v. *Hopkins*:[2]

> "in many of the cases . . . the circumstance of a party selling a particular thing by its proper description, has been called a warranty; . . . but it would be better to distinguish such cases as a non-compliance with a contract which a party has engaged to fulfil; as, if a man offers to buy peas of another, and he sends him beans, he does not perform his contract, but that is not a warranty; there is no warranty that he should sell him peas; the contract is to sell peas, and if he sends him anything else in their stead, it is a non-performance of it".

The concept of the "condition precedent" was basically a question of pleading. If a buyer was sued on the contract for failing to perform his part of the bargain (to accept and pay for the goods), he would plead that delivery of the specified goods, or of goods suitable for his purpose or of merchantable quality, constituted a condition precedent to performance of his obligations and that the seller had not fulfilled the condition in question. An exemption clause in the contract to the effect that no warranties were given as to the goods would enable the seller to deny that he had failed to perform a condition precedent to provide goods suitable for the purpose or of merchantable quality because he had expressly negatived any warranty as to the condition of the goods. However, the exclusion of any warranties would have no effect on the obligation to deliver goods answering the contract description because this condition precedent to the buyer's liability arose, as Lord ABINGER stated, from the contract itself and not from any warranty, express or implied.

Once the undertaking to provide goods answering their description became a condition *in* the contract by virtue of s. 13, it was in theory possible to exclude its operation by a general exemption clause covering all "conditions and warranties, express or implied, by common law, statute or otherwise". By s. 55, where "any right, duty or liability would arise under a contract of sale by implication

---

1 These provisions (now s. 14 (3) and (2)) are dealt with below, pp. 179, 187.
2 (1838), 4 M & W. 339, at p. 404.

of law, it may be negatived or varied" *inter alia* "by express agreement". Such an extraordinary departure from the pre-1893 law has been avoided by the courts refusing to apply general exclusions of liability for "errors and mis-descriptions" to the "fundamental obligation" of the contract of sale which is to supply goods that are properly described by the contract description. However, the existence of s. 13 has created difficulties, not least because of the need to distinguish between different levels of description—those that are fundamental, and those that fall only within s. 13.

In contrast, no such problem is created in relation to the supply of insufficient or too many goods, or of goods mixed with those of a different type, because s. 30 entitles the buyer to reject automatically. There is no need to interpose the intermediate stage of pleading a breach of a condition that the seller had impliedly promised to fulfil.

2 *Sales by description.* According to s. 13 (1) of the Act, it is an implied condition of the contract that the goods should answer their description if the sale is a sale by description. Despite the implication that a sale by description is something unusual, or at least different or distinct, it is accurate enough to regard most sales as being by description. Invariably in a contract negotiated by correspondence, the goods must be given some verbal description. But even if the transaction is effected in a shop, the likelihood is that the contract will be by description. As the Privy Council pointed out in *Grant* v. *Australian Knitting Mills, Ltd.*:[1]

> "There is a sale by description even though the buyer is buying something displayed before him on the counter: a thing is sold by description, though it is specific, so long as it is sold not merely as the specific thing but as a thing coresponding to a description, e.g. woollen under-garments, a hot-water bottle, a second-hand reaping machine, to select a few obvious illustrations."

While this pronouncement makes clear that selection by the buyer of goods displayed in the seller's shop does not prevent the contract being a sale by description, it leaves it far from clear the extent to which the circumstances of the display may affect the nature of the contract. In the traditional High Street shop the fiction could be preserved that the buyer verbally requested a hot-water bottle or a pair of socks rather than selected them from the goods on the counter and handed them to the shop assistant with or without additional verbal communication indicating his (the buyer's) wishes. This fiction was inherent in the dictum of DIXON, J., when the *Australian Knitting Mills* case was before the High Court of Australia:[2]

> "However certainly the identity of the goods may be established, the parties must, since the intention is expressed or communicated, refer in some way to the goods. They must use some 'description' to refer to them. A difficulty, therefore, cannot but arise in determining when the sale is 'by' the description and when not. Apparently the distinction is between sales of things sought or chosen by the buyer because of their description and of things of which the

---

1 [1936] A.C. 85, at p. 100; [1935] All E.R. Rep. 209, at p. 215.
2 (1933), 50 C.L.R. 387, at pp. 417-8.

physical identity is all important. When the ground upon which the goods are selected and identified is their correspondence to a description and when, therefore, it may be said that the buyer primarily relies upon their classification or possession of attributes, then, notwithstanding that they are bought as specific goods ascertained and identified, the goods are bought by description. In the ordinary course of a sale over the counter by a shopkeeper to a customer, who calls for an article of a given description, inspects the specimens produced, and buys one, the transaction is a sale by description."

Acceptance of this approach created a difficulty of classifying sales in a super-market where the customer selects goods and does not ask the assistant to obtain them from the shelves. To a large extent such a difficulty is theoretical rather than practical, because the wording on display shelves, the packaging of the goods, or even (in the case of, say, loaves of bread) their appearance, would seem to constitute an adequate description of the goods for the purpose of a "sale by description". However, the issue was considered sufficiently in doubt to require special mention in the Malony Committee Reports:[1]

"The shop counter across which the customer asks for what he wants has ceased to be the prominent feature of retail establishments it once was. The customer is now encouraged to make his choice unaided by a sales assistant. A very considerable proportion of consumer goods are selected from shelves in self-service stores or from open counters or racks in shops that still maintain some sales staff. It is questionable whether these sales are 'by description' and if not, the customer has no shred of right in law to complain of a defective purchase."

To resolve the difficulty, if in fact one existed, the Supply of Goods (Implied Terms) Act, 1973, s. 2 has renumbered s. 13 of the Sale of Goods Act as s. 13 (1), and added a sub-section (2):

"A sale of goods shall not be prevented from being a sale by description by reason only that, being exposed for sale or hire, they are selected by the buyer."

3 *What constitutes the contract description.* Assuming for the moment that there is an underlying obligation of the contract to supply the goods described, the next step is to decide what exactly it is that forms, and is part of, the contract description. As a purely logical issue, the extent of the seller's obligation to provide goods answering their description is dependent upon the level of abstraction at which that description is stated. The greater the detail in which the goods are described, the more onerous is the obligation placed upon the seller.

However, the courts have shown some reluctance to accept the dictates of logic in their approach to this matter. Support can be found for both a narrow view which would go no further than the classification of the goods, and for a broad view which would include the measurements or even the suita-bility or quality of the goods within the "description". According to the former approach, the seller must supply peas, not beans; chalk not cheese; or pine

---

1 Final Report of the Committee on Consumer Protection (1962) Cmnd. 1781, para. 441.

logs not mahogany logs; but that matters of condition or quality are to be remedied, if at all, within the framework of other provisions of the Act. As Lord WILBERFORCE said in *Ashington Piggeries Ltd.* v. *Christopher Hill Ltd.*:[1]

> "I do not believe that the . . . Act was designed to provoke metaphysical discussions as to the nature of what is delivered, in comparison with what is sold. The test of description, at least where commodities are concerned, is intended to be a broader, more commonsense, test of a mercantile character. The question whether that is what the buyer bargained for has to be answered according to such tests as men in the market would apply, leaving more delicate questions of condition, or quality, to be determined under other clauses of the contract or sections of the Act."

Even if this approach is favoured, however, it is clear that the description can go beyond a general classification of the goods. In an age when technological advances have made it essential that goods, or their components, should be made with the greatest precision, it would be accepted that the description of goods may be applied with equal precision. This proposition seems clear from the decision of the House of Lords in *Arcos, Ltd.* v. *E. A. Ronaasen & Son*,[2] in which B had ordered a quantity of staves from S. Some variation in their length and breadth was provided for in the contract, but the thickness was stated to be $\frac{1}{2}$ in. B rejected the goods on the ground that only about five per cent of the consignment was of this thickness; a large proportion was between $\frac{1}{2}$ in. and $\frac{9}{16}$ in., and a small number exceeded $\frac{5}{8}$ in. in thickness. It was apparent that the staves did not answer the contract description and B was entitled to reject. While "microscopic deviations"[3] which are "so slight as to be negligible"[4] may be disregarded, the general rule is that a contract has to be performed according to its terms. In Lord ATKIN's words:[5]

> "If the written contract specifies conditions of weight, measurement and the like, those conditions must be complied with. A ton does not mean about a ton, or a yard about a yard. Still less when you descend to minute measurements does $\frac{1}{2}$ in. mean about $\frac{1}{2}$ in. If the seller wants a margin he must and in my experience does stipulate for it."[6]

---

1 [1972] A.C. 441, at p. 489; [1971] All E.R. 847, at p. 872. This echoes an earlier pronouncement by Lord DUNEDIN in *Manchester Liners, Ltd.* v. *Rea*, [1922] 2 A.C. 74, at p. 80, [1922] All E.R. Rep. 605, at p. 608:

> "The tender of anything that does not tally with the specified description is not compliance with the contract. But when the article tendered does comply with the specific description and the objection on the buyer's part is an objection to quality alone, then I think that s. 14 . . . settles the standard, and the only standard by which the matter is to be judged."

2 [1933] A.C. 470; [1933] All E.R. Rep. 646.
3 [1933] A.C. 470, at p. 479; [1933] All E.R. Rep. 646, at p. 650, *per* Lord ATKIN.
4 [1933] A.C. 470, at p. 477; [1933] All E.R. Rep. 646, at p. 649, *per* Lord WARRINGTON.
5 [1933] A.C. 470, at p. 479; [1933] All E.R. Rep. 646, at p. 650.
6 In a contract relating to precision equipment the variation would only be in the number of items answering the contract description (say 95 per cent). No "microscopic deviation" in the individual items would be possible because the very existence of such variations could render all the items unusable.

Where doubt exists, because there is a difference of judicial opinion, is whether the contract description can include the quality of goods or their suitability for a particular purpose. Despite the disapproval of this broader view apparently expressed by a number of members of the House of Lords in the *Ashington Piggeries* case, it is noticeable that both Lord GUEST and Lord HODSON did give grudging acknowledgement to the possibility that a "qualitative description" could fall within s. 13.[1] On the other hand, MILMO, J., at first instance in that case,[2] felt that a description could always be qualitative as well as quantitative, and this view seems to have had the support of the Court of Appeal.[3]

Furthermore if one examines Lord ABINGER's judgment in *Chanter* v. *Hopkins*[4] more closely it is apparent that he was of the opinion that if the purpose for which the goods are required is spelt out in the contract as a means of describing the goods, their suitability for that purpose becomes part of the contract description. After his comments about peas and beans Lord ABINGER went on to say[5] that in the case of a man who ordered

> "copper for sheathing ships—that is a particular copper, prepared in a particular manner; if the seller sends him a different sort, in that case he does not comply with the contract: and though this may have been considered a warranty, and may have been ranged under the class of cases relating to warranties, yet it is not properly so".

Despite the reluctance of some of the judges to consider the quality or suitability of goods as falling within the ambit of s. 13, it is clear that the seller's obligations can be classified simultaneously under more than one provision of the Act. Moreover, it takes only a slight alteration in the facts to make classification under one section more appropriate than classification under another. For example, the transaction in *Manchester Liners, Ltd.* v. *Rea, Ltd.*[6] was covered by s. 14 because coal was required for the specific purpose of bunkering the *Manchester Trader*: if the request had simply been for "furnace coal", then a failure to supply such coal would have been a breach of the undertaking relating to description.

4 *The problem of additives.* The goods that are delivered under the contract will not be regarded as answering their description if they include goods which do not comply with that description.

This principle applies in two different ways. In the first place, s. 30 (3) provides:

> "Where the seller delivers to the buyer the goods he contracted to sell mixed with goods of a different description not included in the contract, the buyer may accept the goods which are in accordance with the contract and reject the rest, or he may reject the whole."

---

1 *Per* Lord GUEST, [1972] A.C. 441, at p. 475; [1971] 1 All E.R. 847, at p. 860; and see [1972] A.C., at p. 470; [1971] 1 All E.R., at p. 856, *per* Lord HODSON.
2 [1968] 1 Lloyd's Rep. 457.
3 [1969] 3 All E.R. 1496, at pp. 1510–12.
4 (1838), 4 M. & W. 399.
5 At p. 405.
6 [1922] 2 A.C. 74; [1922] All E.R. Rep. 605.

This is the most obvious application of the principle and it will be dependent upon the degree of particularity with which the goods are described. In *Re Moore & Co. and Landauer & Co.*,[1] S had agreed to supply B with approximately 3,100 cases of Australian canned fruits to be packed in cases containing 30 tins each. When the goods reached London, B refused to accept them on the ground that about half of the cases contained 24 tins each. Having held that, in the circumstances, the way in which the goods were packed formed part of the contract description so that S had been in breach of s. 13, both ROWLATT, J., at first instance, and the Court of Appeal also upheld B's right to reject the whole consignment in accordance with s. 30 (3).

The more difficult question is whether s. 30 (3) can apply to a situation where the goods are physically mixed. In the *Moore and Landauer* case,[2] ROWLATT, J., expressed the opinion that the words " 'mixed with' in sub-s. 3 cannot refer to physical confusion but are equivalent to 'accompanied by' ". The reason behind this pronouncement may be the fact that the sub-section envisages the possibility that the buyer may wish to accept part of the consignment a step which would be more difficult, or even impossible, if the goods were mixed. However, there does not appear to be any reason why the buyer should not, even in such a situation, be given the option of going to the trouble and expense of separating out the goods which do satisfy the contract description and of rejecting the rest.[3]

It may not be possible to apply s. 30 (3) in circumstances where there are not distinguishable goods (i.e. those which do, and those which do not, answer the contract description), but only goods which include some ingredient or additive that makes them totally unsuitable for the buyer's purposes. In a situation of that type, assuming that he cannot rely s. 14 (either because of an exemption clause in the contract or because the buyer is not able to show that he has relied on the seller's skill and judgment), the buyer is thrown back on the argument that the goods plus the "foreign matter" render them something other than those that he contracted to buy.

In *Pinnock Bros.* v. *Lewis and Peat, Ltd.*,[4] B purchased from S a quantity of East African copra cake under the terms of a contract which provided *inter alia* that "the goods are not warranted free from defect rendering them unmerchantable which would not be apparent on reasonable examination". The copra cake was resold and eventually used as a cattle feed. It was subsequently discovered that the cake contained an admixture of castor beans that made it toxic to animals. ROCHE, J., held that B's action for damages succeeded. However widely the exemption clause had been drafted, it could not have

---

1 [1921] 1 K.B. 73; affirmed; [1921] 2 K.B. 519; [1921] All E.R. Rep. 466; see also *Ebrahim Dawood, Ltd.* v. *Heath, Ltd.*, [1961] 2 Lloyd's Rep. 512 (galvanized steel sheets, assorted over 6, 7, 8, 9, and 10 feet long: B held entitled to retain ¼ of consignment which was found to contain 6 foot lengths only).
2 [1921] 1 K.B. 73, at p. 76.
3 See *William Barker (Jr.) & Co. Ltd.* v. *Edward T. Agius Ltd.* (1927), 33 Com. Cas. 120, at p. 132, *per* SALTER, J.
4 [1923] 1 K.B. 690.

protected S because "the goods delivered did not comply with the contract but were totally different from what was contracted for".[1]

This decision should be contrasted with *Ashington Piggeries, Ltd.* v. *Christopher Hill, Ltd.*[2] In March, 1960, B (the appellant) arranged for S to prepare a mink food to be called "King Size". The formula was provided by B. The preparation of animal foods was something S did regularly as part of his business, although he made it clear that he knew nothing about mink food and any special requirements it might have. He did, however, suggest some minor alterations in the ingredients, one being the use of herring meal instead of the slightly more expensive fish meal. During the following 12 months "King Size" was widely distributed and was used apparently without causing any harm. In March, 1961, S purchased a consignment of Norwegian herring meal. Much later it was discovered that a substance in the meal (DMNA) caused acute liver disease in mink, although it was less harmful in such small quantities to other animals. The DMNA content was brought about by a chemical reaction which occurred during processing in a preservative used in the herrings.

It was argued on behalf of B, *inter alia*, that the goods supplied by S had not answered the contract description. In presenting this contention, B was faced with the obvious difficulty that S had supplied goods (i.e. the "King Size" mink food) in accordance with B's own formula. B felt obliged to concentrate the argument on S's selection of the ingredients and to advance the proposition that the herring meal was not in fact herring meal because of the presence of DMNA. This line of reasoning was rejected by the majority of the House of Lords. To them the vital factor in *Pinnock* v. *Lewis* had been that cake which included the addition of an entirely foreign element (the castor seed) was not copra. In the case of the herring meal the addition of the preservative, instead of the salt that had formerly been used, in no way destroyed the identity of the herring meal as herring meal any more than the salt had done. It was not a poisonous substance that had been added but a substance that in processing the herring had produced another substance that proved toxic to mink.[3]

It will inevitably be a matter of some difficulty to decide whether goods supplied that incorporate an additional or modified ingredient can still be regarded as the goods contracted for. Certainly a dissatisfied buyer who wishes to establish that the goods do not answer the contract description will find his task easier if he can point to some foreign matter that has become mixed with the contract goods. The principle is well established and the test applied will usually be a quantitative one.[4] However, despite references emphasising

---

1　At p. 695. ROCHE, J., was in fact referring to the potential effect of a carefully drafted arbitration clause prohibiting a claim not presented in accordance with its terms, but it is clear that what he was saying would be equally applicable to any other sort of term purporting to limit or exclude S's liability, see at pp. 696–7. See also *Robert A. Munro & Co. Ltd.* v. *Meyer*, [1930] 2 K.B. 312, at pp. 327–8; [1930] All E.R. Rep. 241, at p. 245.

2　[1972] A.C. 441; [1971] 1 All E.R. 847.

3　See *per* Lord HODSON, [1972] A.C., at p. 467; [1971] 1 All E.R., at p. 853; *per* Lord Guest, [1972] A.C., at p. 472; [1971] 1 All E.R. at p. 858 *per* Lord WILBERFORCE, [1972] A.C., at p. 489; [1971] 1 All E.R., at p. 872; *per* Lord DIPLOCK, [1972] A.C., at p. 504; [1971] 1 All E.R. at p. 884; Viscount DILHORNE dissented on this point.

4　As in *Robert A. Munro & Co., Ltd.* v. *Meyer*, [1930] 2 K.B. 312; [1930] All E.R. Rep. 241.

the quantitative approach in the *Ashington Piggeries* case,[1] there would seem to be strong reasons for accepting that an addition which, however minute, makes the goods *qualitatively* different should be sufficient to take them outside the contract description. It need hardly be said that a relatively small "addition" can have a more disastrous effect than a much larger quantity of a less harmful substance. In *Wilson* v. *Rickett, Cockerell & Co., Ltd.*,[2] part of a consignment of coal exploded when placed on B's fire. The foreign element that caused this explosion was quantitatively minute in relation to the consignment as a whole, but its presence would have been sufficient to establish a breach of s. 13 had B attempted to rely upon that section in bringing his claim.[3] On the other hand, the buyer's task will be considerably more difficult if he has to persuade the court that the inclusion of a particular ingredient, which has proved to be harmful, in some way destroys the identity of the goods. Only rarely in the latter situation can it be said that the goods no longer satisfy the contract description. The buyer must seek his remedy upon some other basis if one can be found.[4]

4. *Section* 13 (1) *and the doctrine of the fundamental obligation.* If there is no general exception clause in the contract, it will be immaterial whether the court bases its decision on a breach of the condition contained in s. 13[5] or on a failure to perform the obligation of delivering the goods specified.[6] Once a contract contains a clause which appears to exempt the seller from liability for a failure to perform the obligation contained in s. 13, the courts have been obliged to turn to the concept of the fundamental obligation. This area of the law will be explored in more detail later, but for the moment the only further point to be borne in mind is that under the amendments to the Sale of Goods Act introduced by the Supply of Goods (Implied Terms) Act, s. 13 can no longer be excluded by an exemption clause in the case of a consumer sale.[7] Moreover, in other sales, an exemption clause purporting to oust s. 13 "shall . . . not be enforceable to the extent that it is shown that it would not be fair or reasonable to allow reliance on the term".[8]

---

1 Lord GUEST, for example, having stated that the herring meal was "still herring meal notwithstanding that it may have been contaminated", went on to suggest that if "there was a substantial addition to the commodity described, then it might be that the goods plus this addition would not correspond with the description", [1972] A.C., at p. 472; [1971] 1 All E.R., at p. 858.

2 [1954] 1 Q.B. 598; [1954] 1 All E.R. 868.

3 This view was expressed *obiter* by DENNING, L.J., [1954] 1 Q.B., at p. 612, agreeing with Lord EVERSHED, M.R., *arguendo*, at p. 603.

4 Apart from any remedy under s. 14 of the Act, is it not arguable that where goods supplied are so unsuitable as to be positively harmful, a case of fundamental breach may have occurred? See below, p. 241.

5 As in *Ashington Piggeries, Ltd.* v. *Christopher Hill, Ltd.*, [1972] A.C. 441; [1971] 1 All E.R. 847.

6 In *Arcos, Ltd.* v. *E. A. Ronaasen & Sons*, [1933] A.C. 470; [1933] All E.R. Rep. 646, Lord BUCKMASTER, with whom Lord BLANESBURGH and Lord MACMILLAN agreed, decided the case without reference to s. 13; and even the reference to it by Lord ATKIN was solely for the purpose of comparison with other provisions of the Act. Lord WARRINGTON was the only member of the House to reach a decision based upon s. 13.

7 Sale of Goods Act, s. 55 (4), introduced by Supply of Goods (Implied Terms) Act, 1973, s. 4: See below, p. 226.

8 Below, p. 226.

As will be explained later, the new s. 55 (5) of the Sale of Goods contains some general guidance on the circumstances which should be taken into account when considering whether or not reliance on an exemption clause would be fair or reasonable. However, in the context of s. 13, it seems likely that the courts will also be guided by the factors which have always tended to influence their approach to this area of the law.

Prior to 1893 there was a trend that favoured (implicitly rather than explicitly) a distinction being drawn between descriptive words that went to the root of the contract and those that gave no right to the injured party to repudiate the contract, but which might or might not give rise to an action in damages.[1] The effect of s. 13 was to make all descriptive words, which were contractual, conditions of the contract, so that their breach would *prima facie* entitle the buyer to reject the goods.

In *Re Moore & Co. and Landauer & Co.*,[2] the contract was for the sale of about 3,100 cases of Australian canned fruit packed 30 tins to a case. B rejected the consignment when he discovered that half of the cases contained only 24 tins. No evidence was produced that this variation made any difference to B; indeed the umpire in the arbitration had held that there was no difference in the market value of the tins in whichever way they were packed. The Court of Appeal was obviously greatly influenced by s. 13 in deciding in B's favour. It is most unlikely that a court, faced with a similar situation prior to the Act, would have allowed a buyer to reject. SCRUTTON, L.J., made particular mention of a judgment of McCARDIE, J., in which the latter, when deciding that the tender of starch in 220 and 140 lb. bags was not a performance of a contract for the sale of starch in 280 lb. bags, had said, "If the size of the bags was immaterial I fail to see why it should have been so clearly specified in the contract."[3] This approach is clearly correct since 1893: once such a statement of fact is made, it is *prima facie* a contractual term, and s. 13 lays down that it is a condition. Prior to the Act, however, it would have been necessary for the court to have decided whether performance of the "warranty", that the tins were packed 30 to a case, constituted a condition precedent to the seller's liability, or whether it was a collateral undertaking for which the appropriate remedy was in damages. It is likely that, in such circumstances, the latter conclusion would have been preferred.[4]

---

1 The law was a confusion of overlapping concepts: particularly the division between what today are conditions and warranties (discussed below, p. 155); and the idea that breaches of certain terms automatically created a right to repudiate, while with others, the right to repudiate might only arise if the breach were sufficiently serious (see, for example, *Barker* v. *Windle* (1856), 6 E. & B. 675), a dichotomy that is still influential particularly in relation to the fundamental breach doctrine, described below, p. 239.

2 [1921] 2 K.B. 519; [1921] All E.R. Rep. 466.

3 *Manbre Saccharine Co., Ltd.* v. *Corn Products Co., Ltd.*, [1919] 1 K.B. 198, at p. 207; [1918–19] All E.R. 980, at p. 985.

4 In *Makin* v. *London Rice Mill Co., Ltd.* (1869), 20 L.T. 705, the Court of Common Pleas held, on the strength of evidence that the method of packing *was* of importance to rice as an article of commerce in the American market, that the expression "in double bags", attached to the designation "best Siam rice", "affected the quality and description of the thing sold" so that the buyer was entitled to reject rice delivered in single bags.

It could hardly be argued that the failure to pack goods in a particular fashion would be considered as breach of the fundamental obligation to deliver the goods as described in the contract. Similarly, in the absence of evidence clearly establishing the importance of the method of packing to the buyer, it would be unlikely that a court in a "non-consumer sale" would declare an exemption clause void that purported to protect the seller from such a minor breach of s. 13.

b *Delivery of the wrong quantity*

1. *The* de minimis *rule.* What constitutes the quantity of goods due under a contract can give rise to problems where an approximate amount is tendered. It is said that the *de minimis* rule applies, but what is a minute departure from the quantity specified in the contract will depend so much upon the circumstances that it is impossible to offer more than the most general guidance on how the rule operates. The factors that may influence a court are indeed various.

It is simple enough to give illustrations which appear to fall clearly outside or within the ambit of the rule. In *Harland and Wolff, Ltd.* v. *J. Burstall & Co.*,[1] the contract was for 500 loads of timber, and it was held that delivery of 470 loads would have been a non-performance of the contract which would have entitled the buyer to reject. On the other hand, in *Shipton, Anderson & Co.* v. *Weil Bros. & Co.*,[2] where the quantity of wheat specified was 10 per cent more or less than 4,500 tons, it was held that the tender of 55 lb. more than the maximum quantity of 4,950 tons allowable under such a term was nevertheless a "substantial performance" of the contract.

But appearances can be deceptive. In the latter case, LUSH, J., explained that[3]

> "the right to reject is founded upon the hypothesis that the seller was not ready and willing to perform, or had not performed, his part of the contract. The tender of a wrong quantity evidences an unreadiness and unwillingness, but that . . . must mean an excess or deficiency in quantity which is capable of influencing the mind of the buyer".

But what factors might influence this reaction? LUSH, J., continued:

> "The reason why an excess in tender entitles a buyer to reject is that the seller seeks to impose a burden on the buyer which he is not entitled to impose. That burden is the payment of money not agreed to be paid. It is *prima facie* no burden on the buyer to have 55 lbs. more than 4,950 tons offered to him . . . [but if] the sellers had expressly or impliedly insisted upon payment of the 4s. . . . the case would have been different."

If no demand for additional payment is made, it is still possible for the delivery of an excess quantity of the correct goods to impose a burden on the buyer. If he has bought to resell, the additional quantity can give rise to disputes with the sub-buyer. It would cause inconvenience to have to deduct the excess quantity before resale. The excess might not be easily disposed of either by

---

1 (1901), 84 L.T. 324.
2 [1912] 1 K.B. 574.
3 At pp. 577–8.

sale or as waste. Of course, where the quantity tendered falls short of that required by the contract, the seller is hardly in a position to argue that the buyer is receiving what he bargained for, and any diminution of price is only possible with the buyer's agreement.

Another factor that might be relevant in deciding whether the variation was excusable in terms of the *de minimis* rule is the means available for accurate measurement of the amount being delivered. In *Margaronis Navigation Agency, Ltd.* v. *Henry W. Peabody & Co. of London, Ltd.*,[1] a charterer's obligation to load a full and complete cargo of 12,600 tons of maize on a ship was not performed by the loading of 12,588 tons 4 cwt., because the silo from which the loading took place could measure and record the quantity with speed and accuracy. In contrast, though the fact was in no way decisive, in *Shipton, Anderson & Co.* v. *Weil Bros. & Co.*,[2] the excess of 55 lb. occurred because of the need to measure the quantity at the port of loading in kilos but to convert that amount into tons at the port of discharge in performance of the contract.

In cases where there has been a clear departure from the quantity stipulated in the contract, the seller has often attempted to rely on the argument that there was a trade custom, or perhaps an understanding between the parties themselves, that allowed a degree of flexibility in the amount to be delivered. In *Rapalli* v. *K. L. Take, Ltd.*,[3] for example, the contract was for 15 tons of medium sized Parma onions. At a conservative estimate, six or seven per cent were smaller than the 50/70 cm. range regarded as "medium" in size for onions. There was some evidence that, on the Continent, tolerances of up to 10 per cent were allowable on such goods. Such a variation was clearly not part of this particular contract, but it was adduced in an apparent attempt to establish a reasonable allowance in terms of the *de minimis* rule within the trade. This argument was rejected by the Court of Appeal. It would seem that in the Court's view either the practice formed part of the contract by trade usage or from the conduct and dealings of the parties, or it was irrelevant.

The disadvantage to the seller is that, in order to form part of the contract, the usage must be strictly proved[4] or his intention to qualify the contract quantity must be apparent. If he fails to establish either alternatives he will be bound by the statement of amount contained in the contract. In *Harland and Wolff, Ltd.* v. *J. Burstall & Co.*,[5] S had answered B's enquiry with a statement that he (S) had about 500 loads of the wood specified available for shipment, and followed this up by informing B that he had an offer of cargo space for 500 loads. The acceptance telegram and the subsequent contract note were in unqualified terms for 500 loads. S discovered that he only had 470 loads which he nevertheless dispatched. B rejected the goods and his action was held to be

---

1 [1965] 2 Q.B. 430; [1964] 3 All E.R. 333.
2 [1912] 1 K.B. 574.
3 [1958] 2 Lloyd's Rep. 469.
4 As in *Société Anonyme L'Industrielle Russo-Belge* v. *Scholefield & Son* (1902), 7 Com. Cas. 114.
5 (1901), 84 L.T. 324.

justified. The attempt was made to argue (i) that in the trade a seller was entitled to send "about" the quantity named; (ii) that "about" meant "within 10 per cent" and (iii) that, in any case, "about 500 tons" was what was intended by the parties from their negotiations. This contention was rejected by BIGHAM, J.: in his view, no such custom existed, nor could the use of the word "about" in the negotiations be allowed to qualify the interpretation of the document in which the contract was finally expressed.

Where some variation is allowed by the terms of the contract itself, it might be supposed that the courts would be even more reluctant to apply the *de miminis* rule to any but the smallest additional variation. While this supposition might appear logical enough, there is no real evidence that it has had any practical application. In *Payne and Routh* v. *Lillico & Sons*,[1] the contract was for 4,000 tons of South African maize meal, two per cent more or less, with the option available to S of shipping a further three per cent more or less on the contract quantity. It was envisaged that the goods could be sent in more than one consignment. In fact they were sent in two shipments. B refused both orders although only the refusal of the second came before the court. One of the reasons for this action advanced by B was that the total amount consigned exceeded the contract quantity. The excess was not denied although the extent of the variation was disputed. It could have been as great as 100 tons, although ROWLATT, J., was prepared to accept two tons as the difference for the purposes of his decision. He expressed the view that, where the parties agree what is to be the variation, it is not for the court to say that there should be any further variation. While this line of reasoning may appear to support the theory that the courts do adopt a stricter approach to a contract quantity which includes an agreed variation, ROWLATT, J's subsequent words[2] seem inconsistent with any such difference in practice:

> "If it is a matter of ounces or pounds you may disregard it. But this is a matter of tons, and it is a serious amount, [a] real amount, and I do not think that I can regard it as coming within the clause [allowing a variation]."

If the distinction is between a trivial and a real variation or difference, it is difficult to avoid the conclusion that, whether or not the parties allow some variation expressly, the approach adopted by the courts to the problem of deficiency or excess is substantially the same.

Indeed, that no distinction is drawn in practice should not cause surprise. The line of reasoning that the courts should be particularly reluctant to allow any additional variation where the parties themselves have made express provision for some variation is not in itself conclusive on the issue. It could equally well be pointed out that, if the parties contracted for a specific quantity with no variation, they must have intended that amount and that amount alone. In either case, the courts can reasonably take the view that the parties must be taken to have expressed their wishes in the terms of the contract.

---

1 (1920), 3 Ll.L.Rep. 110.
2 At p. 111.

Once it is established that a wrong quantity has been delivered, s. 30 deals with the two alternatives. By sub-s. (1):

> "Where the seller delivers to the buyer a quantity of goods less than he contracted to sell, the buyer may reject them, but if the buyer accepts the goods so delivered he must pay for them at the contract rate."

This principle is based upon two converging lines of authority. If the goods are not what the buyer ordered in quantity, he may reject the entire consignment, but, if he does accept delivery of the incomplete amount, he is both liable to pay for those goods[1] and entitled to recover *pro rata* the part of the price he has overpaid.[2]

In *Behrend & Co., Ltd.* v. *Produce Brokers Co., Ltd.*[3] B had agreed to buy 200 tons and 500 tons of two different types of cotton seed from S to be shipped in one or more vessels from Alexandria and delivered in London. Part of the goods (176 and 400 tons) was sent on a particular vessel. In London the vessel unloaded only 22 and 15 tons of the seed before proceeding to Hull to unload further cargo. The question to be decided was whether B was entitled to refuse to take delivery of the rest of the consignment (i.e. the 154 and 385 tons respectively). It was held that B was entitled to a complete delivery of the goods covered by the bill of lading. Delivery of part only of the goods entitled B, in accordance with s. 30 (1), either to reject the whole shipment, or retain part and reject the rest. As B had chosen to adopt the latter course he was clearly able to recover a substantial part of the price that he had paid against the bill of lading. Similarly, by s. 30 (2):

> "Where the seller delivers to the buyer a quantity of goods larger than he contracted to sell, the buyer may accept the goods included in the contract and reject the rest, or he may reject the whole. If the buyer accepts the whole of the goods so delivered he must pay for them at the contract rate."

2. *Delivery by instalments.* It is fundamental to the notion that the seller is under an obligation to deliver the right quantity that he should, in the absence of an agreement to the contrary, deliver that quantity and not part of it first and the rest later. In *Behrend & Co., Ltd.* v. *Produce Brokers Co., Ltd.*, which has just been considered, S delivered a small portion of the shipment of cotton seed in London and attempted to deliver the rest a fortnight later after the vessel had been to Hull to unload other cargo. It was held that, once delivery had commenced, B was entitled to delivery of the entire shipment. As s. 31 (1) of the Sale of Goods Act states:

> "Unless otherwise agreed, the buyer of goods is not bound to accept delivery thereof by instalments."

---

1 *Oxendale* v. *Wetherell* (1829), 9 B. & C. 386.
2 *Devaux* v. *Conolly* (1849), 8 C.B. 640; quite apart from any question of damages that might arise for breach of the contract.
3 [1920] 3 K.B. 530; [1920] All E.R. Rep. 125.

Although delivery by instalments will obviously be the exceptional case because many goods are simply not susceptible of separate delivery, there are nevertheless certain types of contract in which instalment delivery is implicit. A common situation that gave rise to a good deal of litigation was the practice whereby a buyer agreed to subscribe to a publication that was to be produced in separate numbers over a period of time. Delivery by instalments was inherent in such an agreement.[1]

In other cases, instalment delivery could operate by custom of the trade, or from the very nature of the goods themselves. In this context it should be borne in mind that there can be a number of individual deliveries that together constitute delivery of part or the whole of the goods due. For example, if the National Coal Board undertakes to deliver by road a large amount of coal to a power station on a specified day, it would be obvious that the coal would have to be carried in a number of separate loads. Similarly, where a large number of bags of wheat have to be delivered f.o.b. a named ship, it is not possible to load them all at once. As the Judicial Committee commented in such a case:[2]

> "In many cases of contract to supply a quantity of goods to be delivered within a fixed period, the whole quantity cannot, from the very nature of the case, be delivered at one time."

A common form of contractual undertaking arises when the seller agrees to ship the goods to the buyer by a vessel or vessels sailing within a specified period. It is generally understood that the inclusion of a provision referring to a choice between one ship or several *prima facie* constitutes the parties' agreement to instalment delivery. In *Brandt* v. *Lawrence*,[3] S had entered into two contracts to supply B with 4,500 quarters of Russian oats, both contracts specifying "shipment by steamer or steamers during February". S shipped 5,650 quarters on board one ship and offered to deliver them in satisfaction of one contract and in part satisfaction of the other. The rest of the oats were shipped on another vessel, but this was held to have been outside the period laid down in the contract. B purported to reject both the part delivery from the first ship as well as the remainder in the second ship. The Court of Appeal held that, because the contract said "shipment by steamer or steamers" B was bound by a part shipment within the contract period, even though the rest was shipped outside the contract period. It was clearly a contract which entitled S to deliver by instalments if he wished.

It is clear that this decision must have some limits placed upon it. For example, if a seller intended to complete delivery by one vessel, but had for some reason dispatched an insufficient quantity of goods, it is reasonable to suppose that he cannot then oblige the buyer to accept either the inadequate amount, or

---

1 *Boydell* v. *Drummond* (1809), 11 East 142 (18 numbers containing pictures of scenes from Shakespeare): *Mavor* v. *Pyne* (1825), 3 Bing. 285 ("The History of Royal Residences" in 24 numbers at a guinea each); *Howell* v. *Evans* (1926), 134 L.T. 570 ("The Cries of London", a series of 13 engravings, at 10 guineas each).
2 *Colonial Insurance Co. of New Zealand* v. *Adelaide Marine Insurance Co.* (1886), 12 App. Cas. 128, at p. 138.
3 (1876), 1 Q.B.D. 344.

if the buyer did wish to accept the smaller amount, a subsequent shipment of the rest of the goods. It is arguable that the decision to ship the goods on board one vessel is an election by the seller, from which he cannot later resile, of the way in which he wishes to perform the contract.

In *Reuter, Hufeland & Co.* v. *Sala & Co.*,[1] S agreed to supply B with about 25 tons more or less of black pepper, shipment from Penang to London to be during October and/or November per sailing vessel or vessels; full details to be declared within 60 days from the date of the bills of lading. S declared three bills of lading covering 500 bags of pepper (about 25 tons) on board a vessel called the *Borga*, but one of the bills, in respect of 105 bags of pepper, was dated December. In February, S attempted to declare an alternative 105 bags on board the same vessel, but shipment of which had taken place during November. S acknowledged that the declaration in respect of the alternative 105 bags was out of time but sought to recover damages for non-acceptance of the 395 bags (about 20 tons) which did satisfy the contract requirements. A majority of the Court of Appeal held that B was entitled to reject the 20 tons as well as the subsequent 5 tons. It was true that the use of the words "per sailing vessel or vessels" did show that the goods might be delivered in separate parcels which might arrive in England at different times.[2] However, once "the sellers elect to ship by one vessel the whole quantity contracted to be sold, and declare their election to the buyers ... they cannot, after it is discovered that as to a portion of the quantity shipped it was not shipped in accordance with the terms of the contract ... turn round and call upon them to accept the remaining portion"[3] from another source.

Where delivery by instalments is agreed upon, the question arises whether the party having control of the operation (the matter is usually, although not invariably, at the seller's option) has a complete discretion with regard to the amount that is dispatched in any one or group of instalments. In the absence of any provision in the contract providing for delivery in equal periodic quantities, it is doubtful to what extent the option is fettered.

In *Calaminus* v. *Dowlais Iron Co., Ltd.*,[4] B contracted to buy from S "from 5,000 to 6,000 tons of manganiferous iron ore", delivery by steamers or sailing vessels to be in the port of Cardiff during the months of June, July, August and September. During June, 2,593 tons were delivered and accepted without objection. A number of vessels reached Cardiff exceptionally quickly so that by late July an additional 2,030 tons had been tendered, making 4,623 tons within two months. But by the end of the month a further vessel was ready for unloading, having on board another 767 tons. These vessels were not unloaded until the end of August and the beginning of September. S had to pay substantial

---

1 (1879), 4 C.P.D. 239.
2 At p. 250, *per* Cotton L.J.; at p. 246, *per* Thesiger, L.J.
3 At pp. 246–7, *per* Thesiger, L.J. That the choice of means of delivery constitutes an election is also clear from *Honck* v. *Muller* (1881), 7 Q.B.D. 92, in which, under the contract, B was to decide whether to take 2,000 tons of coal in November, or in three equal instalments in November, December and January. He made no election at all, refusing to take any coal in November. S was held entitled to repudiate and be under no obligation to deliver two-thirds of the coal in December and January.
4 (1878), 47 L.J.Q.B. 575.

sums in demurrage and sought to recover the total amount from B.[1] B claimed that their cargoes were not in fact due until August and, in the case of the last ship to arrive in July, until September. LUSH, J., held that, in the light of the difficulties of guaranteeing the regular shipment of ore to Cardiff, it was hardly surprising that the contract which S had accepted allowed him a good deal of latitude, and certainly could not be interpreted as imposing on him any obligation to tender in any one month an aliquot proportion.

However, although the facts of this case suggest that a seller can tender most, if not all (5,390 tons is between 5,000 and 6,000 tons, although S apparently did intend to make a further delivery), of the goods well within the time set for the delivery of instalments, the judgment does talk in terms of an obligation "to deliver a reasonable proportion"[2] in each of the four months. Taking into account the latitude allowed by the contract and the expeditious voyages completed by the vessels, the jury had found as a fact that the tender of the 767 tons on July 30 had not been unreasonable.

The freedom of choice in the exercise of the option is also illustrated by the facts of *Behrend & Co.* v. *Produce Broker's Co., Ltd.*[3] It will be recalled that the dispute centred upon the unloading of part only of an instalment in London, the ship proceeding to Hull before returning to unload the rest of that instalment. It is interesting to note, however, that the ship was carrying 176 of 200 tons of one type of cotton seed due under one contract, and 400 of 500 tons of another type of cotton seed due under a second contract between S and B. B had made no objection to the tender of such a substantial part of the goods as 176 out of 200 tons under a contract which allowed S to ship the goods by "steamer or steamers".

B. THE DUTIES OF THE BUYER

The counterpart of the seller's duty to deliver the goods is the buyer's obligation "to accept and pay for them" in accordance with the terms of the contract (s. 27).

i Payment

According to s. 28, in the absence of any agreement to the contrary,

> "delivery of the goods and payment of the price are concurrent conditions, that is to say, the seller must be ready and willing to give possession of the goods in exchange for the price, and the buyer must be ready and willing to pay the price in exchange for possession of the goods".

The principle of "cash on delivery" is thus implicit in a contract of sale. It is applicable both to delivery of the goods and to delivery of documents of title because those documents are recognised as representing the goods.

It has already been explained that, under c.i.f. contracts, payment is due against delivery of the bill of lading and the other documents relating to the

---

1 When the case was heard, B paid the demurrage due in respect of the other vessels into court, but still maintained he was not liable to pay in respect of the vessel that arrived at the end of July.

2 47 L.J.Q.B., at p. 578; cp. the division of judicial opinion over the meaning of "Half as soon as possible. Half two months later." in *Bowes* v. *Chaleyer* (1923), 32 C.L.R. 159.

3 (1920), 25 Com. Cas. 286; the record of the facts in [1920] 3 K.B. 530 is incomplete.

carriage of the goods. In *E. Clemens Horst & Co.* v. *Biddell Bros.*,[1] S agreed to supply B with two lots of brewing hops at 90s. per 112 lb., "C.I.F. to London Liverpool or Hull. Terms net cash". A dispute arose over their obligations, B arguing that, as there was no express term providing for payment against the shipping documents he could require physical delivery of the goods for examination before making payment. The House of Lords held, expressly adopting the dissenting judgment of KENNEDY, L.J. in the Court of Appeal,[2] that delivery of the bill of lading while goods were still at sea was equivalent to delivery of the goods themselves: s. 28 was therefore satisfied and payment was due on delivery of the shipping documents.

In a number of the earlier cases[3] there was some dispute whether an action could be maintained by the buyer, who did not plead and could not establish a tender of the price, for non-delivery of the goods. It was finally settled in *Pickford* v. *Grand Junction Rail. Co.*[4] that an actual tender of money was unnecessary: "whenever a duty is cast on a party in consequence of a contemporaneous act of payment to be done by another, it is sufficient if the latter . . . be ready to pay . . . when the other is ready to undertake the duty".[5]

It similarly follows from the principle that delivery and payment are concurrent obligations that the seller does not have to establish an actual tender of the goods, but only a willingness to deliver, in return for the price. Whether property passes on delivery or at some other time, by parting with possession of the goods the seller is surrendering his lien over the goods which entitles him to retain them against payment of the price. If he can show his readiness to deliver other than by an actual tender to the buyer, then he is entitled to sue in respect of an unreadiness by the buyer to pay at the time of delivery.[6] In practice, however, it may be difficult to prove an unwillingness on the buyer's part to pay unless the seller does make a tender of the goods and payment is not forthcoming.

If this unwillingness is made manifest to the seller before the time of performance, a different principle is applicable. The situation is classified as one of anticipatory breach,[7] and the seller has the choice either of continuing to regard the contract as binding or of accepting the repudiation and treating the contract as at an end. If the seller chooses to regard the contractual obligations as continuing, then he is obliged to demonstrate his readiness and willingness to perform at the appropriate time.[8] However, once the seller accepts the repudiation, he releases himself from his obligation to perform, or to show that he was able to perform, the contract.

Although this position would seem to be straightforward, it is somewhat

---

1 [1912] A.C. 18; [1911–13] All E.R. Rep 93.
2 [1911] 1 K.B. 934; [1911–13] All E.R. Rep 93.
3 *Morton* v. *Lamb* (1797), 7 Term. Rep. 125; explained in *Rawson* v. *Johnson* (1801), 1 East 203.
4 (1841), 8 M. & W. 372.
5 At p. 378, *per* PARKE, B., giving the judgment of the Court of Exchequer.
6 See *Paynter* v. *James* (1867), L.R. 2 C.P. 348, applying this principle to a carrier's right to be paid freight on delivery of the goods and surrender of his possessory lien against payment of freight.
7 Dealt with in more detail, below, p. 322,
8 For the time of performance, see below, p. 156.

obscured by the decision of the Court of Appeal in *Braithwaite* v. *Foreign Hardwood Co.*[1] S had agreed to deliver by instalments 100 tons of Honduras rosewood to be shipped c.i.f. London, Hull or Liverpool during 1903. In early October, 1903, B discovered that S had sold a quantity of rosewood to a London merchant contrary to a collateral undertaking B alleged that S had given him. For breach of this undertaking, B purported to repudiate the contract. S nevertheless tendered the bills of lading in respect of the first two shipments, but these were refused by B. B later discovered that the first shipment was not in conformity with the contract because part of the wood was inferior in quality. The Court of Appeal appeared to decide that B could not rely upon the inadequate standard of the first shipment as an excuse for refusing to accept it because B had, by reiterating his refusal to accept on the basis of the alleged collateral undertaking when the bill of lading was presented, waived his right to rely upon the defective nature of the goods.

This approach is in conflict with the well established rule that a party who gives a bad reason for determining a contract is not prevented at a later stage from relying on a good one, whether he only discovers it subsequently, or, presumably, even if he had been aware of it all along.[2] It is possible to effect some degree of reconciliation if one accepts the explanation of the decision put forward by GREER, J., in *Taylor* v *Oakes Roncoroni & Co.* :[3] in his view, *Braithwaite's* case

> "decided that if the buyer wrongfully repudiates his contract, and the seller does not tender performance on his part, but accepts the repudiation and claims damages, the buyer is not released from liability by proving that if he had not repudiated the contract, but called for its performance, the seller would have been unable or unwilling to perform it . . . [or] would have tendered goods which he, the buyer, would have been justified in rejecting".

But even this explanation is unsatisfactory in so far as it was based upon drawing a distinction between an offer to tender the shipping documents and an actual tender of them.[4] However, it does seem possible to accept GREER, J.'s conclusion on the basis that the seller did in fact accept the buyer's repudiation when it was first communicated to him,[5] or at least at some time prior to

---

1 [1905] 2 K.B. 543.
2 *Taylor* v. *Oakes Roncoroni & Co.* (1922), 27 Com. Cas. 261, at pp. 266, 268, *per* GREER, J.; *British and Benningtons, Ltd.* v. *North Western Cachar Tea Co., Ltd.*, [1923] A.C. 48, at pp. 71–2, *per* Lord SUMNER, with whom Lords BUCKMASTER and CARSON concurred; Lord WRENBURY also concurred, presumably also with Lord SUMNER; and for a more recent statement of the rule see *Maredelanto Compania Naviera S.A.* v. *Bergbau-Handel G.m.b.H.* (*The Mihalis Angelos*), [1971] 1 Q.B. 164, at p. 193; [1970] 3 All E.R. 125, at p. 128, *per* Lord DENNING, M.R.
3 (1922), 27 Com. Cas. 261, at pp. 265–6.
4 At pp. 267–8; though this explanation was approved of as being the "key" to the case by SALMON, L.J., in *Esmail* v. *J. Rosenthal & Sons, Ltd.*, [1964] 2 Lloyd's Rep. 447, at p. 466.
  This was in fact argued on the seller's behalf, according to the report in 10 Com. Cas. 189, at p. 193, though the trial judge's finding is reported so sparsely (at p. 191) as to make it impossible to decide whether the repudiation was accepted. SCRUTTON, L.J., who had been the seller's counsel in *Braithwaite's* case, later expressly stated that it was decided on the basis that his client had "promptly accepted the buyer's refusal to perform": *North-Western Cachar Tea Co., Ltd.* v. *British and Benningtons, Ltd.* (1921), 10 Ll. L. Rep. 381, at p. 387.

the tender of the documents. Nevertheless doubts do persist over *Braithwaite's* case. In *British and Benningtons, Ltd. v. North Western Cachar Tea Co.,*[1] Lord SUMNER expressed those doubts in a different form. Either, by his rejection of the bills of lading and his refusal to have anything further to do with the transaction, B was waiving any right to insist upon due performance by S of his part of the contract, or the case was wrongly reported or decided.

If a choice has to be made between different views of *Braithwaite's* case, Lord SUMNER'S suggestion that B was waiving his right to insist upon due performance has much to commend it. If there is a contract for, say, the manufacture of goods to be delivered in instalments, and, after some of them are supplied, the buyer informs the seller that he does not want the rest and will not accept them if they are delivered, the seller is absolved (if he accepts the repudiation) from the obligation of making the goods.[2] "The party must show he was ready; but if the other stops him on the ground of an intention not to perform his part, it is not necessary for the first to go further and do a nugatory act."[3] The buyer has waived his right to insist upon the manufacture and tender of the goods, and the most he can demand of the seller is to demonstrate an apparent readiness to perform at the time the repudiation is accepted. In *Braithwaite's* case, S was apparently in a position to perform: the defects in the goods were irrelevant to the position of the parties, although it would be a factor to be taken into account in the assessment of damages.

ii Acceptance

It will be recalled that according to s. 27, it is the duty of the buyer, "to accept and pay for" the goods. However, while the obligation to pay arises, in the absence of evidence to the contrary, at the time when the goods are delivered, the obligation to accept them does not necessarily operate at that moment. It would be more accurate to expand s. 27 to show that the buyer's duty is more complex: it is to receive the goods (that is, take them into his custody or have them taken into custody on his behalf) and, usually at some later stage, to accept the goods. The duty to accept does come into being on delivery, though the duty is not broken if acceptance is not immediate. Section 34 (1) provides:

> "Where goods are delivered to the buyer, which he has not previously examined, he is not deemed to have accepted them unless and until he has had a reasonable opportunity of examining them for the purpose of ascertaining whether they are in conformity with the contract."

The implication in s. 27 that acceptance as well as payment should occur on delivery is probably a relic of days when sale was a relatively unsophisticated transaction between individuals. This explanation is borne out by s. 34 (2) which appears to be based upon a similar philosophy:

> "Unless otherwise agreed, when the seller tenders delivery of goods to the buyer, he is bound, on request, to afford the buyer a reasonable opportunity

---

1 [1923] A.C. 48, at pp. 70–2.
2 *Cort* v. *Ambergate Rail. Co.* (1851), 17 Q.B. 127, esp. at p. 148.
3 *Jones* v. *Barkley* (1781), 2 Dougl. 684, at p. 694, per Lord Mansfield.

of examining the goods for the purpose of ascertaining whether they are in conformity with the contract."

It is implicit in a number of cases which will be considered shortly[1] that a buyer is entitled to the opportunity of examining the goods and no question was raised that this right is dependent upon any request on his part that he should be allowed to do so. In other words, s. 34 (1) is the guiding principle, and s. 34 (2) is largely ignored in practice.

The buyer retains the right to reject the goods as not being in conformity with the contract (i.e. as not answering a condition of the contract) until he does accept them. What constitutes an acceptance is set out in s. 35:

> "The buyer is deemed to have accepted the goods when he intimates to the seller that he has accepted them, or (except when section 34 of this Act otherwise provides) when the goods have been delivered to him, and he does any act in relation to them which is inconsistent with the ownership of the seller, or when after the lapse of a reasonable time, he retains the goods without intimating to the seller that he has rejected them."

a *Express acceptance*

The first part of s. 35, that an intimation by the buyer that he accepts the goods as being in conformity with the contract amounts to an acceptance of those goods, may appear to be a statement of the obvious. However, unless the buyer actually writes in so many words to inform the seller that he has had an opportunity of examining the goods and that they are in conformity with the contract, a mere acknowledgment of their receipt will not amount to an acceptance under s. 35.[2]

b *Any act inconsistent with the seller's ownership*

1 *Interpretation of B's actions.* At first sight this part of s. 35 may seem straightforward enough. If the buyer, having received goods, indulges in some activity which is tantamount to an assertion of ownership on his part, he will be taken to have accepted them in performance of the contract. In the old case of *Parker* v. *Palmer*[3] B discovered that some samples taken from the bulk of rice he had purchased were inferior in quality to samples that had been shown to him at the time of the contract. B nevertheless went ahead with a proposed auction of the rice. As the bidding did not reach the price B required, the rice was bought on B's behalf. B subsequently refused to pay for the rice on the ground that it was not equal to sample. It was held that, by his conduct, B had accepted the goods so that he was no longer able to reject them as not corresponding with the sample given by S.

The question whether an act is inconsistent with S's ownership will be

---

1 Below, p. 138.
2 See *Saunders* v. *Topp* (1849), 4 Exch. 39; *Abbot & Co.* v. *Wolsey*, [1895] 2 Q.B. 97; on the need to distinguish between a receipt of the goods and an acceptance of them (i.e. any act by the buyer in relation to the goods that recognised a pre-existing contract of sale) within s. 4 of the Act which was repealed by s. 1 of the Law Reform (Enforcement of Contracts) Act, 1954.
3 (1821), 4 B. & Ald. 387; see also *Chapman* v. *Morton* (1843), 11 M. & W. 534.

affected by the circumstances of the case including, in many situations, the issue of whether the goods have been retained for longer than a reasonable time. Retention of the goods as a separate basis of acceptance will be dealt with more specifically below, but, for the moment, an illustration can be given of how the time necessary for a reasonable trial can affect the interpretation to be placed upon B's conduct.

In *Long* v. *Lloyd*,[1] B sought to rescind a contract under which he had purchased a lorry on the ground that a number of statements made by S about the "excellent condition" of the vehicle had proved to be untrue. The Court of Appeal held that, even if a right to rescind had existed,[2] it had been lost. What constituted a reasonable time for inspection required, at least in the circumstances of S's representations about the petrol consumption and speed of which the vehicle was capable, a test drive over some distance. B had in fact driven the vehicle to his home and then on a business run the next day. He had then complained of a number of defects and S had agreed to "go halves" on the cost of a reconstructed dynamo. The Court expressed the view that it was probably at this stage too late for B to reject the goods, but certainly sending the lorry off with his brother on a business run to the north of England "conclusively extinguished" any right of rescission B may have had.[3]

2 *B's right to examine the goods.* A factor which has created the greater difficulty in the application of s. 35, however, has been its relationship with B's right to examine the goods. In the first place, in the absence of anything in the contract or the circumstances that establish the contrary, the place of examination is the place of delivery.

This principle was confirmed on the eve of the passing of the Sale of Goods Act by the Court of Appeal in *Perkins* v. *Bell*.[4] B purchased by sample barley from S under a contract made at S's stall at Leicester market. The barley was to be delivered to a roadside railway station two and a half miles from B's farm. As S thought probable, B resold the goods and had quantities of barley delivered to the sub-buyers. These goods were rejected because the barley was of inferior quality. B sought to set aside his contract with S. It was held that he had lost his right of rejection, *inter alia*, because the railway station was the place at which any inspection should have taken place. S knew of no other place: there was nothing which suggested that an adequate inspection could not have been carried out there. In the Court's own words,[5] there was "no evidence in this case to dislodge the presumption which *prima facie* arises, that the place of delivery is the place for inspection".

But what kind of circumstances will rebut this *prima facie* presumption? It could well be argued that if B, writing from a particular address, contracts with S by correspondence on the basis that the goods are to be delivered at a

---

1 [1958] 2 All E.R. 402.
2 The claim was made on the ground of "innocent misrepresentation", not for "breach of condition" (see further below, p. 259). The Court appears to have been guided by the same principles that would be applicable to decide whether or not goods had been accepted under s. 35.
3 [1958] 2 All E.R., at p. 408.
4 [1893] 1 Q.B. 193.
5 At p. 197.

station for him (B) to collect and to take to his (B's) place of business, then that place will be where any inspection should be carried out. This view was certainly that adopted by the New Zealand Court of Appeal in *Canterbury Seed Co., Ltd.* v. *J. G. Ward Farmers' Association, Ltd.*[1] in which *Perkins* v. *Bell* was distinguished:

> "Where ... a merchant by correspondence orders goods from another at a distance, the purchaser has a right to inspect at the place which will be reasonably supposed to be in the minds of the parties [as] the destination of the goods; and that, in the absence of any special circumstances or incidents in the contract, must ... be taken to be the place where the purchaser carries on business."

As delivery can take place at a variety of places over which the buyer has little control (in some circumstances, when put in the hands of a carrier;[2] sometimes when goods are unloaded at a dock or railway terminal), the presumption linking the place of delivery and the place of inspection should be regarded as one that can readily be rebutted.

Existence of the presumption has been the cause of difficulty in relation to shipping contracts. Under f.o.b. contracts, delivery takes place when the goods are placed on board ship.[3] Does this fact raise an inference that the buyer should inspect at that stage in transit? The view generally expressed is that the goods need not be examined until they are received by the buyer at their destination.[4] However, it is not altogether clear that such a principle can be deduced from the case law.

In *Boks & Co.* v. *J. H. Rayner & Co.*,[5] B had bought 30 tons of palm oil f.o.b. Antwerp. In performance of this contract, S had shipped 79 casks of oil from Antwerp to Liverpool. There B inspected the goods, found 58 casks contained oil not of the contract quality, and purported to reject the whole consignment. The arbitrators held *inter alia* that there was nothing to rebut the normal presumption that the place of inspection was the place of delivery, that is Antwerp where B had a representative who could have examined the goods. They also found a trade custom that under f.o.b. contracts the examination should take place at or before shipment. The Court of Appeal rejected this latter finding, and held that, simply by not taking advantage of an opportunity of inspecting the goods at Antwerp, B did not deprive himself of the right of rejecting at Liverpool.

In contrast, in *J. and J. Cunningham, Ltd.* v. *Robert A. Munro & Co., Ltd.*[6] B had purchased from S 200 tons of bran f.o.b. Rotterdam. After 384 bags had been loaded on the ship named by B, it was discovered that the bran had heated after 14 days lying in barges and B refused to accept any more bags. It is significant in the present context that B made no attempt to reject the 384

---

1 (1894), 13 N.Z.L.R. 96, at p. 108.
2 See above, p. 113.
3 See above, p. 22, n. 3.
4 See, for example, Schmithoff, *Sale of Goods*, 2nd Ed. p. 144; Halsbury, 3rd Ed., Vol. 34, p. 178 (though subject to the "circumstances of the case").
5 (1921), 37 T.L.R. 519; affirmed 37 T.L.R. 800.
6 (1922), 28 Com. Case 42.

bags and it seems to have been assumed by the court that he had already accepted them. Indeed the basis of its interpretation of the rights and obligations of the parties was the principle that, subject to anything in the contract or the conduct of the parties suggesting otherwise, it was for B to reject the goods when S placed them on the ship's rail.[1] The uncertainty that stems from this decision was reflected in the judgment of Lord STERNDALE, M.R., in *J. W. Schofield & Sons v. Rownson, Drew and Clydesdale, Ltd.*:[2]

> "I was at first inclined to think that on a f.o.b. contract there would be a *prima facie* rule that the goods should be examined at the place of destination. But looking at the cases, I doubt very much whether there is any *prima facie* rule at all. I am inclined to think . . . the question of whether there has been reasonable opportunity of examination before shipment where the goods are to be put free on board is a question to be decided in the particular case on its circumstances."

It may be asked whether it is a satisfactory state of affairs that the place of inspection under a f.o.b. contract should be left in such uncertainty. If there is no opportunity, or no reasonable facilities, for inspecting at the port of loading, it is clear that the examination should take place at the destination. But even if the opportunity does exist for examining the goods prior to shipment, there seems to be no obligation on the buyer to carry out an inspection, in the absence of anything expressly stated in the contract or to be implied from the circumstances requiring him to do so. Despite the reluctance of the courts to acknowledge its existence, there would seem to be sound practical reasons favouring a presumption that under a f.o.b. contract the inspection should take place at the destination of the goods.

The final question to be answered, of course, is what is meant by "destination". It is a question which can only be answered in the wider context of where it is reasonable for the buyer to carry out a satisfactory examination. If he has the goods stored at or in the vicinity of the docks prior to resale, then it is his responsibility to give himself the opportunity of, and facilities for, examining the goods. If the goods are held at the docks temporarily in the course of transit to the buyer's premises elsewhere, then much will depend upon the nature of the goods, and even their packing.[3] If the buyer receives a consignment of bacon at the docks, he may not be able to tell whether it is the type of bacon he agreed to buy until he can open up the packaging; and this might be unreasonable for him to do until he takes the bacon to his own premises.[4]

With respect to c.i.f. contracts, there can be no question of inspection (unless specifically provided for in the contract) prior to, or at the time of, shipment. Property passes not on delivery of the goods, but on delivery of the shipping documents.[5] Accordingly the first opportunity that the buyer has of examining

---

1 At pp. 45–6.
2 (1922), 10 Ll. L.R. 480, at p. 482.
3 This aspect is dealt with below in relation to sub-sales: see pp. 142 *et seq.*
4 *B. & P. Wholesale Distributors v. Marko,* [1953] C.L.Y. 3266. It may also be possible for a buyer to reject when he discovers a latent defect which a previous examination failed to reveal: see below, p. 143.
5 See above, p. 113.

the goods is when they are unloaded. The place of that examination will depend upon the type of goods and the circumstances of the case in the same way as under a f.o.b. contract.

There is, of course, a logical difficulty in that the right to examine goods presupposes a right to reject them if they do not satisfy the contract requirements. But how can a right to reject exist if property has already passed in the goods at the time when the documents were transferred to the buyer? The answer to this apparent inconsistency is that a buyer has a right to reject both the documents and the goods. Acceptance of the documents has the effect of passing title, but it is only a conditional title; a title which the buyer is entitled to terminate or convert into a full title by his acceptance of the goods. As DEVLIN, J., explained in *Kwei Tek Chao* v. *British Traders and Shippers, Ltd.*:[1]

> "the true view is that what the buyer obtains, when the title under the documents is given to him, is the property in the goods, subject to the condition that they revest if upon examination he finds them to be not in accordance with the contract. That means that he gets only conditional property in the goods, the condition being a condition subsequent. All his dealings with the documents are dealings only with that conditional property in the goods. It follows, therefore, that there can be no dealing which is inconsistent with the seller's ownership unless he deals with something more than the conditional property".

3. *The position with respect to other sub-sales.* A transaction which would be inconsistent with the seller's ownership (or, as DEVLIN, J., put it in such circumstances, his "reversionary interest") would be a dealing with the goods after they had been delivered at their destination. In *Hardy & Co.* v. *Hillerns and Fowler,*[2] B had taken up the shipping documents and had received part of a cargo of wheat. This portion they sold and dispatched to sub-buyers. It was then discovered that the wheat was not in accordance with the contract. Notice of this fact was given to S within two days of the wheat being unloaded. Even though this was held to be before a reasonable time for examination of the goods had expired, the Court of Appeal was emphatic that the transfer of the goods to the sub-buyers was an act inconsistent with the seller's ownership.

The danger inherent in this decision was that it cast doubt on a number of earlier authorities[3] which had tried to establish a balance between s. 35 and s. 34 by suggesting that, in appropriate circumstances, where a sub-sale was clearly contemplated, the place of ultimate delivery to the sub-buyers would be considered the place of inspection. This danger became apparent with the case of *E & S Ruben, Ltd.* v. *Faire Bros. & Co., Ltd.*[4] B agreed to buy by sample some lengths of rubber material. When B placed this order he had already arranged a sub-sale of the rubber to T, so at the same time B arranged for S to deliver the goods direct to T. When T received the goods he rejected them as being unsuitable and not in accordance with the sample. HILBERY, J., held that B was not entitled to reject the goods himself because he had lost this right.

---

1 [1954] 2 Q.B. 459, at p. 487; [1954] 1 All E.R. 779, at p. 796.
2 [1923] 2 K.B. 490; [1923] All E.R. Rep. 275.
3 These are dealt with below, p. 143.
4 [1949] 1 K.B. 254; [1949] 1 All E.R. 215.

By instructing S to send the goods to T, B must be deemed to have taken delivery at S's place of business. The dispatch of the goods to T was an act, carried out by S on B's behalf, that was inconsistent with S's rights of ownership.

This position in relation to sub-sales was obviously totally unsatisfactory from the buyer's point of view. Hence, rather belatedly, Parliament made some attempt to remedy the position by including in the Misrepresentation Act a provision (s. 4 (2)) which inserts in s. 35 of the Sale of Goods Act, the words

> "(except where s. 34 of the Act otherwise provides)"

before the second part of s. 35:

> "when the goods have been delivered to him, and he does any act in relation to them which is inconsistent with the ownership of the seller".

It cannot be claimed that the attempt was particularly well conceived. Although the criticism was voiced of *Ruben* v. *Faire* that it made s. 34 subject to s. 35, instead of vice-versa, making s. 34 the governing provision in this imprecise way does not provide a complete solution to the difficulties. It is true that s. 34 requires that the buyer should have a reasonable opportunity of examining the goods before he is deemed to accept them. Accordingly, *Ruben* v. *Faire* is no longer correct in so far as it held that, by instructing S to send the goods direct to T, B lost his right to reject because the dispatch of the goods by S on his behalf was an act inconsistent with S's ownership: s. 34 now requires that B should have a reasonable opportunity for examining the goods before he is deemed to accept them. *Hardy* v. *Hillerns* would similarly be affected in that the sale of the portion of the wheat occurred before it was possible to test enough of the wheat to discover whether the consignment as a whole was in accordance with the contract.

However, the amendment to s. 35 does not altogether clear the air as far as another group of decisions is concerned, one of which, *Molling & Co.* v. *Dean & Sons, Ltd.*,[1] was expressly doubted in *Hardy & Co.* v. *Hillerns and Fowler.*[2] In the former case, S, a firm of printers in Germany, contracted to supply B with toy books, some of which were for resale to a New York publisher. The consignment destined for America was specially packed by S for the voyage to New York. B received the packages in London, but sent them straight on to America without examining them. The New York publisher rejected the goods as they were defectively printed. It was held by a Divisional Court that it was not unreasonable for the Official Referee to hold that, as S knew the goods were destined for America and had packed them for the voyage there, the proper place of inspection was the destination of the books (i.e. where they were received by the sub-buyer).

Making s. 35 subject to s. 34 does not affect the situation where goods are delivered to B who refrains from examining them. However, there seems good reason for ignoring the doubts expressed in *Hardy & Co.* v. *Hillerns and Fowler* on the basis that *Molling* v. *Dean* is in keeping with the spirit behind the amend-

---

1 (1901), 18 T.L.R. 217.
2 [1923] 2 K.B., at p. 497; [1923] All E.R. Rep., at p. 278, *per* BANKES, L.J.

ment to s. 35. Indeed the latter decision gains some support from two later judgments at first instance by BAILHACHE, J. In *Van den Hurk* v. *R. Martens & Co., Ltd*,[1] S agreed to supply B with sodium sulphate. He sent it in drums to B in Manchester, but was aware that it was for export. Because of the nature of the substance, it was not possible to open the drums until the time came to use their contents. When the drums reached the sub-buyers in Lyons and Genoa it was discovered that they contained caustic soda of inferior quality which the sub-buyers rejected. The decision concerned the assessment of damages, but in a subsequent case[2] BAILHACHE, J., explained the principle upon which it was based:

> "In order to postpone the place of inspection it is necessary that there should be two elements: the original vendor must know, either because he is told or by necessary inference, that the goods are going further on, and the place at which he delivers must either be unsuitable in itself or the nature or packing of the goods must make inspection at the place unreasonable."

While one can perhaps be critical of some of the phraseology used, the position can be summed up by saying that, either by the apparent agreement of the parties at the outset, or by their assent in performing the contract, the place of inspection can be varied to affect the application of s. 35, even where the buyer has not taken advantage of the possibility of examining the goods once they are in his hands. What is a reasonable opportunity of examining the goods is a factor which operates subject to the apparent intentions of the parties. In *Molling* v. *Dean* the place of examination was established according to those intentions. In *Van den Hurk* v. *Martens*, the place was established by reference to the knowledge of the seller in the context of the nature of the goods and the way in which they had to be "packaged" for transit.

Coupled with the amendment to s. 35, this approach to the existing authorities will give a degree of flexibility to the need to balance the rights of buyer and seller in this type of situation. Similarly the requirement that the opportunity for examination should be reasonable must be viewed in relation to the types of fault such an examination is likely to reveal. It might not be possible until the goods are put into use that certain types of defect become apparent.[3] In such a situation it would be logical to suppose that a "reasonable opportunity" only covers defects which an examination conducted in those circumstances would reveal. Although the question has several times been discussed in relation to comparing the bulk with sample of how thorough the testing can be, there is little authority in relation to latent defects. In *Heilbutt* v. *Hickson*,[4] S contracted to make and supply B with 30,000 army shoes as per sample. The shoes were to be delivered in weekly instalments to a wharf where they were to be examined and their quality approved, and the price was to be paid. It was known by S that the shoes were for delivery to the French army. However, it was not reasonable to inspect quantities of the shoes to discover what filling had been used

---

1 [1920] 1 K.B. 850.
2 *Saunt* v. *Belcher and Gibbons* (1920), 26 Com. Cas. 115, at p. 119.
3 If seed is guaranteed as "good growing seed" it is hardly possible to test it without using it: see *Poulton* v. *Lattimore* (1829), 9 B. & C. 259.
4 (1872), L.R. 7 C.P. 438.

in the soles. B suspected that paper may have been used which would have rendered the shoes useless for army purposes. He only took delivery on the strength of a written undertaking by S to take the shoes back if paper was discovered in them and the French army rejected them. In the event, paper was discovered in a large percentage of the shoes; they were rejected by the French military authorities; and B claimed to be entitled to return them to S. A majority of the Court of Common Pleas held that S's written undertaking varied the terms of the original contract and entitled B to return the shoes to S. With this conclusion BRETT, J., also agreed, but he went on to state that, in his view, even without the written undertaking, B would have been entitled to return the goods. Because of the nature of the defect, the first possible opportunity of an adequate inspection was at their destination. In BRETT, J.'s own words:[1]

> "By the necessary inefficacy of the inspection in London—an inefficacy caused by this kind of fault, *viz.* a secret defect of manufacture which the defendants' servants committed—the apparent inspection in London could be of no more practical effect than no inspection at all. If it could be of no practical effect, there could not . . . be any effective, and, therefore, any real practical inspection until an inspection at Lille."

Although this was a minority opinion expressed by BRETT, J., it has generally been preferred for the very obvious reason that it commends itself to common sense. And it has some support from cases dealing with the principle, considered below, that the question of what is a reasonable time within which the goods must be rejected is dependent in part upon the nature of the defect. If a latent defect comes to light at a subsequent time, whether the buyer can still reject must be considered in relation to the length of time that has elapsed. But it is clear that the existence of a latent defect can be sufficient justification for an earlier "acceptance" of the goods being disregarded.

c *Retention of the goods*

From what has been said already it will be apparent that what is the lapse of a reasonable time is not entirely free from difficulty. It is obvious enough that a comparatively short period will be sufficient to deprive the buyer of his right to reject once he has discovered that the goods are defective. As soon as this discovery is made, many cases refer to a need for an immediate communication of rejection. In *Milner* v. *Tucker*,[2] it was discovered that a chandelier ordered from S was inadequate to light B's assembly rooms as promised. Instead of giving notice immediately, B retained the chandelier for nearly six months. It was held that B could no longer set up a right to reject as a defence to an action for the price. Similarly, if the buyer retains the goods for an unreasonable time before making an examination, he will not be allowed later to reject them.[3]

Perhaps the most difficult problem arises where the defect is latent and a

---

1 At pp. 456–7.
2 (1823), 1 Car. & P. 15; *Cash* v. *Giles* (1828), 3 C. & P. 407.
3 See, for example, *Percival* v. *Blake* (1826), 2 C. & P. 514. The actual time may be limited by custom: *Sanders* v. *Jameson* (1848), 2 Car. & Kir. 557; or, of course, by the contract: *Sharp* v. *Great Western Rail. Co.* (1841), 9 M. & W. 7. The period can also be extended by S's conduct: *Lucy* v. *Mouflet* (1860), 5 H. & N. 229.

considerable time elapses before it is discovered. If BRETT, J's judgment in *Heilbut* v. *Hickson*[1] in fact accurately states the law, the existence of a latent defect can prevent the seller relying upon earlier conduct of the buyer that would normally have constituted an acceptance of the goods. But for how long is the seller subject to this risk (albeit slight) of a buyer rejecting goods months, or even years, later? It would seem that the time for rejection in respect of a latent defect is limited by the overriding test of reasonableness. In *Leaf* v. *International Galleries*,[2] B had purchased a picture, described as a Constable, in 1944. In 1949 he tried to sell it at Christie's and was informed that it was not by Constable. He sought rescission of the contract. The Court of Appeal rejected his claim. Even though he had no idea that the picture was not genuine, his right to reject had been lost after such a long period of time.

C. REJECTION

i What constitutes rejection

If the buyer does not accept goods, and in order that his conduct should not be taken to constitute acceptance, he must notify the seller of his rejection of the goods. However, unless the parties have agreed otherwise, there is no obligation on the buyer to return the goods to the seller. In *Grimoldby* v. *Wells*,[3] S agreed to sell B four quarters of tares. These were delivered to B's cart part of the way between S's premises and B's residence. The tares were thence taken to B's residence, and later transferred to B's barn. B informed S almost immediately that the tares were not equal to sample, but they remained in B's barn until the time of the action. The Court of Common Pleas held that the county court judge had been wrong in holding that B was under a duty to return the goods in addition to making clear to S that he rejected them. This principle was reproduced in s. 36 of the Sale of Goods Act as follows:

> "Unless otherwise agreed, where goods are delivered to the buyer, and he refuses to accept them, having the right so to do, he is not bound to return them to the seller, but it is sufficient if he intimates to the seller that he refuses to accept them."

Even though the buyer is not obliged to return the goods to the seller (unless required to do so by the terms of the contract, or because of some trade usage or course of dealings between the parties), he is still under a duty to make them available for collection by the seller. Hence, the right of rejection is dependent upon the buyer being in possession, or able to resume possession, of the goods in order that the seller should be able to collect them. Accordingly, if the buyer has in fact sold and delivered the goods, and his sub-buyer does not wish to return them, the buyer's right of rejection will be lost and he will be obliged to rely on his remedy in damages. Indeed the judgments of the Court of Appeal

---

1 (1872), L.R. 7 C.P. 438; above, p. 143.
2 [1950] 2 K.B. 86; [1950] 1 All E.R. 693.
3 (1875), L.R. 10 C.P. 391, applying dicta of MARTIN, B., and BRAMWELL, B., in *Lucy* v. *Mouflet* (1860), 5 H. & N., at pp. 233–4; and explaining *Couston* v. *Chapman* (1872), L.R. 2 Sc. & Div. 250, H.L.

in *Hardy & Co.* v. *Hillerns and Fowler*[1] went further in suggesting that, at the time of rejection the buyer must actually be in a position himself to let the seller have the goods. As BANKES, L.J., said:[2]

> "Where under a contract of sale goods are delivered to the buyer which are not in accordance with the contract, so that the buyer has a right to reject them, the seller upon receipt of notice of rejection is entitled to have the goods placed at his disposal so as to allow of his resuming possession forthwith, and if the buyer has done any act which prevents him from so resuming possession that act is necessarily inconsistent with his right. It is not enough that the buyer should . . . be in a position to give the seller possession at some later date, he must be able to do so at the time of the rejection."

ii Position after rejection

Assuming that a rejection has been effectively made, the question arises as to how the parties stand in relation to goods which are in the hands of the buyer. The buyer is clearly a bailee of the goods, but he is no longer buyer under a contract of sale which he has brought to an end. Accordingly any subsequent dealings with the goods would not vivify the contract although the seller could consent, expressly or by implication from his conduct, to what would be a new transaction whether on the same, or different, terms as the original agreement. A subsequent dealing, unless consented to by the seller, would amount to a conversion of the seller's goods, although property could well pass to the sub-buyer under s. 25 (2) of the Sale of Goods Act. The buyer would certainly be a person who had agreed to buy goods, and who had obtained possession of them with the seller's consent, so that a delivery by the buyer to the sub-buyer would be effective to pass title.[3]

If the seller refrains from collecting the goods after rejection, the buyer is in the difficult position of having to decide what rights and obligations he has towards the goods. The buyer must, as part of his duty to take reasonable care of the goods, pay whatever charges are necessary for their storage or upkeep. In order to make the seller liable for such charges, the buyer must show an actual tender of the goods back to the seller, and a refusal by the seller to receive them. However, the seller will only be liable during a reasonable time by the end of which the buyer is entitled to sell the goods and to recover from the seller his loss on the transaction.[4]

iii Reasons for rejection

In the next chapter the discussion will centre on the terms of the contract of sale. By way of introduction it should be borne in mind that a buyer is entitled to reject the goods for a failure by the seller to perform a condition precedent

---

1 [1923] 2 K.B. 490; [1923] All E.R. Rep. 275.
2 [1923] 2 K.B., at p. 496 (the passage does not appear in the very different report of BANKES, L.J.'s judgment in [1923] All E.R. Rep., at pp. 277–8); and *per* ATKIN, L.J., [1923] 2 K.B., at p. 499; [1923] All E.R. Rep., at p. 280.
3 See above, p. 80.
4 *Chesterman* v. *Lamb* (1834), 2 Ad. & E. 129, applying Selwyn, *Nisi Prius*, 8th Ed., Vol. 1, p. 657; see also *Caswell* v. *Coare* (1809), 1 Taunt. 566.

to the buyer's liability to accept and pay for them. Although this breach may take the form of a failure to perform the contract at all,[1] it will more normally arise out of some express or implied undertaking in the contract itself. The extent of the buyer's rights to reject is therefore dependent upon the range of obligations which the seller has accepted as part of the contract of sale.

---

1 See above, pp. 117 *et seq.*

CHAPTER 5

The Bases of the Buyer's Remedies

A REMEDIES BASED UPON THE SELLER'S MISSTATEMENTS[1]

Leaving aside for the moment the question whether the buyer is entitled to reject the goods or has to content himself with a remedy in damages; there are a number of initial problems of classification that have to be resolved. Although a seller may make a variety of statements about the goods to be sold, the position of the buyer, should these statements prove to be inaccurate, depends upon whether or not these statements form part of the contract. If they are part of the contract, their inaccuracy gives the buyer a remedy for breach of contract. If they fall outside the contract, the buyer may be able to sue in tort (for fraud or negligence), or rely upon the provisions of the Misrepresentation Act 1967.

i Representations as terms of the contract

In the course of negotiating a contract, the seller may have made a number of statements about the goods he is offering to the buyer. It is generally held that a distinction must be drawn in such a case between statements which form part of the contract, and those which are "mere representations", having no contractual effect. How such a distinction is made, however, is a question which has produced a number of seemingly inconsistent answers,[2] and some explanation is necessary on the sources of the confusion.

a Historical origins

The remedy available to the buyer who claimed to have bought goods on the strength of a seller's representations which later proved to be false was an action in tort for deceit. At the beginning of the seventeenth century, to take a convenient starting point, it was established that an action on the case for deceit would lie providing the plaintiff pleaded and could establish either (1) that the seller had knowingly made the false assertion, or (2) that he had warranted the goods, thereby assuming responsibility for the truth of what he had said.[3]

---

1 A good deal of the material for this section appeared in (1971), 87 L.Q.R. 179–213.
2 See Cheshire and Fifoot, *Law of Contract*, 7th Ed., pp. 105–10; and cf. 8th ed., pp. 110–15.
3 *Chandelor* v. *Lopus* (1603), Cro. Jac. 4.

148

By this time it was no longer necessary for particular words to be used (such as "I warrant"), but it was essential to show that there had been a representation of fact, and not an expression of opinion.[1] The basis of the action was the deception of the plaintiff. In deciding this issue, the court took account of such factors as whether what the defendant had said concerned a matter likely to be better known to him, and not easily checked by the plaintiff,[2] or whether the representation had the effect of dissuading the plaintiff from making his own inspection.[3]

Sometime around the middle of the eighteenth century actions alleging the falseness of the defendant's warranty began to be pleaded in *assumpsit*.[4] Because of a number of advantages to the plaintiff in this form of action, *assumpsit* rapidly took over the contractual role formerly fulfilled by the action in deceit. However, its affinity with the tort action was still clear from the significance attached in claims for breach of warranty to the need for a statement of fact as the test of whether the statement made was intended to constitute a warranty. In *Power* v. *Barham*,[5] for example, the defendant had signed a bill evidencing the sale of "Four pictures. Views in Venice. Canaletto" to the plaintiff. The plaintiff discovered that the pictures were not by that artist and claimed damages for breach of warranty. COLERIDGE, J.'s direction to the jury, that it was for them to decide whether the defendant gave it as his opinion that the pictures were by Canaletto, or whether, as part of the contract, he had represented that the pictures were by Canaletto, was upheld. The jury's decision in the plaintiff's favour was justifiable, in the opinion of a majority of the Court of King's Bench, on the ground that, Canaletto being then a comparatively modern painter, a statement as to the name of the painter was more likely to be a representation of fact. In most cases, a statement as to the authenticity of an old master would be conjecture.[6]

b Consequences of the change to assumpsit

The concept of warranty did not emerge altogether unscathed from its transposition from tort to contract. The "warranty" which sounded in damages in an action on the case for deceit did not have to be formally "part" of the contract. Providing the statement preceded the contract (or was contemporaneous with it), no problems were created by issues such as the process of negotiation, the time lag between the representation and the contract, and so on. In its new contractual environment, however, the warranty had to be supported by consideration. And in order for the bargain and sale to include (and thus support) the warranty, the courts began to advance the view that the parties must have

---

1 *Leakins* v. *Clissel* (1663), 1 Sid. 146.
2 *Crosse* v. *Gardner* (1688), Carth. 90.
3 See *Williamson* v. *Allison* (1802), 2 East 446, at p. 451 *per* Lord LOUGHBOROUGH, C.J.
4 The first reported case was *Stuart* v. *Wilkins* (1778), 1 Doug. 18, although both ASHURST and BULLER, J.J., referred to the practice as having already been "long established".
5 (1835), 7 Car. & P. 356; on appeal (1836), 4 Ad. & El. 473.
6 As in *Jendwine* v. *Slade* (1797), 2 Esp. 572.

manifested an intention that the seller's statements should form part of the contract.[1]

The transposition also brought into prominence a second, related, issue for the courts to solve: if the warranty was part of the contract, but was not included in a subsequent written document embodying or evidencing the agreement, what was its status in the context of the rules governing the construction of contracts in writing? Although the two questions, whether there was a warranty, and whether evidence of it was admissible, should have been kept distinct, there was a confusing tendency to refer to the terms of the written contract in deciding whether a warranty had *previously* been given. This approach was only possible by distorting the concept of warranty as an assertion of fact about the subject-matter of the contract, and by relying upon the quite arbitrary test of intention.

In *Hopkins* v. *Tanqueray*[2] S dissuaded B from continuing his examination of a horse by assuring him that the animal was "perfectly sound in every respect". The following day B purchased the horse at an auction which was held subject to a condition that no warranty was given unless so stated in the catalogue. No warranty was given in the catalogue, but, when B discovered that the horse was unsound, he sought damages on the basis of S's representation made on the day preceding the sale. The jury held in B's favour. As this decision was clearly in accord with existing authority had the representation been followed by a private sale,[3] the only question for the Court of Common Pleas should have been whether the condition of sale "no warranty unless stated in the catalogue" had the effect of negativing the warranty. However, as leave to move to enter a non-suit was granted to S solely on the issue of whether there had been sufficient evidence of a warranty to go to the jury, the Court was obliged, in reaching what it obviously regarded as the desired conclusion in S's favour, to rely heavily on the subsequent condition of sale as demonstrating the absence of an intention to warrant. In this form the decision was inconsistent with authority and therefore a disturbing influence on the rational development of the law.

The high water mark of the "simple principle" that "an affirmation can only be a warranty provided it appear on evidence to have been so intended"[4] was the decision of the House of Lords in *Heilbut, Symmons & Co.* v. *Buckleton*[5] in which it was referred to as a principle of "elementary law".[6] However, its importance can too readily be overestimated because there are likely to be many situations in which the conduct of the party making the representation would raise the implication that such an intention existed.[7] Furthermore, there has

---

1 The foundation of the alleged rule that there must be an "intention to warrant" is a dictum of BULLER, J., in *Pasley* v. *Freeman* (1789), 3 Term Rep. 51, at p. 57; discussed 87 L.Q.R., at pp. 181–3.
2 (1854), 15 C.B. 130; [1843–60] All E.R. Rep. 96.
3 The parties themselves had been convinced that S's statement amounted to a warranty: see *per* JERVIS, C.J., 15 C.B., at p. 139, and the fuller report in 18 Jur., Pt 1, 608.
4 *Heilbut, Symons & Co.* v. *Buckleton*, [1913] A.C. 30, at p. 38; [1911–13] All E.R. Rep. 83, at p. 86, *per* Viscount HALDANE, L.C.
5 [1913] A.C. 30; [1911–13] All E.R. Rep. 83; for a criticism of this decision see 87 L.Q.R. 179, at pp. 185–8.
6 [1913] A.C. 30, at p. 43; [1911–13] All E.R. Rep. 83, at p. 88; *per* Lord ATKINSON.
7 For example, the contemporaneous House of Lords decision in *Schawel* v. *Reade,* [1913] 2 Ir. R. 81.

been a tendency for the courts to pay lip-service to the decision in *Heilbut* v. *Buckleton* while disregarding its implications.[1]

In the well-known case of *Oscar Chess, Ltd.* v. *Williams*[2] the Court of Appeal had to decide whether S, who had stated that his car was a 1948 model in a conversation with B's salesman, had warranted the truth of his statement as part of the contract under which he had sold the car to B. *Heilbut* v. *Buckleton* was recited with approval, but the decision that no such warranty had been given was reached upon principles that had become clearly established by the nineteenth century. As DENNING, L.J., said in course of his judgment:[3]

> "When the seller states a fact which is or should be within his own knowledge and of which the buyer is ignorant, intending that the buyer should act on it and he does so, it is easy to infer a warranty; see *Couchman* v. *Hill*[4] . . ., where a farmer stated that a heifer was unserved, and *Harling* v. *Eddy*[5] . . ., where he stated that there was nothing wrong with her. So also if the seller makes a promise about something which is or should be within his own control; see *Birch* v. *Paramount Estates, Ltd.*[6] . . . where the seller stated that the house would be as good as the show house. If, however, the seller, when he states a fact, makes it clear that he has no knowledge of his own but has got his information elsewhere, and is merely passing it on, it is not so easy to imply a warranty. Such a case was *Routledge* v. *McKay*[7] . . ., where the seller stated that a motorcycle combination was a 1942 model, and pointed to the corroboration of that statement to be found in the registration book, and it was held that there was no warranty."

In contrast, in *Dick Bentley Productions, Ltd.* v. *Harold Smith (Motors), Ltd.*[8] the apparent knowledge of the seller gave to his representations the status of a warranty. S stated that the Bentley car he was selling to B had done only 20,000 miles since it had been fitted with a replacement engine and gear-box.

---

1 An attitude adopted by successive editors of *Benjamin on Sale*. In the first edition of 1868 Benjamin himself put forward the proposition that, in determining whether a representation made in the course of negotiations amounted to a warranty, "a decisive test is whether the vendor assumes to assert a fact of which the buyer is ignorant, or merely states an opinion or judgment upon a matter of which the vendor has no special knowledge, and on which the buyer may be expected also to have an opinion and to exercise his judgment". This was adopted by the Court of Appeal in *De Lassalle* v. *Guildford*, [1901] 2 K.B. 215, at p. 221; [1900-3] All E.R. Rep. 495, at p. 499. However in *Heilbut* v. *Buckleton*, the test was dismissed as a "serious deviation from the correct principle" by Lord MOULTON, [1913] A.C., at p. 50; [1911-13] All E.R. Rep., at p. 92. Despite this stricture, the test was retained by Kerr in the 6th Ed. (1920), although it was prefaced by the words "a valuable, though not decisive test". See 8th Ed., p. 666.
2 [1957] 1 All E.R. 325.
3 At p. 329; see also *per* HODSON, L.J. at p. 331. A similar theme can be seen running through a number of Australian authorities: *Bulloch* v. *Glasson* (1915), 15 S.R. (N.S.W.) 91; *Gardner* v. *Grigg* (1938), 38 S.R. (N.S.W.) 524; and in *O'Dempsey* v. *Hansen*, [1939] Q.W.N. 34, Case No. 22, *Heilbut* v. *Buckleton* was strongly pressed by counsel as requiring evidence of an intention to warrant, but totally ignored by the members of the Queensland Full Court in giving judgment.
4 [1947] K.B. 554; [1947] 1 All E.R. 103.
5 [1951] 2 K.B. 739; [1951] 2 All E.R. 212.
6 (1956), 16 Estates Gazette 396.
7 [1954] 1 All E.R. 855; and see also *Dunlop* v. *Waugh* (1792), Peake 167, in while the seller of a horse had no more information about the age of the animal than a document given to him by the previous owner.
8 [1965] 2 All E.R. 65; [1965] 1 W.L.R. 623.

As S was a dealer who was in a position to know, or at least to find out, the true history of the car (the new components of which had in fact been fitted 100,000 miles earlier), the Court of Appeal held that his misstatements amounted to a breach of warranty.

ii Relationship to tort

The transfer of the remedy against a seller who had made misrepresentations to his buyer, from deceit to assumpsit, from tort to contract, created one major problem which the courts have significantly failed to solve. The "warranty" which sounded in damages in an action on the case for deceit was never "part" of the contract. When it was received into its new contractual environment, the courts were obliged to discover the necessary consideration to support it.

The most simple and obvious process was to treat the warranty as part of a single contract, e.g. a sale of a horse warranted as sound. However, greater difficulty was experienced in situations where the subsequent sale was by auction, or in circumstances where the warranty was "incidental" to the main object of the contract of sale (e.g. becoming a shareholder in a company); or where the subsequently executed lease or other contractual document made no mention of the earlier warranty.[1]

The solution advanced by Lord MOULTON in *Heilbut, Symons & Co.* v. *Buckleton*[2] to deal with such a situation was that it would have to be possible to construct two contracts, the main agreement to buy shares or to purchase a horse as highest bidder at an auction, and a collateral contract whereby the seller, in return for the buyer entering into the main agreement, warrants the nature of the company or the condition of the horse. In other words, the consideration given by the plaintiff to support the warranty is his entry into the main contract. But even this analysis in which the prior representation inducing a contract is characterised as part of a collateral contract does not altogether solve the problems. The courts have shown great reluctance to enforce the prior representation where it is inconsistent with the terms of the main contract to which the buyer subsequently assents.[3] As was said in a leading Australian case, a

> "distinct collateral agreement, whether oral or in writing, and whether prior to or contemporaneous with the main agreement, is valid and enforceable, even though the main agreement be in writing, provided the two may consistently stand together so that the provisions of the main agreement remain in full force and effect notwithstanding the collateral agreement."[4]

---

1 As in *De Lassalle* v. *Guildford*, [1901] 2 K.B. 215; [1900–3] All E.R. Rep. 495; in which the plaintiff was held entitled to refuse to exchange the counterparts of a lease without the defendant's assurance that the drains were in order; and see *Van Den Esschert* v. *Chappell*, [1960] W.A.R. 114, in which the plaintiff was assured that the house he was about to enter into a contract to buy had no white ants.

2 [1913] A.C. 30; [1911–13] All E.R. Rep. 83.

3 The High Court of Australia has expressed the view that, even if there is no inconsistency, the chief reason why the judges are reluctant to uphold a collateral warranty or contract "is that too often the collateral warranty put forward is one that you would expect to find its place naturally in the principal contract": *Shepperd* v. *Municipality of Ryde* (1952), 85 C.L.R. 1, at p. 13.

4 *Per* KNOX, C.J. in *Hoyt's Pty, Ltd.* v. *Spencer* (1919), 27 C.L.R. 133, at p. 139; *Henderson* v. *Arthur*, [1907] 1 K.B. 10; but cf. *City and Westminster Properties* (1939), *Ltd.* v. *Mudd*, [1959] Ch. 129; [1958] 2 All E.R. 733.

In the auction situation, the method most readily adopted to enforce the representation (in *Couchman* v. *Hill*[1] and *Harling* v. *Eddy*[2] for example) was to hold that the oral undertaking had superseded the conditions of sale; *Hopkins* v. *Tanqueray*[3] being distinguishable on the ground that the representation in that case was made before the sale and was unknown to the auctioneer at the time of the sale. On the other hand, where three different parties are involved, as in the normal hire purchase arrangement, a dealer's representations are readily classifiable as part of a contract that is collateral to the main hire purchase transaction between customer and finance company. The existence of a widely drawn exemption clause in the latter agreement cannot affect the rights of the customer *vis-à-vis* the dealer.[4]

A buyer is able to sue in tort on a seller's "collateral undertaking" if that undertaking is made fraudulently. The ambit of the tort of deceit was restricted by *Derry* v. *Peek*[5] to cases where a statement was made by a representor that he knew to be false or if he made it with a reckless disregard of whether or not it was true. The House of Lords held that the absence of reasonable grounds for belief in the truth of a statement was not in itself a basis for a claim in deceit, although it might be evidence of recklessness as to whether the statement was true or false.[6]

In *Hedley Bryne & Co., Ltd.* v. *Heller and Partners, Ltd.*,[7] however, their Lordships laid down the principle that a negligent misstatement, causing subsequent financial loss to the person to whom the representation was directed and who has acted on the strength of it, gives rise to a remedy in damages. What is not clear from the judgments is in what circumstances a duty of care will exist to avoid making a careless misstatement. More specifically, there is little guidance on the question whether the duty can extend to parties who are negotiating, and who subsequently enter into, a contract.

There is perhaps discernible a tendency to regard actions as lying either in contract or in tort but not in both.[8] Certainly the courts have consistently refused to allow a remedy in tort in actions brought against professional men who owed a contractual duty to their clients, but these decisions[9] are hardly relevant to a discussion of the seller/buyer relationship, except in so far as they

---

1 [1947] K.B. 554; [1947] 1 All E.R. 103.
2 [1951] 2 K.B. 739; [1951] 2 All E.R. 212.
3 (1854), 15 C.B. 130.
4 *Brown* v. *Sheen and Richmond Car Sales, Ltd.*, [1950] 1 All E.R. 1102; *Andrews* v. *Hopkinson*, [1957] 1 Q.B. 229; [1956] 3 All E.R. 422.
5 (1889), 14 App. Cas. 337.
6 See *per* Lord HERSCHELL, at pp. 375–6.
7 [1964] A.C. 465; [1963] 2 All E.R. 575.
8 See *per* Lord REID, [1964] A.C., at p. 483; [1963] 2 All E.R., at p. 581; *per* Lord DEVLIN, [1964] A.C., at pp. 528–9; [1963] 2 All E.R., at p. 610; and *per* Lord PEARCE, [1964] A.C., at p. 539; [1963] 2 All E.R., at p. 617.
9 *Clark* v. *Kirby-Smith*, [1964] Ch. 506; [1964] 2 All E.R. 835; *Bagot* v. *Stevens, Scanlan & Co.*, [1966] 1 Q.B. 197; [1964] 3 All E.R. 577; *Cook* v. *S.*, [1967] 1 All E.R. 299. These decisions follow from earlier authorities: *Bean* v *Wade* (1875), 2 T.L.R. 157, *Groom* v. *Crocker*, [1939] 1 K.B. 194; [1938] 2 All E.R. 394; but cf. Viscount HALDANE, L.C.'s statements in *Nocton* v. *Ashburton*, [1914] A.C. 932, at p. 956; [1914–15] All E.R. Rep. 45, at p. 54, that "the solicitor contracts with his client to be skilful and careful. For failure to perform his obligation he may be made liable at law in contract, or even in tort, for negligence in breach of a duty imposed on him".

demonstrate a reluctance to extend the ambit of the decision in *Hedley Byrne*. McNair, J., did go so far as to state the view[1] (although without giving reasons) that "the submission . . . that the ruling in that case applies as between contracting parties is without foundation". As a buyer may well have a remedy in tort against a seller when the goods cause the buyer physical injury,[2] the only remaining justification for the proposition advanced by McNair, J., is the existence of some distinctive feature about economic loss as opposed to injury or damage to person or property. However, the importance of this distinction was greatly reduced by the judgments in *Hedley Byrne*: indeed Lord Devlin went so far as to say that in his view there was "neither logic nor common sense" in the distinction between physical and economic loss, at least in relation to negligent misstatements.[3]

iii The Misrepresentation Act 1967

To a large extent the question whether a duty of care exists between seller and buyer not to make negligent misstatements is likely to be academic as far as this country is concerned. Because of the degree of uncertainty that could exist, as a result of cases like *Heilbut* v. *Buckleton*, over whether a representation formed part of contract, s. 2 (1) of the Misrepresentation Act 1967 was enacted. It provides:

> "Where a person has entered into a contract after a misrepresentation has been made to him by another party thereto and as a result thereof he has suffered loss, then, if the person making the misrepresentation would be liable to damages in respect thereof had the misrepresentation been made fraudulently, that person shall be so liable notwithstanding that the misrepresentation was not made fraudulently, unless he proves that he had reasonable ground to believe and did believe up to the time the contract was made that the facts represented were true."

In practice, this provision is not likely to have any very dramatic effect because whether a representation amounts to a statement of fact and therefore constitutes a warranty is likely to depend upon factors such as the apparent reasonableness of the representor's belief in what he was saying.[4] However, while claims are pleaded alternatively for breach of warranty or under s. 2 (1), it is less likely that a claim under *Hedley Byrne* will be included.[5]

---

1 In *Oleificio Zucchi S.P.A.* v. *Northern Sales, Ltd.*, [1965] 2 Lloyd's Rep. 496, at p. 519.
2 *Clarke* v. *Army and Navy Co-operative Society*, [1903] 1 K.B. 155; *Andrews* v. *Hopkinson*, [1957] 1 Q.B. 229; [1956] 3 All E.R. 422. In *W. B. Anderson & Sons, Ltd* v. *Rhodes (Liverpool), Ltd.*, [1967] 2 All E.R. 850, Cairns, J., allowed a claim based upon *Hedley Byrne* in circumstances that could readily have been classified as a collateral contract situation.
3 [1964] A.C. 465, at p. 517; and *per* Lord Morris, at pp. 496, 502–3; *per* Lord Pearce, at p. 538; and *per* Lord Hodson, at p. 509. See also *Dutton* v. *Bognor Regis United Building Co., Ltd.*, [1972] 1 All E.R. 462, at pp. 480–1, *per* Sachs, L.J.
4 See *Dick Bentley Productions, Ltd.* v. *Harold Smith (Motors), Ltd.* [1965] 2 All E.R. 65, at p. 67, *per* Lord Denning, M.R.
5 Although there is some slight "authority for the proposition that an opinion, expressed in response to a request for advice may give rise to an action for damages even though it is an opinion which is, in fact, honestly entertained, and *its expression does not involve any misrepresentation* of fact": *per* Taylor, J., in the High Court of Australia in *Mutual Life and Citizens Assurance Co., Ltd.* v. *Evatt* (1968), 42 A.L.J.R. 316, at p. 330, emphasis added; rev. on other grounds [1971] 1 All E.R. 150.

B THE RIGHT TO REPUDIATE

i The status of the terms of the contract

Prior to the passing of the Sale of Goods Act, the term "warranty" was still employed principally in its normal sense of a promise or guarantee given by a contracting party. Where there was a subsequent written agreement, or a document containing the terms which would govern the transaction, the terms contained in the agreement or document were often referred to as "conditions". In the former case the expression was used because of the similarity with the conditions of sale in a contract for the purchase of land; and in latter cases the document might be an auctioneer's "conditions of sale" or a carrier's "conditions of carriage".

It has already been explained[1] that, in order for one party (in the case of the contract of sale usually the buyer) to establish that he was no longer bound by his obligations under the contract, he had to show that the other party (the seller) had failed to perform a condition precedent to his (the buyer's) duty to carry out his part of the bargain. This "condition precedent" was simply the method of pleading the prior obligation of the seller to comply with a certain term or terms of the contract. Hence compliance with a warranty (i.e. a promise) that the goods were of a specific quality would usually constitute a condition precedent to the buyer's obligation to accept the goods. However, compliance with a condition precedent would depend as much on the conduct of the party in breach and the nature of the breach as on the term broken.

In *Bettini* v. *Gye*[2] a useful example, though not a case on sale, the plaintiff had agreed with the defendant to sing in concerts and operas in the United Kingdom for a period of three and a half months from March 30, 1875, and "to be in London without fail at least six days before the commencement of his engagement, for the purpose of rehearsals". Because of illness, the plaintiff only reached London on March 28, but the defendant refused to employ the plaintiff in accordance with the agreement. Whether the plaintiff could recover damages depended upon whether his arriving in London six days before March 30, was "a condition precedent to the defendant's liability, or only an independent agreement, a breach of which will not justify a repudiation of the contract, but will only be a cause of action for a compensation in damages".[3] It was held that, taking into account the length of the engagement, the delay in arrival at the initial rehersals could not amount to a breach of a condition precedent to the defendant's liability to employ the plaintiff.

Because of a tendency to omit the word "precedent" in talking about "conditions precedent", the courts in time began to use the word "condition" more as a type of term breach of which absolved the other party from his obligations under the contract.[4] And in order to describe a lesser term, breach of which would only give rise to a remedy in damages, but would not entitle the injured

---

1 See above, p. 118.
2 (1876), 1 Q.B.D. 183; [1874–80] All E.R. Rep. 242.
3 *Per* BLACKBURN, J., delivering the judgment of the court (1876), 1 Q.B.D. 183, at p. 187; [1874–80] All E.R. Rep. at p. 244.
4 E.g. as in *Behn* v. *Burness* (1863), 3 B. & S. 751.

party to repudiate the contract, there was a trend towards use of the word "warranty". It was this dichotomy between conditions and warranties which Chalmers adopted in drafting the Sale of Goods Act. By s. 62 (1) a warranty is defined as

> "an agreement with reference to goods which are the subject of a contract of sale, but collateral to the main purpose of such contract, the breach of which gives rise to a claim for damages, but not to a right to reject the goods and treat the contract as repudiated".

The effect of the adoption of this distinction between conditions and warranties was to shift the emphasis when a court was deciding upon the rights of the parties. Instead of asking whether the seller's conduct was such as in the circumstances entitled the buyer to repudiate, the courts were required to decide whether the seller's conduct had broken the contract and whether the term broken was a condition or a warranty. The answer to the second question "depends in each case on the construction of the contract" (s. 11 (1) (*b*)).[1] However, as has already been suggested,[2] it is in some cases easier for a buyer to establish a right to repudiate under the Act than it was formerly at common law.

ii Loss of the right to repudiate

However, it does not follow that once a term is classified as a condition, its breach automatically leads to a repudiation of the contract. As s. 11 (1) (*a*) states:

> "Where a contract of sale is subject to any condition to be fulfilled by the seller, the buyer may waive the condition, or may elect to treat the breach of such condition as a breach of warranty, and not as a ground for treating the contract as repudiated".

In other words, it is not open to the buyer who has been notified in advance by the seller that goods are not going to be delivered on time and who has made no attempt to renounce the contract to turn round at the time of delivery and purport to repudiate the contract: he has waived his right to rely upon breach of any condition relating to the time of performance and must be content with his remedy, if any, in damages. Conversely, it is not open to a seller who has been in default and has been sued for damages, to claim that the term broken was a condition and that therefore the buyer was only entitled to repudiate the contract. In fact, although s. 11 does not mention it, a buyer who has suffered loss as a result of a breach of condition is entitled to repudiate the contract *and* to sue for damages if repudiation alone does not provide an adequate remedy.

It is also provided in effect in s. 11 (1) (*c*) that once goods are accepted, unless there is an additional express or implied promise by the seller to allow a subsequent rescission of the contract, the right to repudiate is lost:

---

1 And it is not necessarily conclusive that the parties have used the term warranty instead of condition: *Wallis, Son and Wells* v. *Pratt*, [1911] A.C. 394; [1911–13] All E.R. Rep. 989; or vice-versa: *L. Schuler AG* v. *Wickman Machine Tool Sales, Ltd.*, [1973] 2 All E.R. 39; [1973] 2 W.L.R. 683.
2 See the discussion of *Re Moore & Co. and Landauer & Co.*, [1921] 2 K.B. 519; [1921] All E.R. Rep. 466; above p. 126.

"Where a contract of sale is not severable, and the buyer has accepted the goods, or part thereof, the breach of any condition to be fulfilled by the seller can only be treated as a breach of warranty, and not as a ground for rejecting the goods and treating the contract as repudiated, unless there be a term of the contract, express or implied, to that effect."

In *Long* v. *Lloyd*,[1] it will be recalled, B sought to rescind a contract under which he had bought a lorry from S. He had driven the vehicle home but had then complained of a number of defects. S had agreed to "go halves" on the cost of a reconstructed dynamo. The Court of Appeal expressed the view that it was probably at this stage that B lost his right to reject (i.e. if the claim had been for breach of condition, B would have been deemed to have accepted the goods and been obliged to treat the breach of condition as a breach of warranty).

iii Instalment contracts

Section 11 (1) (c) applies to contracts for the delivery of the goods either in one consignment, or in several instalments where those instalments are not "severable".

a Non-severable contracts

It follows that in an indivisible contract (i.e. where the instalments are not severable), once the first instalment has been accepted, it is no longer possible for the buyer to reject either that instalment, or any subsequent instalment, on the ground that it does not satisfy some condition of the contract. He is obliged, by s. 11 (1) (c), to rely upon his remedy in damages.

1 *Part delivery of the wrong goods.* However, it would seem that s. 11 (1) (c) must be read subject to s. 30 (3), which provides that where the seller delivers the goods contracted for mixed with goods of a different description, the buyer may accept the goods which are in accordance with the contract and reject the rest, or he may reject the whole. In *William Barker (Junior) & Co., Ltd.* v. *Edward T. Agius, Ltd.*,[2] SALTER, J., reluctantly[3] decided that a buyer who had accepted part of a cargo, was entitled to reject the remainder which did not comply with the contract description, but could not reject the entire cargo. B had agreed to buy a quantity of German coal briquettes "size 2 inches". Part of the ship load, carried as deck cargo, did comply with the contract description; this part was sold by B. When the holds were opened it was discovered that the rest of the cargo largely comprised goods not of the size required by the contract. B thereupon purported to reject the *entire* cargo. SALTER, J., held that, although B could have rejected the rest of the cargo, he was not entitled to reject the whole cargo (i.e. including the deck cargo which he had already sold). His notice to S was therefore ineffective to rescind the contract and he was obliged to seek

---

1 [1958] 2 All E.R. 402; [1958] 1 W.L.R. 753, see above, p. 138.
2 (1927), 33 Com. Cas. 120.
3 He felt himself bound by *J. and J. Cunningham, Ltd.* v. *Robert A. Munro & Co., Ltd.* (1922), 28 Com. Cas. 42; and *E. Hardy & Co. (London), Ltd.* v. *Hillerns and Fowler,* [1923] 1 K.B. 658, at p. 666, affirmed; [1923] 2 K.B. 490, at pp. 495–6.

damages instead. In other words, where, in a non-severable contract, an instalment, or an identifiable part of the contract, is in accordance with the contract, but the rest is not, the buyer can rely upon s. 30 (3), but is nevertheless obliged to take those goods which he has already accepted.

However, while such a proposition will hold good in most circumstances, its application is not automatic. In *London Plywood and Timber Co., Ltd.* v. *Nasic Oak Extract Factory and Steam Sawmills Co., Ltd.*[1] B agreed to purchase from S a quantity of timber "to be inspected and taken over by the buyers" before shipment f.o.b. to London. B's agent inspected lengths of timber tendered by S, and branded those which he accepted. When the shipment was discharged at London, B paid for the goods, but subsequently B alleged that the timber delivered was not in accordance with the contract. It was found by the arbitrator that the shipment was not that inspected and taken over by B's agent: less than half the shipment consisted of timber accepted by the agent. In strict logic it was possible to argue that B had accepted part of the goods that had been delivered. However, in this case S had put on one side the parcel of goods accepted by B and had sent him part only of those goods together with a substantial quantity which was not the contract goods. In such circumstances the goods delivered could not be regarded as those alleged to have been accepted.

Too much should not be made of this decision because of the most unusual circumstances that gave rise to it. Acceptance occurs at the time of, or after, the act of delivery. Hence there will normally be no great problem in applying s. 11 (1) (*c*), subject to s. 30 (3). Although examination of the goods can occur at the port of loading, it will surely only be a rare occurrence that the goods examined and approved are not those shipped under the contract. Indeed there is much to be said for the view that such an examination of the goods is presumptive but not decisive. An examination, however thorough, is no protection against a subsequent delivery of the wrong goods, and acceptance can never be complete until a reasonable examination is possible to check that the goods are in fact those contracted for. To this type of situation, s. 11 (1) (*c*), which deals with what occurs after acceptance of the whole or part of the goods, can have no application.

Section 30 (3) does give rise to one rather unsatisfactory distinction. In *Barker* v. *Agius* the part of the goods accepted by B had been in accordance with the contract; it had only been the cargo in the hold that had not answered the contract description. If B had accepted goods which themselves were not in accordance with the contract, he could not reject the rest. In *E. Hardy & Co., (London), Ltd.* v. *Hillerns and Fowler*,[2] B agreed to purchase a quantity of Rosario and/or Santa Fé wheat. When the wheat reached England, B sold a substantial part of it. When B examined the remaining wheat he discovered that it was neither Rosario nor Santa Fé wheat. It was held that B had lost his right of rejection because the resale of part of the cargo had amounted to an

---

1 [1939] 2 K.B. 343.
2 [1923] 1 K.B. 658, affirmed; [1923] 2 K.B. 490; [1923] All E.R. Rep. 275, discussed above, p. 141.

acceptance of the goods within s. 35 of the Act. But how is it possible to distinguish between the two situations?

Unhampered by authority, SALTER, J., in *Barker* v. *Agius* would have applied s. 11 (1) (c) to the exclusion of s. 30 (3), but he felt himself bound to follow dicta in *Hardy* v. *Hillerns and Fowler*, and inferences drawn from *J. and J. Cunningham, Ltd.* v. *Robert A. Munro & Co., Ltd.*[1]

At first instance in *E. Hardy & Co. (London), Ltd.*, v. *Hillerns and Fowler*,[2] GREER, J., had rejected the argument that there could be "acceptance of part and a rejection of the balance" in the circumstances that had arisen, but acknowledged that it could be done

> "when a portion of the goods is obviously in accordance with the contract and another part is not, but where the same objection applies to the whole quantity, and a portion has been accepted notwithstanding the objection, there cannot be a rejection of the part".

This obiter pronouncement was expressed to be "probably quite right" by BANKES, L.J., in the Court of Appeal[3] who thus accepted the possibility of a buyer being able to reject part of a cargo and to accept the remainder.

It is this reference to a part *cargo* which may provide a better line of distinction to these cases than the application or non-application of s. 30 (3). To take an obvious point about that provision, it has no application at all to the situation where the condition broken relates to the quality and not the description of the goods. This proposition has the strong support of the Scottish case, *Aitken Campbell & Co., Ltd.* v. *Boullen and Gatenby*[4] in which the Court of Session held emphatically that a buyer was not entitled to reject part of a consignment of maroon twill which was not equal to sample, and that s. 30 (3) could not apply in such circumstances. Nevertheless, in *Cunningham* v. *Munro* it was held that a buyer was entitled to reject the portion of wheat that had yet to be loaded under a f.o.b. contract once it was discovered that the wheat had overheated.

Despite the suggestion by GREER, J., and BANKES, L.J., in *Hardy* v. *Hillerns and Fowler* that *Cunningham* v. *Munro* had something to do with s. 30 (3), no reference was made to s. 30, nor indeed to any other provision of the Act, in the latter case. The Divisional Court held that there was no evidence that the buyer had accepted any of the wheat other than the quantity actually loaded on board. No comment at all was made with respect to counsel's argument that, as a matter of law, the buyer could not take part of the goods and not the rest. There must be a suspicion that the case is wrongly decided. It would seem justifiable, if at all, either on the ground that the Court was dealing only with the issues presented to it by the arbitration board (and there had been no evidence of an actual acceptance by the buyer of the goods that had yet to be loaded); or on

---

1 (1922), 28 Com. Cas. 42.
2 [1923] 1 K.B., at p. 666.
3 (1923), 29 Com. Cas. 30, at p. 37 (the shorter report in [1923] 2 K.B. 490 does not contain this passage); [1923] All E.R. Rep., at p. 278.
4 (1908), 15 S.L.T. 776.

the basis that some special rule applies to f.o.b. contracts.[1] It could be argued, for example, that, as property passes once the goods are loaded, the buyer is entitled to refuse to accept delivery on board of the rest of a cargo that is not of the standard required by the contract.

2 *Part delivery of incorrect amount.* If s. 30 (3) is applicable to situations where an acceptance of part of the goods would normally bring s. 11 (1) (*c*) into play, the same should be true of s. 30 (1) and (2) which cover the cases where the seller delivers less or more than the quantity of goods specified in the contract. Although both sub-sections deal with "the goods" in terms of a single delivery, it would appear to be unsatisfactory if a buyer is unable to make use of his power to reject the wrong quantity in instalment contracts. Although there is no real authority on the point, the issue may in fact depend upon inferences from the conduct of the parties, their course of dealings, or even the custom in their particular trade (see s. 30 (4)). In some circumstances a buyer might be entitled to say that his acceptance of the earlier instalments was conditional upon the right total quantity being delivered: in other cases, it might be difficult to avoid the conclusion being drawn that the buyer was accepting those goods whatever the total amount eventually delivered. Although this division may well be that which lies between severable and non-severable contracts in many situations, the dividing line will not necessarily be identical. There are a number of cases where the contract has been treated as severable for some limited purpose,[2] for example, as we have seen, where the buyer has been entitled to reject part only of the goods in a contract which may not even have envisaged delivery by instalments.

The expression "whatever total amount is eventually delivered" needs some amplification. It will be remembered that the courts have construed the contract quantity strictly: if a seller wishes a "margin of error" he should stipulate for it in the contract. It may be that, in instalment contracts, the courts would, in the absence of evidence suggesting a contrary intention, allow some "margin of error" in deciding whether the goods delivered by the seller approximated sufficiently to the total goods ordered to make the buyer's acceptance of the earlier instalments binding on him so far as those instalments were concerned.

---

1 It may be that contracts involving the loading and discharge of cargo require the application of different principles. *Barker v Agius* was not an unsatisfactory decision on the facts, but its rationale, that s. 30 (3) was an exception to the application of s. 11 (1) (*c*), created a number of anomalies. It could perhaps now satisfactorily be justified in more general terms: a buyer who, in the course of discharge, accepts part of a cargo which is in conformity with the contract of sale is entitled to reject the rest when he has the opportunity of examining them and discovers that the remaining goods are not in conformity with the contract. Such a rule would not be subject to the limitation of s. 30 (3) that the buyer is not entitled to reject unless the remaining goods do not answer the contract description. Reconciling the rule with the Act presents no problems because many of the special principles of shipping contracts are recognised to fall, by commercial practice, outside specific provisions of the Act.

2 As Lord WRIGHT pointed out in giving the judgment of the House of Lords in *Ross T. Smyth & Co., Ltd.* v. *Bailey, Son & Co.* (1940), 45 Com. Cas. 292, at p. 308, in many c.i.f. contracts (which perhaps constitute the majority of instalment contracts, certainly that come before the courts) there "is still only one contract and one contract quantity, though for certain purposes in the way of performance particular instalments or shipments and parcels may be treated in separation from the others".

A buyer would not of course be bound by such acceptance (unless he had so dealt with the goods as to make rescission impossible) if there was a substantial difference in the total goods delivered because he could not be regarded as having bargained on such a basis.

By ascribing the solution of problems arising out of delivery of the wrong quantity in instalment contracts to the apparent intention of the parties, one is at least able to avoid the conflict that exists between s. 11 (1) (c) and s. 30 (1). Where the delivery is of a quantity larger than that contracted for, s. 30 (2) can more readily be applied because it expressly states that the buyer can either accept the goods contracted for; or reject all the goods delivered; or accept them all, paying for them at the contract rate. Nevertheless there may be situations in which a buyer, having accepted a series of instalments, is suddenly faced with a much larger final instalment than was provided for by the contract. At this stage, is he obliged to take at least the amount that makes up the contract quantity, or can he reject the entire instalment but retain those already delivered? Some principle outside s. 11 (1) (c) or s. 30 (2) would be necessary to enable him to take the latter step which in certain circumstances might well be his most reasonable course of action. The application of the apparent intention of the parties under s. 30 (4), would enable a court to uphold such an action by the buyer in an appropriate case.

b Severable contracts

By s. 31 (2), contracts "for the sale of goods to be delivered by stated instalments, which are to be separately paid for", are made subject to different principles from those contracts where, even though the contract may be performed by instalment deliveries, the contract is essentially an entire whole. However, it has already been pointed out that many contracts which appear to be non-severable have been treated as if they were in some respects severable, so that the suspicion is raised that these severable contracts (i.e. those where because of separate payment and delivery, each instalment can be regarded as a separate contract) are not so very distinctive. Indeed this suspicion is increased when one takes account of two factors: first the fact that s. 31 (2) itself gives no real guidance on how differently this type of instalment contract should be treated; and secondly the tendency of the courts to employ reasons to support the conclusion that a particular contract is severable which do not provide any clear dividing line between the different types of instalment contract.

As far as the wording of s. 31 (2) is concerned, it is drafted in general terms:

> "Where there is a contract for the sale of goods to be delivered by stated instalments, which are to be separately paid for, and the seller makes defective deliveries in respect of one or more instalments, or the buyer neglects or refuses to take delivery of or pay for one or more instalments, it is a question in each case depending on the terms of the contract and the circumstances of the case, whether the breach of contract is a repudiation of the whole contract or whether it is a severable breach giving rise to a claim for compensation but not to a right to treat the whole contract as repudiated."

It goes without saying that a refusal to pay for an instalment is an issue that can only arise under a contract where each instalment is to be separately paid for. However, the consequences of a defective instalment by the seller or a refusal by the buyer to take delivery of an instalment are surely subject to "the terms of the contract and the circumstances of the case" whichever type of instalment contract is being dealt with. To suggest that there is something distinctive and unique about instalment contracts involving separate payment for each delivery is a most unfortunate piece of legislative drafting. As has already been pointed out, even under an entire contract where the goods, in the process of what is almost a continuous single delivery, are handed over in successive "parcels", there have been occasions on which the courts have been prepared to treat the different parcels as severable instalments "in the circumstances of the case".

As far as the second factor is concerned, the approach frequently adopted is for the courts to decide that a particular contract is severable because the parties could not have intended the consequences that would follow from its being an entire contract.[1] No difficulty can arise under c.i.f. contracts where the seller is to ship goods from overseas because, if he is entitled to send them in different shipments,[2] they will be dispatched under separate bills of lading and payment will be due against each bill as it is tendered.[3] If, however, the contract provides for the supply and delivery of goods to the actual premises of the buyer (a situation more likely to occur in internal trade, or perhaps where the shipment of the goods is a minor part of the operation) there is no such standard practice which can operate within the terms of the contract, but it is still for the court to draw such inferences as it can from those terms and the circumstances of the case.

In *Jackson* v. *Rotax Motor and Cycle Co.*,[4] B, a London dealer in motor car accessories, ordered 609 motor horns of varying specification, "delivery as required", from S in Paris. The goods were delivered in 19 cases at various dates during May and June, 1909. When the last consignment arrived, B inspected the goods and discovered that they were unmerchantable. He purported to reject all but case 2 which he had already sold to retailers. When S commenced this action, B paid into court the price of cases 1, 3 and 4 which had been delivered at the same time as case 2 (the price of which he had already paid to S). Assuming that the goods were unmerchantable, the right to reject was dependent upon whether the delivery of each case constituted performance

---

1 For an overt admission of this approach see *Jackson* v. *Rotax Motor and Cycle Co.*, [1910] 2 K.B. 937, esp. at p. 947 *per* FARWELL, L.J., citing the dissenting (on a matter of construction) judgment of BRETT, L.J., in *Reuter* v. *Sala* (1879), 4 C.P.D. 239, at p. 256. In other cases such a consideration will operate tacitly or perhaps even subconsciously: see *Tarling* v. *O'Riordan* (1878), 2 L.R. Ir. 82, the Irish case followed in *Jackson* v. *Rotax*.

2 Of course, if S purports to send the goods by one ship he may be bound by this election: *Reuter* v. *Sala & Co.* (1879), 4 C.P.D. 239, discussed above, p. 132. It is a question of construction whether two parcels on the same vessel under separate bills of lading can be regarded as severable: *Esmail* v. *J. Rosenthal & Sons, Ltd.*, [1964] 2 Lloyd's Rep. 447 (held not to constitute separate shipments); *Ross T. Smyth and Co., Ltd.* v. *Bailey, Son & Co.*, [1940] 3 All E.R. 60.

As in *Millars Karri and Jarrah Co.* v. *Weddel, Turner & Co.* (1908), 100 L.T. 128.

[1910] 2 K.B. 937.

of a separate contract; or alternatively the court might have been prepared to consider each separate instalment of cases (e.g. the first four) as constituting a separate contract. The conclusion reached by the Court of Appeal was that B was entitled to reject each batch (i.e. he was liable to pay for the first four cases having accepted case 2 which was delivered with them). "Delivery as required" created an obligation upon S to treat the contract as severable if B gave instructions (as he had done) for the delivery of different horns at different times. In a severable contract, therefore, the buyer's treatment of the first instalment is not crucial, even if those goods are defective. If he accepts it, he is not necessarily bound to take a subsequent delivery of goods that are defective.

However, s. 31 (2) deals with a slightly different problem, namely that of deciding whether delivery of a defective instalment entitles the buyer to repudiate the contract *as a whole,* or whether a refusal of the buyer to take part of the goods is a sufficient ground for the seller to refuse to make further deliveries. The reason why the sub-section was drafted so broadly was the existence of a number of conflicting authorities which could be reconciled, if at all, only in the most general terms.[1] It was based upon a test, suggested by COLERIDGE, L.C.J., in *Freeth* v. *Burr*[2] that the question should be asked "whether the acts and conduct of the party evince an intention no longer to be bound by the contract", and amplified by Lord SELBORNE, L.C., in the following words in *Mersey Steel and Iron Co.* v. *Naylor, Benzon & Co.*:[3]

> "You must look at the actual circumstances of the case in order to see whether the one party to the contract is relieved from its future performance by the conduct of the other; you must examine what that conduct is, so as to see whether it amounts to a renunciation, to an absolute refusal to perform the contract, such as would amount to a rescission if he had the power to rescind, and whether the other party may accept it as a reason for not performing his part."

In practice there is probably some difference in approach where there has been a refusal to perform rather than a defective performance. In the case of a non-performance, whether in relation to delivery, acceptance or payment, some explanation would almost certainly be given by the defaulting party for his conduct. In *Freeth* v. *Burr*,[4] the goods (250 tons of pig iron) were to have been delivered in two equal instalments. The first instalment was delivered late in separate parcels over a period of time. The buyer continued to press for delivery of the remainder, but, to put pressure on the seller, refused to pay for the goods already delivered until he received the rest. It was held that his refusal to pay was clearly a breach of contract, but it was far from demonstrating any intention to put an end to the contract. If the buyer had not been pressing for performance of the contract and had given no reason for his failure to pay, his conduct would

---

1 In *Mersey Steel and Iron Co. Ltd.* v. *Naylor, Benzon and Co.* (1882), 9 Q.B.D. 648, at p. 666, LINDLEY, L.J., commented that he despaired of reconciling *Hoare* v. *Rennie* (1859), 5 H. & N. 19; *Simpson* v. *Crippen* (1872), L.R. 8 Q.B. 14; and *Honck* v. *Muller* (1881), 7 Q.B.D. 92.
2 (1874), L.R. 9 C.P. 208, at p. 213.
3 (1884), 9 App. Cas. 434, at pp. 438–9.
4 (1874), L.R. 9 C.P. 208.

have been strong evidence of an intention not to proceed with further performance of the contract.[1]

Some guidance in assessing whether a breach by the other party is sufficient grounds for a party to treat the contract as at an end may be provided by the proportion that the controversial instalment bears to the total contract quantity.

In *Simpson* v. *Crippen*,[2] for example, S agreed to supply B with 6,000 to 8,000 tons of coal to be delivered into B's wagons at S's collieries in equal monthly instalments over a period of 12 months. During the initial month B sent wagons sufficient to load only 158 tons. Thereupon S informed B that, as B had been in breach of contract, S did not intend to deliver any more coal. It was held that, this being a severable contract, breach in respect of the first instalment did not necessarily involve a substantial breach of the contract as a whole. Accordingly S's refusal to make further deliveries of coal had been unjustified.

By way of contrast, in *Robert A. Munro & Co., Ltd.* v. *Meyer*,[3] the contract was for the sale of 1,500 tons of bone meal, to be shipped at the rate of 125 tons monthly in equal weekly quantities. 611 tons were delivered and found not to be in accordance with the contract. It was held that "where the breach is substantial and so serious as the breach in this case and has continued so persistently, the buyer is entitled to say that he has the right to treat the whole contract as repudiated".[4]

The law was succinctly summarised by Lord HEWART, C.J., giving the judgment of the Court of Appeal in *Maple Flock Co., Ltd.* v. *Universal Furniture Products (Wembley), Ltd.*,[5] when he stated that:

> "The main tests to be considered . . . are, first, the ratio quantitatively which the breach bears to the contract as a whole, and secondly the degree of probability or improbability that such a breach will be repeated."

In the New Zealand case of *Hammer and Barrow* v. *Coca-Cola*,[6] B purchased 200,000 wooden "yoyos" to be delivered in instalments. Of the first 85,000 delivered to B's order, over 60,000 were returned as defective. B therefore purported to rescind the contract. It was held that "the ratio quantitatively which the breach bore to the contract . . . was very considerable as it affected some 80 per cent. of the 85,000 yoyos delivered . . . out of a total contract quantity of 200,000".[7] In the circumstances, there was a great risk that B would have an

---

1 A breach amounting to a repudiation can often occur when the repudiating party alleges that the other party's conduct entitles him to repudiate but the court holds that the conduct of the other party would only be a basis for an action in damages: *Simpson* v. *Crippen* (1872), L.R. 8 Q.B. 14 (see below); *Dominion Coal Co., Ltd.* v. *Dominion Iron and Steel Co., Ltd.*, [1909] A.C. 293.

2 (1872) L.R. 8 Q.B. 14; *Maple Flock Co., Ltd.* v. *Universal Furniture Products (Wembley), Ltd.*, [1934] 1 K.B. 148; [1933] All E.R. Rep. 15 (the 16th of the first 20 instalments of 100 ton parcels of rag flock was the only one not up to Government standards: buyer not entitled to repudiate).

3 [1930] 2 K.B. 312; [1930] All E.R. Rep. 241.

4 [1930] 2 K.B. 312, at p. 331; [1930] All E.R. Rep. 241, at p. 247.

5 [1934] 1 K.B. 148, at p. 157; [1933] All E.R. Rep. 15, at pp. 18–19.

6 [1962] N.Z.L.R. 723.

7 At p. 726.

expensive advertising campaign ruined by further unsatisfactory deliveries.[1] B had therefore been justified in rescinding the contract.

C IMPLIED OBLIGATIONS

The Act deals with a number of situations in which, subject to the over-riding intention of the parties, terms may be implied into contracts for the sale of goods.

i Stipulations as to time

Section 10 (1) is rather a curious provision. It lays down:

> "Unless a different intention appears from the terms of contract, stipulations as to time of payment are not deemed to be of the essence of a contract of sale. Whether any other stipulation as to time is of the essence of the contract or not depends on the terms of contract."

It is undoubtedly true that, although a seller can withold delivery against payment,[2] he cannot immediately repudiate the contract unless some term of the contract (expressed or implied) entitles him to do so.[3] However, it is well established that in commercial contracts for the sale of goods time will usually be of the essence as far as *delivery* is concerned.[4] Hence if goods are to be shipped during a particular period, failure to do so will constitute breach of the seller's obligations under the contract of sale.[5] Similarly, if the buyer fails to collect the goods by the day appointed, the seller will be entitled to repudiate the contract.[6]

Where the time of delivery is only ascertainable by reference to the time of dispatch (as often happens in contracts where the goods are to be shipped from overseas), then it is the time of shipment which must be strictly conformed to.[7] The position is complicated where no precise time of shipment is given, as would be the case with the familiar words that the ship carrying the goods is "expected ready to load" by a specified date or during a specified period. Failure to load by or during the time stipulated will not in itself constitute a breach of the contract if, at the time the contract was formed, the expectation in the vessel's loading date was reasonable.[8]

---

1 Citing the following passage from the judgment of BIGHAM, J., in *Millars' Karri and Jarrah Co.* v. *Weddel, Turner & Co.* (1908), 14 Com. Cas. 25, at p. 29; "If the breach is of such a kind, or takes place in such circumstances as reasonably to lead to the inference that similar breaches will be committed in relation to subsequent deliveries, the whole contract may there and then be regarded as repudiated . . .".
2 Delivery and payment being concurrent conditions by s. 28, see above, p. 133.
3 *Martindale* v. *Smith* (1841), 1 Q.B. 389; and see below, p. 315.
4 *Hartley* v. *Hymans*, [1920] 3 K.B. 475, at p. 484; [1920] All E.R. Rep. 328, at p. 332, *per* McCARDIE, J.
5 *J. Aron & Co. (Inc.)* v. *Comptoir Wegimont*, [1921] 3 K.B. 435; whether or not the buyer had suffered any loss: *Bowes* v. *Shand* (1877), 2 App. Cas. 455.
6 *Harrington* v. *Browne* (1917), 23 C.L.R. 297.
7 *Bowes* v. *Shand* (1877), 2 App. Cas. 455.
8 *Sanday & Co.* v. *Keighley, Maxted & Co.* (1922), 91 L.J.K.B. 624; *Finnish Govt.* v. *Ford & Co., Ltd.* (1921), 6 Ll. L. Rep. 188; see 89 L.Q.R. 93, at pp. 99–100.

It is possible for a party to waive a condition relating to the time of delivery (as he can any other condition of the contract).[1] The most likely situation giving rise to such a waiver is where the buyer continues to press for delivery after the contract date has passed. In *Hartley* v. *Hymans*,[2] S agreed to supply B with 11,000 lbs. of cotton yarn at the rate of 1,100 lbs. per week, delivery to commence in September, 1918. On this basis delivery would have been complete by mid-November, 1918. However S did not start deliveries until the end of October and then he only delivered about half the stipulated amount for each instalment. By the end of February, 1919, S delivered seven further instalments, which averaged about half the 1,100 lbs. Throughout this period B exhorted S to make better deliveries, and from time to time warned S that B's own customer might cancel, thus leaving B no alternative but to cancel his contract with S. In mid-March, B purported to cancel the order and refused to accept the instalment then ready for delivery. McCardie, J., held[3] that B was not entitled to reject delivery under the contract because he had waived his right to enforce the condition as to time.

If compliance with a time clause has been waived, the buyer (or seller) is entitled once again to make time of the essence by giving the other party reasonable notice of the time for performance.[4] There exist a number of older authorities which suggested that it was in some way necessary to imply a new agreement to the effect that the contract period should be extended until the party waiving his rights gave notice requiring delivery within a reasonable period.[5] This seems rather a clumsy way of justifying the right to give notice. The better view was that advanced by the Court of Appeal in *Charles Rickards, Ltd.* v. *Oppenheim*[6] that the interests of the parties are best safeguarded by reference to the reasonableness of the notice. In considering this criterion such factors can be taken into account as[7] the time specified by the notice in relation to the contract itself; whether the party has been pressing for speedy delivery of the goods; and, of course, whether time was originally of the essence. And it follows from this last consideration that the court was recognising that time may, by reasonable notice, be made of the essence, even if originally it was not a condition of the contract.[8]

---

1 Section 11 (1) (*a*) deals only with waiver by the buyer; but it is equally possible for a seller to waive a condition, for example, that the buyer should make available a confirmed letter of credit before delivery commences: *Panoutsos* v. *Raymond Hadley Corporation of New York*, [1917] 2 K.B. 473; [1916–17] All E.R. Rep. 448.

2 [1920] 3 K.B. 475; [1920] All E.R. Rep. 328.

3 He also held that B was estopped from claiming that the contract had ceased to be valid after mid-November 1918: see also to the same effect *Charles Rickards, Ltd.* v. *Oppenheim*, [1950] 1 K.B. 616, at p. 623; [1950] 1 All E.R., 420, at p. 423, *per* Denning, L.J.

4 A rule as applicable to contracts of sale as to contracts for work and materials: *Charles Rickards, Ltd.* v. *Oppenheim* (above).

5 It was probably bound up in the need to satisfy the requirement of evidence in writing by virtue of s. 4 of the Sale of Goods Act: see the review of the authorities by McCardie, J., in *Hartley* v. *Hymans*, [1920] 3 K.B. 475; [1920] All E.R. Rep. 328.

6 [1950] 1 K.B. 616; [1950] 1 All E.R. 420.

7 [1950] 1 K.B. 616, at p. 624; [1950] 1 All E.R. 420, at p. 424; *per* Denning, L.J., citing *Stickney* v. *Keeble*, [1915] A.C. 386, at p. 419, *per* Lord Parker.

8 See also *per* Singleton, L.J., [1950] 1 K.B. 616, at p. 628; [1950] 1 All E.R. 420, at p. 426.

ii As to title

Section 1 of the Supply of Goods (Implied Terms) Act 1973 has amended s. 12 of the 1893 Act in a manner which is not entirely consistent with the definition of the contract of sale in s. 1 of the 1893 Act.[1] According to that definition, a contract of sale of goods is "a contract whereby the seller transfers or agrees to transfer the property in goods to the buyer".[2] According to the new s. 12 there are now clearly established two types of contract for the sale of goods: the "normal" type and the type falling within s. 12 (2).

The contracts in the latter category are those where "there appears from the contract or is to be inferred from the circumstances of the contract an intention that the seller should transfer only such title as he or a third person may have". In other words, s. 12 (2) envisages contracts of sale in which the "property" transferred will not necessarily be full ownership of the goods in question.

a *Contracts to which s. 12 (2) does not apply*

Unless unscrupulous traders look upon s. 12 (2) as an invitation to include terms in contracts of sale to restrict their liability for breach of s. 12 (1) by suggesting that they are selling some right less than ownership of the goods, most contracts of sale will fall within s. 12 (1). Accordingly most buyers will be able to rely upon the following.

1 *A condition that S has a right to sell.* By s. 12 (1) (a) there is:

> "an implied condition on the part of the seller that in the case of a sale, he has a right to sell the goods, and in the case of an agreement to sell, he will have a right to sell the goods at the time when the property is to pass".

Without wishing to over-emphasis the point already raised about the nature of a contract of sale in relation to the concept of property, s. 12 (1) (a) does at least make clear that, in every contract of sale, unless it is a case covered by s. 12 (2), such a condition is implied. Furthermore, as s. 55 (3) declares void any term purporting to exclude s. 12, it will only be possible to oust s. 12 (1) (a) by a clause which specifically points to the seller's possible defect in title, or by circumstances that clearly show that the seller may not be selling as owner.

By establishing that a contract of sale was based upon the concept of a transfer of ownership through the rather crude medium of an implied *condition,* the Sale of Goods Act created problems not just of a possible conflict between s. 1 and s. 12. A condition is a term of the contract for breach of which certain remedies lie, and in particular the remedy of rescission or repudiation. But, if there is a breach of s. 12, is the buyer's right to set aside the contract and to obtain his money back affected by the provisions of s. 11 (1), and in particular by s. 11 (1) (c) which limits the buyer's right to that of seeking damages if he has already accepted the goods?

The leading authority on this point is *Rowland* v. *Divall*[3] in which S sold B a car which four months later was discovered to have been stolen. In the course of

---

1 See also above, p. 15.
2 Unless the word "property" is taken to include "special property" (i.e. some right less than ownership) in, as well as full ownership of, goods.
3 [1923] 2 K.B. 500; [1923] All E.R. Rep. 270.

the case it was argued that the use of the car had made *restitutio in integrum* impossible and that there had been an acceptance of the vehicle by the buyer. Nevertheless the Court of Appeal held that B was entitled to his money back in full. He was not obliged to treat the breach of condition as a breach of warranty because he had not obtained what he had bargained for, namely ownership of the vehicle, so that there had been a total failure of consideration.

The principle upon which this decision was based is equally applicable to goods held under a hire purchase agreement. If it transpires that they were not the property of the original owner, nor therefore of the finance company to which they were transferred as part of the hire purchase transaction, the hirer is entitled to set aside the agreement and to recover his deposit and any instalments he may have paid under the contract.[1]

Under a contract of sale there is a breach if the seller has not a right to sell at the time the contract is entered into, or, if it is an agreement to sell, there is a breach if he does not have the right to sell at the time when property is to pass. As a consequence the buyer is entitled to repudiate even if he has not been dispossessed. Furthermore, once he has repudiated, even if the seller acquires title (or a right to pass title by buying out the rights of the true owner), the buyer is still entitled to recover the price he has paid. In *Butterworth* v. *Kingsway Motors, Ltd.*,[2] H, the hirer of a car under a hire purchase agreement, sold the vehicle, but continued to pay the instalments due on it to O, the finance company. Subsequently the car was sold to S who then sold it to B. At a later date H discovered that she had no right to sell the car and informed O of what had occurred. O thereupon contacted B and asked for the return of the vehicle. Immediately B notified S that the car had not been S's to sell and that therefore he (B) wanted his money returned. Shortly afterwards H completed the payments due under the hire purchase agreement with O and O accepted the final payment as a discharge of its interest in the vehicle. Nevertheless PEARSON, J., held that the facts were covered by *Rowland* v. *Divall* notwithstanding B's possession of the car for eleven months and the fact that, at the time the writ was issued, there was no likelihood of an adverse claim being made.

The position of the buyer who had repudiated may be contrasted with the intermediate buyers who had not taken any steps to avoid their contract by the time H paid out O. PEARSON, J., went on to hold that H acquired title as between herself and O and "that the title so acquired went to feed the previously defective titles of the subsequent buyers and enured to their benefit".[3] Although this proposition creates a curious distinction between a buyer who has, and one who has not, repudiated at the critical moment, it is supported by strong persuasive authority,[4] and it does provide the unfortunate parties, caught up in such a chain of transactions, some measure of protection.

---

1 *Karflex, Ltd.* v. *Poole*, [1933] 2 K.B. 251; [1933] All E.R. Rep. 46.
2 [1954] 2 All E.R. 694.   3 At p. 701.
4 PEARSON, J., relied particularly upon dicta of members of the Court of Appeal in *Whitehorn Bros.* v. *Davison*, [1911] 1 K.B. 463, at pp. 475, 481, 486. The principle has since been applied by an appeal court in New South Wales: *Patten* v. *Thomas Motors Pty., Ltd.* (1965), 66 S.R. N.S.W. 458, which also relied on a number of dicta from Australian cases, notably *Guthrie* v. *Motor Credits, Ltd.* (1963) 37 A.L.J.R. 167, at. p. 168.

Under a hire purchase transaction where the "owner" hiring out the goods turns out to have no title, the same principle is applicable. Under the existing hire purchase legislation,[1] there is an implied condition that the "owner" will have a right to sell *at the time when property is to pass*. This moment will depend on when, in accordance with the contract, the hirer is entitled to exercise his option to purchase. However, in *Karflex, Ltd.* v. *Poole*[2] the view was taken by ACTON and GODDARD, J.J., that, on the terms of the agreement, there was also a condition, implied if not express, that the *"owner" was the true owner*, and this approach was also adopted in *Warman* v. *Southern Counties Car Finance Corporation, Ltd.*[3] On the other hand, in *Mercantile Union Guarantee Corporation, Ltd.* v. *Wheatley*,[4] GODDARD, J., changed his mind and adopted the principle that it was only *at the time of delivery* of the goods to the hirer that such a condition operated.

Despite this slight area of uncertainty, it is apparent that, if the tenor of these cases is taken as authoritative, a hirer can set aside the hire purchase transaction before he makes any attempt to exercise his option. The finance company is in no better position than a seller whose buyer's possession has not been disturbed. It cannot be claimed that this consequence of the application of legal logic is altogether satisfactory.

It was argued in *Rowland* v. *Divall* that a party who obtained temporary use of goods cannot claim that the consideration has totally failed. The cases cited in support of this contention concerned a lessee who was dispossessed by the true owner of the premises,[5] and the user of a patent who discovered that the person who had licensed his use of an invention was not entitled to patent rights in the equipment in question.[6] While there may well be a sound basis for distinguishing these decisions in a case involving the relationship between buyer and seller, there is less ground for distinguishing them in the case of the hirer under a hire purchase agreement.

In *Warman* v. *Southern Counties Car Finance Corporation, Ltd.*,[7] this point was placed squarely before the court when the finance company whose title had proved defective, sought payment from the hirer for his seven month use of the vehicle. It is undoubtedly true that a hire purchase agreement involves the renting of the goods for a certain length of time. Nevertheless, FINNEMORE, J., held that, as the real object of such a transaction was to acquire title to the goods, once "the option to purchase goes, the whole value of the agreement to the hirer has gone with it".[8]

---

1 On this point, s. 8 of the Supply of Goods (Implied Terms) Act 1973, now introduces provisions substantially similar to the redrafted s. 12 of the Sale of Goods Act. By s. 8 (1) (*a*), unless it appears from the agreement or is to be inferred from the circumstances that the owner will be transferring only such title as he or a third person may have, there is in every hire-purchase agreement "an implied condition on the part of the owner that he will have a right to sell the goods at the time when property is to pass".
2 [1933] 2 K.B. 251; [1933] All E.R. Rep. 46.
3 [1949] 2 K.B. 576; [1949] 1 All E.R. 711.
4 [1938] 1 K.B. 490; [1937] 4 All E.R. 713.
5 *Hunt* v. *Silk* (1804), 5 East 449.
6 *Taylor* v. *Hare* (1805), 1 B. & P. N.R. 260; *Lawes* v. *Purser* (1856), 6 E. & B. 930.
7 [1949] 2 K.B. 576; [1949] 1 All E.R. 711.
8 [1949] 2 K.B. 576, at p. 582; [1949] 1 All E.R. 711, at p. 714.

The consequence of this line of authority is that the law has reached an unfortunate state of rigidity. It has already been pointed out that the warranty of title was a comparatively late development in the law of sale of goods.[1] For that reason many of the possible implications of regarding it as a *condition* of the contract had not arisen by the time the law was codified in 1893. For a breach of warranty to give rise to a right to reject, it had to be shown that the conduct of the defaulting party amounted to a breach of some condition precedent to the other party's obligations under the contract. It was by no means automatic that a breach of warranty would amount to a breach of a condition precedent. The circumstances to be taken into account in making this judgment would include both the conduct giving rise to the alleged breach and its consequences.

While the decision in *Rowland* v. *Divall* might seem to follow inexorably from the wording of s. 12, some degree of latitude should surely be allowed in cases where no loss results from the breach. Apart from time clauses, in which, once time is of the essence, damage arising from a breach by one party is irrelevant if the other party wishes to rescind (a rule dating from before the Act[2] but not incorporated in the Act), the Act has been unfortunate in establishing this sort of inflexibility.[3] It would not be impossible for the courts to rephrase the question, has that condition been broken, and to ask instead whether the conduct of the defaulting party in the circumstances amounts to a breach of the condition. In *Butterworth* v. *Kingsway Motors, Ltd.*,[4] for example, while the seller did not have a right to sell, could it not be said that, as long as the buyer was in undisturbed possession, and with the possibility of his title being established, he was not entitled to set aside the contract: that there had been no actual breach of the implied condition?

In fact, s. 12 (1) (or s. 12 (1) (*a*) as it has now become) was not an exact reproduction of the common law in one further respect. Although *Eichholz* v. *Bannister*,[5] had established as a general principle that a sale of goods carried with it a guarantee of title, the way in which this undertaking was phrased varied from one case to another. Chalmers included these obligations within s. 12 (the condition that the seller has the right to sell in sub-s. (1); the warranty of quiet possession in sub-s. (2);[6] and the warranty of freedom from charge or incumbrance in sub-s. (3)), as a means of incorporating the common law undertaking as to title into the Act. Prior to 1893 a breach of this general undertaking could either constitute a condition (precedent) in appropriate circumstances or would be treated as a collateral undertaking (such as the warranty of quiet possession) for which damages only would lie.

2 *The warranty of quiet possession.* Under the redrafted s. 12 (1) (*b*), there is an implied warranty "that the buyer will enjoy quiet possession of the goods

---

1 Above p. 16. And it was a *warranty* of title: see *Morley* v. *Attenborough* (1849), 3 Exch. 500.

2 *Bowes* v. *Shand* (1877), 2 App. Cas. 455.

3 For the other obviously absurd situation, see *Re Moore & Co. and Landauer & Co.*, [1921] 2 K.B. 519; [1921] All E.R. Rep. 466, dealt with above, p. 126.

4 [1954] 2 All E.R. 694; [1954] 1 W.L.R. 1286.

5 (1864), 17 C.B. N.S. 708; above p. 16.

6 These "warranties" are now in one paragraph, s. 12 (1) (*b*), by virtue of s. 1 of the 1973 Act.

except so far as it may be disturbed by the owner or other person entitled to the benefit of any charge or encumbrance" disclosed to the buyer before the contract was made.

The existence of this warranty creates two major inter-related problems: the first being one of definition or description; the second being that of distinguishing it from the condition covering the right to sell in s. 12 (1) (*a*). It has already been pointed out that prior to 1893 the nascent undertaking as to title was referred to in a number of different forms, including a warranty of quiet possession.[1] This tendency was hardly surprising in view of the obvious similarity of terminology with the covenants for title and for quiet enjoyment in conveyances and leases.[2] However, it should be stressed that at most it was an analogy, and not one that is to be taken too far.

In *Mason* v. *Burningham*,[3] B purchased a typewriter from S for £20 and subsequently spent £11.10s on having it repaired. It was then discovered that the typewriter was in fact "stolen goods" and B had to return it to the owner. B sought to recover the £11.10s as well as the £20 on the ground that there had been a breach of warranty of quiet possession. On the basis of the trial judge's finding that the repairs were "the ordinary and natural thing" for her to have done, it was held that her claim succeeded. The argument advanced on S's behalf that the warranty did not apply to disturbance of possession by the true owner, by analogy with the title paramount principle of conveyancing law, was rejected. As Lord GREENE, M.R., pointed out,[4] the covenant for quiet enjoyment set out in the second schedule of the Law of Property Act 1925, contained words excluding from its ambit the situation where the disturbance was by title paramount. However, no such limitation appeared in s. 12 of the Sale of Goods Act; no authority suggested such a limitation existed; and the Court was not prepared to introduce such a gloss on the wording of the Act.

This conclusion is acceptable enough, but it should not follow from this approach that the wording of s. 12 (1) (*b*) should be applied in its widest sense. It would be totally unreasonable to suppose that a seller was guaranteeing the buyer's possession against every disturbance that might occur. If there exists some nexus between the seller and the disturbance, either because the title passed was defective, or because the seller himself interfered with the buyer's possession,[5] then the warranty is broken. If there is no such nexus, for example the goods are seized by a party who alleges that the buyer had sold them to that party, then there is no breach flowing from the contract of sale.

It is clear that the warranty of quiet possession is wider in compass than the condition that the buyer has a right to sell. The condition is broken at the time

---

1 See the early N.S.W. case of *Fitzgerald* v. *Luck* (1839), 1 Legge 118, at p. 122, *per* DOWLING, C.J., cited *per* WINDEYER, J., in *Healing (Sales) Pty., Ltd.* v. *Inglis Electrix Pty., Ltd.* (1968), 42 A.L.J.R. 280, at p. 291.
2 See *Howell* v. *Richards* (1809), 11 East 633, at pp. 642–3; *Baynes & Co.* v. *Lloyd & Sons*, [1895] 1 Q.B. 820, at p. 824; *Niblett, Ltd.* v. *Confectioners' Materials Co., Ltd.*, [1921] 3 K.B. 387, p. 403; [1921] All E.R. Rep. 459, at p. 465; *per* ATKIN, L.J.
3 [1949] 2 K.B. 545; [1949] 2 All E.R. 134.
4 [1949] 2 K.B., at p. 563; [1949] 2 All E.R., at p. 144.
5 As in *Healing (Sales) Pty., Ltd.* v. *Inglis Electrix Pty., Ltd.* (1968), 42 A.L.J.R. 280, where the seller wrongfully seized the goods.

of sale, or at the time when property is to pass under an agreement to sell. The warranty of quiet possession can only be broken at the time the disturbance takes place. It is not unreasonable that the buyer should be protected by the latter provision long after the limitation period for breach of the former may have run. Furthermore, the warranty can provide protection against disturbance by the seller himself, in a situation where there is no question of the condition that he had a right to sell being broken.[1] Of course in such a case the action for breach of warranty would be an alternative remedy to an action in tort.

On the whole these differences are slight. The likelihood is that a breach of the condition will also involve a breach of the warranty, though the converse is not necessarily true. A defect in the seller's title will usually give rise to a disturbance of the buyer's possession but a disturbance of possession could equally well arise because of some charge or encumbrance over the goods held by a third party. This possibility will be considered shortly, but the degree of overlap between the condition and the warranty is in part due to the fact that the condition is broader than a covenant of title. In *Niblett, Ltd.* v. *Confectioners' Materials Co., Ltd.,*[2] B purchased a consignment of tins of milk under a c.i.f. contract. Payment was made against the shipping documents, but when the goods were received B was notified that they infringed the Nestlé's trade mark. Before he could obtain possession of them, B was obliged to remove the offending labels from all the tins. As a consequence he could only sell the goods at a loss. There was no doubt that S had "owned" the goods in question, but the Court of Appeal held that he nevertheless lacked the "right to sell" them because the Nestlé's company could have restrained him from so doing. Accordingly there had been a breach of the implied condition. As to the warranty of quiet possession, neither BANKES, nor SCRUTTON, L.J.J., was willing to commit himself, but ATKIN, L.J., was prepared to hold that it had been broken.[3] B could hardly enjoy quiet possession if, in order to deal with the goods, he was obliged to remove the label on each tin.

3 *A warranty of freedom from encumbrances.* In addition to setting out the warranty of quiet possession, s. 12 (1) (*b*) also provides for:

> "an implied warranty that the goods are free, and will remain free until the time when the property is to pass, from any charge or encumbrance not disclosed or known to the buyer before the contract is made."

The occasions on which a breach of this part of s. 12 will occur will be rare for the obvious reason that charges or encumbrances unprotected by possession of goods are relatively few; and even more rarely will there be a breach of the warranty of freedom from encumbrances that will not also involve a breach of the warranty of quiet possession, a fact recognised by the redrafting of s. 12 to bring the former two sub-ss. ((2) and (3)) together into the one paragraph.

In *Lloyds and Scottish Finance, Ltd.* v. *Modern Cars and Caravans (Kingston), Ltd.,*[4] S had bought a caravan from a debtor against whom a writ of fi. fa. had

---

1 See above, n. 5, p. 171.
2 [1921] 3 K.B. 387; [1921] All E.R. Rep. 459.
3 [1921] 3 K.B., at p. 403; [1921] All E.R. Rep., at p. 403.
4 [1966] 1 Q.B. 764; [1964] 2 All E.R. 732.

been issued and a warrant served. Soon afterwards S learnt of the position but nevertheless sold the caravan to B, a finance company, as part of a hire purchase transaction. The sheriff seized the caravan from the hirer. It was held, *inter alia*, that, although S had transferred a good title to B, he had been in breach of both warranties implied by s. 12.

In this case, B had remained the owner of the goods under the hire purchase transaction, indeed he became the owner by virtue of it. However, if the buyer in such a situation had himself transferred title in the goods (for example, if the hirer had exercised his option to purchase), then it could hardly be said that his (B's) possession had been disturbed. He would therefore be obliged to rely upon the warranty of freedom from encumbrances alone.[1]

The final point that should be noticed about these warranties (and indeed the condition in s. 12 (1) (*a*)) is that they operate irrespective of the seller's knowledge of the true situation. Hence in *Lloyds and Scottish Finance, Ltd.* v. *Modern Cars and Caravans (Kingston), Ltd.*, the fact that the seller to the finance company had been aware by the date of that transaction of the "charge or encumbrance" was irrelevant.[2]

b *Where the sale is only of such title as the seller or a third party might have*

Section 12 (2) is an entirely new provision which regulates the situation where:

> "there appears from the contract or is to be inferred from the circumstances of the contract an intention that the seller should transfer only such title as he or a third person may have."

Under the previous s. 12 the condition in (1) and the warranties in (2) and (3) were excluded altogether if the circumstances of the contract showed a contrary intention. Thus, if a sale of a debtor's goods took place on behalf of the sheriff, the circumstances would demonstrate that the sale was only of such interest that the debtor himself possessed. Section 12 was ousted, and there was no protection afforded by the Act to a buyer of the debtor's goods.

The new s. 12 (2) (*a*), however, provides for:

> "an implied warranty that all charges or encumbrances known to the seller and not known to the buyer have been disclosed to the buyer before contract is made".

It will be realised that the protection is not as wide as that offered by s. 12 (1) (*b*) because of the limitation that the charges or encumbrances to be disclosed are only those "*known to the seller* and not known to the buyer".

And s. 12 (2) (*b*) implies a warranty that neither:

> "(i) the seller; nor
> (ii) in a case where the parties to the contract intend that the seller should transfer only such title as a third person may have, that person; nor

---

1 As in the unreported Australian case of *Steinke* v. *Edwards*, a brief note of which appears in (1935), 8 A.L.J. 368.
2 See *Steinke* v. *Edwards* in which the parties had been totally ignorant of the unpaid tax on the vehicle which led to its being seized from a purchaser from the buyer in the case.

> (iii) anyone claiming through or under the seller or that third person otherwise
> than under a charge or encumbrance disclosed or known to the buyer
> before the contract is made"

will disturb the buyer's quiet possession of the goods. In other words the protection of the buyer's quiet possession is restricted. It would not provide him with a remedy if the interference was from the true owner, not being the seller or the third person.

iii Correspondence with description

By s. 13 (1) of the Act:

> "Where there is a contract for the sale of goods by description, there is an implied condition that the goods shall correspond with the description; and if the sale be by sample, as well as by description, it is not sufficient that the bulk of the goods corresponds with the sample if the goods do not also correspond with the description."

And s. 13 (2) makes clear that

> "A sale of goods shall not be prevented from being a sale by description by reason only that, being exposed for sale . . ., they are selected by the buyer."

There has already been a good deal of discussion of how a failure to provide goods answering the contract description amounts to a failure to perform the contract rather than a breach of any term implied in the contract.[1] It has been suggested that the effect of s. 13 is to divide, or at least to reinforce the division of, the idea of a contract description into two aspects: the fundamental obligation to perform the contract, and the ancillary parts of the description that do not go to the root of the contract. Prior to 1893, the subsidiary parts of the contract would not have been regarded as constituting a condition precedent, if indeed they were regarded as being contractual at all.

A useful illustration, though not a case on sale, is *Windle* v. *Barker*.[2] In a charterparty, the ship was described as 180 to 200 tons or thereabouts, but, as the owners' agents who negotiated the contract admitted to the charterer, they had no certain information as to the exact size of the vessel. When the ship reached the port of loading the charterer measured it and discovered that it was nearly 258 tons.[3] He thereupon refused to load. The Court of Exchequer Chamber held that this action was without justification: as the parties well knew, the agents had no precise knowledge of the size of the ship so that there was no basis for arguing that the description of the size of the vessel was a term in the contract.[4] However, individual members of the Court pointed out that the charterer would not have been under an obligation to load if the difference had been unreasonably great. The principal reason given was that the condition precedent that would have been broken would not have been a contractual

---

1 Above, pp. 125–7.
2 (1856), 25 L.J.Q.B. 349.
3 A ton is a measurement of space not weight. It equals 100 cubic feet of enclosed space.
4 A decision which was clearly correct: the agents' statment was one of their opinion, and did not amount to an assertion of fact: see above, p. 149.

term, but the underlying principle that the charterer would have obtained something quite different from what he had contracted for. If the description of the vessel's tonnage had been a contractual obligation, then of course there would have been a breach in providing a vessel larger than that described, although here again the difference would not have been so substantial or material as to have excused the charterer from loading. He would have been limited to a remedy in damages for losses incurred, if any.

In contracts of sale, the effect of s. 13 was to make breach of the obligation to provide goods answering the contract description automatically a basis upon which the buyer could, if he wished, repudiate the contract. Failure to satisfy an ancillary part of the description even one of minor significance, would entitle the buyer to take this course. In *Re Moore & Co. and Landauer & Co.*,[1] the goods were in keeping with the main part of the contract description—they were Australian canned fruit—but they were not all packed 30 tins to the case as was also specified in the contract. The fact that some were packed 24 tins to the case made no commercial difference to their value, but it was nevertheless held to be a sufficient ground for the buyer to reject because, by s. 13, the term broken was a condition of the contract.

While it is possible to accept this decision as an unfortunate consequence of the drafting of the 1893 Act, the possibility that s. 13 can give contractual effect to a representation that does not amount to a term in the contract according to common law principles should be resisted. A representation of opinion cannot, in theory, become a statement of fact by the operation of s. 13. Nevertheless, in *Beale* v. *Taylor*,[2] the Court of Appeal used s. 13 in such a way as to suggest that it could create a contractual obligation out of what appeared to be a statement of opinion. S, a private motorist, advertised his car for sale in a motoring journal as a "Herald convertible, white, 1961, twin carbs". Unknown to either party the vehicle was a reconstruction of halves from two "Heralds", one of which was of an earlier date. On anything but a detailed examination of the underneath of the car it looked what it was said to be. Unfortunately S did not have legal representation. The argument which prevailed in *Oscar Chess, Ltd.* v. *Williams*,[3] that a statement by a private seller on a matter not within his knowledge and on which the buyer could just as well exercise his own skill and judgment, was not raised. On the issue of whether a warranty (i.e. a contractual term) existed, *Oscar Chess* was clearly correct. But the questions must be asked (1) whether the pleading of s. 13 in that case would have produced a different result; and (2) whether the existence of an advertisement thus describing the vehicle in *Beale* v. *Taylor* made the case distinguishable from *Oscar Chess*.

It is submitted that s. 13 cannot turn non-contractual statements of *opinion* into terms of the contract. The only error in the reasoning employed in *Oscar Chess* was to suggest that the means of knowledge and the skill and judgment in the representor were the test of an intention to warrant, rather than of an intention to make a statement of fact. The absence of such knowledge, and of

---

1 [1921] 2 K.B. 519; [1921] All E.R. Rep. 466.
2 [1967] 3 All E.R. 253; [1967] 1 W.L.R. 1193.
3 [1957] 1 All E.R. 325; [1957] 1 W.L.R. 370; see above, p. 151.

skill and judgment, should have led the Court of Appeal to conclude in *Oscar Chess* that the seller had merely made a statement of opinion about the age of his car. It would not therefore have been possible for s. 13 to have operated. Does the fact that the statement of the age of the car by the non-expert seller, who has no accurate source of information, is contained in an advertisement make any difference? It would seem that the decision in *Beale* v. *Taylor* can be supported, if at all, only on this basis. By making the statement in the advertisement, the implication is that the statement serves to identify the subject-matter by reference to the age and make of the vehicle. Whether this deduction is correct is uncertain because, unfortunately, the Court itself gave no adequate explanation of the grounds for its decision.

iv Conditions of merchantable quality and fitness for purpose

Under the 1893 Act, the conditions that the goods should be suitable for the buyer's purpose and of merchantable quality were covered by s. 14 (1) and (2). As well as adding to them and amending them the Law Commission, for no very good reason,[1] decided to alter the arrangement of these provisions. Under the amendments introduced by the Supply of Goods (Implied Terms) Act 1973, the undertaking as to merchantable quality now appears before that of suitability for purpose, though it retains its original numbering (s. 14 (2)); the introductory words of s. 14 have been redrafted separately as s. 14 (1); while the condition of suitability now appears as s. 14 (3).

a *No condition or warranty as to quality or fitness except by statute*

By s. 14 (1):

> "Except as provided by this section, and section 15 of this Act and subject to the provisions of any other enactment, there is no implied condition or warranty as to the quality or fitness for any particular purpose of goods supplied under a contract of sale."

The Law Commission, in drafting this sub-section, recommended no change in its effect.[2] While it is true that the provision has not had a restrictive effect, it should at least be realised that it could be prejudicial to the buyer. The Law Commission observed[3] that it was "of obviouus importance in cases where the seller is not acting in the course of business". While sub-ss. (2) and (3), as we shall see, apply only in sales in the course of a business, it should not necessarily be accepted that terms cannot be implied from the circumstances of a particular case into sales between private individuals.

In *Sullivan* v. *Constable*,[4] B and S had been negotiating the sale of S's yacht.

---

1 As the case law on the old s. 14 is bound to be relevant in a number of ways to the interpretation of the new s. 14, the advantage of retaining the numbering of the original sub-ss. (1) and (2) would seem far to outweigh any technical preferences for the new arrangement.
2 Exemption Clauses in Contracts: First Report (1969) (Law Com. 24), para. 29.
3 *Loc. cit.*
4 (1932), 48 T.L.R. 369.

S adamantly refused to guarantee its condition. In an attempt to conclude matters, B sent S a cheque for the price together with a letter stating that he would take the yacht guaranteed on the terms he had been seeking. It was held that, by receiving and retaining the payment, S must, by implication, be taken to have accepted the terms set out in the letter.

There is a close analogy between this case and the situation where a buyer asks for something for an expressed purpose. A contract then entered into by a seller who does not disavow the fitness of the goods should in principle include a term guaranteeing their suitability. If one takes s. 14 (3) in conjunction with s. 14 (1). it is arguable that an express statement of a specific purpose by a buyer followed by a sale creates only an "implied term", and then only if "the seller sells goods in the course of a business". Despite the logical force of this contention, such an approach would be patently unsatisfactory because it would place terms relating to the suitability of goods on a different basis from those covering other aspects of the goods. It can hardly be supposed that, had the buyer in *Sullivan* v. *Constable* stated that he would take the yacht guaranteed for ocean racing, he would have lost the case on the ground that, where the purpose is expressly revealed, s. 14 prevents claims against a private owner.

The explanation of this possible area of conflict is that, unwittingly, the expression "implied condition" has been used in different ways. In s. 14 (1) it deals only with terms that arise from the fact of the sale itself (and this is also its meaning in s. 14 (2) covering the condition of merchantability). In s. 14 (3), however, the "implied condition" applies both to terms implied from the fact of a sale (e.g. where the buyer asks for an item the use of which is obvious), and to express terms which arise from the conduct of the parties (i.e. the situation referred to above where the seller, by acting on the buyer's request for goods for an expressed special purpose, may be said to assent by implication to suitability for that purpose being an *express* term in the contract).

b *Sales "in the course of a business"*

The conditions as to merchantability and suitability are to be implied into sales "in the course of a business"; and "business" includes "a profession and the activities of any government department . . . local authority or statutory undertaker" (s. 62 (1)).[1]

In the original s. 14 there was a regrettable difference of wording between the two conditions. Under the condition as to suitability, the goods had to be "of a description which it is in the course of the seller's business to supply"; while in relation to merchantability the seller had only to deal in goods of the description. There was a degree of uncertainty about the meaning of both limitations.

In *Ashington Piggeries, Ltd.* v. *Christopher Hill, Ltd.*,[2] S was a manufacturer of and dealer in animal feeding-stuffs. He had never made a feedstuff for mink,

---

1 Section 14 will also apply to a sale by an agent in the course of a business *unless* his principal is not selling in the course of a business *and* either B is aware of this fact or reasonable steps were taken before the contract was made to bring the fact to B's attention (s. 14 (5)).

2 [1972] A.C. 441; [1971] 1 All E.R. 847; see also above, p. 124.

as he made clear to B, but he agreed to make up such a compound from a formula provided by B. Could it be said (1) that the goods were of a description which it was in the course of the seller's business to supply; or (2) that the seller dealt in goods of that description?

The Court of Appeal[1] applied the word "description" in the strict sense of the contract description. As S had never compounded mink food before, the goods were not those which it was in the course of his business to supply,[2] nor did he deal in goods of that description.

The House of Lords was unanimous in rejecting the narrow interpretation of the words "of a description which it is in the course of the seller's business to supply". Indeed, the use of a general form "of *a* description" made a restrictive interpretation difficult to accept. As Lord HODSON pointed out, S's business "was to make up compounds for animal feeding" and he was only using raw materials which he regularly handled.[3]

When it came to the condition of merchantability, however, the requirement that S should deal in "goods of that description" was given a wide range of interpretations. The majority view was that, as long as the seller dealt in goods of that kind, it did not matter that he had not dealt before in goods of the contract description. On the other hand, Lords HODSON and DIPLOCK agreed with the Court of Appeal that the word "description" in this sub-section should be strictly applied and limited to the "contract description".

This case does illustrate the urgent need for reform that existed when the 1973 Act was before Parliament. The terminology used in 1893 had created unnecessary difficulties. In the classic pre-1893 statement of the law by MELLOR, J., in *Jones* v. *Just*[4] it is significant that for either term to be implied the goods had to be those which the supplier manufactured or produced, "or in which he deals". As Lord WILBERFORCE suggested in the *Ashington Piggeries* case,[5] there was no reason to suppose that the Act was designed to introduce a change in the law when it used different phrases in the two sub-sections. Nor did his Lordship see any obstacle to regarding a seller as dealing in goods of such a description if the goods in question were being supplied for the first time.

Under the new s. 14 these problems are resolved. It is irrelevant if the goods are not those in which a seller has dealt in the past, as long as the sale is in the course of business. If a manufacturer of metal goods suddenly decides to produce electrical trouser presses,[6] the conditions in s. 14 will be implied at the time of the first sale. Nor will it be possible to argue that ancillary "dealings" are not

---

1 *Sub nom. Christopher Hill, Ltd.* v. *Ashington Piggeries, Ltd.*, [1969] 3 All E.R. 1496.
2 Purporting to apply, though in fact adopting a very restrictive view of, *Spencer Trading Co., Ltd.* v. *Devon*, [1947] 1 All E.R. 284, at p. 286.
3 [1972] A.C. 441, at p. 469; [1971] 1 All E.R. 847, at p. 855. Although there was overall general agreement on the conclusion, there were contrasting ways of reaching that goal: cf. Lord DIPLOCK, [1972] A.C. 441, at p. 505; [1971] 1 All E.R. 847, at p. 885; with Lord WILBERFORCE [1972] A.C., at p. 494; [1971] 1 All E.R., at p. 876.
4 (1868), L.R. 3 Q.B. 197, at pp. 202–3.
5 [1972] A.C. 441, at pp. 494–5; [1971] 1 All E.R. 847, at p. 876.
6 The facts of *Robertson (Australia) Pty., Ltd.* v. *Martin* (1956), 94 C.L.R. 30, in which there was a sharp difference of opinion between DIXON and WILLIAMS, JJ., as to whether the former s. 14 applied.

covered. If the Post Office sells one of its surplus vehicles, the sale will clearly be in the course of its general "business activities":[1] it would have been less easy to demonstrate that the Post Office "dealt in" such goods.

The fact that a "business" is defined to include a "profession" can give rise to borderline cases. The doctor's car is run as part of his "business" and is subject to tax relief accordingly. If, when he purchases a new vehicle, he sells off the old, the sale is presumably in the course of his business; although scarcely related to it. But what if he hands it over to his wife for her use, but to be available for himself in an emergency? For tax and insurance purposes, the use is perhaps 20 per cent business and 80 per cent private. When the next new car is due, the second car is sold. If it is traded in for a new one to be used in his practice, the trade in sale would presumably be in the course of the "business", but, if it is sold privately, is the sale in the course of a business or not? The fact that the vehicle was available for business use means that any dealing with it has some connection with the business because of the tax and depreciation factors. On the other hand, would the courts not take the transaction at face value, that is as a normal sale by a private seller?

The use of the expression "in the course of" could in fact be given alternative interpretations. It could mean, if the transaction is related to the business. Hence, if it is dealt with as part of the paper work involved in the business, the sale is in the course of business. Alternatively, where the transaction is out of the normal run of business activities, its apparently private nature takes it out of the course of business.

This issue may be one that the courts will have to resolve. If any criticism is to be aimed at the drafting of this aspect of the legislation, it could be said that its ambit is too wide. In this respect the Molony Committee recommendation may have been preferable, when it suggested[2] that the test should be whether the seller "sells by way of trade to the particular purchaser".

c *The condition of merchantable quality*

By s. 14 (2):

> "Where the seller sells goods in the course of a business, there is an implied condition that the goods supplied under the contract are of merchantable quality, except that there is no such condition—
>
> (*a*) as regards defects specifically drawn to the buyer's attention before the contract is made; or
>
> (*b*) if the buyer examines the goods before the contract is made, as regards defects which that examination ought to reveal."

1 *The definition of merchantable quality.* A variety of definitions of "merchantable quality" had been advanced by judges, but the Law Commission felt the

---

1 The expression "part of his business activities" was that used by the Law Commission in explanation of "in the course of a business": see First Report on Exemption Clauses in Contracts, para. 31, n. 30.
2 Final Report of the Committee on Consumer Protection (1962), Cmnd. 1781, para. 443.

time had come for the Sale of Goods Act itself to include a definition. Accordingly s. 7 (1) of the 1973 Act inserts a new s. 62 (1A) into the 1893 Act:

> "Goods of any kind are of merchantable quality within the meaning of this Act if they are as fit for the purpose or purposes for which goods of that kind are commonly bought as it is reasonable to expect having regard to any description applied to them, the price (if relevant) and all the other relevant circumstances; and any reference in this Act to unmerchantable goods shall be construed accordingly."

The reason advanced by the Law Commission for including this definition was that it was "not satisfactory for an Act which purports to codify a whole branch of the law to use a technical term the meaning of which is far from self-evident and becomes meaningful only when the case law is looked at".[1] It remains to be seen whether the statutory definition makes a great deal of difference in this respect. It is said to be based upon a dictum of DIXON, J., in *Australian Knitting Mills* v. *Grant*,[2] as approved by a majority of the House of Lords in *Henry Kendall & Sons* v. *William Lillico & Sons, Ltd.*[3] Accordingly it would seem almost unavoidable that the courts will seek guidance from the pre-1973 pronouncements of the judges on what the legislature intended by s. 62 (1A).

In deciding whether goods are merchantable, it is essential that one takes account of the description of the goods and the purpose for which they are required. This relationship was made very clear by Lord REID in *Kendall* v. *Lillico* :[4]

> "If the description in the contract was so limited that goods sold under it would normally be used for only one purpose then the goods would be unmerchantable under that description if they were of no use for that purpose. But if the description was so general that goods sold under it are normally used for several purposes, then goods are merchantable under that description if they are fit for any one of those purposes."

However, this pronouncement is an over-simplification. Even if the contract description is in general terms it could well be that the parties had in mind some type of purpose (without the seller guaranteeing the suitability of the goods for that purpose) against which the merchantability of the goods should be tested. In the Australian case of *H. Beecham & Co. Pty., Ltd.* v. *Francis Howard & Co. Pty., Ltd.*,[5] B had made known to S that he (B) wanted quantities of timber for use in making pianos. The contract was finalised in the form that B was to be allowed to select the wood from S's yard. It was later discovered that much of the wood that had been selected, although it had no external signs that anything was wrong, was in fact infected with dry rot. Although no condition of suitability could be implied in the circumstances, it was held that B was entitled to rely upon s. 14 (2):[6]

---

1 Final Report on Exemption Clauses, para. 42.
2 (1933), 50 C.L.R. 387, at p. 418.
3 [1969] 2 A.C. 31; [1968] 2 All E.R. 444.
4 [1969] 2 A.C. 31, at p. 77; [1968] 2 All E.R. 444, at p. 452.
5 [1921] V.L.R. 428.
6 At p. 435.

"A large proportion of the timber was not merchantable in any reasonable sense of the word. That it is all saleable I have no doubt, but I am satisfied that no business man, having a contract to buy spruce timber either for resale or for purposes of manufacture, would think for a moment of accepting this timber, its condition being known, without a very large reduction upon current market price. The plaintiff's witnesses deposed that the infected timber could all be sold for making boxes, and that box-making is one of the purposes for which spruce is commonly used. But it is obvious that box-making must afford opportunity for using timber of a wide range of quality and condition, according to the purposes which the boxes are to fulfil. It seems to me that the evidence of the plaintiff's manager himself on the question of values goes far to dispose of the suggestion that fitness for box-making may be taken as a test of merchantable quality under the present contract."

This decision has had an indirect influence on the law in this country because it was expressly referred to by DIXON, J., when he made the following often quoted statement in *Australian Knitting Mills* v. *Grant*:[1]

"The condition that goods are of merchantable quality requires that they should be in such an actual state that a buyer fully acquainted with the facts and, therefore, knowing what hidden defects exist and not being limited to their apparent condition would buy them without abatement of the price obtainable for such goods if in reasonably sound order and condition . . . "

It was not until the matter was raised in *Kendall* v. *Lillico*[2] that there had been any real discussion in the English courts of the significance of price in this context. The test of merchantability advanced by Lord REID and quoted above[3] was obviously deficient in this respect. As Lord GUEST pointed out in that case,[4] if the test is "that the article is fit for no use few goods would be unmerchantable because use can always be found for goods at a price" (to which one might add, even under the contract description).

In *B. S. Brown & Son Ltd.,* v. *Craiks, Ltd.,*[5] the issue of price was placed squarely before their Lordships. B had ordered large quantities of rayon cloth to his own specification. Some months after deliveries commenced, S was astounded to discover that B had intended to use the cloth for making dresses, for which it was unsuitable. It was admitted that the price was rather high for industrial fabric (36·25d. a yard against 30d. a yard for which it would normally sell). Their Lordships, while suggesting that the DIXON test was too wide, in that there would have to be a substantial difference in the price for which the goods could actually be sold to render them unmerchantable, were prepared to accept that price was a relevant consideration. On the facts, however, it was held that the difference was not so great as to render the goods unmerchantable.

It is obvious from this brief survey that, prior to 1973, the test of merchantability was not altogether easy to define. However, the wording of s. 62 (1A) is

---

1 (1933), 50 C.L.R. 387, at p. 418.
2 [1969] 2 A.C. 31; [1968] 2 All E.R. 444.
3 Above, p. 180.
4 [1969] 2 A.C. 31, at p. 108; [1968] 2 All E.R. 444, at p. 477. See also *per* Lord PEARCE, [1969] 2 A.C. 31, at p. 118; [1968] 2 All E.R. 444, at p. 486.
5 [1970] 1 All E.R. 823.

more of an attempt to bring together the threads of the case-law then to provide an authoritative definition in its own right. This tendency is apparent from its references to purpose, description and price (as well as to "other relevant circumstances") as criteria for the courts to take into account.

Even more striking is the use of the phrase "reasonable to expect". The reference to reasonableness appears to be an attempt to bring in what is regarded as an altogether different test, namely that advanced by Farwell, L.J., in *Bristol Tramways, etc. Carriage Co., Ltd.* v. *Fiat Motors, Ltd.*,[1] according to which merchantable quality meant that:

> "the article is of such quality and in such condition that a reasonable man acting reasonably would, after a full examination, accept it under the circumstances of the case in performance of his offer to buy that article whether he buys for his own use or to sell again."

Although the principal authority cited for this proposition related to saleability under the contract description,[2] the test put forward by the Lord Justice was much wider in ambit. B had ordered an omnibus together with six omnibus chassis. The trial judge had held that B had fully made known to S that the vehicles were to be used for the carriage of passengers in and around Bristol— i.e. for heavy duty work in a hilly district—and that the omnibus and the chassis had proved unsuitable for this purpose. While the Court of Appeal was unanimous in upholding the decision in B's favour for breach of the condition of suitability, only Farwell, L.J., was of the opinion that, in the circumstances, a claim under s. 14 (2) was also available.[3]

Although the test advanced by Farwell, L.J., was adopted by *Benjamin on Sale*,[4] it was defective in that it contained no reference to the price at which the goods were being sold. On the other hand, although the Dixon approach was an attempted synthesis of Farwell L.J.'s dictum and the decision in *Beecham* v. *Howard*,[5] it cannot be claimed that as a statement of principle it was particularly helpful. The Law Commission, through s. 62 (1A), has at least provided an alternative synthesis that makes obvious what factors should be regarded as important. Merchantable quality is inseparable from reasonable suitability of the goods for their common purpose or purposes; and the test of reasonableness is dependent upon any description applied to the goods (and not necessarily *the contract description*), the price being paid and other factors that might be relevant. In order for the buyer to succeed, he must show that the goods are

---

1 [1910] 2 K.B. 831, at p. 841; [1908–10] All E.R. Rep. 113, at p. 117–8.
2 A statement by Lord Ellenborough in *Gardiner* v. *Gray* (1815), 4 Camp. 144, at p. 145: "The intention of both parties must be taken to be that it shall be saleable in the market under the denomination mentioned in the contract between them."
3 "In the present case the materials used, especially as regards the size and strength of necessary fittings, were not of merchantable quality": [1910] 2 K.B. 831, at p. 841; [1908–10] All E.R. Rep. 113, at p. 118.
4 6th Ed. (1920), p. 730; 8th Ed. (1950), p. 645.
5 Two of the four cases cited by Dixon, J., in *Australian Knitting Mills* v. *Grant* (1933), 50 C.L.R. at p. 418, were *Bristol Tramways, etc. Carriage Co.* v. *Fiat Motors, Ltd.* and *H. Beecham & Co.* v. *Francis Howard & Co.*

unsuitable for their only usual purpose,[1] or that, if they are unsuitable for his purpose, though not unsuitable for others, the difference in purpose makes the goods different in character, by reference to description or price or other circumstances, from those he reasonably believed he was ordering.

2 *Defects to which s.* 14 (2) *does not apply*. The implied condition of merchantability does not apply in two circumstances:

> "as regards defects specifically drawn to the buyer's attention before the contract is made" (s. 14 (2) (*a*)).

On the face of it, the Law Commission's argument[2] that it is "desirable in the interests of both buyer and seller to provide that where the seller specifically draws the buyer's attention to defects in the goods, the implied condition of merchantable quality should not apply to such defects" is unexceptionable. However, a note of caution should perhaps be sounded. If the seller notifies the buyer that the goods have a certain defect, but the defect is much more serious than it appeared to be, should the seller be protected? The courts may be faced by difficult questions of whether the defect to which attention was drawn was in fact the defect which rendered the goods unmerchantable. Discolouration and blotches in the bodywork of a car may be the symptoms of a defect leading to such a deterioration of the paintwork that the vehicle as a whole needs respraying. The car is thereby rendered unmerchantable, but it would have to be argued that the true defect had not been called to the buyer's attention. In this type of situation the buyer may be assisted by the fact that s. 14 (2) (*a*) requires the defect to be *specifically* drawn to his attention, a fact which suggests that the precise nature of the defect must be revealed.[3]

> "if the buyer examines the goods before the contract is made, as regards defects which that examination ought to reveal" (s. 14 (2) (*b*)).

This exception is substantially identical with the proviso to the former s. 14 (2) although, as will be discussed shortly, there is a slight, though significant, change of one particular word. It was retained by the Law Commission despite the very obvious criticism that it placed the lazy buyer who made no examination of the goods in a stronger position than one who did make some sort of inspection of the goods. The principal reason why the Commission took this line was that it did not view favourably the alternative approach of making the exception relate to defects which should have come to light if the buyer had taken advantage of whatever opportunity of examining the goods had been made available to him.[4] Of the arguments that can be advanced in favour of the

---

1 As the High Court of Australia observed in *George Wills & Co.* v. *Davids* (1957), 98 C.L.R. 77, at p. 88, before "goods can be characterised as unmerchantable it must be shown that, *as goods of that description or character,* they are defective though no doubt, in many cases, proof of their unfitness for some particular and obvious purpose may well establish that the goods are defective".
2 Final Report, p. 118, para. 49.
3 Inevitably the need to be "precise" will give rise to problems of evidence as to exactly what the seller did say: it is unfortunate therefore that the Law Commission rejected the suggestion that written notice of defects should be required: see *loc. cit.,* para. 50.
4 Final Report, p. 17, para. 48.

Commission's rejection of this alternative, the most telling is the difficulty of assessing what defects would be brought to light by an examination by the particular purchaser in the circumstances under which any examination could have been carried out.

What is more surprising is why the Commission could not have settled for the rule that a seller was only protected as regards defects which the buyer's examination actually revealed. It would seem, as a matter of proof, easier to establish what he did or did not discover than it would be first to establish what sort of inspection he conducted and then to assess what defects such an examination should have revealed.

It is also surprising that the Commission's Report made no reference to one difficulty of interpretation that had actually arisen in respect of the proviso. In *Thornett and Fehr* v. *Beers & Sons*,[1] the parties agreed that their representatives should meet at a warehouse so that the goods (barrels of glue) could be inspected. In fact B's representatives did not turn up at the appointed time, but arrived while S's agent was absent attending to other business. B's representatives had a look at the outside of the barrels, but did not have any of them opened. The following day, B said that he had inspected the goods and made an offer to S's agent. This offer was not accepted, although subsequently a price was agreed between the parties. It was established that, had B's representatives looked in the barrels, the defect complained of would have been discovered. On this basis, BRAY, J., held in S's favour on the ground that there was no condition of merchantability implied in such circumstances.

This decision is difficult to reconcile with the wording of the section. In an Australian case[2] involving the sale of a motor car which had at least one major defect that the buyer had not discovered on inspecting the vehicle, the judge reviewed the magistrate's decision in accordance with the strict wording of the Act:[3]

> "In order to ascertain whether the proviso operated the magistrate should have considered first whether the buyer did in fact examine the car before he agreed to buy it, and then (if he—the magistrate—decided that the buyer had in fact examined the car before the sale) whether the defects which had been proved to exist were such that they ought to have been revealed to the buyer by the examination which he made."

What then is to be made of the decision in *Thornett and Fehr* v. *Beers & Sons*? BRAY, J., seemed unduly influenced by the pre-1893 Common Law position where the condition of merchantability did not apply if the goods were available for the buyer's inspection. He remarked that the position had been changed by the Act so that the condition was excluded "if the buyer has examined the goods". It is true, as the above quotation from the Australian case demonstrates, that there are two questions to be considered of which the first is whether there was an examination, but the approach of BRAY, J., was to place undue emphasis on what amounted to an examination. In his view, once it could be shown that the

---

1 [1919] 1 K.B. 486.
2 *Frank* v. *Grosvenor Motor Auctions Pty., Ltd.,* [1960] V.R. 607.
3 At p. 609.

goods were examined, that examination should have revealed the defects complained of. In other words, either the buyer had examined the goods or he had not; if he had examined the goods then there was such a "thing" as an "examination" that would reveal certain defects. In this case the opportunity was there; the buyer's representatives had looked at the goods; the buyer had purchased on the strength of an "inspection"; an examination had therefore taken place and (it would therefore seem to follow) the buyer could not then say that his inspection was so cursory as not to reveal an obvious defect. Or, as *Benjamin on Sale* puts it,[1] "the condition of merchantable quality will be excluded, not, as at common law, by the existence of an opportunity of examination, but only by an actual examination, and then only as regards *discoverable* defects".

This approach is clearly a gloss upon s. 14 (2) and it is to be hoped that by altering the word "such" (i.e. an examination of that kind) to "that" (i.e. the examination which actually took place), the Law Commission has come down firmly against the line adopted by BRAY, J. Whether the amendment has achieved this consequence, however, must depend upon what view the courts adopt towards it.

3 *The quality of second-hand or substandard goods.* I has been a source of some dispute whether and, if so, to what extent, the former s. 14 (2) applied to second-hand or substandard goods. As the Sale of Goods Act draws no distinction between new and top quality goods on the one hand and second-hand or "seconds" on the other, the answer to the first part of the question is simple enough: the implied terms, and more particular that relating to merchantability, do apply to sales of second-hand or sub-standard items. The more difficult question is *how* the condition of merchantability should operate on such transactions.

In *Bartlett* v. *Sidney Marcus, Ltd.*,[2] B had purchased a second-hand car on which, in addition to trading in his own car, he was given the choice of paying £575 and S carrying out some repair work on the clutch, or £550, in which case B was to pay for the repairs to be done. B chose the second arrangement. A written contract was drawn up which noted the repairs to be carried out. In fact it was later discovered that the defects were more substantial and the

---

1 7th Ed. p. 668; 8th Ed. p. 644. The view adopted by Chalmers, *Sale of Goods*, 17th Ed., pp. 105–6, is that where the buyer's conduct shows "that he was willing to take the risk of any defects not revealed by a partial inspection which would have been apparent upon a full one . . . in such a case the seller will not be liable for such defects". In order to use *Thornett and Fehr* v. *Beers & Sons* as support for this proposition it is stated to have been based on the situation "where a full examination was agreed to and an opportunity for such an examination was afforded to the buyer, but without the seller's knowledge the buyer failed to avail himself of it". The obstacle to this interpretation is the difficulty of explaining upon what basis such an "argument" can operate (except perhaps as one of estoppel which clearly was not the basis of BRAY, J's decision; see at p. 489) as the contract was only made *after* the examination had taken place. Furthermore if the buyer was indeed assuming the risk, the principle to be applied would not have been s. 14 (2) of the Act and the proviso thereto, but the contrary intention of the parties. However, BRAY, J., specifically stated (at p. 490) that the case fell within the proviso.

2 [1965] 2 All E.R. 753; [1965] 1 W.L.R. 1013.

cost of the more radical repairs came to £45. It was held by the Court of Appeal that, in the circumstances, there had been no breach of either of the conditions implied by s. 14. However, Lord DENNING, M.R. did comment on the extent to which s. 14 (2) could be applied to sales of second-hand goods. Having put forward the proposition that[1]

> "the article may be of some use though not entirely efficient use for the purpose. It may not be in perfect condition but yet it is in usable condition. It is then, I think, merchantable."

His Lordship went on to state that it

> "means that, on a sale of a second-hand car, it is merchantable if it is in usable condition, even though not perfect."

In this case

> "the car was far from perfect. It required a good deal of work to be done on it; but so do many second-hand cars. A buyer should realise that, when he buys a second-hand car, defects may appear sooner or later; and, in the absence of express warranty, he has no redress. Even when he buys from a dealer the most that he can require is that it should be reasonably fit for the purpose of being driven along the road."

These dicta were probably too sweeping under the original drafting of s. 14 (2). In *Frank* v. *Grosvenor Motor Auctions Pty., Ltd.,*[2] the Supreme Court of Victoria had no hesitation in holding that a second-hand car with the gear box and differential split was not of merchantable quality. In fact, the fallacy in Lord DENNING'S reasoning lies in the failure to deal with the relevance of price.[3] If one is called upon to deal with the merchantability of second-hand or substandard goods, the test of quality must be related to the price paid compared with what one would normally pay for new and top quality goods. As Lord PEARCE said in *Kendall* v. *Lillico :*[4]

> "The suggestion, without more, that goods are merchantable unless they are of no use for any purpose for which they would normally be used and hence would be unsaleable under that description may be misleading, if it contains no reference to price. One could not say that a new carpet which happens to have a hole in it or a car with its wings buckled are of no use for their normal purposes and hence would be unsaleable under that description. They would no doubt, if their price was reduced, find a ready market. In return for a substantial abatement of price a purchaser is ready to put up with serious defects or use part of the price reduction in having the defects remedied. In several classes of goods there is a regular retail market for 'seconds', that is, goods which are not good enough in the manufacturer's or retailer's view to fulfil an order and are therefore sold off at a cheaper price. It would be wrong to say that 'seconds' are necessarily merchantable."

---

1 [1965] 2 All E.R., at p. 755.
2 [1960] V.R. 607, at p. 611.
3 Though this factor was alluded to by SALMON, L.J., [1965] 2 All E.R., at p. 756.
4 [1969] 2 A.C. 31, at p. 118; [1968] 2 All E.R. 444, at p. 486.

The Molony Committee on Consumer Protection acknowledged that the law was unsatisfactory in this area and, while accepting the principle that sales should in most circumstances automatically include a condition of merchantability, proposed that retailers should be allowed to relieve themselves from liability on sales of second-hand, shop-soiled or imperfect goods.[1] The Law Commission refused to follow this line of thinking[2] but attempted to deal with the matter by

> "so defining merchantable quality that it should not operate unfairly in the case of used or imperfect goods. We have tried to reach this result by incorporating in the definition of merchantable quality a specific reference to the description under which goods are sold; and we have linked this reference to another specific one pointing to the price of the goods. In our expectation this formula will put the honest seller of used or imperfect goods out of any danger of unfairness. If he has described the goods as used, second-hand, substandard or otherwise inferior or if this can reasonably be inferred from the fact that the price itself is patently lower than that at which new goods of that type are obtainable in the market, then the standard of fitness involved in the condition of merchantable quality will not be higher than is appropriate to the kind of used or inferior goods with which the particular transaction is concerned."[3]

As has already been suggested,[4] the effect of the definition now included in the Sale of Goods Act, is to clarify and incorporate a number of trends that were already appearing in the law of sale in the hands of the judges. It is believed that this observation is particularly relevant in this context. There was already authority that could be employed to advance the proposition that merchantable quality should be assessed by balancing the defects existing in the goods with their description and price. The new s. 62 (1A) gives statutory blessing to this line of legal development.

d *The condition of suitability*

It will already have been realised that, as merchantability relates to the suitability of goods for some purpose, there is bound to be a degree of overlap with a condition that deals with the suitability or fitness of goods for a particular purpose. Formerly it is probable that a distinction was drawn between the two undertakings. Thus, in an early formulation of them, BEST, C.J., said[5] that if a man "sells an article, he thereby warrants that it is merchantable—that it is fit for some purpose . . . If he sells it for a particular purpose, he thereby warrants it fit for that purpose". By the time the Sale of Goods Act was drafted, however, the two undertakings were used indiscriminately and s. 14 reflected the degree of overlap that existed between the two. Despite representations made to the Law Commission that a clear line should be re-established between them, the Commission decided in favour of the *status quo*: "although we readily concede

---

1 Cmnd. 1781, pp. 144–5, para. 445.
2 Final Report, pp. 18–19, paras. 51–52.
3 *Ibid.*, p. 19, para. 52.
4 Above, p. 182.
5 In *Jones* v. *Bright* (1929), 5 Bing. 533, at p. 544.

the attraction of this approach as a matter of elegance, we think that the attraction is outweighed by the proven utility of the overlap in practice".[1]

Indeed, although s. 14 (1) now appears as s. 14 (3) in the Sale of Goods Act as a result of s. 3 of the 1973 Act, and although a number of alterations have been made to its wording, the new provision is not substantially different in effect from the old. It now reads:

> "Where the seller sells goods in the course of a business and the buyer, expressly or by implication, makes known to the seller any particular purpose for which the goods are being bought, there is an implied condition that the goods supplied under the contract are reasonably fit for that purpose, whether or not that is a purpose for which such goods are commonly supplied, except where the circumstances show that the buyer does not rely, or that it is unreasonable for him to rely, on the seller's skill or judgment."

1 *Where the purpose is obvious.* In many instances, the purpose for which goods are required will be obvious. If one buys food,[2] or underclothing,[3] or a hot-water bottle,[4] there is no need to specify in express words the purpose for which the goods are required because the purpose is made known by implication. As COLLINS, M.R., said in *Preist* v. *Last*:[5]

> "In a case where the discussion begins with the fact that the description of the goods, by which they are sold, points to one particular purpose only, it seems to me that the first requirement of the sub-section is satisfied, namely, that the particular purpose for which the goods are required should be made known to the seller. The fact that, by the very terms of the sale itself, the article sold purports to be for use for a particular purpose cannot possibly exclude the case from the rule that, where goods are sold for a particular purpose, there is an implied warranty that they are reasonably fit for that purpose."

There is usually little difficulty for the buyer who requires goods for their normal purpose to be able to show that he has relied on the seller's skill and judgment. In *Godley* v. *Perry*,[6] a six year old boy purchased a toy plastic catapult. While he was using it, the catapult broke and he lost the use of one eye which was damaged by part of the catapult. The boy's action against the shopkeeper was successful:[7] a customer is entitled to rely upon a shopkeeper's skill and judgment in the selection of his stock.

This conclusion is in accord with the following comment by Lord WRIGHT giving the opinion of the Judicial Committee in *Grant* v. *Australian Knitting Mills Ltd.*:[8]

---

1 Final Report, p. 14, para. 39.   2 *Chapronière* v. *Mason* (1905), 21 T.L.R. 633.

3 *Grant* v. *Australian Knitting Mills, Ltd.*, [1936] A.C. 85; [1935] All E.R. Rep. 209.

4 *Preist* v. *Last*, [1903] 2 K.B. 148.

5 [1903] 2 K.B. 148, at p. 153; a view of the law approved in *Grant* v. *Australian Knitting Mills, Ltd.*, [1936] A.C. 85, at p. 99; [1935] All E.R. Rep. 209, at p. 215: "There is no need to specify in terms the particular purpose for which the buyer requires the goods . . . because it is the only purpose for which any one would ordinarily want the goods."

6 [1960] 1 All E.R. 36; [1960] 1 W.L.R. 9.

7 For the action by the retailer against the wholesaler and by the wholesaler against the importer under s. 15, see below, p. 204.

8 [1936] A.C. 85, at p. 99; [1935] All E.R. 209, at p. 215.

"It is clear that the reliance must be brought home to the mind of the seller, expressly or by implication. The reliance will seldom be express: it will usually arise by implication from the circumstances: thus to take a case like that in question, of a purchaser from a retailer, the reliance will be in general inferred from the fact that a buyer goes to the shop in the confidence that the tradesman has selected his stock with skill and judgment: the retailer need know nothing about the process of manufacture: it is immaterial whether he be manufacturer or not: the main inducement to deal with a good retail shop is the expectation that the tradesman will have bought the right goods of a good make."

The only reservation that must be made to this observation is to regret the reference to a "good" retail shop. Even if, one can say particularly if, a buyer purchases goods from a discount store which has a rather dubious reputation, he should be entitled to rely on s. 14 (3) if he has made known to the store's salesman the purpose for which the goods are required, or if the purpose for which the goods are required is obvious. Lamentably, Lord REID in *Henry Kendall & Sons* v. *William Lillico & Sons, Ltd.*[1] saw fit to approve this very aspect of Lord WRIGHT's comments when his Lordship remarked that a "shopkeeper's goodwill consists largely in his reputation of being reliable—the better the shop the easier it is to draw this inference".

2 *Disclosure of a particular purpose.* Where the buyer has in mind some special purpose, or some special requirement that the goods should possess, he must reveal that purpose or that requirement to the seller. In *Griffiths* v. *Peter Conway, Ltd.*,[2] B was a woman with an abnormally sensitive skin. Without revealing this fact to S, she bought a Harris Tweed coat. The affect of the cloth on her skin was to cause dermatitis. However, as there was nothing in the cloth that would have affected the skin of a normal person, the Court of Appeal held that S was not in breach of s. 14. As DENNING, L.J., said in a later case,[3] "the implied term as to fitness is dependent upon proper disclosure by the customer of any relevant peculiarities known to her".

3 *Need to establish reliance.* Under the pre-1973 Act wording of this section there had been uncertainty as to whether disclosure alone of the purpose for which the goods were required established that reliance was being placed upon the seller's skill and judgment. The basis of the uncertainty lay in the requirement, explicit in s. 14, that the buyer had to make known the particular purpose for which the goods were required *so as to show* that he was relying on the seller's skill or judgment.

In *Manchester Liners, Ltd.* v. *Rea, Ltd.*,[4] B ordered coal expressly for use in a specified ship. The coal supplied by S proved unsatisfactory. The House of Lords was unanimously of the opinion that B was entitled to say that he had relied on the seller's skill and judgment in the selection of suitable coal. However,

---

1 [1969] 2 A.C. 31, at p. 82; [1968] 2 All E.R. 444, at p. 455.
2 [1939] 1 All E.R. 685; see also *Bristol Tramways etc., Carriage Co., Ltd.* v. *Fiat Motors, Ltd.*, [1910] 2 K.B. 831; [1908–10] All E.R. Rep. 113, above, p. 182; *Baldry* v. *Marshall*, [1925] 1 K.B. 260; [1924] All E.R. Rep. 155, below, p. 199.
3 *Ingham* v. *Emes*, [1955] 2 Q.B. 366, at p. 374; [1955] 2 All E.R. 740, at p. 742.
4 [1922] 2 A.C. 74; [1922] All E.R. Rep. 605.

it is clear that their Lordships were of opinion that this presumption woud not necessarily operate in all situations where the buyer made known his purpose to the seller, for reference was made to SLATER, J.'s decision at first instance that "the mere disclosure of a purpose *may* amount to sufficient evidence of reliance".[1]

The Law Commission decided to dispense with the apparent need to show reliance[2] on the ground that in most cases reliance was readily inferred from the fact that the buyer's purpose had been communicated to the seller. The revised version of s. 14 (3) makes clear that, once the purpose is made known, there is an implied condition that the goods are fit for that purpose, "except where the circumstances show that the buyer does not rely, or that it is unreasonable for him to rely, on the seller's skill or judgment". In other words the Commission was trying to formulate the law as it was applied in practice rather than being content to allow the courts to apply what it obviously considered to be an artificial interpretation of the wording of the original provision.

In justifying its approach, the Commission was influenced by the decision of the House of Lords in *Henry Kendall & Sons* v. *William Lillico & Sons, Ltd.*,[3] a case which will also be pertinent to the future interpretation of the revised s. 14. A large quantity of ground nut extract was imported from Brazil to England. Much of it was supplied to various manufacturers of cattle and poultry foods. The ultimate buyers of a quantity of meal containing the extract lost a large number of their young pheasants and partridges. It was discovered that the cause of the loss was the abnormally high concentration of a poisoncus substance in the extract. The suppliers had known from their previous course of dealings with the manufacturers of the meal in question that they (the manufacturers) only made poultry foods, and for this purpose the extract had obviously been unsuitable. But had the manufacturers relied upon the suppliers' skill and judgment?

HAVERS, J., held[4] that it was "established by *Manchester Liners, Ltd.* v. *Rea* . . . that if the particular purpose is made known by the buyer to the seller, then, unless there is something in effect to rebut the presumption, that in itself is sufficient to raise the presumption that he relies on the skill and judgment of the seller", but that in this case as the parties were members of the London Cattle Food Trade Association a sale between them was not likely to be in reliance on the skill and judgment of the seller. The Court of Appeal, by a majority, reversed this decision,[5] holding that, although the parties were members of the Association, there was nevertheless reliance upon the skill and judgment of the seller. There was, however, no dissent from the opinion expressed by HAVERS, J., on *Manchester Liners, Ltd.* v. *Rea.*

The House of Lords upheld[6] the conclusion reached by the Court of Appeal,

---

1 Emphasis added: SLATER, J., had cited *Gillespie Bros. & Co.* v. *Cheney, Eggar & Co.,* [1896] 2 Q.B. 59, in support of this proposition.
2 Final Report, p. 13, para. 35.
3 [1969] 2 A.C. 31; [1968] 2 All E.R. 444.
4 *Sub nom. Hardwick Game Farm* v. *Suffolk Agricultural and Poultry Producers Association, Ltd.,* [1964] 2 Lloyd's Rep. 227, at p. 272.
5 [1966] 1 All E.R. 309. DIPLOCK, L.J., dissented; see below, p. 191, n. 5.
6 Lord GUEST dissenting; see below, p. 191.

but differing opinions were advanced on whether such a presumption did arise. Only Lord PEARCE was prepared to accept that if "a particular purpose is made known, that is sufficient to raise the inference that the buyer relies on the seller's skill and judgment unless there is something to displace the inference".[1] The other members of the House were more cautious,[2] but they did not dissent from the general proposition that, by making known the purpose for which the goods are required, the inference will usually be that the buyer is relying on the seller's skill and judgment. As Lord MORRIS said,[3] the "object of stating or making known a particular purpose will usually be to ensure that the seller only sells something that is reasonably fit for the purpose". And this is emphatically the position under the redrafted s. 14 (3). However, the more complex the transaction, the more precisely would it be necessary for the seller to be made aware of the buyer's purpose. In the words of Lord WILBERFORCE, the authorities demonstrate that s. 14 (3) is "readily and untechnically applied to all sorts of informal situations—such as retail sales over the counter of articles whose purpose is well known—and . . . applied rather more strictly to large scale transactions carried through by written contracts".[4]

It would seem that the main difference in theory, though perhaps it will not create any problems in practice, is that the new s. 14 (3) gives rise to a presumption in all cases where the buyer's purpose is made known to the seller. In some situations, under the former wording, it was possible to have a case where reliance could not be inferred, for example, because of the standing of the parties towards each other. Then it would have been necessary to look at the circumstances of the case as a whole in order to decide whether, nevertheless, the fact that the seller was aware of the purpose for which the goods were required would be sufficient to establish reliance. Now, if the seller *makes known* the purpose, the condition is implied, unless the circumstances suggest otherwise. In other words, the burden of proof may have been reversed.

Kendall v. *Lillico* was in fact a case in which the circumstances may have suggested that the presumption should be rebutted. The parties were both members of a trade association a fact which tended to raise a contrary inference, i.e. that normally there would be no such reliance on the seller's skill and judgment. Indeed, it was on this point that both DIPLOCK, L.J., in the Court of Appeal and Lord GUEST in the House of Lords dissented, holding that on international commodity markets there could be no basis for implying a term of suitability for purpose in reliance upon the seller's skill or judgment. Members of the Association, buying in such a market, did so in reliance upon their own skill or judgment.[5] However, as Lord WILBERFORCE explained:[6]

---

1 [1969] 2 A.C. 31, at p. 115; [1968] 2 All E.R. 444, at p. 483; his Lordship added that there was "no need for a buyer to 'make known' that which is already known".
2 See especially Lord REID's comment on the *Manchester Liners* case, [1969] 2 A.C. 31, at p. 81; [1969] 2 All E.R. 444, at p. 455.
3 [1969] 2 A.C. 31, at p. 94; [1968] 2 All E.R. 444, at p. 465.
4 [1969] 2 A.C. 31, at p. 123; [1968] 2 All E.R. 444, at p. 490.
5 DIPLOCK, L.J., had earlier expressed the same view in *C.E.B. Draper & Son, Ltd.* v. *Edward Turner & Son, Ltd.*, [1965] 1 Q.B. 424; [1964] 3 All E.R. 148; and it had been on this basis that HAVERS, J., had decided the present case at first instance.
6 [1969] 2 A.C. 31, at pp. 124–5; [1968] 2 All E.R. 444, at pp. 491–2.

> "On many commodity markets, where business or speculative dealings take place between persons on the market, it would no doubt be true that each buyer relies on his own judgment and it would be wrong to seek to impose on sellers an implied condition based on reliance. To do so would impede the play and working of the market and would be in opposition to commercial reality. That does not mean, however, that in individual cases the possibility of reliance may not exist. If a buyer can show that a particular purpose was made known so as to show reliance, the condition may attach."

Having pointed out that the buyer's task in such circumstances would not be an easy one, his Lordship continued:

> "In seeking to discharge it, it is not sufficient merely to show that the seller knew the purpose. Of course he may. Business men do not work in a vacuum, they know their trade and their customers and they are not to be saddled with conditions merely because they are competent and knowledgeable. The purpose must be made known so as to show reliance."

What established the reliance in this case was that it had been the first occasion upon which Brazilian ground nut extract had been imported, and the buyers had made the purchase principally because they relied upon Kendall "not to sell anything he knew was rubbish".

Obviously considerations of this sort will be highly relevant under the redrafted s. 14 (3). Theoretically, at least, the buyers task may be made easier by the presumption that, if the buyer makes known the purpose, then the condition will be implied because it is only by exception that this rule may be ousted. However, in practical terms the wording of the exception would seem to reduce any such advantage to a minimum. While it may be difficult to show that the buyer did not rely upon the seller's skill or judgment, it would be much easier to demonstrate that it was unreasonable for him to do so. The buyer in the commodity market should, in normal circumstances, rely upon his own judgment rather than on the reliability of the seller, though it would not be unreasonable for him to do so if the goods were new to the market so that the buyer has little alternative but to rely upon the seller's selection of suitable goods.

Some difficulty may still be experienced in a situation where the seller was aware of the buyer's purpose, although the buyer cannot show that he himself made known that purpose to the seller. In view of the Law Commission's intention to clarify the position by redrafting s. 14, it may appear unfortunate that the opportunity was not taken to deal with this particular point especially as it had been discussed in *Kendall* v. *Lillico*. Lord WILBERFORCE's comment had already been quoted[1] in which he said that businessmen "do not work in a vacuum, they know their trade and their customers and they are not to be saddled with conditions merely because they are competent and knowledgeable". Knowledge was equated with the purpose being "made known" not only where the purpose was obvious from the nature of the goods, but also, apparently, where there was some special or particular purpose the existence of which was

---

1 [1969] 2 A.C. 31, at p. 125; [1968] 2 All E.R. 444, at p. 492.

known to the seller. Under the former s. 14, the safety valve was the need to establish that knowledge established the reliance. If the expression "makes known" in the new s. 14 (3) is regarded as equivalent to the same wording in the former provision, there is no equivalent safety valve in s. 14 (3). Once again the seller is obliged to fall back on the exception that the implied condition does not apply if it was unreasonable for the buyer to rely on the seller's skill or judgment.

4 *Partial reliance.* The Law Commission left untouched the position that, as long as the buyer has placed *some* reliance on the seller, it does not matter that he may have relied to a greater extent on his own view of the goods, or even on the opinion of a third party. Any dispute as to whether the buyer did rely, or the extent or reasonableness of his reliance, fall to be considered within the exception to the application of the condition. This reluctance to consider the more technical and difficult problems raised by s. 14, as opposed to the more obvious discrepancies between the wording and the operation of the section, is particularly regrettable. In the present context, the Commission should not be criticised for their Final Report which was presented to Parliament in 1969, before the House of Lords decision in *Ashington Piggeries, Ltd.* v. *Christopher Hill, Ltd.*[1] However no regard appears to have been paid to this case in that the 1973 Act was based on the largely unamended Law Commission's recommendations.

It went without saying that a buyer could not, under the former s. 14, claim that he relied upon a seller's skill or judgment when the seller supplied goods to the buyer's specifications and the goods proved unsuitable because of some error in those specifications. Under s. 14 (3) the seller can now show that the buyer had not relied on his skill or judgment. However, reliance would not be negatived if certain matters were left to the discretion of the seller and it was in respect of one of those matters that goods failed to suit the purpose for which they were required. In *Cammell Laird & Co., Ltd.* v. *Manganese Bronze and Brass Co., Ltd.,*[2] B ordered two ship's propellers to be made by S to B's design and specifications. The thickness of the blades was left to the skill and judgment of S and it was the unsuitable thickness of one of them which caused undue noise when the propellers were used. The House of Lords had no doubt that S was liable for failing to supply goods that were suitable for B's purpose: the defect related to a part of the work which fell within S's sphere of judgment.

There was an obvious similarity between *Cammell Laird* and *Ashington Piggeries,* the facts of which have already been given,[3] in that in the latter case the formula for the mink food was prescribed by the buyer but the supply of ingredients was left to the discretion of the seller. The main point of difference, however, was the fact that, as the seller had disclaimed any sort of knowledge of what was suitable for mink, he could reasonably argue that he could hardly be said to have exercised any skill or judgment upon which the buyer could rely.

This view of the facts was endorsed by the Court of Appeal,[4] but the House of

---

1 [1972] A.C. 441; [1971] 1 All E.R. 847.
2 [1934] A.C. 402; [1934] All E.R. Rep. 1.
3 Above, p. 124. 4 [1969] 3 All E.R. 1496.

Lords was unanimous in deciding that, despite the seller's disclaimer of any knowledge of what was suitable for mink, he was nevertheless liable. According to Lord Hodson, the condition of suitability included an undertaking that the ingredients would not contain poison: the herring meal contained a poison at a level sufficiently high to be lethal to mink which was an animal "to which herring meal can properly be fed". Presumably what was important was that although mink were "more sensitive to DMNA than most other animals all animals are sensitive to a greater or less degree to this form of poisoning".[1] Even more emphatic was Lord WILBERFORCE with whom Lord GUEST agreed: the "critical question" was "whether the appellants [the buyers] proved enough to show that their mink died because of some general, i.e. non-specific, unsuitability of the herring meal through contamination".[2] In his Lordship's view, the buyers had succeeded in establishing their case.

This distinction between specific unsuitability, for which a seller may be able to show the absence of reliance or even that his goods satisfied the requirement, and a general unsuitability, is of importance and could be overlooked. In the Australian case of *David Jones, Ltd.* v. *Willis*,[3] B had asked for a pair of walking shoes for herself and had also informed the saleswoman of the store that she (B) wanted a shoe which would go comfortably over a bunion on her foot. The shoes selected on the woman's advice proved very comfortable, but the heel of one of them collapsed while B was walking in them, and B fell, breaking her leg. Of the members of the High Court who considered whether the condition of suitability applied,[4] STARKE, J., flirted with the bizarre view that, by making known to the seller the particular purpose for which the goods were required (i.e. that they should be comfortable over B's bunion), no undertaking could be implied that the goods should be suitable for their general (and normal) purpose (i.e. walking in).[5] On the other hand, neither RICH, J., nor McTIERNAN, J., saw any such obstacle to the application of the condition of fitness for a general purpose. Indeed, in this case, B had actually asked for shoes suitable for their normal purpose. As McTIERNAN, J., pointed out:[6]

> "It is conceivable that a pair of shoes may be required for some purpose other than for general wear or for walking. But it would be drawing a strange distinction to hold that a buyer . . . is entitled to the benefit of the condition implied by the sub-section if he says that he requires the goods for some special or odd purpose but not if he discloses that his particular purpose is their ordinary use."

5 *The burden of proof.* It has already been mentioned[7] that the new s. 14 (3) establishes a presumptive rule that, once the buyer makes known to the seller the purpose for which the goods are required, the condition is implied. However

---

1 [1972] A.C., at p. 468; [1971] 1 All E.R., at p. 885; distinguishing *Griffiths* v. *Peter Conway, Ltd.*, [1939] 1 All E.R. 685 (see above, p. 189) in which the tweed coat would not have affected a normal buyer.
2 [1972] A.C., at p. 491; [1971] 1 All E.R., at p. 873.
3 (1934), 52 C.L.R. 110.
4 DIXON, J., with whom GAVAN DUFFY, C.J., agreed, held that, as there was evidence of a cause of action under s. 14 (2), it was unnecessary to consider the point.
5 At p. 122.   6 At p. 128.   7 Above, p. 191.

in most cases this will make no very real difference from the former position in which, once the buyer made known the purpose, his reliance on the seller's skill and judgment was presumed.

There was an area of uncertainty in the burden of proof in relation to cases where the goods had been supplied to the buyer's specifications. It was the existence of this degree of uncertainty which contributed to one rather strange feature of the *Ashington Piggeries* decision. It will be recalled[1] that the House of Lords held that there had been no breach of s. 13 because the seller had made clear his lack of knowledge of mink food so that he could not be said to have been guaranteeing the suitability of the food for mink as part of the contract description. However, it was held that s. 14 did apply because the ingredient in question was not necessarily suitable as an animal food and was in fact unsuitable for mink. The narrow line of distinction between these two propositions is to some extent explicable by a consideration of the burden of proof.

A buyer can usually establish that he made known to the seller the purpose for which the goods are required without difficulty. He was then obliged to rely upon the presumption (readily made) that he was relying upon the seller's skill and judgment. Under the new s. 14 (3) this presumption is made clear. It is then for the seller to rebut this presumption, and one way of doing this will be for him to show that he was making goods to the buyer's specifications or formula.

It is at this point that the difficulties really begin. By rebutting the initial presumption in this way, under the former s. 14, the burden of proof was placed squarely back upon the shoulders of the buyer. As Lord WRIGHT said in *Cammell Laird & Co., Ltd.* v. *Manganese Bronze and Brass Co., Ltd.*,[2] in which the seller had made propellers to the buyer's specifications:

> "The more difficult question remains whether the particular purpose was not merely made known, as I think it was, by the appellants to the respondents, but was made known so as to show that the appellants as buyers relied on the seller's skill and judgment. Such a reliance must be affirmatively shown."

Once the buyer, in such a situation, could establish that, despite the existence of the specifications or formula, the seller had an area of discretion and that the defect related to a matter falling within that area of discretion and over which the seller could be expected to exercise his judgment, the burden shifted back to the seller.

This explanation of the situation is reasonably straightforward, but Lord DIPLOCK in *Ashington Piggeries* advanced the view that the decision of other members of the House of Lords in that case had the effect of establishing that the burden of proof on the ancillary point of whether the matter was within the field of competence of the buyer or of the seller lay with the *seller*.[3] Not only is this proposition difficult to reconcile with Lord WRIGHT's statement,[4] but

---

1 See above, p. 124.
2 [1934] A.C. 402, at p. 423; [1934] All E.R. Rep. 1, at p. 11.
3 [1972] A.C. 441, at pp. 508–9; [1971] 1 All E.R. 847, at p. 888.
4 Lord DIPLOCK opined that the point had been left open in the *Cammel Laird* case, but it seems that Lord DIPLOCK was in reality asserting that, under the former s. 14, reliance had to be disproved.

it is not substantiated by the other judgments in *Ashington Piggeries*, nor indeed by Lord DIPLOCK's own line of reasoning.

All that their Lordships decided was that, because the selection of ingredients fell outside the buyer's sphere of competence, and was a matter in which they relied upon the seller, the onus then lay on the seller. No issue could have arisen had the purpose been mink food and if the seller's undertaking of suitability related to mink food: patently the ingredients had been unsuitable for mink. However, in this case, the purpose which was relevant to the buyer's claim could not be fitness for mink because the seller had disclaimed all knowledge of the special characteristics of mink food.

The buyer succeeded because the seller did have expertise in preparing animal food so that the herring had to be suitable for at least that general purpose. It would have been absurd if the seller could have argued that the herring meal in question might have been harmful to a variety of other animals but he was not liable as he had given no undertaking as to its suitability for the particular needs of mink. On the issue of whether the food was suitable for other animals (a secondary issue which arose only because of the unusual circumstances of the case) there seems to have been a clear division of opinion on where the burden of proof lay. Lord WILBERFORCE, while emphasising the necessity for avoiding loose use of the term "toxic" for fear of prejudging the question in issue, gave it the status of something akin to a term of art:[1]

> "Where an element in feeding stuffs is shown to be (i) lethal in some quantities to one or more species (ii) damaging in other quantities to one or more species and in more than one respect and (iii) when it is not suggested that in any circumstances the chemical is beneficial . . . there is every justification for describing it as toxic, and, which is the relevant consideration, for placing responsibility for its exclusion firmly on the seller. I am satisfied that DMNA was shown to be toxic in this sense."

This dictum[2] makes clear that the onus is certainly on the buyer to show the general unsuitability (toxicity) of the food and is certainly not the same thing as requiring the seller, in Lord DIPLOCK's words,[3] to "prove affirmatively that the herring meal was of a quantity suitable for use in compound feeding stuffs for domestic animals and poultry other than mink".

In the light of these uncertainties it is not possible to suggest that s. 14 (3) offers any guidance as to how they can be resolved. Once the purpose is made known to the seller by the buyer, the onus is clearly upon the seller to rebut the presumption of reliance. To achieve this he must be able to point to *circumstances* which show that the buyer did not rely (or that it was unreasonable for him to rely) on the seller's skill or judgment. The Law Commission clearly thought that the burden (and presumably not just the initial onus of pointing to circumstances which give rise to the inference that the buyer was not relying on the seller's skill or judgment) was being placed on the seller. Referring to the formula contained in the earlier Working Paper, the Commission said:[4]

---

1 [1972] A.C. 441, at pp. 491–2; [1971] 1 All E.R. 847, at pp. 873–4.
2 See also the words cited above, p. 192, reference given at n. 2.
3 [1972] A.C. 441, at p. 509; [1971] 1 All E.R. 847, at p. 888.
4 Page 13, para. 37.

"We had perhaps gone too far in requiring the seller to prove *total* absence of reliance on his skill or judgment. We think that the seller's burden of proof could, without undue prejudice to the buyer, be lightened by providing an alternative to proving strictly that the buyer *had not* relied upon the seller's skill and judgment. We suggest that it should be sufficient for the seller to prove that in all the circumstances it was not reasonable for the buyer to rely upon the seller's skill and judgment."

However, even if a court were able to refer to the Law Commission's recommendations in interpreting the Act, it is difficult to see how the neutral phraseology actually used requires the seller to do more than demonstrate the existence of circumstances that show (or even just tend to show) that there had been no reliance. At this stage it could well be that a court would regard the onus as having shifted back once more to the buyer.

It is apparent that whatever effect the redrafting has on the initial presumption, it does not seem to be directly relevant to the situation that is reached once the seller is able to point to circumstances that tend to rebut that presumption. For example, if he was able to point to the fact that the specifications or formula he was to follow in making the goods were provided by the buyer, it could be argued that one is thrown back to the common law position. Under the original version of s. 14 it was not altogether clear whether, once the seller had pointed to the existence of the specifications or formula, he also had to show that the matter at issue fell within the area covered by the specifications or formula, or whether their existence threw back on the buyer the need to show that the matter was within the ambit of the seller's discretion. The *Cammell Laird* decision[1] appeared to lay down that, in such a situation, the onus lay on the buyer to establish reliance. The effect of the *Ashington Piggeries*[2] case was to create uncertainty. The Law Commission did not deal with the problem, although it is arguable that the courts will accept s. 14 (3) as an indirect indication that it is for the seller to point to all the circumstances at each stage which show the absence of reliance.

The alternative part of the exception, that the circumstances should show that it is unreasonable for the buyer to rely upon the seller was introduced largely to protect the seller in a situation where he had intimated to the buyer that he should not rely upon his (the seller's) skill or judgment. In the *Ashington Piggeries* case, it would have been unreasonable for the buyer to have relied upon the seller in the preparation of mink food, if the ingredients had been unsuitable only for mink. Under s. 14 (3) the circumstances of the disclaimer would certainly have showed *prima facie* that it was unreasonable for the buyer to have relied upon the seller's skill or judgment. There is nothing in the section that suggests that the seller should then be required to demonstrate the general suitability of the goods. In other words, the answer to the question where the onus of proof lies at this stage is still dependent upon how one reads the decision in the *Ashington Piggeries* case.

6 *Relationship with general contractual principles.* Mention has already been made of the unfortunate tendency of the courts to look at the provisions of the

---

1 [1934] A.C. 402; [1934] All E.R. Rep. 1.   2 [1972] A.C. 441; [1971] 1 All E.R. 847.

Sale of Goods Act in isolation from each other and from contractual principles. What is now s. 14 (3) has suffered particularly from this attitude. Two examples will illustrate the way in which the sub-section has been treated as if it existed in a vacuum outside the general law of contract.

In the first place, as has already been explained,[1] a statement would only be regarded as one of fact, and therefore as a warranty, if the representor had, or appeared to have, superior knowledge about the subject-matter of the contract and about the particular aspect of it that was covered by the representation. If a statement could only in those circumstances be treated as an *express* warranty, it is hardly likely that, in the absence of actual or apparent superior skill or judgment, a warranty of suitability for a particular purpose would be implied. Nevertheless, in *Teheran Europe Co., Ltd.* v. *S. T. Belton (Tractors), Ltd.* DONALDSON, J., held[2] that the fact that the seller of air compressors knew that they were to be exported to Persia raised an inference that he warranted their suitability for that purpose. The Court of Appeal reversed this absurd conclusion.[3] As DIPLOCK, L.J., rightly pointed out:[4]

> "Where a foreign merchant . . . buys by description goods . . . for re-sale in his own country, of which he has no reason to suppose the English seller has any special knowledge, it flies in the face of common sense to suppose that he relies on anything but his own knowledge of the market in his own country and his own commercial judgment as to what is saleable there. To hold the contrary would mean that whenever anyone known by the seller to be a foreign merchant bought from a seller in England goods for sale in his own country there would rise automatically an undertaking on the part of the seller, unless he expressly disclaimed it, that the goods would be suitable for sale in the market of which the foreign buyer knew everything and he, the seller, knew nothing. With great respect that would be nonsense."

In such a situation under the revised wording of s. 14, the seller would have no difficulty in pointing to the circumstances as showing how unreasonable it was for the buyer to rely upon the seller's judgment of how suitable his goods would be under Persian conditions.

There are some cases in which the question of reliance will be irrelevant. The possibility that a term may become part of the contract even though the seller might not be acting in the course of any business had already been considered. In addition, if the buyer spells out with precision his needs, there is another alternative, namely that suitability for the purpose would constitute part of the contract description.[5] Even in its redrafted form, s. 14 (3) should not be regarded as excluding the buyer from a remedy under other provisions of the Act or under the general law of contract.

7 *The relevance of a trade name.* Under the former s. 14 there was a proviso that "in the case of a contract for the sale of a specified article under its patent

---

1 See above, pp. 148–52.
2 [1968] 1 All E.R. 585.
3 [1968] 2 Q.B. 545; [1968] 2 All E.R. 886.
4 [1968] 2 Q.B. 545, at pp. 560–1; [1968] 2 All E.R. 886, at p. 894.
5 See above, pp. 120–2.

or other trade name, there is no implied condition as to fitness for any particular purpose". The Law Commission's view[1] was that the proviso should be excluded: hence the redrafted s. 14 (3) contains no reference to it.

The opinion of the Law Society was that the proviso should have been retained as it served to sound a note of caution in a situation where the condition of fitness should not too readily by implied. In the light of *Baldry* v. *Marshall Ltd.*,[2] however, the Law Commission felt that a warning was unnecessary on the ground that the proviso had been rendered meaningless. In that case, B asked a firm of motor dealers for a car that would be suitable for touring and they recommended a Bugatti. A contract of sale was entered into for a Bugatti, but after he had used it, B found that it was not suitable for touring purposes. The Court of Appeal had no hesitation in holding that the dealers were in breach of the condition that the car should fit for B's purposes. In order for the proviso to protect the seller the question had to be asked:

> "Did the buyer specify it under its trade name in such a way as to indicate that he is satisfied, rightly or wrongly, that it will answer his purpose, and that he is not relying on the skill or judgment of the seller, however great that skill and judgment may be?"[3]

As s. 14 (3) establishes a condition of fitness once the buyer makes known his purpose to the seller, and it is then for the seller to point to circumstances which suggest that there was not, or should not have been, reliance on the part of the buyer, one can predict that the Law Commission's decision to omit the proviso will have the effect of preserving the existing position. Unless the use of the trade name demonstrates the absence of reliance, the condition of suitability will be implied into the contract.

In one respect, the omission of the proviso might have a beneficial effect. It has already been pointed out[4] that the existence of reliance in respect of one aspect of goods, should not exclude reliance if the goods prove generally unsuitable. In *Wilson* v. *Rickett, Cockerell & Co., Ltd.*,[5] B ordered a quantity of "Coalite". The "Coalite" delivered contained an explosive substance. Thus, when B used some of the "Coalite", his house was damaged. The Court of Appeal held that, as B had ordered the goods by their patent or trade name, there had been no reliance upon S's skill or judgment. With respect, this decision seems wrong. The use of the name "Coalite" certainly demonstrated an absence of reliance as to the characteristics and qualities of the goods, but it surely did not absolve S from his responsibility to provide goods that were generally suitable in a way that "Coalite" was generally suitable. In its revised form,

---

1 Final Report, p. 12, para. 33.
2 [1925] 1 K.B. 260; [1924] All E.R. Rep. 155. See also *Bristol Tramways, etc. Carriage Co., Ltd.* v. *Fiat Motors, Ltd.*, [1910] 2 K.B. 831, [1908–10] All E.R. Rep. 113.
3 *Per* BANKES, L.J., [1925] 1 K.B., at p. 267; [1924] All E.R. Rep., at p. 158. This approach has been followed in Australia: *Johnston and Wilmot Pty., Ltd.* v. *Kaine* (1928), 23 Tas L.R. 43 (a lorry required for carting potatoes to coastal ports ordered as a "Guy Motor Truck"), *Criss* v. *Alexander* (1928), 28 S.R. (N.S.W.) 587 (a lorry capable of carrying five tons over long distances and holding its own with other lorries on the road ordered as a "five-ton Berliet lorry").
4 See above, p. 194.
5 [1954] 1 Q.B. 598; [1954] 1 All E.R. 868.

it could be argued that s. 14 (3) would require S to point to circumstances which established the absence of reliance on B's part on S to provide "Coalite" generally suitable for its purpose.

8 *The condition is that "the goods supplied under the contract are reasonably fit for the purpose."* The wording of the condition does raise two points that were equally relevant under the former s. 14.

In the first place, the condition relates to goods "supplied under the contract" and *not* just the goods actually purchased. Hence it is no defence for the seller to plead that the goods themselves were fit for the purpose if the container in which they were packed has the effect of rendering them unfit. In *Geddling* v. *Marsh*,[1] B purchased some mineral water in a bottle. The bottle exploded and injured her. S argued that, as the bottle remained the property of the manufacturers, he could not be liable for breach of a contract of sale. This argument was rejected. B had bought the mineral water and the bottle had clearly been "supplied" under that contract. The Sale of Goods Act therefore applied and S was in breach of s. 14: the bottle had not been fit for its purpose.

Similarly, the seller would be liable if, in addition to the goods answering the contract description, he supplied some impurity which was unsuitable. In *Wilson* v. *Rickett, Cockerell & Co., Ltd.*,[2] as we have seen, S supplied B with a quantity of "Coalite" which contained an explosive substance. The Court of Appeal refused to accept the contention that S had not sold B the offending substance: it had been supplied under the contract of sale and that was sufficient to bring s. 14 into play, even though, on the facts, S was held not liable for breach of s. 14 (3).

The second point is that the condition does not require that the goods be absolutely fit for the buyer's purposes, but only that they should be *reasonably* so. Accordingly, the seller is entitled to require the buyer to treat the goods properly. In one case,[3] for example, B had bought some pork chops. Properly cooked they would have caused no harm, but he only partly cooked them and became ill after eating them. It was held that the chops had been reasonably fit for his purpose.

e *The period of merchantability or suitability*

It is implicit in the notion that the goods should be of merchantable quality, or "reasonably fit" for the buyer's purpose, that the goods should remain so for a reasonable time after the sale. A hot-water bottle should not burst after only five days' use;[4] and a consignment of goods should remain suitable for sale or consumption for a period of time sufficient to allow both for delivery in the normal course of transit and for ultimate disposal of the goods.[5]

In *Mash and Murrell, Ltd.* v. *Joseph I. Emanuel, Ltd.*,[6] B purchased a quantity

---

1 [1920] 1 K.B. 668; [1920] All E.R. Rep. 631.
2 [1954] 1 Q.B. 598; [1954] 1 All E.R. 868.
3 *Heil* v. *Hedges*, [1951] 1 T.L.R. 512.
4 *Preist* v. *Last* [1903] 2 K.B. 148.
5 *Beer* v. *Walker* (1877), 46 L.J.Q.B. 677; [1874–80] All E.R. Rep. 1139.
6 [1961] 1 All E.R. 485; [1961] 1 W.L.R. 862.

of Cyprus spring potatoes from S under a c. & f. contract. The potatoes were sound when they were loaded, but were unfit for human consumption when they reached England. It was held that S was liable for breach of s. 14 (2) because, in a contract of this type involving transit, the goods had to be fit to retain their quality during the period of the journey and for a reasonable time thereafter to allow for their ultimate disposal. The decision in B's favour was reversed on appeal[1] on the ground that s. 14 could only apply if the conditions in transit were what were reasonably to be expected. In this case, however, the vessel had called at an intermediate port where the holds had been open to several days of hot sunshine. The conditions had not been at all reasonable and S could not be taken to guarantee the quality of the goods against deterioration in such circumstances.

The question of what consistutues a reasonable period has not been the subject of any real examination by the English courts, although the issue was raised in the context of the grocery trade in the Australian case of *George Wills & Co.* v. *Davids.*[2] A wholesaler had purchased a number of cases of beetroot canned in vinegar. Fourteen to seventeen months later it was found that the beetroot had become unmerchantable. The trial judge held that, in order to be merchantable, canned foodstuffs must possess *inter alia* "lasting qualities far and away beyond that of the article in its natural state", and that the lasting qualities required of canned beetroot should be tested against the life span of other tinned vegetables in the light of the needs of the grocery trade. This decision was upheld by the New South Wales Full Court:[3]

> "It was open to his Honour to find that it was a circumstance attending the sale that the only purpose of the transaction was to distribute throughout New South Wales the commodity by methods ordinarily associated with a wholesaler, and that such distribution was to be made over a period of time to retail grocers and thence through the housewife or restaurant keeper or other agency to the ultimate consumer. It was clearly not sold for immediate consumption by the respondent. It was consequently open to his Honour to decide as a question of fact that, as understood in the world of commerce, the canned beetroot was to have a reasonable life or prospect of preservation which was to be commensurate with its known ultimate destination. The period of preservation which is to be regarded as reasonable differs, no doubt, to some extent with the class of goods put up in tins. Doubtless some keep longer than others. But in the wholesale grocery trade, according to his Honour's findings, it is understood that canned beetroot possessed the characteristic of preservation similar to canned beetroot of earlier seasons or of any other canned goods, or canned vegetables at any rate, so that such food would be estimated to remain fit for consumption and in a state of freshness when in the normal course it should reach the consumer."

The High Court of Australia did not dissent from the basic principle that goods should remain merchantable for a reasonable period after the sale, but it reversed the decision upon the ground that, as the beetroot had deteriorated no more

---

1 [1962] 1 All E.R. 77.
2 (1957), 98 C.L.R. 77.
3 (1956), 56 S.R. (N.S.W.) 237, at p. 243.

quickly than other beetroot similarly tinned, the seller had not been in breach of s. 14. Although the principle remains the same on whichever side of the line these facts are held to fall it would seem that, as this particular defect in beetroot tinned in vinegar was not fully realised at the time of sale, the buyers should surely have been entitled to suppose that the goods would remain suitable or merchantable for a period similar to that of other canned vegetables. On the facts, therefore, the decision of the lower courts appears preferable to that of the High Court.

v Correspondence with sample

a *When is a sale by sample?*

Section 15 (2) implies certain conditions into contracts of sale by sample, but, before these conditions can be impled, it has to be shown that the contract is in fact a sale by sample. Under s. 15 (1) a "contract of sale is a contract for sale by sample where there is a term in the contract, express or implied, to that effect". In other words, the mere fact that a sample has been given is not sufficient: there must be agreement to that sample setting the standard for the contract goods. Unlike ss. 12, 13 and 14, which imply conditions in all contracts of sale falling within the appropriate fact situations, the test of a sale by sample is a question of law.

The position of the buyer may be made more difficult if the contract is reduced to writing, because there is authority[1] which suggests that if there is a written memorandum of the contract, the term relating to the sale by sample should be included in it. If these cases are correct, they constitute an exception to the normal limitation on the parol evidence rule that such evidence is freely admissible if the written document does not purport to set out the full terms of the contract. Where the document does appear to be a complete record of the transaction, then it must contain a reference to the sample in order for s. 15 to apply.

In the Australian case of *L. G. Thorne & Co.* v. *Thomas Borthwick & Sons (A'sia), Ltd.*,[2] for example, B had purchased fifty drums of neatsfoot oil by a written document which set out "with a considerable degree of particularity" the details of the agreement. A majority of the New South Wales Full Court held that, as the contract was complete on the face of it, parol evidence was not admissible to establish that the parties had intended the sale to be one by sample and that the oil delivered was not equal to sample:

> "The mere fact that a sample has been shown by the intending vendor to the prospective purchaser during the course of negotiations leading up to a sale does not necessarily make the final contract a contract of sale by sample. If the contract is reduced to writing after the sample has been shown and makes no reference to this fact, then the written contract, if it be a complete contract, cannot have the added term incorporated in it."[3]

---

1 *Meyer* v. *Everth* (1814), 4 Camp. 22; *Gardiner* v. *Gray* (1815), 4 Camp. 144.
2 (1956), 56 S.R. (N.S.W.) 81; but cf. *R. W. Cameron & Co.* v. *L. Slutzkin Pty., Ltd.* (1923), 32 C.L.R. 81, in which such evidence was declared admissible in order to identify the subject matter of the contract.
3 56 S.R. (N.S.W.), at p. 87, *per* STREET, C.J.

In its preliminary Working Paper, the Law Commission canvassed the amendment of s. 15 (1) to dispense with the need to show that the sale was one by sample by the terms of contract itself and to avoid the problems created by the parol evidence rule. The reaction to these proposals was unfavourable:

> "It was thought that to make the seller liable under the conditions implied by sub-section (2) merely because a sample had been exhibited might lead to unjust results; as for the requirement of writing, it has been urged upon us that while there was an obvious case for its reconsideration, this could be better done within the framework of a comprehensive study directed to the respective merits of written and parol evidence and not, incidentally as it were, in relation to one particular section of one particular statute."[1]

These reasons do not seem particularly persuasive. In the commercial world, it is true, the business man will be, or should be, aware of the need to comply with s. 15 (1) in order to have the benefit of s. 15 (2). The private buyer will not be aware that, in addition to being shown a sample, he must be able to demonstrate that, as part of the contract, the goods are to comply with the sample and that, if a written note of the contract is made, that note must refer to the goods as per sample. It would have been a reasonable, and not an unjust, amendment, to have given the buyer under a consumer sale the additional protection. Very often goods ordered are not of the standard of those on display though they are merchantable and suitable within s. 14. Furthermore, in the light of the slow pace and erratic results of the movement for law reform, it is most unsatisfactory that the parol evidence rule must be explored in all its manifestations before any attempt can be made to set right a defect which exists in relation to sales by sample.

b *The terms applicable to sales by sample*

Once it is established that the sale is one by sample, s. 15 (2) implies three conditions into the contract:

> "(a) . . . that the bulk shall correspond with the sample in quality:[2]
> (b) . . . that the buyer shall have a reasonable opportunity of comparing the bulk with the sample:
> (c) . . . that the goods shall be free from any defect, rendering them unmerchantable, which would not be apparent on reasonable examination of the sample."

The purpose of, and the basic philosophy behind, a sample was explained by Lord MacNaghten in the following classic statement in *Drummond* v. *Van Ingen*:[3]

> "the office of a sample is to present to the eye the real meaning and intention of the parties with regard to the subject matter of the contract which, owing

---

1 Final Report, p. 21, para. 58.
2 It will be recalled that under s. 13, above, p. 174, "if the sale be by sample as well as by description it is not sufficient that the bulk of the goods corresponds with the sample if the goods do not also correspond with the description".
3 (1887), 12 App. Cas. 284, at p. 297.

to the imperfection of language, it may be difficult or impossible to express in words. The sample speaks for itself. But it cannot be treated as saying more than such a sample would tell a merchant of the class to which the buyer belongs, using due care and diligence, and appealing to it in the ordinary way and with the knowledge possessed by merchants of that class at the time. No doubt the sample might be made to say a great deal more. Pulled to pieces and examined by unusual tests which curiosity or suspicion might suggest, it would doubtless reveal every secret of its construction. But that is not the way in which business is done . . ."

Two propositions follow from this statement. First, the buyer cannot, by unreasonable examination, escape from his liability to accept the goods by demonstrating that in some unusual respect the goods do not correspond with the sample. In *Hookway* v. *Alfred Isaacs & Sons*,[1] the practice of the London Shellac[2] market under delivery contracts was that all shellac should be certified by a Committee as conforming to certain standards; and, apart from tests to establish the resin content, the quality of the shellac was determined by visual examination alone. Because increasing amounts of shellac reaching the market were proving unsuitable for some purposes, B had a quantity of shellac that was tendered to him analysed. The analysis showed that in one particular respect the shellac was not equal to the standard sample. Nevertheless, DEVLIN, J., held that such a test was inadmissible to show that s. 15 (2) (*a*) had not been complied with because the quality of the goods referred only "to such qualities as are apparent on an ordinary examination of the sample as usually done in the trade".[3]

The second proposition which follows from Lord MACNAGHTEN's words is contained in s. 15 (2) (*c*), namely that the goods must be free from any defect rendering them unmerchantable which a reasonable examination of the sample would not have revealed. In *Drummond* v. *Van Ingen* itself, "worsted coatings" were supplied to cloth merchants which were equal to samples previously examined. It was later discovered that the cloth, when made up into garments by customers of the merchants, split at the seams and was therefore unmerchantable for the purposes for which it was required. It was held that the fact that the cloth was equal to sample did not protect the manufacturer where, as in this case, the defect was not discoverable by any reasonable examination.

That the reasonability of the examination is dependent on the circumstances of the case is vividly illustrated by *Godley* v. *Perry*.[4] A six year old boy was held entitled to recover damages from a retailer who had sold him a catapult which broke causing injury. The question arose whether the retailer could recover from the supplier and so on down the chain of purchases. It was clear that the catapult

---

1 [1954] 1 Lloyd's Rep. 491.
2 A gum obtained from a type of insect: the gum is widely used in the making of gramophone records.
3 [1954] 1 Lloyd's Rep, at p. 511. Such a test was admissible to establish that the goods were unmerchantable. On the facts, this argument also failed because B could not show that the purchase had been destined for one particular purpose: the shellac was clearly merchantable for other purposes.
4 [1960] 1 All E.R. 36; see above, p. 188.

was unmerchantable, but should a reasonable examination have revealed the defective nature of the toy? In EDMUND DAVIES, J's words:[1]

> "Counsel for the fourth party demonstrated that by squeezing together the two prongs of the catapult in the hand they could be fractured, and further suggested that by holding the toy down with one's foot and then pulling on the elastic its safety could be tested and, as I understand it, its inherent fragility would thereby inevitably be discovered. True, the potential customer might have done any of these things. He might also, I suppose, have tried biting the catapult, or hitting it with a hammer, or applying a lighted match to ensure its non-inflammability, experiments which, with all respect, are but slightly more bizarre than those suggested by learned counsel. But, looking at the matter realistically, as one must, in my judgment none of these tests is called for by a process of 'reasonable examination', as that phrase would be understood by the common-sense standards of everyday life. All these suggested tests were doubtless practicable, but the Act speaks not of a 'practicable', but of a 'reasonable' examination. In my judgment, to pull back the elastic . . . was all that could be reasonably expected of any potential customer, and such an examination wholly failed to make apparent to [the successive buyers], or even render them alive to the possibility of, such a defect as undoubtedly existed in the accident catapult."

Whether the goods are equivalent to sample is a question of fact for the court to decide. However it is permissible for the contract itself to provide for this issue to be determined by some other person. In *Hookway* v. *Isaacs*,[2] it was argued by the sellers that the Committee which issued the certificate that the shellac was equal to the standard sample had by implication a power to determine conclusively whether the contract had been performed in this respect. DEVLIN, J., rejected this contention on the ground that there clearly were grounds upon which the Committee's certification could be upset—the presence of adulterating matter contrary to the standard form contract being the most obvious.[3]

Not only is it possible for a third party to be given a power conclusively to decide whether the goods are in accordance with the contract, but it is also possible (though rare) for the contract to specify that one of the parties should have the power to decide the matter. In the Australian case of *Briscoe* v. *Victorian Railways*,[4] S supplied B with canvas under a contract for the supply of stores which included a term that "the chief storekeeper shall have full power to reject any of such stores, or any portion thereof, which in his judgment are not in every respect in accordance with this contract". Another term provided that where "no particular make of stores is specified the contractor may supply the stores of any make provided that they (in the judgment of the chief storekeeper) be of the very best quality and strictly in accordance with the order and sample and in every respect to the satisfaction of the chief storekeeper". The argument

---

1 At pp. 40–1.
2 [1954] 1 Lloyd's Rep. 491; see also *Rolimpex* v. *Dossa & Sons, Ltd.*, [1971] 1 Lloyd's Rep. 380.
3 [1954] 1 Lloyd's Rep, at p. 509.
4 [1907] V.L.R. 523.

that the canvas supplied was strictly in accordance with the sample did not help the plaintiff because the final decision on whether it was equal with the sample had been granted by the terms of the contract to the chief storekeeper.

One final point: if the goods do not correspond to the sample, it is no excuse for the seller to plead that, with little inconvenience, the buyer could himself remedy the defect. In *E. & S. Ruben, Ltd.* v. *Faire Bros. & Co., Ltd.*[1] it was held that S had failed to deliver rolls of rubber equivalent to sample because the rubber was "crinkly and folded in some cases". It was argued that these faults could have been corrected by warming the rubber and pressing out the crinkles. But, as HILBERY, J., pointed out, it was "no compliance with a contractual obligation for an article to be delivered which is not in accordance with the sample but which can by some simple process, no matter how simple, be turned into an article which is in accordance with the sample on which the contract was made".[2]

vi By custom or usage, or the conduct of the parties

A contract of sale, like any other contract, will be construed against a background of the dealings between the parties and of the trade customs with which they are familiar. As the implication of some additional term depends upon a construction of the contract in its widest sense,[3] it will not be possible to prove a usage or custom which is inconsistent with the terms of the written agreement. In addition, of course, it is necessary to show that the contract was made in the light of custom or usage pleaded. In *Summers* v. *Commonwealth*,[4] the plaintiff had agreed to supply a specified number of blocks of marble for Australia House in London: the size of each block was to be "full enough to admit of its being marked and polished in London without blemish on every side if need be, to the sizes set out in the schedule". The plaintiff sent blocks that were larger than the sizes set out, claiming that a custom in the trade allowed slabs of marble to be larger than the size specified as long as they were not unreasonably so. His argument was rejected for two reasons. In the first place, he was not "in the trade" nor, even if he had been, was it a usage sufficiently "well known and acquiesced in that it may be reasonably presumed to have been an ingredient tacitly imported by the parties into their contract".[5] And, the express terms of the contract made such an interpretation as that contended for impossible. The marble was to be just large enough to be polished down to size; many of the blocks in this case would have needed cutting first.

It should be realised of course that trade usages or customs, or inferences from the actions of the parties, may affect different aspects of the contract of sale. A statement of the quantity of goods to be delivered may be interpreted in the light of a trade usage. In *Société Anonyme L'Industrielle Russo Belge* v.

---

1 [1949] 1 K.B. 254; [1949] 1 All E.R. 215.
2 [1949] 1 K.B. 254, at p. 260; [1949] 1 All E.R. 215, at pp. 218–9.
3 *Produce Brokers Co., Ltd.* v. *Olympia Oil and Coke Co., Ltd.,* [1916] 1 A.C. 314; [1916–17] All E.R. Rep. 133.
4 (1918), 25 C.L.R. 144; affirmed (1919), 26 C.L.R. 180, P.C.
5 *Per* ISAACS, J., 23 C.L.R., at p. 148, citing *Juggomohun Ghose* v. *Manickchund* (1859), 7 Moo. Ind. App. 263, at p. 282.

Scholefield & Son,[1] the Court of Appeal allowed evidence to establish a custom in the Newcastle coal trade to the effect that the word "about" allowed sellers a margin of up to 5 per cent in either direction on the amount of coal proferred. And s. 14 (4) of the Sale of Goods Act specifically provides that an "implied warranty or condition as to quality or fitness for a particular purpose may be annexed to a contract of sale by usage".[2]

In contrast, a practice might be shown which excludes the operation of the conditions implied by the Act.[3] Similarly, the rules as to the passing of risk may be affected by a custom operating within the particular trade.[4]

---

1 (1902), 7 Com. Cas. 114.
2 See *Jones v Bowden* (1813), 4 Taunt. 847.
3 See *Cointat* v. *Myham & Son* (1914), 110 L.T. 749; 30 T.L.R. 282; reversing [1911–13] All E.R. Rep. 724.
4 See above, p. 113, in relation to c.i.f. contracts the rules applicable to which are based upon commercial practice.

CHAPTER 6

Factors Affecting Liability

A. MISTAKE: FRUSTRATION AND THE CONCEPT OF RISK

If a contract, at the time when it was made, was impossible to perform, it is not unreasonable to regard the contract, *prima facie* at least, as void. Similarly, if, at some subsequent stage, the contract becomes impossible to perform, through no fault of the parties, it is perhaps the most just solution to regard the future rights and obligations of the parties as being avoided. Viewed in the narrow confines of impossibility of performance, both mistake (initial impossibility) and frustration (subsequent impossibility) are dealt with in the Sale of Goods Act. Unfortunately, however, they are dealt with in such a way as to suggest that the Act is exclusive of any other possible application of the doctrines of mistake and frustration, whereas at common law both doctrines are potentially or in fact of wider application.

i Mistake

The only circumstance covered by the Act is that of specific goods which have perished. By s. 6:

> "Where there is a contract for the sale of specific goods, and the goods without the knowledge of the seller have perished at the time when the contract is made, the contract is void."

a *The origin of the rule*

Even if one accepts the fact that, in 1893, the law relating to "mistake" was uncertain and of limited application, it cannot be claimed that the inclusion of this section was a particularly helpful rationalisation of the existing law. Chalmers, in drafting the Act, claimed that the section reproduced the decision in *Couturier* v. *Hastie*. S, the plaintiffs, and chartered a vessel to carry a cargo of corn from Salonica to a safe port in the United Kingdom. The corn was loaded and a bill of lading issued whereby freight was payable by S or his assigns as per charterparty. The charterparty and the bill of lading duly indorsed were sent to S's London agent. He effected an insurance on the cargo and placed the charterparty, the bill of lading and the policy in the hands of the defendant, A, a corn factor, who sold under a del credere commission to B. B then discovered that, before he had entered into the contract with A, the corn had become over-heated and had been sold off at an intermediate port.

208

He, therefore, repudiated the contract on the ground that the cargo had not existed at the time of the sale. As he later went bankrupt, S brought this action for the price against A, who, acting as a del credere agent, impliedly guaranteed any sale that he might arrange. The crucial question was whether B would have been liable, or whether his repudiation had been justified.

The case came before four different courts, and it is quite clear that they each regarded the matter as depending either primarily, or entirely, upon the construction of the contract. At first instance MARTIN, B., held that the contract implied that, at the time of sale, the corn was in existence as such and was capable of delivery.[1] A majority of the Court of Exchequer entered a verdict for the plaintiffs on the ground that the third party had bought the cargo, if it existed at the date of the contract: but, if it had been damaged or lost, he had bought the benefit of the insurance.[2] The Court of Exchequer Chamber reversed this judgment.[3] COLERIDGE, J., giving the Court's decision, accepted that the case turned "entirely on the meaning of the contract" made between the defendant and the third party. It was the Court's view, however, that the basis of the contract was for the sale and purchase of goods, and it was not a contract for goods lost or not lost.[4] The House of Lords refused to interfere with this conclusion.[5]

It is clear that the decision in this case turned not upon any different view of the law by the various judges involved in the hearings, but in their application of the law, which they all regarded as fairly clear, to a contract the precise interpretation of which was far from obvious. In the course of giving the judgment of the Court of Exchequer, which was later reversed, PARKE, B., admitted that "when there is a sale of specific chattel . . . there is an implied undertaking that it exists; and if there were nothing in this case but a bargain and sale of a certain cargo . . . there would be an engagement by the vendor, or a condition, that the cargo was in existence at that time."[6] This statement is no different from the opinions of the majority of the judges involved in the case, who departed from PARKE, B., only in their interpretation of the contract. If the contract is treated as a straightforward contract for the sale of goods then, normally, the existence of the subject matter will be the basis upon which the parties contract.

b *The consequences of the rule*

Even on the basis of this assumption, it is possible to imagine more than one consequence if that assumption is not fulfilled. In the first place, the buyer clearly will not be liable for the price. This result was emphatically endorsed by the Court of Exchequer Chamber and the House of Lords in *Couturier* v. *Hastie*.

---

1 (1852), 8 Exch. 40, at p. 47.
2 (1852), 8 Exch. 40.
3 *Hastie* v. *Couturier* (1853), 9 Exch. 102; [1943–60] All E.R. Rep. 280.
4 9 Exch., at p. 107; [1943–60] All E.R. Rep., at p. 283.
5 (1856), 5 H.L. Cas. 673; [1843–60] All E.R. Rep. 284.
6 (1852), 8 Exch., at p. 54.

But can the disappointed buyer sue the seller for non-delivery or for return of the price if already paid? These possibilities were not considered in *Couturier* v. *Hastie* but, as the judges were unanimously of opinion that the terms, whether express or implied on the basis of the parties' apparent intentions, of the contract were all important, it would appear that they would have been prepared to accept a contract by the terms of which the seller had guaranteed the existence of the goods.

In *McRae* v. *Commonwealth Disposals Commission*,[1] the plaintiff had purchased from the defendants an oil tanker lying on Jourmand Reef, which was said to be 100 miles north of Samarai. It was later discovered that no such vessel had ever existed, and the plaintiffs were put to a considerable expense in fitting out a salvage expedition and in a fruitless search for the non-existent tanker. The trial judge held on the strength of *Couturier* v. *Hastie* that, as there was no tanker, there was no contract. The High Court of Australia reversed the decision on this point. DIXON and FULLAGER, J.J., exhaustively analysed the various judgments in *Couturier* v. *Hastie* and concluded that that case had depended essentially on a matter of construction. Similarly, in this case, there was no automatic principle to be applied simply because the subject-matter of the contract did not exist. On a true construction of its terms it was clear that the defendants had implicitly promised that the tanker did exist. The non-existence of the vessel was therefore not a reason for holding the contract void, but was the reason for holding the defendants liable in damages for breach of their contract.

On the facts of *McRae's* case, of course, s. 6 did not apply because the goods never had existed so they had not "perished" within the wording of that section. If there had been evidence that the tanker had once been on the reef specified, strictly speaking the Court would have been obliged to apply s. 6 and to hold the contract void. Such a conclusion might not be in accord with what is felt to be the justice of a particular case. Indeed, as the rule is not an accurate statement of the law as laid down in *Couturier* v. *Hastie*, it is to be hoped that the courts would not feel precluded by the wording of s. 6 from interpreting contracts in the light of what the parties seem to have intended.

While implementation of this suggestion may be desirable, it is less obvious upon what legal grounds the courts could justify such a course of action. There are a number of possibilities:

1 *To read s. 6 subject to a contrary intention.* Under s. 55, where any "right, duty, or liability would arise under a contract of sale by implication of law, it may be negatived or varied by express agreement or by the course of dealing between the parties, or by usage, if the usage is such as to bind both parties to the contract". It is doubtful whether as a matter of strict interpretation s. 6 can be classified as a rule arising by implication because it appears to be one of automatic application. The way round this obstacle might be to argue that s. 6 should be read in the light of the previous common law rule, and not in derogation from it. Admittedly this solution would involve some distortion of the actual words used in the section, but it would then have something in

---

1 (1951), 84 C.L.R. 377.

common with the more flexible attitude of the courts to the doctrine of frustration of which s. 7 is but a part.[1]

2 *To treat the implied promise that the goods exist as a separate contract.* The argument that, the main contract of sale being rendered void by s. 6, a collateral contract would fail for want of consideration, is not an insuperable barrier to this analysis. If the parties see some value in entering into a transaction that may be void there is surely sufficient consideration to support the collateral or preliminary promise. In the situation that arose in the *McRae* case, tenders for the tanker were called for by advertisements in the Press. It would clearly have been possible to construe a contract along the lines of a promise by the Commission that there was a tanker at the place stipulated as an inducement to the public at large to put in tenders. Whether there was such a tanker would of course be immaterial to an unsuccessful tenderer, but an action on this preliminary or collateral agreement would be maintainable by the party whose tender was accepted as the basis of the main contract. The *consideration* for the preliminary contract would not have been the main contract, so, even if there had been a tanker which had been destroyed by storms, the failure of the main contract by the application of s. 6 would not have affected the validity of the preliminary agreement and the enforceability of the preliminary promise.

3 *To regard the contract as a sale of a chance and not a sale of goods at all.* There is a suggestion in *Couturier* v. *Hastie* that a sale of an article which may or may not be in existence, where the buyer assumes the risk of getting the article or of obtaining only the benefit of the insurance (or even nothing at all), is not a sale of goods. In the course of giving the judgment of the Court of Exchequer Chamber, COLERIDGE, J., distinguished between a sale of goods on the one hand, and a purchase of an adventure or contract for goods lost or not lost on the other. It was clearly acknowledged that a purchase of an adventure in which the risk of the goods already having been lost was assumed by the buyer was not void: it was not a contract for the sale of goods. Is it possible to argue that a sale of an article in which the seller guarantees its existence is not a sale of goods, or at least not a sale of goods within s. 6 of the Act?

c *If the goods are not specific*

There is of course no need to apply s. 6 automatically to situations where the goods involved are not, strictly speaking, specific. It is nevertheless likely that, where the continued existence of the source from which the goods were to be obtained was by implication fundamental to the contract, the "perishing" of the source will have the effect of avoiding the contract.[2] The example was given by Chalmers[3] of a contract to sell "five dozen of the '74 champagne now

---

1 See Lord WRIGHT's discussion of what is "just and reasonable" in *Joseph Constantine Steamship Line, Ltd.* v. *Imperial Smelting Corporation, Ltd.*, [1942] A.C. 154, at pp. 183–6.
2 This would certainly be the case under s. 7, see below, p. 221.
3 *The Sale of Goods Act* 1893, 6th Ed. (1905), p. 21; *Sale of Goods*, 16th Ed., p. 73.

in my cellar", when unknown to the parties all but three dozen had been destroyed by fire. Although there was no authority on the point, it was Chalmers' view that the contract would be void. While this conclusion will normally be the case, the reason is not the application of s. 6, but the interpretation of the terms of the contract in the light of the parties' apparent intentions. There may be circumstances in which the seller might be liable for a failure to supply the order—for example, if he had never had five dozen bottles of that vintage but believed that he had them and was impliedly promising that he was able to provide them.

d *The meaning of "perish"*

The application of s. 6 is also dependent upon the goods having "perished". This superficially straightforward word conceals a fundamental problem. The wider the interpretation placed upon it, the greater the excuse s. 6 might offer to the defaulting seller. In the New Zealand case of *Rendell* v. *Turnbull & Co.*,[1] S sold B all the table-potatoes in S's paddock, estimated quantity 75 tons. Six hundred sacks (weighing just over 54 tons) were delivered; forty-nine sacks were ready for delivery; and sixteen tons were still in the ground. B gave notice that he did not want any more of the potatoes. In an action by S for the price of the 600 bags and for damages for non-acceptance of the rest, B pleaded: (1) that the goods had perished without the knowledge of the parties; (2) that they were not of merchantable quality; and (3) that they did not answer the description of "table-potatoes." It was held that the potatoes had been suffering from a second growth at the time of the contract and that, being unfit to eat, their character as table potatoes was destroyed. The contract was thus void under s. 6. S's claim failed, but, on this interpretation of the facts, B could not succeed in his counter-claim for damages for breach of S's implied undertaking that the goods were merchantable.[2]

If such a decision were followed, the implications would be far-reaching, because it suggests that, if the defects are sufficient to render the goods in a different merchantable category from that contracted for, the ignorant seller (i.e., one who is not aware of the condition of the goods) will escape liability. To avoid such a wide immunity being created, it is obviously necessary to limit the scope of s. 6 by placing a restrictive interpretation on the word "perish". In *Horn* v. *Minister of Food*,[3] on facts not all that dissimilar to the *Rendell* case, MORRIS, J., held that s. 7 did not apply because, "however grave was the deterioration of their condition", the potatoes still answered their description as such and could not be said to have perished.[4]

The dividing line between goods which retain their characteristics as the goods described and those which have so altered as to become something altogether different is based in part on a decision in a case not directly related to a contract of sale at all. In *Asfar & Co.* v, *Blundell*,[5] a cargo of dates was shipped under bills of lading by which freight was payable on right delivery of the goods to the port of London. Before discharge the ship had been struck by another vessel

---

1 (1908), 27 N.Z.L.R. 1067.   2 At pp. 1073–4.
3 [1948] 2 All E.R. 1036.   4 At p. 1039
5 [1896] 1 Q.B. 123.

and had sunk. By the time she was raised, the dates had become saturated with sewage and were in a fermenting condition. They were condemned as unfit for human consumption and were not allowed to be unloaded in London. However, a large portion of them retained the appearance of dates and were of considerable value for distilling purposes. They were in fact resold, transhipped and exported. The question for the Court of Appeal was whether freight was payable in whole or in part, or whether, from an insurance angle, there had been a total loss of the freight on the goods. The Court had no hesitation in holding that there had been a total loss of the dates. The argument to the contrary was ridiculed by Lord ESHER, M.R.:[1]

> "The ingenuity of the argument might commend itself to a body of chemists, but not to business men. We are dealing with dates as a subject-matter of commerce; and it is contended that, although these dates were under water for two days, and when brought up were simply a mass of pulpy matter impregnated with sewage and in a state of fermentation, there had been no change in their nature, and they were still dates. There is a perfectly well known test which has for many years been applied to such cases as the present —that test is whether, as a matter of business, the nature of the thing has been altered. The nature of the thing is not necessarily altered because the thing itself has been damaged; wheat or rice may be damaged, but may still remain the things dealt with as wheat or rice in business. But if the nature of the thing is altered, and it becomes for business purposes something else, so that it is not dealt with by business people as the thing which it originally was, the question for determination is whether the thing insured . . . has become a total loss. If it is so changed . . . as to become an unmerchantable thing . . . then there is a total loss."

This decision is regularly cited[2] in connection with ss. 6 and 7 and there would seem ample justification for so doing. In *Couturier* v. *Hastie*, there had almost certainly been a constructive total loss of the goods; that is, they had been in imminent danger of becoming an actual total loss as a result of overheating and they had been abandoned by the sale on the owner's behalf. Chalmers, who also drafted the first Marine Insurance Bill of 1894,[3] was very likely thinking of the insurance analogy when he used the word "perish" in the Sale of Goods Act. However, a moment's reflection will serve to bring out how inappropriate the analogy is in interpreting a provision which purports to lay down a rule of law and not a presumption dependent upon the circumstances of the case.

If an importer had agreed to sell dates to a merchant in circumstances similar to those that arose in *Asfar & Co.* v. *Blundell*, would the contract have been void under s. 6 or would there have been a breach of a fundamental term of the contract? It would be a startling proposition to suggest that, if the seller knew, or perhaps should have been aware of the possible deterioration of the dates, he would be liable for breach of contract, but if not, he was exempt from any

---

1 At pp. 127–8.
2 Atiyah, *op. cit.*, 4th Ed., p. 141; Fridman, *Sale of Goods*, p. 46; Benjamin, *op. cit.*, 8th Ed., p. 143.
3 Several bills were introduced between 1894 and 1906 when the Marine Insurance Act was eventually passed.

obligation to perform. Indeed, in the latter circumstance, a seller would be in a more advantageous position if the goods had reached an advanced stage of deterioration than if their defects were relatively slight so that they retained their existing identity.

The problem of distinguishing between a breach of contract and a void contract also arose in *Barrow, Lane and Ballard, Ltd.* v. *Phillip Phillips & Co., Ltd.*,[1] in which "perish" was given a novel interpretation. S had agreed to sell to B 700 bags of ground nuts which were stated to be lying in a warehouse. B gave S two bills of exchange for the price and received in return a delivery order for the goods. Later B sent orders to the warehouse in respect of 150 bags and these were duly delivered. When B sent two further orders, however, they were returned "Goods not available". It was discovered that at the date of the contract only 591 bags had been in store, 109 having disappeared; and that during the following two months all but the 150 delivered had also been irregularly taken. By this time the warehouse company was in liquidation so that S and B were obliged to settle between themselves where the loss should lie. Was S in breach for failing to deliver 700 bags? Or had B accepted the goods and waived his right to set aside the contract for delivery of the wrong quantity? WRIGHT, J., would accept neither of these alternatives. If all 700 bags had been stolen prior to the contract date without the knowledge of the parties, or if they had been destroyed by fire, s. 6 could undoubtedly have applied. In this case, not all 700 had been destroyed: 591 had remained at the contract date. However, a contract for a parcel of 700 bags was something different from a contract for 591 bags; the parties were therefore contracting about a subject matter which, at the time of the contract, had ceased to exist.

It cannot be claimed that this decision is any more satisfactory than some of the other situations that have been dealt with in this context. It implies that, providing the parties are dealing with a specific consignment of goods, which unknown to them has been reduced in size, the contract of sale entered into between them is void. Stated in that form the principle verges on the absurd. It clearly must yield to a contrary intention in the large number of situations where the transaction involves a transfer of the bill of lading. Indeed in the commercial world a buyer can justifiably feel aggrieved if the onus is not placed on the seller to "deliver the goods".

This area of the law of sale is an unsatisfactory state. That it has not produced more problems in litigation is undoubtedly due to the reluctance of parties to rely upon a provision which, applied according to its letter, could create havoc with commercial transactions. It would also appear unlikely that the courts would countenance the frequent invocation of s. 6. Nevertheless, the decision in *Barrow, Lane and Ballard, Ltd.* v. *Phillip Phillips & Co., Ltd.* is a salutary remainder that the existence of the section cannot be dismissed as a matter of no consequence. It does exist and it is a threat, particularly if the word "perish" is too readily given an extended meaning and if it is regarded as a rule of law rather than a presumption that can be negatived by the apparent intentions of the parties.

---

1 [1929] 1 K.B. 574; [1928] All E.R. Rep. 74.

ii Frustration: the concept of risk

a *The scope of s. 7*

If the goods perish after the contract has been formed, the agreement *may* be terminated.

By s. 7:

> "Where there is an agreement to sell specific goods, and subsequently the goods, without any fault on the part of the seller or buyer, perish before the risk passes to the buyer, the agreement is thereby avoided."

As with s. 6, in order for this provision to operate, the goods must be specific. Hence, difficulty has arisen as to whether a contract for the sale of goods from a stipulated or implied source can be frustrated.

In *Howell* v. *Coupland*,[1] a contract for the purchase of 200 tons of potatoes from S's land at Whaplode was held to be avoided when most of the crop was destroyed by blight. It was the view of the Court of Appeal that, the contract being for part of a specific crop, its destruction without fault on the part of S fell within the principle laid down in *Taylor* v. *Caldwell*.[2]

While *Howell* v. *Coupland* is generally regarded as good law, it must be said that it is not covered by the strict wording of s. 7, which relates to specific and not future goods. It has been suggested[3] that the principle has been preserved by s. 5 (2) which provides that there "may be a contract for the sale of goods, the acquisition of which by the seller depends upon a contingency which may or may not happen". Alternatively, it is not unreasonable to treat goods from a specific source as being the equivalent of specific goods for the purposes of s. 7.

As far as the use of the word "perish" is concerned, that term should presumably have the same meaning (whatever that might be) as under s. 6. However, there seems less danger to the wide application of s. 7 than there is if s. 6 were interpreted too broadly.

b *The relationship between s. 7 and the concept of risk*

1. *The general principle applies unless "otherwise agreed"*. Goods are said to be at the risk of a particular party when the cost of their loss or depreciation falls on him. The principles attributing that loss are distinct from the rules governing liability for non-performance of the contract. In the case of s. 7, however, the principles dealing with the risk are directly related to the rules covering liability.

The general principle attributing the risk is stated in s. 20:

> "Unless otherwise agreed, the goods remain at the seller's risk until the property therein is transferred to the buyer, but when the property therein is transferred to the buyer, the goods are at the buyer's risk whether delivery has been made or not."

---

1 (1874), L.R. 9 Q.B. 462; *on appeal* (1876), 1 Q.B.D. 258; [1874–80] All E.R. Rep. 878.
2 (1863), 3 B. & S. 826; [1861–73] All E.R. Rep. 24 (performance of a contract for the hire of a music hall and gardens excused when, without fault on the part of the owners, the hall was destroyed and the gardens badly damaged by fire).
3 See *per* McKenna, J., in *H. R. & S. Sainsbury, Ltd.* v. *Street*, [1972] 3 All E.R. 1127, at p. 1133.

An obvious case where the risk is by arrangement to pass before the property is a transaction on approval or on sale or return. In such contracts it is usually specified that the risk is to pass on delivery of the goods to the would-be buyer,[1] but even in the absence of express agreement a term to that effect may be implied from the usage of a particular trade.[2] By usage also, in c.i.f. contracts, the property passes when the shipping documents are transferred to the buyer, although the risk passes as soon as the goods cross the ship's rail at the port of loading.

As the property in goods cannot pass until they are identified (i.e. either that they were specific goods or that they were unascertained goods that have been appropriated to the contract), the risk is not usually upon the buyer in the case of unascertained and unappropriated goods. To this principle there is one notable, but imprecise, exception.

In *Sterns, Ltd.* v. *Vickers, Ltd.*,[3] S had acquired 200,000 gallons of white spirit in a tank belonging to a storage company on terms that he was to have free storage for the month of January. S then sold 120,000 gallons to B, B to make his own arrangements about storage after January 31. B resold the spirit, received a delivery warrant for the spirit and endorsed it in favour of the sub-buyer. The sub-buyer arranged to have the oil kept in the same tank, but when he took delivery he discovered that it had deteriorated. There was no doubt that property could not have passed in the 120,000 gallons because there had been no severance from bulk,[4] but was it not arguable that the risk of deterioration had passed from S to B? Certainly, as SCRUTTON, L.J., pointed out, some interest must pass on such a transaction because it had been decided by the House of Lords in *Inglis* v. *Stock*[5] that the buyer of part of an undivided bulk obtained an insurable interest in the goods. He then continued:[6]

> "Whether the property passes or not, the transfer of the undivided interest carries with it the risk of loss from something happening to the goods, such as a deterioration in their quality, at all events after the vendor has given the purchaser a delivery order upon the party in possession of them, and that party has assented to it. The vendor of a specified quantity out of a bulk in the possession of a third party discharges his obligation to the purchaser as soon as the third party undertakes to the purchaser to deliver him that quantity out of the bulk."

This decision was approved by two members of the House of Lords in *Comptoir d'Achat, etc. du Boerenbond Belge S/A* v. *Luis de Ridder Limitada* (*The Julia*), Lord NORMAND commenting that[7]

---

1 Such an allocation of risk is entirely reasonable; but "the parties can agree to some purely artificial allocation of the risk and if they express that agreement in suitable language in the contract it must somehow be given effect": *per* Lord NORMAND in *Comptoir d'Achat, etc. du Boerenbond Belge S/A* v. *Luis de Ridder Limitada* (*The Julia*), [1949] A.C. 293, at p. 319; [1949] 1 All E.R. 269, at p. 281.
2 *Bevington and Morris* v. *Dale & Co., Ltd.* (1902), 7 Com. Cas. 112.
3 [1923] 1 K.B. 78; [1922] All E.R. Rep. 126.
4 See above, p. 18.
5 (1885), 10 App. Cas. 263.
6 [1923] 1 K.B. 78, at pp. 84–85.
7 [1949] A.C. 293, at p. 319; [1949] 1 All E.R. 269, at p. 281; also *per* Lord PORTER, [1949] A.C., at p. 312; [1949] 1 All E.R., at p. 274.

> "In those cases in which it has been held that the risk without the property
> has passed to the buyer it has been because the buyer rather than the seller
> was seen to have an immediate and practical interest in the goods, as for
> instance when he has an immediate right under the storekeeper's delivery
> warrant to the delivery of a portion of an undivided bulk in store."

While the exception thus has some authority to support it, it is worth asking
whether it might not be preferable to fit the decision into the existing framework
rather than to treat it as an anomaly. In this respect the importance ascribed by
Lord NORMAND to the attornment of the storekeeper is unfortunate. The
attornment was given less prominence in the judgment of SCRUTTON, L.J., in
Sterns, Ltd. v. *Vickers, Ltd.* itself. It would not appear unreasonable to consider
the passing of the risk as having occurred with the agreement of the parties.
From a certain date it was for the buyer to make his own arrangements with the
storekeeper. Whether he did so, or even presented the delivery warrant, could
have been regarded as irrelevant to the decision on the facts. It was implicit in
the arrangement between the parties that the risk was upon the buyer.

2 *Risk of deterioration in transit.* It is also possible for the property to pass before
the risk. The property in specific or ascertained goods may have passed to the
buyer before delivery, yet the risk of deterioration rendering them unsuitable
or unmerchantable remains on the seller to allow a reasonable period for delivery
and use. In *Beer* v. *Walker*,[1] S agreed to send rabbits each week by rail from
London to B in Brighton. Although sound when put in the hands of the railway,
they were unfit when they were delivered in Brighton. It was held that the risk of
deterioration rendering the goods unfit lay on the seller:

> "The implied warranty extended to the time at which, in the ordinary course
> of transit, the rabbits should reach the [buyer], and not only to that time, but
> that it continued until the [buyer] should have a reaonable opportunity of
> dealing with them in the ordinary course of business".[2]

This decision was approved and applied by DIPLOCK, J., in *Marsh and Murrell,
Ltd.* v. *Joseph I. Emanuel, Ltd.*,[3] but it must give rise to some difficulty in
relation to s. 33 of the Act:

> "Where the seller of goods agrees to deliver them at his own risk at a place
> other than that where they are when sold, the buyer must, nevertheless,
> unless otherwise agreed, take any risk of deterioration in the goods necessarily
> incident to the course of transit."

Section 33 establishes a rule which is inconsistent with the principle accepted
by DIPLOCK, J., in the following passage:[4]

> "I have so far travelled through my legal life under the impression, shared
> by a number of other judges . . . that when goods are sold under a contract
> such as a c.i.f. contract, or f.o.b. contract, which involves transit before use,
> there is an implied warranty not merely that they shall be merchantable at

---

1 (1877), 46 L.J.Q.B. 677.
2 At p. 679.
3 [1961] 1 All E.R. 485.
4 At p. 488.

> the time when they are put on the vessel, but that they shall be in such a state that they can endure the normal journey and be in a merchantable condition on arrival."

The inconsistency is even more striking when one considers the fact that the Court of Appeal reversed[1] the decision on the ground that in the circumstances the voyage had not been a normal one[2] so that the principle was not applicable. It was the abnormality of the voyage which threw the risk on to the buyer, not the normal incidents of transit suggested by s. 33.

It could be contented that s. 33 contains the exception "unless otherwise agreed" and that in the case of c.i.f. and f.o.b. contracts, there is implied agreement as to the allocation of the risk. However, there is no reason to doubt the correctness of *Beer* v. *Walker*, nor to limit the principle to sea-carriage. Of course, s. 33 deals with a specific situation where S has accepted the risk by undertaking to deliver the goods. In such a situation the property will normally also pass on delivery, but there seems little place today for a rule that in such a limited area the buyer must take the risk of deterioration necessarily incident to the course of transit.

3 *Delay in delivery*. Despite the number of exceptions to the application of s. 20, normally risk does pass with the property. However, even in a normal case the application of the section can be affected by the two circumstances included as provisos. Section 20 continues:

> "Provided that where delivery has been delayed through the fault of either buyer or seller the goods are at the risk of the party in fault as regards any loss which might not have occurred but for such fault.
>
> Provided also that nothing in this section shall affect the duties or liabilities of either seller or buyer as a bailee of the goods of the other party."

In *Demby Hamilton & Co., Ltd.* v. *Barden*,[3] S agreed to process and supply B with 30 tons of apple juice in accordance with sample, to be delivered to X in weekly truckloads. With the last apples of the season S prepared the juice and put it into casks. Deliveries commenced but, at X's request, B asked for a halt to them. Two further deliveries were made, but, despite repeated requests for instructions by S, no further deliveries were accepted. The contents of the casks became putrid and had to be thrown away. It was held that, although property in the undelivered juice remained with S, after the delay the risk passed to the buyer under the first proviso to s. 20.

Its application can give rise to questions of causation. In the Australian case of *Sharp* v. *Batt*,[4] S had been instructed to have 100 cases of standard grade apples ready to ship on April 22. He picked the apples in readiness, but then received instructions to postpone delivery until May 20. Before that date the apples developed a fungal disease which would not have occurred if S had wrapped the apples, but he had left them unwrapped. The Supreme Court of Tasmania held

---

1 [1962] 1 All E.R. 77; [1962] 1 W.L.R. 16.
2 The hatches to the hold had been open in the hot sun at the intermediate port in Cyprus: see above, pp. 200–1.
3 [1949] 1 All E.R. 435.
4 (1930), 25 Tas. L.R. 33.

that B had no claim for S's failure to deliver standard grade apples because the deterioration would not have occurred had it not been for the delay caused by B. Even though property in the apples had not passed, the apples were at B's risk under the first proviso to s. 20. It was true that S was under a duty to take care of the apples, but, as the time for delivery had passed, he could only be liable as a gratuitous bailee, that is, for gross negligence. On the facts, it was held that, although S had certainly been negligent, his conduct did not amount to gross negligence.

Some of the difficulty of deciding whether the first proviso applies is avoided by its wording. It is not loss that "would not have occurred" but loss which "might not have occurred". In *Sharp* v. *Batt*, B was *prima facie* at risk because the loss might not have occurred but for the delay he had occasioned. However the second proviso stipulates that "*nothing* in this section" is to affect the duties or liabilities of buyer or seller as bailee of the goods on behalf of the other party. In other words, even the delay altering the risk of loss or deterioration was not to affect the position of S as bailee.

However, *Sharp* v. *Batt* was squarely based upon the proposition advanced by Benjamin[1] that on principle "a seller in possession of the buyer's goods is, until the expiration of the period limited for delivery, in the position of a bailee for reward, and is liable for ordinary negligence only, as the price of the goods should include their custody by the seller till the time fixed for delivery or for a reasonable time. Afterwards he would be a gratuitous bailee". Although the proposition is difficult to reconcile with the wording of the second proviso, the issue may have been rendered largely academic because of the tendency of the courts today to regard the duties of all bailees within one general, though variable, standard of care dependent upon all the circumstances of the case.[2] The current approach would not be to categorise the bailee/seller's conduct as negligent, or not grossly negligent, but to ask whether he owes a duty of care not to act towards the goods in the way he has done. In answering this question, the delay in taking delivery would be a relevant factor.[3]

4 *A concept of risk, or are there different "risks"?* Once it is realised that the risk and the property can be separated and indeed that different aspects of the risk can be vested in different parties, it will be apparent that s. 7 is something of an over-simplification. All that is required for that section to operate is that, without fault of the parties, the goods should perish before *the risk* passes to the buyer. It would seem that in this case the "risk" relates to the risk of loss. However obvious this statement might appear, it is nevertheless necessary to

---

1 *Op. cit.*, 7th Ed., p. 427; citing 3 Salk. 61; and the American case of *Koon* v. *Brinkerhoff* (1886), 39 Hunt 130: see 25 Tas. L.R., at pp. 55–6.
2 *Houghland* v. *R. R. Low (Luxury Coaches), Ltd.*, [1962] 1 Q.B. 694; [1962] 2 All E.R. 159.
3 In *Sharp* v. *Batt*, the judge applied the correct test, "that degree of care and diligence which men of common prudence generally bestow on their own property" in words drawn from *Koon* v. *Brinkerhoff* (above), but reached a somewhat strange conclusion. He accepted as demonstrating the absence of "gross" negligence evidence that S had 135 cases left to fulfil the order and that S had not therefore minded if a few of the apples deteriorated: he had simply misjudged the number that had become diseased. For the "prudent owner" test, see also *Wiehe* v. *Dennis Bros.* (1913), 29 T.L.R. 250; applying *Bullen* v. *Swan Electric Engraving Co.* (1907), 23 T.L.R. 258.

cover the situation where property has passed to the buyer but the risk, as bailee, remains with the seller. Destruction of the subject matter without fault would fall outside the seller's range of liability, but it could not be claimed that the contract was frustrated because the remainder of the risk clearly lies with the buyer.

The position is more complicated where delay in delivering goods might throw back liability on the seller. The risk has already passed: does the seller resume the entire risk, as suggested by the first proviso ("as regards any loss which might not have occurred but for such fault"); or is he only responsible for negligence as a bailee (for reward) under the second proviso? Does part of the risk remain with the buyer? Or is it still possible for s. 7 to operate?

The better view would seem to be that, once the property (and thereby usually the risk) has passed, it places a heavy burden on the buyer to show that destruction of the subject-matter is still at the seller's risk. There is no direct authority because on the whole it would appear very difficult for a buyer who has obtained property in the goods to argue that the contract is frustrated. And then if he could argue this successfully, as frustration only operates from the moment of the frustrating event, the buyer could still find himself liable for the price. As a purely practical matter, therefore, s. 7 does not figure in his assessment of his legal position. In the Australian case of *Maine* v. *Lyons*,[1] a quantity of potatoes was bought under a contract which provided that their acceptance was subject to their being passed by the Tasmanian government's inspector, and, if exported to another State, to their being similarly passed in that State. If the potatoes were rejected by an inspector, the buyers had a right to avoid the contract. The potatoes were passed in Tasmania, and were exported to Victoria but, before an inspection could take place, the importation of Tasmanian potatoes into Victoria was prohibited. The buyers were obliged to re-ship the potatoes and to sell them at a loss in Tasmania. The High Court held that, as the property in the potatoes had already passed to the buyers, the condition relating to the inspection of the potatoes was a condition subsequent, the failure of which to operate rendered the contract absolute. Even if the importation of Tasmanian potatoes into Victoria was a frustrating event,[2] it could not operate on a contract under which property had already passed.

5 *The automatic application of s.* 7. The role that can be played by the concept of risk makes it less significant whether s. 7 can be ousted by a contrary intention along the lines suggested in the context of s. 6. It would be inappropriate if destruction of the goods without fault after contract but before performance invariably terminated the contract. There should be no barrier to allocating the risk of loss or destruction to one of the parties in appropriate circumstances. In the case of the buyer, this allocation is clearly within the terms of s. 7. For the seller to assume the risk of safe keeping, i.e. of guaranteeing the continued existence of the goods, certainly falls outside the scope of the doctrine of frustration.

---

1 (1913), 15 C.L.R. 671.
2 Which it was not, as the contract of sale left open where the seller was going to resell the goods.

c *Situations falling outside s. 7*

It goes without saying that a contract may be frustrated by events other than destruction of the goods. In addition, s. 7 applies only to sales of specific goods, but it is possible for a sale of unascertained goods to be frustrated, for example, where the seller intends to fulfil his contract with the buyer by obtaining goods from a particular source. What is the effect if he is cut off from that source, or that source is destroyed?

All would seem to depend upon the terms of the contract in the light of the knowledge of the parties. If the source is specified then the contract is frustrated by the failure of that source as in the case of the potato crop from the seller's land at Whaplode.[1] Similarly, in *Re Badische Co., Ltd.*,[2] where S dealt exclusively in goods on behalf of a German manufacturer, it was held that a contract to supply dyestuffs to B was frustrated by the outbreak of war in 1914.

In contrast, in *Blackburn Bobbin Co., Ltd.* v. *T. W. Allen & Sons, Ltd.*,[3] it was held that as, in a contract for the sale of 700 standards of Finland birch timber, B did not know how S intended to fulfil his contract, whether by direct import or by purchase of the goods from sources in this country, the contract was not discharged by a complete halt in trade with Finland following the outbreak of war between Britain and Germany. And, in *Tsakiroglou & Co., Ltd.* v. *Noblee Thorl G.m.b.H.*,[4] the House of Lords held that a contract for the sale of unascertained goods, namely groundnuts, to be shipped from the Sudan to Europe, was not frustrated by the closing of the Suez Canal for some six months although it meant that the seller would, under the terms of the contract, incur additional expense by having to despatch the goods via the Cape of Good Hope. Their Lordships took the view that though the route via the Cape involved a change in the method of performance of the contract, it was not such a fundamental change from that envisaged under the contract as to entitle the seller to say the contract was frustrated.

d *The effects of frustration*

Once it is established that a contract has been frustrated, then the rights and obligations of the parties are determined as they existed at the moment when the frustrating event occurred.

1. *The position at common law.* The original position is well illustrated by the Australian case of *Re Continental C. and G. Rubber Co. Pty., Ltd.*,[5] in which S agreed to make certain machinery for B. Progress payments were to be made by B to S and £6,000 was in fact paid. When war broke out in August, 1914, the contract was discharged because nearly all the shares in B were held by enemy aliens so that any contract with B became illegal. The questions in dispute were (1) whether any claim for damages lay against B for work carried out by S; (2) whether B was entitled to recover the £6,000, or perhaps just the £3,000 of

---

1 *Howell* v. *Coupland* (1876), 1 Q.B.D. 258, above p. 215.
2 [1921] 2 Ch. 331.
3 [1918] 2 K.B. 467; see also *Monkland* v. *Jack Barclay, Ltd.*, [1951] 2 K.B. 252, at p. 258, *per* ASQUITH, L.J.
4 [1962] A.C. 62; [1961] 2 All E.R. 179.
5 (1919), 27 C.L.R. 194.

the advance payments that had been made before the outbreak of war; or
(3) whether B was entitled to the machinery actually constructed by S in pursuance of the contract. On (1), the High Court held that the only rights that
accrued to S were to progress payments made under the contract. If S's costs
and expenses exceeded that amount, there was no entitlement to them. Once the
performance of the contract became impossible, all further liabilities under the
contract were at an end. As to (2) B's claim also failed. The common law rule[1]
was that, where both parties were excused from further performance of the
contract by a frustrating event, neither had a cause of action in respect of what
might be termed inchoate rights. There was no basis upon which a claim would
lie for total failure of consideration.[2] In the case of (3), the same principle
applied. B was only entitled to delivery of the machinery in final performance of
the contract: at the time of discharge no right to the machinery or any part of it
had arisen.

At common law, the doctrine of frustration thus drew a sharp division between accrued rights which remained enforceable and those that were dependent
upon further performance of the contract. It was a division which created the
most glaring injustices as was demonstrated by the Court of Appeal decision in
Chandler v. *Webster*.[3] In that case, it was held that the hire of a room from which
to view the 1902 Coronation procession had been frustrated by the cancellation
of the procession. However, as the sum of £141 15s. had been payable in advance
before the time when the procession was cancelled, the defendant was entitled
to retain the £100 already paid and to claim the £41 15s. as money still due
under the contract.

This conclusion was strongly criticised, and the opportunity was taken by the
House of Lords in the *Fibrosa* case[4] to mitigate some of its apparent harshness.
B was a Polish company which had contracted to buy machinery from S, an
English company. B had paid £1,000 of the contract price in advance when the
German occupation of Poland rendered further performance of the contract
illegal. The House of Lords overruled *Chandler* v. *Webster* and laid down the
principle that even under a frustrated contract, where there had been a total
failure of consideration, the party who had paid a sum such as the £1,000 was
entitled to recover it in quasi-contract on the ground that he had got nothing
of what he had bargained for.

2 *The Law Reform (Frustrated Contracts) Act* 1943. This development did not
solve all the problems nor make for a just solution in all cases. In the first place,
no recovery would be possible in a case where there had not been a total failure

---

1 *Appleby* v. *Myers* (1867), L.R. 2 C.P. 651 (The plaintiffs had erected part of the
 machinery which they had contracted to build on the defendant's premises when the
 premises were destroyed by fire: it was held that both parties were excused from further
 performance, but that the plaintiffs had no action to recover the cost of work already
 carried out as the contract only provided for payment on completion).
2 As far as sums paid after the outbreak of war were concerned, there were the additional
 reasons for non-recovery that the money had been paid under a mistake of law and that
 it had been paid under a contract that had become illegal.
3 [1904] 1 K.B. 493.
4 *Fibrosa Spolka Akcyjna* v. *Fairbairn Lawson Combe Barbour, Ltd.*, [1943] A.C. 32;
 [1942] 2 All E.R. 122.

of consideration: if the person seeking to recover sums already paid under the contract had received some benefit, however small, no action would lie. And, secondly, by enabling the party who had made payments under the contract to recover them, the courts might be causing hardship to the other party. In the *Fibrosa* case itself, for example, the English company had already commenced making the machinery, although no benefit had been received by the Polish company. The machinery might have been saleable elsewhere, but there is no guarantee that this will always be the case. In an attempt to remedy this unsatisfactory situation Parliament passed the Law Reform (Frustrated Contracts) Act 1943. However the Act did not lay down a coherent code to cover all cases of frustration because a number of classes of contract were excluded from its operation, most notably in the present context:

> "any contract to which s. 7 of the Sale of Goods Act, 1893 . . . applies, or . . . any other contract for the sale, or for the sale and delivery, of specific goods, where the contract is frustrated by reason of the fact that the goods have perished" (s. 2 (5) (*c*).

For such cases, the common law position as modified by the *Fibrosa* decision is preserved.

In all other cases, that is where the contract does not relate to specific goods or in all contracts which are frustrated by an event other than the perishing of the goods, the Act does apply. By its provisions:

(x) Sums paid under the contract may be recoverable, and sums still due under the contract may be withheld (s. 3 (2)). The result of this provision is to reverse the *Chandler* v. *Webster* solution completely. However, the Act does not adopt the *Fibrosa* alternative in its entirety because the proviso to s. 1 (2) goes on to state that:

> "if the party to whom the sums were so paid or payable incurred expenses before the time of discharge in, or for the purpose of, the performance of the contract, the court may, if it considers it just to do so having regard to all the circumstances of the case, allow him to retain or, as the case may be, recover the whole or any part of the sums so paid or payable, not being an amount in excess of the expenses so incurred".

In the *Fibrosa* case it had not been possible for the House of Lords to make any allowance for the work that the English company had carried out under the contract. Such an allowance is possible under the Act. However, it should be noted that it is only payments made or work carried out *before* the time of discharge that can be recovered or taken into account under s. 1 (2).

(xx) Where a party has "obtained a valuable benefit" by partial performance of a contract which is frustrated before payment is due, the party providing the benefit may recover "such sum (if any), not exceeding the value of the said benefit to the party obtaining it, as the court considers just" (s. 1 (3)). This provision is designed to cover the situation in which the frustrating event occurs before the obligation to pay for goods delivered or materials supplied under the contract materialises. The application of s. 1 (3) appears straightforward enough, but there may be some uncertainty whether it covers the

Appleby v. *Myers*[1] situation in which the goods or materials perish as a result of a frustrating event. There has been some debate over whether the party receiving the goods or materials can be said to have received any benefit at all from the contract. The opinion has been expressed, however, that, as he would have an insurable interest in goods or materials received by him, this interest should be equated with a valuable benefit whether or not he had taken advantage of it by insuring the goods.[2] Once this benefit exists of course a court is not bound to make an award in favour of the seller or supplier. The court has a discretion to allow the seller or supplier such sum, if any, as it considers just. If the other party has not *in fact* benefited from the transaction, the court may consider it just to make no award at all.

B EXEMPTION CLAUSES

i The general position

An exemption clause is a term which purports in general terms to curtail or exclude the liability of a party which would otherwise arise if he fails to perform his obligations, or some aspect of them, under the contract.

The reason why it is necessary to define an exemption clause as one drafted in general terms is that, if the limitation on liability is specific, in the sense that it cuts down the scope of a principal or fundamental obligation of the contract, then it redefines the contract rather than excludes liability for what would otherwise be a breach of contract. For example, in the discussion of the underlying obligation to deliver the goods described by the contract it was pointed out that, if goods are described as 1,000 cases of Australian canned peaches, no exemption clause drafted in general terms could protect a seller who delivered a cargo of, or including, tins of pears. On the other hand, a specific clause which absolves the seller from liability for delivering cans including tins of pears in effect redefines the fundamental obligation of the contract to deliver tinned peaches only.[3]

The fundamental obligation apart, a general exemption clause can operate on all aspects of the contract. At common law it can exclude altogether, or restrict in extent, liability, whether for breach of some implied term or in respect of the inaccuracy of a statement which would otherwise have taken effect as an express term in the contract. Indeed, it was because exemption clauses excluding liability for breach of the terms implied into sales of goods by the 1893 Act, and even for breach of express undertakings given by the seller, became so widespread that Parliament has in recent years enacted legislation designed to curtail the power of contracting parties thus to limit their obligations.

Because the common rules in some circumstances co-exist with, and in other areas have not been affected by, the recent legislation, it is still necessary to consider in detail those common rules as well as the statutory innovations.

---

1 (1867), L.R. 2 C.P. 651, above, p. 222, n. 1.
2 Glanville Williams, *Law Reform (Frustrated Contracts) Act 1943*, pp. 48–51.
3 See above, pp. 118–9; 125–7.

However, before embarking upon a more detailed examination of specific aspects of the law, it is perhaps desirable to provide a more general framework into which those various aspects can be fitted.

(a) If the claim is based on an alleged breach of s. 12 of the Sale of Goods Act, no exemption clause can limit or exclude liability if it would otherwise arise, whether the sale is a consumer sale, or a non-consumer sale (s. 55 (3)).

(b) If it is based on alleged breaches of ss. 13 to 15, the position is governed by s. 55 (4):

(1) If the transaction was a consumer sale, the exemption clause is void.

(2) If it was not a consumer sale, the court must consider whether it can be shown that it would not be fair or reasonable to allow reliance on such terms. However, the court might also be addressed with arguments on the buyer's behalf suggesting that the exemption clause did not apply in the circumstances on the basis of the existing common law rules relating to the interpretation and application of such clauses.

(c) If the breach is allegedly related to some usage, custom, or course of dealing between the parties, the distinction between a consumer and a non-consumer sale could still be vital. Section 14 (4) allows a condition of quality or fitness to operate by "usage". In the original version of s. 14, any such condition was dependent upon a "trade usage". However, the new provision is clearly wider in the sense that a usage could include a local custom. And it might be possible to argue that a regular course of dealings between two parties, even if one of them is a private buyer, could amount to a usage. If the condition as to quality or fitness is covered by s. 14 (4), an exemption clause which, it is claimed, excludes its operation is void. If, however, the condition is not covered by s. 14 (4) then of course the buyer must seek to rely upon the common law rules to avoid the exemption clause.

(d) If the buyer seeks to rely upon some express representation of the seller, the buyer is entitled to rely upon s. 3 of the Misrepresentation Act which lays down that certain types of exemption clause are of no effect "except to the extent (if any) that, in any proceedings arising out of the contract, the court or arbitrator may allow reliance on it as being fair and reasonable in the circumstances of the case".

(e) Usually a representation by the seller will form a term in the contract in which case it would seem that the buyer can rely not only on the common law rules for interpreting and avoiding an exemption clause, but also on s. 3 of the Misrepresentation Act.

ii The effects of the 1973 Act

a *The general approach*

The 1973 Supply of Goods (Implied Terms) Act has made substantial alterations to a limited area of the law. By the original s. 55 of the 1893 Act:

> "Where any right, duty, or liability would arise under a contract of sale by implication of law, it may be negatived or varied by express agreement or by

the course of dealing between the parties, or by usage, if the usage be such as to bind both parties to the contract."

This now appears as s. 55 (1), but the following words have been added to the end of it:

"but the foregoing provision shall have effect subject to the following provisions of this section".

The principal changes are then incorporated into the 1893 Act as s. 55 (3) and (4). By sub-s. (3):

"In the case of a contract of sale of goods, any term of that or any other contract exempting from all or any of the provisions of section 12 of this Act shall be void."

In other words, unless a person is expressly or by clear inference transferring only such title as he or a third person may have, he is guaranteeing his right to sell, etc. under s. 12 (1), and even if he is only selling such title as he or a third party has, he is still unable to exclude liability for breach of the warranties implied by s. 12 (2).

By sub-s. 4:

"In the case of a contract of sale of goods, any term of that or any other contract exempting from all or any of the provisions of section 13, 14 or 15 of this Act shall be void in the case of a consumer sale and shall, in any other case, not be enforceable to the extent that it is shown that it would not be reasonable to allow reliance on the term."

To make quite clear that s. 55 contemplates no exemption from its application it reinforces the point by laying down that it covers both the contract itself "or any other contract" (s. 55 (3), (4)), so that it is not possible to evade s. 55 by means of a collateral contract. Nor can the seller rely upon any collateral term incorporated in the contract by virtue of any term in the contract of sale (s. 55 (10)). Furthermore, s. 55 (6) preserves the right of a court to decide that a purported exemption clause does not in fact form part of the contract.[1] Finally, s. 55A is included to make certain that a seller does not attempt to evade the provisions of ss. 12 to 15 and s. 55 by substituting the law of some other country as the proper law of the contract in a case where in the absence of an express choice of law, the proper law of the contract of sale would be the law of a part of the United Kingdom.[2]

---

1 For a discussion of the application of the "ticket" cases to contracts of sale, see below, pp. 232 *et seq.*
2 According to the principles of private international law applied in this country it is possible for the parties to select a system of law either directly by the terms of their contract, or indirectly (e.g. by selecting the courts of a particular country as the arbiters of their rights under the contract), whether or not that law system has any real connection with the contract, either through the parties or by reason of the place of making or performance of the contract: *Vita Foods Products, Inc.* v. *Unus Shipping Co., Ltd.,* [1939] A.C. 277; [1939] 1 All E.R. 513.

Contracts for the sale of goods are, in relation to ss. 13 to 15 of the Sale of Goods Act, divided into two categories:

(i) consumer sales; and
(ii) others.

However, it should be borne in mind that, if the attempt is made to oust other provisions of the Act, or terms imported into the contract by commercial usage (for example as to the time of delivery), or to alter the seller's obligations thereunder, the existing judge-made rules for interpreting and applying exemption clauses may still be relevant. As has already been pointed out, even in the context of ss. 13 to 15, it may be that the courts will be called upon to decide whether the principles laid down in s. 55 are superseded by, or coexist with, the common law rules as far as non-consumer sales are concerned. Nor, in relation to consumer transactions, is the position altogether clear. Section 55 (4), on the fact of it, suggests that any term in such a sale, which exempts from s. 13, 14 or 15, is void *in its entirety*. In other words, it is arguable that, if an exemption clause in a consumer sale does exclude, for example, "all conditions and warranties, express or implied", that clause is void even in so far as it covers conditions and warranties not contained in ss. 13–15. To avoid such a conclusion would require the word "term" to be interpreted as meaning a part only of a clause in order to allow severance of the offending from the valid parts. To give s. 55 (4) the wider meaning would certainly be an added incentive to business sellers to curtail their use of broadly drawn exemption clauses, although it is almost certain that neither the Law Commission nor Parliament had the possibility of the wider application of the first part of s. 55 (4) in mind in drafting or examining the bill.

b *Consumer sales*

First, however, it is necessary to consider what is meant by a "consumer sale". By s. 55 (7) of the amended Sale of Goods Act:

> "In this section 'consumer sale' means a sale of goods (other than a sale by auction or by competitive tender) by a seller in the course of a business where the goods—
>
> (*a*) are of a type ordinarily bought for private use or consumption; and
> (*b*) are sold to a person who does not buy or hold himself out as buying them in the course of a business."

And s. 55 (8) provides that the "onus of proving that a sale falls to be treated for the purposes of this section as not being a consumer sale shall lie on the party so contending".

The definition contained in s. 55 (7) is based upon three main criteria:

1 *The status of the seller.* A sale "in the course of a business" is of wide application because a business is defined to include "a profession and the activities of any government department, local authority or statutory undertaker". There are, therefore, a large number of individuals whose activities might well be caught by this formula. The example has already been given of the person

such as a doctor,[1] who purchases a vehicle primarily for use in his work, and who later sells it. It could well be difficult to decide whether or not that sale was in the course of a business. On the other hand, there is no doubt that a sale by a firm or public authority of vehicles surplus to their operational requirements would, as far as the status of the seller is concerned, qualify under s. 55 (7).

2 *The status, or apparent status, of the buyer.* Similar problems can arise in relation to the status of the buyer under s. 55 (7) (*b*): for the sale to be a consumer sale the goods must be sold "to a person who does not buy or hold himself out as buying them in the course of a business". There is, however, the complicating factor of having to decide what constitutes a "holding out" as buying in the course of a business. To take the example of a doctors' group practice: by arrangement between themselves, each partner buys his own vehicle. *Prima facie* at least this is not a purchase in the course of a business. But what if the doctor announces to the seller that he is a doctor and that, therefore, he needs a reliable car? Is he thereby holding himself out as buying in the course of his profession and therefore in the course of a business?

3 *The type of goods being purchased.* But even if it appears both that the seller *was* acting in the course of a business and that the buyer *was not* purchasing in the course of a business, so that the transaction falls within the first part of s. 55 (4), the seller may still avoid the operation of that provision, if he can show that the goods are not "of a type ordinarily bought for private use or consumption".

It is certainly no easy matter to decide what goods are of a "type ordinarily bought for private use". In the first place is 'type' meant to be all embracing so that, as long as some goods of a particular type are ordinarily for private use, it does not matter if the particular sort bought are not usually for such use? Until recently purchase tax regulations drew a very unreal distinction between domestic and commercial freezers, no tax at all being imposed on freezers above a certain size. Hence, a wide range of freezers, categorised as commercial for purchase tax purposes, were in fact bought for private use. However, domestic users did not purchase freezers in the commercial range greater in size than about 20 or 25 cubic feet. If a private purchaser does buy one that is 30 cubic feet, would this transaction fall within s. 55 (4): is the freezer, being goods of a *type* that is ordinarily bought for private use, covered even though it is far larger than is ordinarily bought for such a purpose?

To take an example of a different kind, in this age of "do-it-yourself", there is an increasing range of goods purchased for private use. Is paint "ordinarily" for private use? The buyer's position is strengthened by the fact that the onus is on the seller. Even so, the quantity being ordered might be a relevant factor. Drums of paint are usually used commercially: tins can more easily be regarded as "ordinarily for private use"; though to make this distinction the word "type" must in this situation be interpreted to refer to the "packaging" of the goods rather than to their basic characteristics.

---

1 Similar problems can of course arise with a wide variety of people: farmers, partners in or employees of an estate agent's business, and a variety of self-employed people like decorators, freelance journalists or salesmen.

But what if the handyman wishes to repair his roof? Tiles or guttering are not ordinarily for private use. Similarly, if our handyman turns his attention to his car: spare parts are presumably not capable of being covered by a "consumer sale", though the car itself most probably would have been.

It is unfortunate, therefore, that an additional clause was not included in s. 55 (7) to the effect that a purchase of goods not ordinarily for private use would nevertheless constitute a consumer sale if the seller was aware that the goods were in fact for private use.

c *Non-consumer sales*

It follows from the way in which the 1973 Act was drafted that contracts of sale are either consumer sales or they are not. No particular name is adopted for the "other" category so that non-consumer sale would seem to be appropriate enough. It covers all sales which are not covered by the definition, already considered, of a consumer sale.

The effect of an exemption clause purporting to limit or exclude liability under ss. 13 to 15 in relation to non-consumer sales is set out in s. 55 (4):

> "Any term of that or any other contract exempting from all or any of the provisions of section 13, 14 or 15 of this Act . . . shall, in any other case [than a consumer sale], not be enforceable to the extent that it is shown that it would not be fair or reasonable to allow reliance on the term."

This provision was essentially a compromise. Throughout its deliberations the Law Commission had been divided on whether "business" sales should be subject to restrictions on "contracting out". However, even those members of the Commission most opposed to the idea were prepared to accept a limitation based upon the concept of reasonableness if restrictions were to be imposed. Hence, once it was decided as a matter of policy that exemption clauses in non-consumer sales should be subject to legal controls, as part of the compromise the onus of proof was placed on the party (who will normally be the buyer) seeking to show that it would not be fair or reasonable to allow reliance on the clause in question.

Despite the general consensus on the "fair and reasonable" test, it was open to the criticism that it could create uncertainty. Accordingly, in its Final Report, the Law Commission listed a number of factors which were considered relevant to the application of such a test, and a number of these factors were incorporated as s. 55 (5) of the amended Sale of Goods Act. Hence, when the "fair and reasonable" principle is applied by the courts, "regard shall be had to all the circumstances of the case and in particular to the following matters—".

1 *The bargaining position of the parties.* One of the principal justifications for judicial hostility towards exemption clauses was the fact that in many situations there was no "freedom of contract". The ordinary consumer in the vast majority of cases was obliged to accept the goods with his right against retailer or manufacturer severely limited. For this reason the 1973 Act made attempts to contract out of ss. 13 to 15 of the 1893 Act absolutely void in the case of consumer sales. However, "freedom of contract" can be equally illusory in the commercial

world. Despite legislation in recent years aimed at preventing undesirable restrictive trade practices and the creation of monopolies, a retailer might have little or no choice in his selection of supplier. Accordingly, when the 1973 Act was finally passed, it included a clause specifically calling the courts' attention to the availability of alternative sources of supply when deciding what is "fair and reasonable".

By s. 55 (5) regard is to be had to:

> "(*a*) the strength of the bargaining positions of the seller and buyer relative to each other, taking into account, among other things, the availability of suitable alternative products and sources of supply".

And to:

> "(*b*) whether the buyer . . . in accepting [the term] had an opportunity of buying the goods or suitable alternatives without it from any source of supply".

2 *Inducement to accept the exemption clause.* Clause (*b*) of s. 55 (5) is an awkward piece of drafting because the first part of it deals with a totally different criterion to be taken into account, namely:

> "whether the buyer received an inducement to agree to the term".

Presumably the fact that an inducement has been provided to persuade the buyer to accept the term in question will not in itself make reliance on the term "fair and reasonable". The buyer may have been given some small discount on the goods, or may have been given an option to buy future supplies at a lower price than would normally apply. In order for the inducement to operate it must in itself be a "fair price", that is, fair compensation, for acceptance of the term and the risks that might be entailed.

3 *Knowledge of the term and its effects.* It is still open to a court to hold that a particular exemption clause does not form part of the contract of sale at all: in relation to clauses which purport to exclude or restrict any of the provisions of ss. 13, 14 or 15, this power is reiterated by s. 55 (6). However, as will be discussed shortly, there is still a degree of uncertainty in the rules for ascertaining whether a particular document does form part of a contract. It is possible for a party to find himself bound by a term of which he was not aware, or of the precise terms of which he was ignorant. Hence s. 55 (5) (*c*) directs attention to:

> "whether the buyer knew or ought reasonably to have known of the existence and extent of the term (having regard, among other things, to any custom of the trade and any previous course of dealing between the parties)".

Although s. 55 (6) instructs the court that sub-s. (5) is not to *prevent* it from holding that a term is not part of the contract, it must be asked whether sub-s. (5) should *influence* the court in reaching its decision on whether the term is contractual. Although the directive in sub-s. (6) is presumably designed to avoid the possibility of a court interpreting sub-s. (5) (*c*) to exclude the operation of rules for deciding whether a document is part of the contract, the word "prevent" could suggest that it is nevertheless left open to the courts to decide whether sub-s. (*c*) should affect those rules. If this is a possibility in theory, it is certainly true that in practice the courts might be less concerned in *contracts of sale* to avoid the application of exclusion clauses on the ground that they are non-contractual. The decision is more likely to be along the lines that "if necessary, we would hold that the clause is not (or perhaps that it is) part of the contract, but in any case it is neither fair nor reasonable that the seller should be allowed to rely upon it in the circumstances of the case". For the moment, at any rate, as the Law Commission has not yet reported on, let alone the stage having been reached for legislation to be introduced with regard to, exemption clauses in other types of contract, the inclusion of sub-s. (5) (*c*) is unlikely to affect the overall content of the rules designed by the courts for deciding whether a particular document or term forms part of the contract.

4 *Exemption if the buyer does not comply with condition specified.* By s. 55 (5) (*d*) regard shall also be had to the following situation:

> "where the term exempts from all or any of the provisions of section 13, 14 or 15 of this Act if some condition is not complied with, whether it was reasonable at the time of the contract to expect that compliance with that condition would be practicable".

The most frequent type of condition attached to clauses regulating liability relates to the time within which notice of defects must be given. When discussing what constituted a reasonable examination of the goods in relation to their acceptance by the buyer,[1] it was pointed out that the extent to which a buyer was bound by his acceptance depended to a large extent on the nature of the defect and the opportunities for examining the goods. Similarly, under s. 55 (5), if an attempt is made to restrict or exclude the buyer's rights under ss. 13–15 unless notice of the defect is given within a specified period of delivery, the extent to which the seller would be entitled to rely upon such a term would be dependent upon whether compliance with the condition as to notice appeared reasonably practicable at the time of the contract. This enables the court to exercise some degree of latitude in dealing with such terms. However, in one important respect, s. 55 (5) (*d*) is unduly restrictive. A court might find it difficult to refuse reliance on the term if the period of notice proved unsatisfactory because of some unexpected defect in the goods that only manifested itself outside the period of notice stipulated. The reasonableness and practicability must be viewed as at the time the contract is made, not when the defect is discovered.

5 *When the goods are made or adapted to the buyer's orders.* The final factor to be taken into account is given in s. 55 (5) (*e*):

> "whether the goods were manufactured, processed, or adapted to the special order of the buyer".

It may be the case that a buyer will provide specifications for goods that will suggest that he is not relying upon, or that it is unreasonable for him to rely,

---

1 See above, p. 143.

on the seller's skill and judgment so that there will be no implied condition of fitness within s. 14 (3). However, s. 55 (5) (*e*) goes much further by laying down that, where a buyer has placed a special order for goods (whether or not they are to be made to the buyer's precise specifications), such a circumstance is to be taken into account in deciding whether reliance on an exemption clause relating to ss. 13–15 is "fair and reasonable". What para. (*e*) does not make clear is whether the circumstance of a special order is a factor which makes it less or more reasonable for the seller to rely upon an exemption clause. In making an assessment the court would take account of the surrounding circumstances, like the degree to which the buyer has specified his requirement (thus limiting the scope of discretion in carrying out the work open to the seller), or perhaps more significantly, the nature of the seller's business.

It will be recalled that the implied conditions of suitability and merchantability are no longer dependent upon the seller being a dealer[1] (whether as manufacturer or not). Under the former s. 14, there was some uncertainty whether a person dealing for the first time in goods of the particular description could be a seller within the section. In applying s. 55 (5) (*e*) it would seem to be at least a relevant factor in his favour that the seller imposing the term was manufacturing, processing or adapting such goods for the first time. In contrast, if he had made the same goods to special order on previous occasions, or had wide experience in dealing with special orders, these would be circumstances militating against reliance on the term being upheld as fair and reasonable.

iii The common law approach to exemption clauses

It has already been pointed out that the common law rules governing the application and effect of exemption clauses have been overlaid by special statutory provisions dealing with attempts to contract out of ss. 12, and 13–15 of the Sale of Goods Act, and of liability with respect to misrepresentations in general. Since the coming into force of the Supply of Goods (Implied Terms) Act on May 18, 1973, the common law rules are of no importance in relation to attempts to exclude liability for breach of s. 12 of the 1893 Act in any contract made after May 18, 1973, or for breach of ss. 13–15 in consumer sales after that date. But in the case of non-consumer sales the common rules co-exist with the "fair and reasonable" test propounded by the 1973 Act. Moreover, the common law rules continue to be relevant in cases of a contract including a term based upon some express representation made during the negotiations that led to the formation of the contract, notwithstanding the fact that the Misrepresentation Act 1967 provides the representee with a remedy based upon the inaccuracy of the representation.

a *Is the clause part of the contract?*

1 *Consumer transactions.* The question whether a particular document forms part of the contract has been a source of much litigation in relation to contracts

---

1 There was in fact a difference in terminology between the former s. 14 (1) and s. 14 (2); the word "dealer" is used because the distinction between the two forms of wording was not important in relation to this particular problem. In any case that particular distinction is now only of academic interest except with regard to contracts made before May 18, 1973, when the Act came into operation.

of bailment and carriage, but it has not given rise to the same problems in the context of the contract of sale. It is true that, in purchases of new motor vehicles, the buyer is almost invariably asked to sign a delivery order which sets out the terms of the contract. But, in the majority of transactions, a written document is not usually produced for signature at the time of the contract, and the seller will rarely attempt to rely upon notices[1] or receipts, or the other paraphernalia which cause difficulties in contracts of bailment, and even carriage.

The type of document most frequently met with in consumer transactions stems from the dual nature of the buyer's rights, principally against the retailer on the contract of sale itself, but also against the negligent manufacturer in tort.[2] It is the common practice of manufacturers to include with their products "guarantees" or "warranties" which are usually designed in an attempt to limit the rights of the buyer against both retailer and manufacturer in exchange for what is often a minimal obligation on the part of the manufacturer to put right certain defects in the goods should they occur within a specified period from the date of purchase.

Although pressure from consumer groups has led to a gradual amelioration in the harshness (from the buyer's standpoint) of many of the exemption clauses contained in these documents, the motor car trade remained largely unmoved by representations and protests by these groups. Indeed, as it was in the car trade that greatest care was taken to ensure that these documents would be binding on the buyer, the Supply of Goods (Implied Terms) Act of 1973 has been described as a piece of legislation that the car trade brought on itself by its refusal to heed the representations made to it.

In relation to other types of consumer goods, the manufacturers have rarely been able to organise their retail outlets to such a high degree of efficiency in bringing the guarantee and its terms to the attention of customers. In many cases the buyer may find himself in the position of having bought goods without having had his common law rights impaired. It is only later that he discovers the guarantee card and finds that, to take "advantage" of its terms, it has to be sent to the manufacturers within a certain period (of days or weeks) in order for the guarantee to be "registered".

Needless to say the advice that should be given to the buyer is that he should only send in the card if the manufacturer is offering more extensive rights than those that would be available at common law. But what is the position if the buyer has sent in the card and has, on the face of it, relinquished rights against the seller? In order for the seller to rely on the exemption clause he must show that he was a party to the contract and gave consideration for the buyer's promise. Hence the guarantee card must be capable of being construed as part of the main contract of sale or as dependent on it. The buyer must have been aware of the existence of a guarantee or of the fact that the goods were guaranteed so that his subsequent acknowledgment of the terms of the guarantee can be "attached" to

---

1 One does see notices such as "Sale goods will not be exchanged"; or "Gramophone records must be examined before purchase as they will not be exchanged", but a buyer who wishes to *reject* the goods should have no difficulty under the *contra preferentem* rule, see below.

2 See further, below, p. 247.

the contract of sale. If he was unaware of the guarantee, it would seem that the only contract can be between buyer and manufacturer: "In exchange for you, the manufacturer, offering the service set out on the card, I, the buyer, renounce my rights against the seller and any other rights I may have against you." Upon such an arrangement the seller, not being a party, could not rely.

To a large extent the significance of the guarantee has been reduced by the 1973 Act. Guarantees are of most importance in consumer transactions upon which the Act will operate to render void clauses which purport to exclude the operation of ss. 13–15 of the 1893 Act. However, in so far as a guarantee may purport to exclude liability for express undertakings[1] or affect liability in respect of other provisions of the 1893 Act, the principles whereby the courts decide whether a particular document is contractually operative between two parties still have some relevance.

2 *Commercial transactions.* In many sales, particularly in the commercial field, the crucial question may well be whether the seller can rely upon a past course of dealings between himself and the buyer in order to incorporate an exemption clause into the present contract. In order to do so, the seller must be able to show (1) that the buyer had knowledge of the clause on a past occasion and (2) that the dealings had a sufficient degree of regularity.

The extent of the buyer's knowledge required is not altogether clear from the authorities. It may be that where the buyer is unfamiliar with the ways of business "previous dealings are relevant only if they prove knowledge of the terms, actual and not constructive, and assent to them".[2] However, this dictum should not be applicable[3] in the commercial world in which parties who have received sale notes on previous occasions can expect similar terms to be applied to their contracts on later occasions. Indeed, the requirement of a degree of regularity in the dealings between the parties may be no more than an amplification of the first requirement as to notice or knowledge.

In *Henry Kendall & Sons* v. *William Lillico & Sons, Ltd.*[4] it will be recalled, a quantity of Brazilian ground nut extract was used in a poultry food which poisoned young pheasants. At one stage in the chain of supply there was a contract between one buyer and seller which, S claimed, included a term that B accepted responsibility for any latent defects. B and S had dealt with each other several times a month over a period of approximately three years. On each occasion the agreement had been made verbally, but then S had sent B a sold note including the term in question. B claimed that he had never looked at the term on the note and did not know its contents. On this occasion there had been no departure from this regular practice. The House of Lords held that it was reasonable for S to assume that the contract was being made on terms he had apparently made known to B and to which B had made no objection.

In other words, once one is operating on the basis of a *regular* course of dealings, a buyer is not allowed to rely upon an absence of actual notice. Reasonable

---

1 Subject of course to the provisions of the Misrepresentation Act, 1967, see below, p. 242.
2 *McCutcheon* v. *David MacBrayne, Ltd.*, [1964] 1 All E.R. 430, at p. 437; [1964] 1 W.L.R. 125, at p. 134; *per* Lord DEVLIN.
3 Though see *D. J. Hill & Co. Pty., Ltd.* v. *Walter H. Wright Pty., Ltd.*, [1971] V.R. 749.
4 [1969] 2 A.C. 31; [1968] 2 All E.R. 444.

access to the terms of the contract and an absence of protest are sufficient to imply assent to those terms on subsequent occasions. To situations of that type, Lord DEVLIN's dictum about actual, as opposed to constructive, notice being required is not applicable.

But what of the occasional business transaction, as opposed to the regular dealings that occurred in *Kendall* v. *Lillico*? In *Hollier* v. *Rambler Motors (A.M.C.), Ltd.,*[1] the Court of Appeal took the view that three or four transactions in the course of five years was not sufficient to establish a course of dealing. However, the transactions in question were the repair of a private car by the defendant garage. It does not follow that three or four contracts of sale, particularly of substantial quantities of goods, or where the goods in question are not obtained by the buyer from other sources of supply, would not qualify as a course or dealing.

Another factor that will clearly be relevant is the precise procedure followed on the occasion out of which the dispute arises. In *Kendall* v. *Lillico* an oral agreement was followed, as on the previous occasions, by the contract note. If there has been, through oversight on the part of the seller's employees, a break in the normal practice, this is just the circumstance in which the seller would like to rely on past practice. However, the case of *McCutcheon* v.*McBrayne* strongly suggests that the break with the normal procedure is fatal to the seller's case.

In *McCutcheon* v. *David MacBrayne, Ltd.,* O had arranged through A, his brother-in-law, to have his car shipped to the Scottish mainland. The contract was made verbally at C's office on the island, although A was handed a receipt, which he did not read, containing a statement that the goods were carried subject to the conditions specified on C's sailing bills and notices. Normally consignors of goods were asked to sign a "risk note" by which they expressly agreed to be bound by C's conditions which were printed on the note, but, through an oversight, a risk note was not presented to A for signing. The vessel upon which the car was carried struck a rock and sank. The car was damaged beyond repair. It was admitted that the accident occurred through negligent navigation, but C pleaded a clause in the conditions of carriage exempting them from liability in respect of negligence. The judges of the Court of Session[2] were unanimously of opinion that the receipt for the freight was no more than a receipt and certainly was not reasonable notice[3] of the existence of conditions of carriage. However, it was clear that O and A were aware that conditions were usually imposed in such circumstances, so the crux of the case was whether this knowledge, gleaned from a past course of dealings in which both of them had shipped goods on C's services, was sufficient to establish the exemption clause as part of the contract. The House of Lords held,[4] reversing the decision of the Court of Session, that the knowledge of O and A of the existence of conditions in previous contracts

---

1 [1972] 2 Q.B. 71; [1972] 1 All E.R. 399.
2 1962 S.C. 506.
3 A fact recognised by C's own practice in regarding the "risk note" as the notification to the consignor of the terms of carriage: see 1962 S.C., at p. 513.
4 [1964] 1 All E.R. 430; [1964] 1 W.L.R. 125.

of carriage did not avail C because there had been a departure from the previous course of dealings between the parties in that no "risk note" had been signed on this occasion.

Taken at face value this decision would be unfortunate. In the business world it would not necessarily be satisfactory to allow a defect of procedure by the seller to allow a buyer to escape the limiting of his rights by an exemption clause which was normally part of their dealings. A preferable view of *McCutcheon* v. *MacBrayne* would therefore be to relate the procedural defect to the other circumstances of the case. Lord REID had called attention to the irregularity of the dealings in that the goods to be carried had more usually been cattle (three times) than a car (once) and that they had been sent by A sometimes as agent, and sometimes as principal. In the circumstances therefore there was no sufficiently regular course of dealings with which to remedy the defect, although it is arguable that, had there otherwise been a regular course of conduct, the absence of the signed "risk note" would not have been fatal to the seller's defence. There would seem to be support for taking this view of the case in *Hollier* v. *Rambler Motors (A.M.C.), Ltd.*,[1] although it must be admitted that it is not in accord with the attitude of at least one of their Lordships in *Kendall* v. *Lillico*.[2]

b *The contra preferentem rule*

Once it is established that a document containing an exemption clause does form part of the contract, it is a basic principle of the common law that the clause should be construed *contra preferentem*. A seller who had excluded reliance by the buyer on any "guarantee or warranty statutory or otherwise" would still be liable for breach of a condition implied into the contract by s. 14 of the Sale of Goods Act.[3] Nor would it make any difference if the buyer had accepted the goods so that, by s. 11 (1) (c), he is obliged to treat the breach of condition as a breach of warranty, and not as a ground for rejecting the goods; the term broken would still remain a condition that would not be affected by a clause excluding "warranties, express or implied."[4] Similarly, a term in the contract of sale excluding all warranties, conditions and liabilities implied by statute, common law or otherwise, will have no affect on an express term of the contract to deliver a new, as opposed to a second-hand, car.[5]

The *contra preferentem* rule is of no assistance against a carefully drawn exclusion clause. In the well-known case of *L'Estrange* v. *Graucob*,[6] B signed a sales agreement for the purchase of an automatic slot machine which contained

---

1 In the way the facts of *McCutcheon* v. *David MacBrayne, Ltd.* are set out in the principal judgment of SALMON, L.J., [1972] 1 All E.R. 399, at pp. 403–4.
2 [1969] 2 A.C. 31, at pp. 104–5; [1968] 2 All E.R. 444, at p. 474, *per* Lord GUEST; and less obviously, [1969] 2 A.C., at p. 113; [1968] 2 All E.R., at p. 481, *per* Lord PEARCE.
3 *Baldry* v. *Marshall*, [1925] 1 K.B. 260; [1924] All E.R. Rep. 155.
4 *Wallis, Son and Wells* v. *Pratt and Haynes*, [1911] A.C. 394; [1911–13] All E.R. Rep. 989.
5 *Andrews Bros. (Bournemouth), Ltd.* v. *Singer & Co., Ltd.*, [1934] 1 K.B. 17; [1933] All E.R. Rep. 479. Where the contract makes no reference to whether the goods are to be new or secondhand, it may be possible to show that new goods were intended: see *Marcus Clark (Vic.), Ltd.* v. *Brown* (1928), 40 C.L.R. 540; but cp. *Hope* v. *R.C.A. Photophone of A'lia Pty., Ltd.* (1937), 59 C.L.R. 348.
6 [1934] 2 K.B. 394; [1934] All E.R. Rep. 16.

the following clause: "This agreement contains all the terms and conditions under which I agree to purchase the machine specified above and any express or implied condition, statement, or warranty, statutory or otherwise not stated herein is hereby excluded." The machine failed to work properly. It was held that, in the absence of fraud or misrepresentation[1] (which did not exist in this case), B could not be heard to say that she was not bound by the terms of a document which clearly protected S from a claim for breach of condition of warranty.

c *Fundamental term and fundamental breach*

1 *The concept of the fundamental term.* Prior to the Misrepresentation Act, 1967, a representation made before the time of the contract could be excluded by the terms of the contract,[2] though if it was made in order to induce a contract in a way which suggested that it superseded or amended the written agreement, it would be enforceable notwithstanding the exclusion clause.[3] However, in the last resort the court could well be faced with a clause which, to all appearances, protected the seller from having broken his contract. In this situation the courts turned to the concept of the fundamental obligation to which attention has already been directed.[4] By failing to deliver the goods described in the contract, the seller is not failing to perform some term in the contract, but failing to perform the contract itself.

The idea that there is a fundamental obligation of a contract of sale to deliver the goods contracted for is apparently straightforward. If S contracts to sell B "copra cake" as a cattle food, he would not be fulfilling the contract to supply cake which was so adulterated with castor oil as to be poisonous.[5] But at what stage do the goods, which appear to be the contract goods, or which answer the same general description, cease to satisfy *the* contract description?

In *Karsales (Harrow), Ltd.* v. *Wallis,*[6] B had inspected and then agreed to take on hire purchase terms a Buick car. In the hire purchase contract between the defendant and the finance company was a term stating that "no condition or warranty that the vehicle is roadworthy or as to its age, condition or fitness for any purpose is given by the owner or implied herein". The car was delivered surreptitiously, and when the defendant inspected it he discovered that it had been badly damaged. The tyres had been taken off and old ones put on; the radio had been removed; the chrome around the body had been stripped off; the cylinder head was off, the valves were burnt out, and there were two broken pistons. The car was no longer in working order. Was the defendant justified in refusing to take delivery of the vehicle?

---

1 For the circumstances in which a party may be able to rely on the plea of *non est factum,* see *Saunders* v. *Anglia Building Society,* [1971] A.C. 1004; [1970] 3 All E.R. 961. But even when a party was not mistaken as to the nature of the document, he would not be bound by individual terms the effect of which were misrepresented by the other party: *Curtis* v. *Chemical Cleaning and Dyeing Co.* [1951] 1 K.B. 805; [1951] 1 All E.R. 631; and see below, p. 243, where the effect of the Misrepresentation Act is considered.
2 A factor which largely influenced the court in *Hopkins* v. *Tanqueray* (1854), 15 C.B. 130; [1843–60] All E.R. Rep. 96; see above, p. 150.
3 *Harling* v. *Eddy,* [1951] 2 K.B. 739; [1951] 2 All E.R. 212; and see above, p. 150.
4 See above, pp. 119 *et seq.*
5 *Pinnock Bros.* v. *Lewis and Peat, Ltd.,* [1923] 1 K.B. 690.
6 [1956] 2 All E.R. 866.

Denning, L.J., pointed out[1] that under an agreement of this kind where an inspection has actually been made, there was an obligation on the supplier to deliver the goods in the same condition as when they were seen.[2] A failure to satisfy this obligation constituted a breach going to the root of the contract, and disentitled the other party from relying upon the exemption clause. Parker, L.J., also expressly treated the case as one of a breach of a fundamental term because the vehicle delivered was in effect "not properly described . . . as a motor vehicle . . . By that I am not saying that every defect in a car which renders it for the moment unusable on the road amounts to a breach of a fundamental term; but where, as here, a vehicle is delivered incapable of self propulsion except after a complete overhaul . . . it seems to me that it is abundantly clear that there was a breach of a fundamental term."[3]

This decision may be contrasted with the later case of *Charterhouse Credit Co., Ltd.* v. *Tolly*.[4] The hirer under a hire-purchase agreement took delivery of a Vauxhall car which he then discovered had a defective back axle, as a result of faulty repair work, and a number of less serious defects including the need to replace two of the tyres. The vehicle was unroadworthy and unsafe to drive. The agreement contained an exemption clause in the widest terms. The hirer paid none of the instalments. The Court of Appeal refused to disturb the county court judge's finding that there had been a fundamental breach of the contract.

There is a tendency on the part of the judges to treat "breach of a fundamental term" and "fundamental breach" as synonymous. It is believed, however, that there is a strong case for distinguishing between the two, a proposal that gains support from the judgments of Viscount Dilhorne and Lord Upjohn in the *Suisse Atlantique* case.[5]

It is rare for the contractual description itself to be phrased in such a way as to cut down expressly and clearly the contractual obligation. An example of such a limitation in the description would be a contract for the delivery in London of a consignment of Australian canned peaches in which there is a statement to the effect that, although the goods are believed to comprise solely peaches, up to 50 per cent might in fact be pears and/or pineapples. In such a situation, a lower percentage of pears and pineapples would not take the consignment as a whole outside the contract description. On the other hand, if the contract were for peaches subject to a clause exempting the seller from liability for all errors of description, it is clear that a similar consignment including pears and pineapples would not constitute a delivery in accordance with the contract.

As, in cases involving breaches of the fundamental term or obligation of a contract of sale, the exemption clause will be an attempt to restrict rights created by the contract, it is possible to interpret the contractual obligation independently

---

1 At p. 868.
2 Unless, in a contract of sale, the risk had already passed to the buyer when the seller could only be liable, if at all, as a bailee of the goods.
3 At p. 871.
4 [1963] 2 Q.B. 683; [1963] 2 All E.R. 432; and see *Farnworth Finance Facilities, Ltd.* v. *Attryde*, [1970] 2 All E.R. 774, [1970] 1 W.L.R. 1053.
5 *Suisse Atlantique Societe d'Armement Maritime, S.A.* v. *N.V. Rotterdamsche Kolen Centrale*, [1967] 1 A.C. 361; [1966] 2 All E.R. 61.

of the exemption clause. One can, therefore, accept the proposition that "where there is a breach of a fundamental term the person in breach cannot rely on clauses of exclusion to protect him as against the other party".[1]

2 *The doctrine of fundamental breach.* Whereas a breach of a fundamental term, unless such breach is waived, entitles the aggrieved party to a remedy irrespective of any exemption clause in the contract, a fundamental breach of the contract may not have such a far-reaching effect. The words "fundamental breach" have been described as "no more than a convenient shorthand expression for saying that a particular breach of breaches of contract by one party is or are such as to go to the root of the contract which entitles the other party to treat such breach or breaches as a repudiation of the whole contract".[2] In other words, it is not that the fundamental obligation has been broken, but that the breach or breaches which have occurred together strike at the root of the contract.

This distinction can be further illustrated by reference to two cases already considered. In *Karsales (Harrow), Ltd.* v. *Wallis*, the vehicle delivered had become so much transformed from its former state (the condition it was in at the time of inspection) that it could no longer be regarded as a car within the terms of the parties' contract. On the other hand, in *Charterhouse Credit Co., Ltd.* v. *Tolly*, the vehicle delivered was still a car within the terms of the agreement, although it was a defective one. There had not been, therefore, a breach of a fundamental term, but the principal defect was so serious that it constituted a fundamental breach. In other words, it was the breach, and not the term that was broken, which was fundamental.

While the fundamental term in a contract of sale (or of hire purchase) is to be deduced from the contract description, which will be ascertainable independently of the terms of any exemption clause, the question whether a breach is fundamental can only be decided from the terms of the contract as a whole. In *Suisse Atlantique*, the House of Lords expressed approval of a dictum of PEARSON, L.J., in an earlier case:[3]

> "... there is a rule of construction that normally an exception or exclusion clause or similar provision in a contract should be construed as not applying

---

1 *Per* UPJOHN, L.J., in *Charterhouse Credit Co., Ltd.* v. *Tolly*, [1963] 2 Q.B. 683, at p. 709; [1963] 2 All E.R. 432, at p. 442; Similarly *per* HOLROYD PEARCE, L.J. in *Yeoman Credit, Ltd.* v. *Apps* [1962] 2 Q.B. 508, at p. 520; [1961] 2 All E.R. 281, at p. 291; and *per* PARKER, L.J., in *Karsales (Harrow), Ltd.* v. *Wallis*, [1956] 2 All E.R. 866, at p. 871; [1956] 1 W.L.R. 936.

2 *Per* Lord UPJOHN in the *Suisse Atlantique* case, [1967] 1 A.C., at pp. 421–2; [1966] 2 All E.R., at p. 86.

3 *U.G.S. Finance, Ltd.* v. *National Mortgage Bank of Greece*, [1964] 1 Lloyd's Rep. 446 at p. 453. It is clear that the House of Lords took this statement as a correct expression of the approach to be adopted to "fundamental breach" situations in contradistinction to circumstances in which there has been a breach of a fundamental term. However, PEARSON, L.J., was obviously confusing the two because he went on to give the example of a typical breach of fundamental term situation, namely, a sale of the ton of cheese under a contract which included a provision that no failure of the goods to correspond with the contract description should entitle the buyer to reject the goods or recover damages: to suggest that a seller would thereby be entitled to deliver a ton of chalk "would be an absurd result, which the parties as reasonable men cannot have intended".

to a situation created by a fundamental breach of the contract. This is not an independent rule of law imposed by the Court on the parties willy-nilly in disregard of their contractual intention. On the contrary it is a rule of construction based on the presumed intention of the contracting parties."

In deciding whether a breach or breaches are "fundamental" one must look at the terms of the contract in the light of the circumstances of the case. Even an exemption clause dealing with a particular defect might be disregarded if the seller has deliberately created the situation in which that defect has become a source of complaint. If the seller of a second-hand car were to undertake to carry out certain repairs, a widely drawn exemption clause referring to the condition of the car and the standard of work carried out could well exempt him from liability in respect of his own or his servants' negligence, but not in respect of a deliberate failure to put the car into reasonable order. As the Privy Council suggested in *Sze Hai Tong Bank, Ltd.* v. *Rambler Cycle Co., Ltd.*[1] in reference to a number of cases,[2] including *Karsales (Harrow), Ltd.* v. *Wallis*:

"In each of those cases it could reasonably be inferred that the servant or agent deliberately disregarded one of the prime obligations of the contract. He was entrusted by the principal with the performance of the contract on his behalf: and his action could properly be treated as the action of his principal. In each case it was held that the principal could not take advantage of the exemption clause. It might have been different if the servant or agent had been merely negligent or inadvertent."[3]

The circumstances do not only include the situation at the time of the contract, but also the consequences that flow from the breach. In *Harbutt's Plasticine, Ltd.* v. *Wayne Tank and Pump Co., Ltd.*,[4] the defendants had designed and installed equipment in the plaintiff's factory for providing a supply of molten stearine. The defendants had used a form of plastic pipe in the installation that was totally unsuitable for the purpose. In order to have a supply of the stearine for a test run on the following day, the defendants turned on the heating part of the equipment. The piping distorted and molten stearine escaped causing a fire which destroyed the entire factory. The Court of Appeal held that the nature of the breach, in the light of the catastrophic consequences, rendered it fundamental; accordingly the clause limiting the defendant's liability to the cost of the contract (£2,300) had no application and the defendants were liable for the whole of the loss (nearly £173,000). As Lord DENNING, M.R., explained:[5]

"It was suggested that, in order to determine whether a breach is fundamental or not, one must look at the quality of it, and not at the results. I do not accept

---

1 [1959] A.C. 576, at pp. 588–9; [1959] 3 All E.R. 182, at p. 186.
2 *Bontex Knitting Works, Ltd.* v. *St. John's Garage,* [1944] 1 All E.R. 381n.; *Alexander* v. *Railway Executive,* [1951] 2 K.B. 882; [1951] 2 All E.R. 442.
3 Certainly according to Lord REID in the *Suisse Atlantique* case, [1967] 1 A.C., at p. 398; [1966] 2 All E.R., at p. 71, "the fact that the breach was deliberate might be of great importance". See also *J. Spurling, Ltd.* v. *Bradshaw,* [1956] 2 All E.R. 121, at p. 124, *per* DENNING, L.J.
4 [1970] 1 Q.B. 447; [1970] 1 All E.R. 225.
5 [1970] 1 Q.B., at p. 466; [1970] 1 All E.R., at p. 235: see also [1970] 1 Q.B., at pp. 471–2; [1970] 1 All E.R., at pp. 239–40, *per* WIDGERY, L.J.; [1970] 1 Q.B., at p. 475; [1970] 1 All E.R., at p. 241, *per* CROSS, L.J.

this suggestion. It is not the breach itself which counts so much, but the event resulting from it. A serious breach might have slight consequences. A trivial breach grave ones. Take this very case. The specification of durapipe was, no doubt, a serious breach; but it would not have done much harm if it had been discovered in time and replaced by stainless steel. In that event the plaintiffs could not repudiate the contract or treat it as at an end. But it did, in fact, do great harm because of the consequences. The results were so grave as to bring the contract to an end. One must, therefore, look not only at the breach but also at the results of it."[1]

The advantages of maintaining a distinction between fundamental breach and breach of a fundamental term may be further illustrated by reference to the decision in *Ashington Piggeries, Ltd.* v. *Christopher Hill, Ltd.*[2] It will be remembered that the House of Lords held the seller liable for a breach of s. 14 of the Sale of Goods in that one of the ingredients used in preparing a food for mink had, in processing, become not only toxic to mink but also toxic to other animals to a similar or lesser degree; but not liable for breach of s. 13 because "suitable for mink" did not form part of the contract description as the seller had expressly disclaimed any knowledge of what was suitable for mink as he had never before prepared mink food. Furthermore, the majority view had been that the inclusion of a normal, though unfortunately toxic, ingredient could not affect the description of the goods, unlike the case of *Pinnock Bros.* v. *Lewis and Peat, Ltd.*[3] in which the presence of an additional toxic substance (castor beans) had destroyed the identity of the goods as "copra cake".

Although one can appreciate that it is very much easier for a court to decide that an "addition" is not covered by the contract description than it is for it to accept that the inclusion of a "normal", though in fact harmful, ingredient in some way destroys the identity of the goods, the question must nevertheless be asked what the position would have been in *Ashington Piggeries* had an exemption clause had the effect of excluding liability for breach of s. 14. In such a situation the concept of fundamental breach could well have helped the buyer, because there is a close parallel with *Harbutt's Plasticine*. In that case, if the work and materials proved unsuitable, the contract limited the contractor's liability to the total contract "price". In *Ashington Piggeries* an exemption clause excluding the operation of s. 14 would have, *prima facie*, left the buyer without a remedy had the food proved unsuitable. However, in both cases, because of the disastrous effects of the breach—in one case the destruction of the factory, in the other the widespread destruction of the mink—it was equally arguable that there had been a fundamental breach of contract. It was not that the seller in *Ashington Piggeries* had failed to supply "herring meal" as part of the King Size mink food, and thus broken a fundamental term of the contract, but that he had supplied goods which proved so dramatically unsuitable that he had fundamentally broken the contract.

---

1 Citing *Hong Kong Fir Shipping Co., Ltd.* v. *Kawasaki Kisen Kaisha, Ltd.* [1962] 2 Q.B. 26, at pp. 68–9; [1962] 1 All E.R. 474, at pp. 486–7, *per* DIPLOCK, L.J.
2 [1972] A.C. 441: [1971] 1 All E.R. 847: above p. 124.
3 [1923] 1 K.B. 690.

iv Express statements

Where a party, usually the seller, has made a statement in the course of negotiations which induces the other party to enter into a contract, that other party may have a number of remedies available to him:

(1) for breach of contract, if he can show that the statement constituted a term in the contract;[1]

(2) an action in deceit, if he can show that the statement was made fraudulently;

(3) an action in negligence, if he can show that the first party owed him a duty of care and that, in making the misstatement, the latter had broken that duty;[2]

(4) an action for damages under s. 2 of the Misrepresentation Act;[3]

(5) a claim to rescind the contract for innocent misrepresentation, a situation now covered by s. 1 of the Misrepresentation Act.[4]

Where the contract subsequently concluded by the parties contains an exemption clause, s. 3 of the Misrepresentation Act provides the representee with a means of circumventing its effects:

> "If any agreement . . . contains a provision which would exclude or restrict—
>
> (a) any liability to which a party to a contract may be subject by reason of any misrepresentation made by him before the contract was made; or
>
> (b) any remedy available to another party to the contract by reason of such a misrepresentation;
>
> that provision shall be of no effect to the extent (if any) that, in any proceedings arising out of the contract, the court or arbitrator may allow reliance on it as being fair and reasonable in the circumstances of the case."

Commentators on this section have been perplexed by its wording and have expressed uncertainty as to its true effects. Among the difficulties raised are:

a *To what representations does s. 3 apply*

The section states that it is dealing with "any liability to which a party may be subject by reason *of any misrepresentation*" or "any remedy available . . . by reason of such a misrepresentation". The suggestion has been advanced that s. 3 only applies to render of no effect exemption clauses in situations where the representee is basing his claim on the misrepresentation outside the terms of the contract itself. In other words, s. 3 is only operative if the representation did not become part of the contract, or (perhaps) if the party suing bases his claim on remedies available other than those for breach of contract.

It is undoubtedly true that the Act was passed in part to rectify problems that were likely to arise out of the belief shared by both the judiciary and legal writers that there could be statements of fact about the subject-matter of the contract that did not amount to terms of the contract. However, it did not follow that those who drafted the Act subscribed to that belief to the extent of seeking in

---

1 See above, p. 148.
2 See above, p. 153.
3 See below, p. 154.
4 See below, pp. 258 *et seq.*

s. 3 to distinguish between exemption clauses covering non-contractual misrepresentations and such statements which could be held to form part of the
contract. It must be acknowledged that the draftsman may have produced consequences which they did not foresee. However, in their First Report on Exemption Clauses, the Law Commission seemed in no doubt that s. 3 was equally
applicable to representations which formed part of the contract. In relating s. 3
to the Commission's proposals on exemption clauses purporting to exclude
ss. 13–15, the Report stated:[1]

> "It would produce highly anomalous results to forbid contracting out of
> liability for misrepresentation, as section 2 of the Misrepresentation Act 1967
> has done . . . while permitting contracting out of the statutory conditions and
> warranties in business sales. The two are inextricably interwoven, and where
> there is a breach of section 13 of the Sale of Goods Act there will necessarily
> have been a misrepresentation also, as will often be the case where there is a
> breach of section 14 (1) and sometimes where there is a breach of section 15."

It would certainly be an extraordinary result if a person making a misrepresentation were in a stronger position if his statement formed part of the contract
containing the exemption clause, than if his statement was held to fall outside
the contract. As the wording of the section is not altogether clear, one can say
with some confidence that the courts would not adopt an interpretation which
would give effect to such an absurdity.[2]

b *To what clauses does s. 3 apply*
The ambit of s. 3 is potentially extremely wide: it applies to "any agreement"
that "contains a provision which would exclude or restrict . . . any liability . . .
or . . . any remedy".

   1 *Agreed damages clauses.* There are some provisions which do not, strictly
speaking, exclude or restrict liability. It is, for example, open to the parties to
include in their contract an "agreed damages" clause. Such a clause is *prima
facie* for the benefit of both parties, and would not be construed *contra preferentem*, but what is its position in relation to s. 3?

The most obvious illustration is a demurrage clause in a charterparty: the
shipowner is entitled to be paid *freight* in respect of cargo carried, and *demurrage*
in respect of delay in loading the vessel beyond a reasonable period (usually
expressly provided for as so many "lay days"). In the *Suisse Atlantique* case,[3]
the shipowner alleged that the charterer had been so dilatory in loading and
shipping goods that the demurrage payments bore no relation to the freight that

---

1 Page 42, para. 109 (d). The reference to s. 14 (1) was to the original version of the Act:
  see now s. 14 (3).
2 Ironically, if the courts were to adopt such an interpretation of s. 3, they would be
  likely to increase the strictness of the "test" of when a representation became part of
  the contract (see above pp. 148–52). *Heilbut Symons & Co.* v. *Buckleton*, [1913] A.C.
  30; [1911–13] All E.R. Rep. 83; would be restored to favour; and *Hopkins* v. *Tanqueray*
  (1854), 15 C.B. 130; [1843–60] All E.R. Rep. 96; in which the presence of an exemption
  clause led to the court concluding that a statement about the horse which led to the
  potential buyer discontinuing his inspection was not a warranty, would be the leading
  illustration of how to create a situation for s. 3 to operate!
3 *Suisse Atlantique Societe D'Armement Maritime S.A.* v. *N.V. Rotterdamsche Kolen
  Centrale*, [1967] 1 A.C. 361; [1966] 2 All E.R. 61.

should have been carried, and that the charterer's conduct had therefore amounted to a fundamental breach of contract. The claim was rejected. There certainly had been delay in performing the contract, but it was from a cause that the parties had expressly provided for by the demurrage clause. The doctrine that a party to a contract cannot, in certain circumstances, rely on an exemption clause inserted for his benefit had no application in this case because it was

> "confined to clauses which are truly clauses of exception or limitation, that is to say, clauses essentially inserted for the purpose only of protecting one contracting party from the legal consequences of other express terms of the contract or from terms which would otherwise be implied by law or from the terms of the contract regarded as a whole . . . But if it is inserted for the benefit of both, I know of no authority—and none has been cited—which entitles one party unilaterally to disregard its provisions. In my opinion, the demurrage clause with which we are concerned is a clause providing for agreed damages and is different from a clause excluding or limiting liability for damage by breach of contract by one party. An agreed damage clause is for the benefit of both; the party establishing breach by the other need prove no damage in fact; the other must pay that, no less but no more."[1]

This decision may not be the most helpful guide, however, for two reasons. In the first place, it may be difficult to demonstrate that a provision in a contract of sale is an agreed damages clause, particularly where the clause in question operates to the disadvantage of the representee. In the case of a demurrage clause, there is a presumption that it is an agreed damages provision. In a contract of sale there would be no such presumption unless one were created by the terms of the contract.

Secondly, although the courts might not apply the *contra preferentem* rule to such clauses, it must be admitted that this is no reason why s. 3 should not apply. In some situations an agreed damages clause undoubtedly will "restrict" the extent of the representee's claim (and it is in just such a case that he may seek to rely upon s. 3). Furthermore, in so far as an agreed damages clause, rather than affecting liability, excludes or restricts "any remedy", for example, cuts down or excludes the possibility of the representee rescinding the contract, the clause will fall foul of s. 3. A demurrage clause in a charterparty has the effect of limiting the liability of the party, who has broken the contract through a delay in loading, to payment of the stipulated damages. In a contract of sale both the question whether a provision was an agreed damages clause and whether it by implication restricted the right to rescind would be matters of construction for the court to decide. In general, agreed damages clauses by implication do restrict the remedies available to the party not in breach (or in this case the representee). Obviously enough, if there were a term specifically limiting the remedy to one of damages that term would be caught by s. 3.

2 *Disclaimers of responsibility*. There exist a variety of circumstances in which a seller might utter words of caution the precise relationship of which to s. 3 is uncertain. In the leading case on negligent mis-statements, *Hedley Byrne & Co., Ltd.* v. *Heller and Partners, Ltd.*[2] the representor was held not liable because

---

1 *Per* Lord UPJOHN, [1967] 1 A.C. 361, at p. 420; [1966] 2 All E.R. 61, at p. 85.
2 [1964] A.C. 465; [1963] 2 All E.R. 575.

the representation, though made in circumstances that would otherwise have been categorised as creating a duty of care, had been made with a disclaimer of responsibility. The view has been advanced[1] that such a disclaimer is not within the ambit of s. 3 "for even though the misrepresentee may subsequently enter into a contract on the strength of the misrepresentation in that sort of situation, the exclusion provision does not exclude or restrict any liability of 'a party to a contract' by reason of 'a misrepresentation made by him', nor does it exclude or restrict a remedy available to a party to the contract by reason of 'such a misrepresentation'." With respect, this contention seems far from conclusive. If the representor and representee enter into a contract on the strength of the representation, there is no reason why the disclaimer should not be regarded as much a part of the contract as the representation itself. The disclaimer is then a provision of the contract which does "exclude or restrict" liability. Indeed, in view of the increasing habit of making representations and at the same time disowning responsibility for them,[2] it would appear to be necessary, as a matter of policy, to apply s. 3. This step is possible without violating the wording of the section, and it is clearly in keeping with its spirit and intention.

However, some caution must be exercised in looking at the circumstances in which a disclaimer is given. The misrepresentation must be a misrepresentation of fact, and not of opinion, in order for the representation to give rise to a cause of action under the 1967 Act or for breach of contract. If the "disclaimer" takes the form of words which warn the buyer that the seller (or his agent) has no firm basis upon which the seller can assert the true position with any confidence, the representation could well be one of opinion rather than one of fact.

c *The effects of s. 3*

The other aspect of s. 3 that has to be considered is its effect once it has been decided that a contractual provision does fall within its scope. It will be remembered that s. 55 (4) of the Sale of Goods Act declares an offending clause in a non-consumer sale not to be "enforceable to the extent that it is shown that it would not be fair or reasonable to allow reliance on the term" (i.e. the onus is on the buyer to show it would not be fair or reasonable to allow reliance). In contrast s. 3 of the Misrepresentation Act provides that the offending provision "shall be of no effect to the extent (if any) that . . . the court or arbitrator may allow reliance on it as being fair and reasonable in the circumstances of the case" (in other words it is for the party relying on the provision, i.e. usually the seller, at least to point to circumstances showing that reliance on it would be fair and reasonable). Furthermore, like s. 55 (4) dealing with exclusion clauses in non-consumer sales, but unlike the part of s. 55 (4) dealing with consumer sales which declares void clauses purporting to exclude ss. 13–15 of that Act, a clause caught

---

1 By Atiyah, *op. cit.*, 4th Ed., p. 129.
2 This iniquitous trend is particularly to be seen in transactions involving land. Estate agents issue details of a house but then disclaim liability for any errors or misdescriptions. Even more reprehensible is the practice of surveyors, for whose services the potential purchaser pays to have a survey carried out on a property, of disclaiming liability for any losses that might be incurred by the purchaser if he acts in reliance on their report.

by s. 3 is only affected to an *extent*, not absolutely. Whereas it is arguable that s. 55 (4) renders void in its entirety a clause which only in part purports to exclude ss. 13–15 in a consumer sale, there is no such problem about severance under s. 3, or under s. 55 (4) as far as it deals with non-consumer transactions. Though the onus of proof is different, both provisions allow reliance to the extent that it is fair and reasonable. It would be perfectly fair and reasonable to allow an exemption clause to operate on other aspects of the contract, even if it was not adjudged fair and reasonable that it should exclude or restrict liability for a misrepresentation.

C THE POSITION OF THIRD PARTIES: PRODUCT LIABILITY

A major defect in the law of sale in England is that it is based almost exclusively in contract. Accordingly the rights of the user of defective goods depend principally upon whether he can show the existence of a contract between himself and the party he wishes to sue. Sections 13–15 of the Sale of Goods Act are of no assistance to the user if (i) he was not the person who bought the goods (unless he can show that the buyer bought as his agent); or (ii) he wishes to sue someone other than the seller.

i The non-contracting plaintiff

There is a clear distinction between the contracting party who can rely upon the seller's skill and judgment in providing suitable (and not defective, or even harmful) goods, in which case the seller's obligation is strict; and the non-contracting party who must establish negligence on the part of the seller, or manufacturer, in order to succeed in his claim.

The problem often arises in the domestic sphere, and involves specific loss or injury to a particular individual. If the family washing machine fails to operate soon after purchase, it does not matter who bought it, because that person can press for its repair, or for compensation if the machine proves totally useless. But if a member of the family other than the buyer is injured, then the buyer himself is only entitled to recover with respect to his own losses. If he bought a teddy bear for his child who suffered internal injuries from swallowing one of the animal's eyes, the parent could readily recover his own limited losses, but the child's remedy against the seller would depend on whether negligence could be established.

In the case of *Preist* v. *Last*,[1] B wanted to buy a hot-water bottle which he hoped would relieve his wife's cramp. He asked S, a retail chemist, for a hot-water bottle, mentioning a special purpose, but not specifying what that purpose was. S showed him a bottle, but warned him that it would take hot water, but not boiling water. B purchased the bottle. It was used by his wife for only four or five days before it burst, scalding her. B's claim was limited to recovering his expenses incurred in having his wife's injuries treated. There was no question of his recovering in respect of her actual injuries.

The arbitrary nature of this principle is thus apparent. It will usually be fortuitous whether a husband or wife purchases a particular item for general

---

1 [1903] 2 K.B. 148.

domestic use. And in the case of goods causing injury to children, it will seldom happen that the child in question would have been the buyer. If a hair shampoo or a toy proves unsuitable or defective, the child will have to claim in tort, not in contract, and to establish negligence against the seller (who often has no greater opportunity of assessing the merits of goods than his buyer) will be no easy task. It is, as we shall see in a moment, easier to sue the manufacturer in negligence, but what if the manufacturer's operations are conducted entirely overseas? In *Preist* v. *Last*, the wife could scarcely have hoped to succeed against the retailer who supplied the hot-water bottle, but a claim against the manufacturer was ruled out for the very practical reason that his activities were carried out in the United States.

The illogicality of the present situation may be further illustrated by reference to the case of *Godley* v. *Perry*.[1] A six year old boy, who was blinded in one eye by a stone from his defective catapult, was able to succeed in a claim against the local retailer because it was the boy himself who had made the purchase and not one of his parents. If a parent, or anyone else, had made the purchase,[2] no remedy would have existed in contract and it would have been extremely difficult to sue the seller in tort. Indeed, as the goods had been manufactured overseas, the boy may have been left without any practical remedy at all.

ii Claims against the manufacturer

a *The manufacturer's duty of care*

Damage or injury caused by goods to a non-buyer will not normally give rise to a claim for damages against the seller because of the difficulty of being able to establish negligence on his part. Indeed, if a chattel is defective, unless it is reasonable for the seller to examine it before reselling, the responsibility to the ultimate user should lie with the manufacturer.

In the Scots case of *Gordon* v. *M'Hardy*,[3] B sought to recover damages from S, a grocer, for the death of B's son who was poisoned by a tin of salmon B had purchased from S. The action failed, the Lord Justice-Clerk remarking that he did not see how S could have been expected to examine the tins "without destroying the very condition which the manufacturer has established in order to preserve the contents, the tin not being intended to be opened until immediately before use". In commenting upon this decision in *Donoghue* v. *Stevenson*,[4] Lord THANKERTON expressed the view[5] that he would be "sorry to think that the meticulous care of the manufacturer to exclude interference or inspection by the grocer in that case should relieve the grocer of any responsibility to the consumer without any corresponding assumption of duty by the manufacturer".

This "assumption of duty" was laid down in *Donoghue* v. *Stevenson* in sub-

1 [1960] 1 All E.R. 36; [1960] 1 W.L.R. 9; above p. 188.
2 Unless it could be agreed that a person buying goods for apparent use by a child is acting as his agent. But what if the goods are intended as a gift? How would one distinguish between the two situations? Presumably the agency argument would only succeed if the money used in the purchase belonged to the child.
3 (1903), 6 F. (Ct. of Sess.) 210.
4 [1932] A.C. 562; [1932] All E.R. Rep. 1.
5 [1932] A.C. 562, at p. 604; [1932] All E.R. Rep. 1, at p. 22.

stantially similar terms by the three Lords of Appeal (Lords ATKIN, THANKERTON and MACMILLAN), who found in the pursuer's favour on the basis of the facts alleged. However, the duty was not the strict obligation arising under a contract to supply merchantable goods, but only a duty to take care. Carelessness in itself is not enough, the law "concerns itself with carelessness only where there is a duty to take care and where failure in that duty has caused damage. In such circumstances carelessness assumes the legal quality of negligence".[1] Between manufacturer and ultimate consumer or user there is normally the nexus to establish the necessary duty of care. In the words of Lord ATKIN:[2]

> "a manufacturer of products, which he sells in such a form as to show tha he intends them to reach the ultimate consumer in the form in which they left him with no reasonable possibility of intermediate examination, and with the knowledge that the absence of reasonable care in the preparation of the products will result in an injury to the consumer's life or property, owes a duty to the consumer to take that reasonable care".

b *Intermediate examination*

There is an area of uncertainty created by the reference (by the three Lords of Appeal) to the absence of a "reasonable possibility of intermediate examination". In its most extreme form this limitation on liability was framed by Lord MACMILLAN in the following terms:[3]

> "It may be a good general rule to regard responsibility as ceasing when control ceases. So, also, where between the manufacturer and the user there is interposed a party who has the means and opportunity of examining the manufacturer's product before he re-issues it to the actual user."

In *Donoghue* v. *Stevenson* itself the opportunity of examining the contents of a sealed, opaque bottle did not occur: the control of the manufacturer over that which was delivered to the consumer was not broken. Similarly, in *Grant* v. *Australian Knitting Mills, Ltd.*,[4] a pair of underpants was "issued to the world" in the state in which it was packed by the manufacturer: it was not contemplated that any examination should be conducted by the retailer, certainly not an investigation thorough enough to have revealed the traces of sulphur dioxide which caused the ultimate user's dermatitis.

But would it be sufficient to escape liability for the manufacturer to be able to establish that some examination was likely before use? In *Grant's* case, even if the retailer normally did look the garments over, such an examination would not have revealed the latent defect in the goods. Hence it is reasonable to suppose that the examination to be expected must be of a type that would reveal the defect in question. While such a supposition would appear to be correct in principle, it provides little guidance on how it would apply in practice.

If meat in a tin, or a loaf of bread, is in part badly discoloured, by some fault

---

1 [1932] A.C. 562, at pp. 618–9; [1932] All E.R. Rep. 1, at p. 29.
2 [1932] A.C. 562, at p. 599; [1932] All E.R. Rep. 1, at p. 20; see also *per* Lord THANKERTON, [1932] A.C., at p. 603; [1932] All E.R. Rep., at p. 22.
3 [1932] A.C. 562, at p. 622; [1932] All E.R. Rep. 1, at p. 31.
4 [1936] A.C. 85; [1935] All E.R. Rep. 209.

in the manufacturing or packaging process, the discolouration may be obvious to the mother who opens the tin or takes the loaf out of its wrapping. But is she supposed to interpret the discolouration as a sign of deterioration? Does it make any difference to the situation if she is poor and ill-educated? If she cuts off the discoloured portion, and it is the rest which, when fed to her children, makes them seriously ill, has she acted reasonably? Is the reasonableness of her conduct relevant to the responsibility of the manufacturer? In other words, is an examination by the person who opens the tin or wrapping, or uncorks the bottle, an intermediate examination within the rule? The most that can be suggested is that, in an obvious case where the suspicion should have been raised, even to a person having no knowledge of the goods in question, that the goods were defective, the circumstances may entitle the manufacturer to plead contributory negligence if the plaintiff himself examined the goods, or to seek contribution from the person who examined the goods if the injury was suffered by a third party consuming or using the goods.

Hence, it would seem that, in order to qualify as an intermediate examination that would *absolve* the manufacturer from liability, the examination should at least be limited to the type of inspection that would be commercially foreseeable.[1] However, it does not follow that any inspection that occurs within the distributive framework of the manufacturer's business should enable the manufacturer to escape liability if a defective chattel does "slip through the net".

It is well known that motor car manufacturers lay down a detailed pre-delivery service for their dealers to carry out on all new vehicles. Not only are many defects not picked up by the system of inspection operated within the factory, but some of these defects escape the vigilance (or lack of it) of the mechanic in the dealer's workshop. If a new car is delivered to the buyer with a defect to its braking system as a result of which the buyer's wife is seriously injured when the car fails to stop and crashes, is her remedy against the dealer or the manufacturer? There is no doubt that a road user, and not just someone driving the car, would fall within the scope of a duty owed by the repairer of a vehicle if, through carelessness in carrying out the work, the vehicle caused damage or injury to that user.[2] But, in the case of the defective new car, by whom is the duty owed? The dealer should certainly be responsible for overlooking a defect, rendering the car unroadworthy, that should have been picked up by his examination. If one regards the references in *Donoghue* v. *Stevenson* to "no possibility of intermediate examination" as sacrosanct it would therefore follow that the manufacturer in such a situation is not liable.

Such a conclusion would be unfortunate, and can be supported only on the basis of faulty classification. The injury arose because of two instances of negligence. The car was negligently made by the manufacturer and negligently

---

1 GODDARD, L.J., expressed the view in *Haseldine* v. *C. A. Daw & Son, Ltd.*, [1941] 2 K.B. 343, at p. 376; [1941] 3 All E.R. 156, at p. 183; that "when Lord Atkin used the expression 'reasonable possibility' with relation to inspection, he meant possibility in a commercial sense", though whether the suggested alternative "probability" is much improvement is doubtful: see also *Paine* v. *Colne Valley Electricity Supply Co., Ltd.*, [1938] 4 All E.R. 803.
2 *Stennett* v. *Hancock and Peters*, [1939] 2 All E.R. 578.

examined by the dealer. The fact that the dealer examined the goods is irrelevant to the primary question of causation. He did not interfere with the goods and thus render them harmful. There is something to be said for reinterpreting Lord ATKIN's words to mean "without intermediate interference",[1] and such an approach is in line with the meaning subsequently placed upon the notion of "control" which formed part of Lord MACMILLAN's judgment and to which Lord ATKIN also alluded. According to the Judicial Committee in *Grant* v. *Australian Knitting Mills, Ltd.*,[2] this concept of "control" was a convenient shorthand expression employed "to emphasise the essential factor that the consumer must use the article exactly as it left the maker, that is in all material features, and use it as it was intended to be used". Although this explanation was not exactly the same as that advanced in the High Court of Australia by EVATT, J.,[3] both definitions are consistent in that they emphasise the absence of interference.

There is a further analogy to be drawn with *Grant's* case. Liability was ultimately imposed because the manufacturer's system of checks had failed to detect the quantity of potentially harmful sulphur dioxide that remained in the material at the end of the manufacturing process. It is arguable that the pre-delivery service carried out by the dealer is part of the manufacturer's system of safeguards to ensure that a defective vehicle is not handed over to a buyer. It would not absolve a manufacturer from liability if he employs an independent contractor, instead of, or in addition to, his own servants, to carry out his own inspection process. And it should make no difference to the legal position if the independent contractor also happens to be one link in the chain whereby the manufacturer's goods are distributed to the ultimate user or consumer.

c *Breach of duty: evidence of negligence*

1 *Inference of negligence.* So far the duty of care has been considered, and also the question of identifying who owes the duty. However, it is also essential to establish a breach of that duty, in other words to show that the manufacturer's activities had been carried on carelessly. If the plaintiff had to show precisely how the defect occurred that led to his injuries, he might well be faced with an impossible task. However, if he is able to point to the defect as one that should not have been present in the goods, he is entitled to rely upon this fact as raising an inference of negligence.

---

1 Though it does not solve the problem of the situation in which the "intermediary's" knowledge and failure to act on that knowledge constitutes a *novus actus interveniens*: *Taylor* v. *Rover Co., Ltd.*, [1966] 2 All E.R. 181; [1966] 1 W.L.R. 1491, see below, p. 254. Nor is the suggestion in the text easy to reconcile with *Buckner* v. *Ashby and Horner, Ltd.*, [1941] 1 K.B. 321, unless one takes the view that the contractors were, in the circumstances of that case, entitled to rely upon the subsequent inspection: the construction had been carried out on behalf of the party who should have carried out the adequate inspection, whereas a car dealer is only participating in the manufacturer's own system of safeguards.
2 [1936] A.C. 85, at p. 104; [1935] All E.R. Rep. 209, at p. 217.
3 *Australian Knitting Mills, Ltd.* v. *Grant* (1933), 50 C.L.R. 387, at p. 438: "the idea of 'control' . . . was intended to describe such action on the part of a manufacturer as was intended to, and would ordinarily secure, that the manufactured article should reach the ultimate consumer in precisely the same condition as when it left the manufacturer".

Once the defect itself raises that inference, the manufacturer should have a heavy burden placed upon him to displace it. He should not be able to point to his system of safeguards alone, because, in theory at least, the fact that the defect has slipped through undetected only demonstrates that the system did not work. The logic of this argument appears to have been accepted by the Privy Council in *Grant's* case.[1]

> "According to the evidence, the method of manufacture was correct: the danger of excess sulphites being left was recognised and was guarded against: the process was intended to be foolproof. If excess sulphites were left in the garment, that could only be because someone was at fault. The appellant is not required to lay his finger on the exact person in all the chain who was responsible, or to specify what he did wrong. Negligence is found as a matter of inference from the existence of the defects taken in connection with all the known circumstances: even if the manufacturers could by apt evidence have rebutted that inference they have not done so."

2 *The range of foreseeability*. Taken in its broadest sense this dictum appeared to apply *res ipsa loquitur* in practice even though there was no express reliance on the principle. Furthermore, if one accepts the proposition that, once there is a defect, the manufacturer is faced with having to show, at least to the extent of rebutting the initial presumption, that the defect did not arise through want of care on his part, the test of a manufacturer's duty to the ultimate user of his goods would seem to fall more within the broader test of negligence liability, the so-called "neighbour" principle also laid down by Lord ATKIN in *Donoghue* v. *Stevenson*.[2] According to that principle, now increasingly regarded as of general application,[3] one must take reasonable care to avoid acts or omissions which one can reasonably foresee would be likely to injure persons who are so closely and directly affected by the act or omission that one ought reasonably to have them in contemplation as likely to be so affected.

Even though such a development might be desirable in the interests of the consumer, it must be admitted that in the decade following *Donoghue* v. *Stevenson*, there was a tendency to adhere closely to the narrower test of a manufacturer's liability and to apply even that with caution. In *Lockhart* v. *Barr*,[4] the plaintiff's son had purchased a bottle of aerated water for his mother. When she drank the water she claimed it had contained phenol which burnt her lips and mouth, and made her sick. In holding the manufacturing company which made and bottled the water liable, the Court of Session looked at the nature

---

1 [1936] A.C., at p. 101; [1935] All E.R. Rep., at p. 216; superseding Lord MACMILLAN's statement in *Donoghue* v. *Stevenson*, [1932] A.C., at p. 622; [1932] All E.R. Rep., at p. 31; that there "is no presumption of negligence in such a case as the present, nor is there any justification for applying the maxim, *res ipsa loquitur*".

2 [1932] A.C. 562, at p. 580; [1932] All E.R. Rep. 1, at p. 11: once this principle is applied to a manufacturer, the failure of a subsequent party in a chain of supply to examine the goods would entitle the injured user to sue both parties; it would not absolve the manufacturer from liability: see *Grant* v. *Sun Shipping Co., Ltd.*, [1948] A.C. 549; [1948] 2 All E.R. 238.

3 *Home Office*, v. *Dorset Yacht Co., Ltd.* [1970] A.C. 1004; [1970] 2 All E.R. 294; *Dutton* v. *Bognor Regis Urban District Council*, [1972] 1 Q.B. 373; [1972] 1 All E.R. 462.

4 1941 S.L.T. 414; affirmed H.L. 1943 S.L.T. 266.

of the precautions that could reasonably be required of the defendants. In doing so the Court resurrected *Mullen* v. *Barr & Co., Ltd.*,[1] the authority of which had been doubted in *Donoghue* v. *Stevenson,* and compared it with *Grant* v. *Australian Knitting Mills, Ltd.*[2]

> "When a manufacturer of beverages intended for human consumption knowingly uses as containers of that beverage 'second-hand' or returned bottles, any one of which may, for all he knows, contain a poisonous substance capable, even in very small quantities, of causing injury or death, I do not think that it is unreasonable to exact from him a very high standard of diligence in relation to the plant which he supplies, the system of working, including inspection and check, and the care and skill displayed by his employees in performing their duties. The standard of care may firstly be said to vary directly with the risk of contamination, and in this respect the present case stands midway between *Grant* v. *Australian Knitting Mills, Ltd.* and *Mullen* v. *Barr & Co., Ltd.* In *Grant* the maker knew that all the articles in question had been deliberately impregnated with sulphite, and that this sulphite must be rendered innocuous. In *Mullen* v. *Barr & Co., Ltd. a priori* grounds for believing that a ginger-beer bottle had been chosen as a habitat by a mouse were relatively slender, for such a thing had never happened in over fifty years. In the present case every bottle was potentially contaminated by some deleterious substance which might vary from microbe-bearing dirt to the most virulent poison and every bottle was supposed to be treated in the cleaning plant on this footing."[3]

The manufacturer's liability arose because his system did not provide adequate safeguards against operatives who could too easily remove bottles from an incoming batch and place them in the batches for filling, thus by-passing the cleaning process altogether.

The approach adopted by the Court in this case does demonstrate the need for the user or consumer to be able to rely on something more than the inference of negligence raised by the existence of the defect itself. Even if he does not have to point his finger at the stage in the manufacturing process at which "something went wrong" he must be sure that the manufacturer cannot show that the probability/possibility was that a defect occurred at a time when the goods were out of his control.

The degree of likelihood (i.e. probability/possibility) depends upon the circumstances. There comes a stage (in time and in amount of use) when a defect can no longer be attributed with any certainty to the manufacturer. In *Phillips* v. *Chrysler Corporation of Canada, Ltd.*,[4] one person was killed and a number injured when the steering unit of the car in which they were travelling became locked and the vehicle crashed. The accident occurred eighteen months after the car was first purchased by which time the car had travelled about 14,000

---

1 [1929] S,C. 461. The headnote to *Donoghue* v. *Stevenson* states that *Mullen* v. *Barr* was overruled, but it may only have been overruled in so far as negligence had been proved: see [1932] A.C., at p. 607; [1932] All E.R. Rep., at p. 24; *per* Lord MACMILLAN.
2 [1936] A.C. 85; [1935] All E.R. Rep. 209.
3 1941 S.L.T., at p. 417.
4 (1962), 32 D.L.R. (2d) 347.

miles. It was held by the Ontario High Court that the injured parties could not recover against the manufacturer, nor indeed from the distributor.

> "If the consumer . . . claims inherent defect or defective and improper material or adjustments, there must be an element of time and nature involving the thing which precludes any other cause from having intervened . . . [T]oo many months have elapsed, too many miles have been travelled by that product claimed to have been defective, from the time it has left the possession, the control, the responsibility of the vendors."[1]

3 *The relevance of control.* The Chrysler case highlights another way in which the manufacturer's duty test as laid down in *Donoghue* v. *Stevenson* can prove too unsophisticated in the modern industrial world. Not only is it possible for the manufacturer's "control" to cease at some stage after delivery to the "user", but it is also possible, in theory, for a defect to occur at a stage prior to that over which the manufacturer has actual control.

In the motor car industry, as in many other production processes, the manufacturer of the vehicle makes use of a large number of components produced by completely separate companies. Some of these components are received as independent units which are simply fitted as they are into the vehicles. Although it may be true that the user who is suing for injuries suffered because of a defective product does not have to lay his finger on the point in the chain where the defect occurred, it may be open to the manufacturer to show that the defect existed in a unit (such as the steering assembly in the *Chrysler* case) which was manufactured by a third party. It is at this point that the concept of "control" assumes great significance. The car maker cannot be expected to test the sealed units he receives from his supplier, but can he, or perhaps should he, be held liable for defects in them?

There is no authority on this point in English Law, although two of their Lordships in *Donoghue* v. *Stevenson*[2] commented favourably on the decision of CARDOZO, J., in *MacPherson* v. *Buick Motor Co.*[3] In that case, a car manufacturer was held liable when the plaintiff was injured by an accident caused by the collapse of a defective wheel. This conclusion was reached despite the fact that the wheel had been purchased from another manufacturer, the view being taken that a manufacturer is responsible for the finished product although parts may have been obtained from a reputable supplier.

Acceptance of this principle would seem necessary for the very practical reason that all manufacturers use materials supplied by others, if not actual

---

1 At pp. 359, 360, per LANDREVILLE, J. The fact that a toughened windscreen had been in a car 1 'r a year was a relevant factor in a case brought against the manufacturer of the screen: *Evans* v. *Triplex Safety Glass Co.*, [1936] 1 All E.R. 283, at p. 286, *per* PORTER, J.; see below, p. 254.
2 Lord ATKIN, [1932] A.C. 562, at p. 598; [1932] All E.R. Rep., at p. 20; and Lord MACMILLAN, [1932] A.C. 562, at pp. 617–8; [1932] All E.R. Rep. 1, at p. 29.
3 (1916), 111 N.E. 1050. This decision was clearly based upon the classification of an automobile as a thing imminently dangerous to life and health, an aspect of the case emphasised by Lord BUCKMASTER in his dissenting judgment in *Donoghue* v. *Stevenson*, [1932] A.C., at p. 577; [1932] All E.R. Rep., at pp. 9–10, and see also *Ross* v. *Dunstall* (1921), 63 D.L.R. 63. However, the case was the origin from which sprang the rule in the United States establishing absolute liability on the part of a manufacturer for the safety of his product if properly used.

component units. If the manufacturer can point to the existence of a defect in the unit supplied by a third party, it should be possible to establish the liability of the third party without the manufacturer himself being absolved from liability. However, in many cases it may be difficult or even impossible to establish a claim against the original manufacturer of a unit. Hence the liability of the manufacturer of the finished product should be independent of the liability of the maker of the unit. Even if the unit is not opened for examination by the car manufacturer, it is nevertheless in his hands for fitting into the car body or engine. It could be all too easy for the original maker to point to the work carried out by the manufacturer as taking the unit out of his (the maker's) control. In *Evans* v. *Triplex Safety Glass Co., Ltd.*,[1] the plaintiff incurred loss and expenses when the windscreen of his car shattered while he was driving. It was held that the makers of the windscreen could not be held liable. It was more likely that the human failure had occurred when the windscreen was being fitted into the vehicle by the car manufacturer than in the actual process of making the screen.

For *Donoghue* v. *Stevenson* to operate satisfactorily in the increasingly complex world of modern industrial processes, it is obvious that it must be applicable against the ostensible manufacturers, i.e. the person who brings all the component parts together as the finished product. He will therefore be liable for a defect arising at any stage in the manufacturing processes, whether through his own carelessness or that of his supplier. Furthermore, in so far as *Grant's* case allowed by implication the use of *res ipsa loquitur*, there seems no obstacle to its general application to the process of manufacture as a whole.[2]

4 *The duty to protect against novel and unforeseen hazards.* One final aspect of the system of checks and precautions built in to the manufacturing process is that a manufacturer may be able to escape liability if the defect which occurred was of a novel and unforeseeable kind. In other words, although the manufacturer is expected to have a competent technical and design staff, he cannot be held responsible if the defect was not one that scientific research had come across as a possible factor to be taken into account in the manufacture of his product. It has only been in the last twenty years that problems of metal fatigue have come to be more properly understood. At one time, therefore, tests to discover the fatigue factor would have, not unreasonably, been far less exacting than they should be today.[3] Similarly, injury can occur from a chemical reaction in the ingredients of food,[4] or perhaps in the materials from which refrigerators, cars, etc. are made that causes early disintegration.

---

1 [1936] 1 All E.R. 283.
2 Where two parties could have been negligent, *res ipsa loquitur* raises a *prima facie* case against both: *Walsh* v. *Holst & Co., Ltd.*, [1958] 3 All E.R. 33; [1958] 1 W.L.R. 800.
3 Cf. the system of inspection on ships in *Union of India* v. *N.V. Reederij Amsterdam*, [1962] 1 Lloyd's Rep. 539 (McNair, J.); [1962] 2 Lloyd's Rep. 336, C.A.; [1963] 2 Lloyd's Rep. 223, H.L.
4 As in *Ashington Piggeries, Ltd.* v. *Christopher Hill, Ltd.*, [1972] A.C. 441; [1971] 1 All E.R. 847 (effect of heating); *Albacora S.R.L.* v. *Westcott and Laurence Line, Ltd.*, 1966 S.L.T. 253 (bacteria multiplying in salted fish not kept in refrigeration).

Many of the difficulties facing the injured user are brought out by the facts of the Thalidomide "case". A British company had manufactured under licence from a German company a sedative drug called Thalidomide. It was widely prescribed and used. Later it was discovered that its use by women at a certain stage of pregnancy caused damage to the foetus. As a consequence a large number of children were born with incomplete limbs. If indeed an unborn child has a right of action in tort under English law (i.e. can be classified as a foreseeable "user" of the goods),[1] could he succeed in establishing negligence against any of the parties involved?

The pharmacist would not be in breach of any duty by obtaining goods from a recognised source, particularly as he could hardly be expected to analyse and test products which he dispensed.[2] Nor in prescribing the drug would the doctor necessarily be in breach of a duty not to give negligent advice: like the pharmacist, he has no means of checking on the usefulness and safety of the vast number of drugs available on the market.

The obvious defendant was therefore the British manufacturer who had put the drug into general use under its own brand name of "Distival". However, the injured user's chance of success still depended upon a number of factors. The original German producer had assured the British company of the drug's safety. Although the information given to the British company was incomplete, none of the tests carried out by either firm covered the possibility that the drug might be capable of crossing the placental barrier. Should the British company have tested (i.e. taken all precautions) against such a possibility? How far were they absolved from their duty by relying upon assurances from the German firm? As far as the second question is concerned, the company was clearly the manufacturer within the rule in *M'Alister (or Donoghue)* v. *Stevenson*, and therefore *prima facie* liable for defects, even those occasioned by the faulty parts or design or formula provided by a third party. As for the first question, it is well established that the precautions to be taken must be measured against the risk and the degree of harm that could possibly result from a failure to take those precautions.[3] In this case the problem was whether the risk was ever foreseeable. If all risks foreseeable at that time had been eliminated by tests, how could it be negligent on the part of the manufacturer not to have carried out other, more complex and intensive tests, to guard against an eventuality that had not been imagined?

d *The present law and its future development*

To attempt to answer this question, or to consider the evidence supporting the company's view or the arguments that could be adduced on behalf of the persons harmed by use of the drug, is beyond the scope of this book. However, it does bring out one aspect of the difficulties that might face the plaintiff under the

---

1 A question undecided by the Courts in England, but answered in the affirmative in a number of other common law jurisdictions.
2 Certainly the retailer is entitled to rely upon his supplier in the absence of circumstances suggesting that the goods might be defective: see *Mason* v. *Williams and Williams, Ltd.*, [1955] 1 All E.R. 808; [1955] 1 W.L.R. 549.
3 *Paris* v. *Stepney Borough Council*, [1951] A.C. 367; [1951] 1 All E.R. 42.

manufacturer's liability rule laid down in *Donoghue* v. *Stevenson*. Even with the advantage of the inference of negligence that the existence of a defect can raise, liability is far from being the strict liability imposed by the law or contract. The occasions upon which a manufacturer has been held to have a contractual relationship with a person buying or obtaining his goods from a third party have been few in English law.[1] But even the benefit of such a collateral contract does not assist the injured user who was never a purchaser of the goods. At present therefore the remedies available to the person suffering loss or injury as a result of using defective goods are severely limited. Without the assistance of the contractual remedies based upon the failure of the drug "Distival" to satisfy the requirements of s. 14 of the Sale of Goods Act, the subsequently born malformed child was faced with all the uncertainties of an action in negligence.

But herein lies the irony of the present law. If the drug had been *purchased* by the pregnant woman, and if the injuries had been suffered by her, the retail chemist would have owed her absolute duties to see that the goods were merchantable and reasonably suitable for their purpose. As has already been pointed out, however, the retailer can rarely have the opportunity or expertise to assure himself of the satisfactory nature of the goods he sells, particularly those that are the more complex. In fact, even if goods are not ordered by the name of the manufacturer, his name rather than that of the retailer is usually a factor which weighs most heavily with the buyer in the selection of a wide range of goods. As the Ontario Law Reform Commission reported recently:[2]

> "It has often been remarked that in the modern marketing milieu it is the manufacturer who plays the dominant role. It is he who is responsible for putting the goods into the stream of commerce and, in most cases, of creating the consumer demand for them by continuous advertising. The retailer is little more than a way station. It is the manufacturer who endows the goods with their characteristics and it is he who determines the type of materials and components that shall be used and who establishes the quality control mechanism. It is also he who determines what express guarantees shall be given to the consumer and who is responsible for the quality control mechanism. It is also he who determines what express guarantees shall be given to the consumer and who is responsible for the availability of spare parts and the adequacy of servicing facilities. Almost all the consumer's knowledge about the goods is derived from the labels or markings attached to the goods or the sales literature that accompanies them—and these too originate from the manufacturer."

In short, it is therefore unrealistic that our "consumer law", like the Canadian, should still be based principally on the philosophy of a code that grew out of a trading system based upon personal contact between manufacturer and buyer and upon a genuine power of selection by the retailer as to whose products he purchased to supply his customers.

---

1 See *Shanklin Pier, Ltd.* v. *Detel Products, Ltd.*, [1951] 2 K.B. 854; [1951] 2 All E.R. 471; *Wells (Merstham), Ltd.* v. *Buckland Sand and Silica Co., Ltd.*, [1965] 2 Q.B. 170; [1964] 1 All E.R. 41.
2 *Report on Consumer Warranties and Guarantees in the Sale of Goods*, Toronto, June 1972, Chapter 5, para. 1a.

In the United States, the courts in a number of jurisdictions overcame the difficulty of the privity of contract doctrine and held the manufacturer liable on the same or similar implied warranties that operated between customer and retailer. In *Henningsen* v. *Bloomfield Motors Inc.*,[1] B purchased a new Plymouth car, manufactured by M (the Chrysler Corporation), from S, the first defendants. Ten days later, with less than 500 miles "on the clock", the car was being driven by B's wife, T, when it veered wildly out of control, and crashed into a wall. As it was impossible to tell from the smashed remains of the car if there had been a defect in the steering mechanism, the trial judge held that there was not sufficient proof to establish a *prima facie* case of negligence against S or M. It was held, however, that T was entitled to recover on the basis of an implied warranty of merchantability running in her favour. The Supreme Court of New Jersey upheld the decision on the warranty issue, refusing to accept the argument that T was neither the buyer of the goods (i.e. in North American terminology, that there had been no "horizontal privity"), nor M the actual seller (i.e. that there had been no "vertical privity"):

> "With the advent of mass marketing . . . it became obvious that the consumer was the person being cultivated. Manifestly, the connotation of 'consumer' was broader than that of 'buyer'. He signified such a person who, in the reasonable contemplation of the parties to the sale, might be expected to use the product. Thus, where the commodities sold are such that if defectively manufactured they will be dangerous to life or limb, then society's interests can only be protected by eliminating the requirement of privity between the maker and his dealers and the reasonably expected ultimate consumer."[2]

This approach was accepted in part by sec. 2–318 of the Uniform Commercial Code which extended the seller's warranties "to any natural person who is in the family or household of his buyer or who is a guest in his home if it is reasonable to expect that such a person may use, consume or be affected by the goods and who is injured in person by breach of the warranty".[3] In a number of states which adopted the Code, the class of third party beneficiaries was extended to cover any person who might reasonably be expected to use, consume or be affected by the goods.

However, this proposed statutory innovation did not cover the position of the manufacturer as the potential defendant. Furthermore, despite the generally hostile attitude of the American judiciary to exclusion clauses whether their benefit was claimed by sellers or manufacturers, warranties implied in the contract of sale, or in relation to such a contract, could still to an extent be excluded.[4] It was, however, but a short step from the language of the court in *Henningsen's* case referring to protecting "society's interests" to the imposition

---

1 (1960), 161 A. 2d 69; 32 N.J. 358.
2 161 A. 2d, at pp. 80–1.
3 A not dissimilar provision was included in the first Working Party proposals issued
   by the English and Scottish Law Commissions, but it was not included in the First
   Report on Exemption Clauses in Contracts because it was felt, on balance, that such a
   suggestion should be considered in the context of the law on products liability as a
   whole: see First Report, pp. 22–3.
4 See Uniform Code, sec. 2–316, 302.

of a strict liability in tort based upon the concept of public policy. This step was first taken by the Supreme Court of California in the case of *Greenman* v. *Yuba Power Products Inc.*,[1] and soon after a provision along similar lines was introduced into the Second Restatement on Torts, namely sec. 402A, which reads in part:

> "1. One who sells any product in a defective condition unreasonably dangerous to the user or consumer or to his property is subject to liability for physical harm thereby caused to the ultimate user or consumer, if
>   (a) the seller is engaged in the business of selling such a product, and
>   (b) it is expected to, and does, reach the user or consumer without substantial change in the condition in which it is sold."

This suggestion has been enacted in a substantial number of states. Under such a provision the user has a remedy available against anyone (even a manufacturer) who sells goods, whether the individual product that caused the damage was sold to the user, or to someone of his acquaintance, or to a wholesaler or retailer. Even damage caused by a free sample could create liability if that product had been sold at some stage by someone "engaged in the business of selling such a product".

In England, the judges have not exercised the same freedom to develop the law as their American counterparts. An express warranty once gave rise to an action in tort, but today the doctrine of privity reigns supreme. Claims against the manufacturer must continue to depend upon the tort of negligence because of the excessive compartmentalisation that has been allowed to encompass the law of civil remedies. Only by statute will it be possible (short of a revolution in judicial thinking) for the present anomalies to be removed and to place primary or at least equal responsibility upon the manufacturer of the goods rather than upon the retailer; and to remove the unsatisfactory legal consequences that flow from the accident of who in fact bought the defective goods.

D RESCISSION FOR INNOCENT MISREPRESENTATION

i The position at common law

Prior to 1967 when the Misrepresentation Act introduced changes into this area of the law, there was much debate on the question of whether a contract for the sale of goods could be rescinded for a misrepresentation on the part of the seller which had induced the buyer to enter into the contract. The issue aroused controversy because of attempts by dissatisfied buyers to avoid the consequences of two principles of law—

   (1) that there were circumstances in which a misrepresentation of fact inducing the contract would not be treated as a warranty; and
   (2) that, in an unconditional contract for the sale of specific goods, the right to rescind for breach of condition was lost by the operation of s. 11 (1) (c) of the Sale of Goods Act as soon as the contract was made.

---

1 (1963), 377 P. 2d 897; 59 Cal. 2d 57.

It has already been explained[1] that the divergence between a statement amounting to a "warranty", i.e. a contractual promise, and a statement being classified as a "mere representation" arose solely because of the erroneous acceptance of the belief that a warranty could only exist if there was an intention to warrant on the part of the representor. Once this misapprehension is corrected it will become apparent that a court of equity granted rescission on grounds substantially similar to those for which a court of law would award damages for breach of warranty.

This similarity of approach may be illustrated by the well known case of *Bisset* v. *Wilkinson*.[2] The appellant, the plaintiff in the original proceedings, was seeking to recover money payable under a contract for the sale of land which had been purchased by the respondents. The respondents had counterclaimed for rescission of the contract, or alternatively for damages for fraud or for breach of warranty. The representation upon which the respondents based their counter-claim was to the effect that the land in question would carry 2,000 sheep. The Judicial Committee stated the law as follows:

> "In an action for rescission, as in an action for specific performance of an executory contract, when misrepresentation is the alleged ground of relief of the party who repudiates the contract, it is, of course, essential to ascertain whether that which is relied upon is a representation of a specific fact, or a statement of opinion, since an erroneous opinion stated by the party affirming the contract, though it may have been relied upon and have induced the contract on the part of the party who seeks rescission, gives no title to relief unless fraud is established."[3]

The Judicial Committee then pointed out that a particular statement could only be classified as one of fact or as one of opinion in the light of the circumstances in which it was made. As BOWEN, L.J., had said in an earlier case:[4]

> "It is often fallaciously assumed that a statement of opinion cannot involve a statement of fact. In a case where the facts are equally well known to both parties, what one of them says to the other is frequently nothing but an expression of opinion . . . But if the facts are not equally known to both sides, then a statement of opinion by the one who knows the facts best involves very often a statement of a material fact, for he impliedly states that he knows facts which justify his opinion."

In the present case, as the trial judge had pointed out, a statement by an owner about the farm he has also been occupying would usually be regarded as a statement of fact, but the appellant, as the respondents knew, had never carried on sheep farming on the land as a whole. Hence they were not justified in regarding what the appellant had said about the sheep-carrying capacity of the land as anything other than a statement of opinion. As to the claim for breach of warranty, this conclusion was "sufficient to dispose of the whole case of

---

1 See above, pp. 150–1.
2 [1927] A.C. 177; [1926] All E.R. Rep. 343.
3 [1927] A.C. 177, at pp. 181–2; [1926] All E.R. Rep. 343, at p. 346.
4 *Smith* v. *Land and House Property Corporation* (1884), 28 Ch.D. 7, at p. 15.

misrepresentation, whether as grounding a claim for rescission or a claim for damages".[1]

Once there was a statement of fact that proved to be untrue, the buyer had at law a right of rejection providing the performance by the seller of the promise contained in the statement constituted a condition precedent to his own obligations under the contract. And if he had no right of rejection he could still fall back on his remedy in damages. There was, therefore, no need for equity to provide an alternative remedy of rescission. Indeed there is strong authority for the proposition that, outside transactions involving land, rescission was only available in circumstances in which, at law, a court would declare a contract void for mistake. As the Court of Queen's Bench said in *Kennedy* v. *Panama, etc. Mail Co.*,[2] "where there has been an innocent misrepresentation . . . it does not authorise a rescission, unless it is such as to show that there is a complete difference in substance between what was supposed to be and what was taken, so as to constitute a failure of consideration". In the circumstances there is much to be said for the view that s. 61 (2) of the Sale of Goods Act, by expressly retaining the rules of common law except "in so far as they are inconsistent with the express provisions of this Act, and in particular the rules relating to the . . . effect of fraud, misrepresentation, duress . . . mistake or other invalidating cause" as applicable to contracts for the sales of goods, was recognising that equity had no part to play in such contracts.[3]

It is certainly true that in a number of cases where factors (1) or (2) above led litigants to rely upon a claim to rescind for innocent misrepresentation the Court of Appeal refrained from deciding conclusively that such a claim was not available. However, in no case did the representee succeed. In *Leaf* v. *International Galleries*[4] it was held that after a delay of five years any claim to rescind that might have existed was lost; and in *Long* v. *Lloyd*[5] it was held that a similar claim to reject a lorry was barred by "acceptance" of the goods.

ii The position since 1967

Even if the remedy of rescission was available, there was a further doubt whether it was applicable to an executed, as opposed to a purely executory, contract. Despite criticism of the so-called *Rule in Seddon's* case,[6] it had never been

---

1 [1927] A.C., at p. 181; [1926] All E.R. Rep., at p. 345. Similarly, in *Smith* v. *Land and House Property Corporation* (above), BOWEN, L.J., held that a statement that certain property was let to a most desirable tenant was "not a guarantee that the tenant will go on paying his rent, but it is to my mind a guarantee of a different sort, and amounts at least to an assertion that nothing has occurred in the relations between the landlords and the tenant which can be considered to make the tenant an unsatisfactory one".

2 (1867), L.R. 2 Q.B. 580, at p. 587: applied by the House of Lords in *Bell* v. *Lever Bros. Ltd.*, [1932] A.C. 161: [1931] All E. Rep. 1.

3 This view was taken in the New Zealand case of *Riddiford* v. *Warren*, [1901] 20 N.Z.L.R. 572, and adopted by the Victorian Full Court in *Watt* v. *Westhoven* [1933] V.L.R. 458.

4 [1950] 2 K.B. 86: [1950] 1 All E.R. 693; see above p. 145.

5 [1958] 2 All E.R. 402; [1958] 1 W.L.R. 753; see above, p. 157.

6 *Seddon* v. *North Eastern Salt Co.*, [1905] 1 Ch. 326. It was a rule devised for the dissimilar circumstances of conveyancing law under which a conveyance or lease, once executed, could only be set aside for fraud, but not for innocent misrepresentation: see *Armstrong* v. *Jackson*, [1917] 2 K.B. 822, at p. 825.

expressly over-ruled until abolished by s. 1 (*b*) of the 1967 Misrepresentation Act. Section 1 reads:

> "Where a person has entered into a contract after a misrepresentation has been made to him, and—
> (a) the misrepresentation has become a term of the contract; or
> (b) the contract has been performed;
> or both, then, if otherwise he would be allowed to rescind the contract without alleging fraud, he shall be so entitled, subject to the provisions of this Act, notwithstanding the matters mentioned in paragraphs (*a*) and (*b*) of this section."

It is almost as if this section had been drafted with deliberate obscurity to leave in doubt whether a contract of sale could be rescinded for innocent misrepresentation. The matters mentioned in (*a*) and (*b*) are not to affect matters if the representee would otherwise be allowed to rescind without alleging fraud. However, the most likely interpretation to be placed upon s. 1 is that it is designed to make available the remedy of rescinding any contract including one for the sale of goods for a misrepresentation of fact that induced the contract. The only supposition that makes sense of the provision is that the factors (*a*) and (*b*) rendered nugatory by the section were the principal obstacles to the general availability of the remedy of rescission.

Apart from the general limits that exist on rescission as a remedy (e.g. the need for *restitutio in integrum* without affecting the interests of third parties), s. 2 (2) gives the court a discretion to award damages in lieu:

> "Where a person has entered into a contract after a misrepresentation has been made to him otherwise than fraudulently, and he would be entitled, by reason of the misrepresentation, to rescind the contract, then, if it is claimed, in any proceedings arising out of the contract, that the contract ought to be or has been rescinded, the court or arbitrator may declare the contract subsisting and award damages in lieu of rescission, if of opinion that it would be equitable to do so, having regard to the nature of the misrepresentation and the loss that would be caused by it if the contract were upheld, as well as to the loss that rescission would cause to the other party."

This restriction on the right to rescind is necessary for the obvious reason that, otherwise, a party might be able to allege that a misrepresentation not going to the root of the contract should entitle him to rescind by virtue of s. 1, whereas, formerly, if it had been pleaded as having formed a term in the contract, it would have entitled him only to a remedy in damages for breach of warranty. Section 2 (2) makes sure that the misrepresentee is not going to be better placed by basing his claim on the 1967 Act, rather than on his position at common law.

E CRIMINAL REMEDIES

i The Trade Descriptions Act

Even though civil remedies may exist whereby a buyer can enforce his rights against a seller who has made misrepresentations about the goods, the buyer may be unwilling to embark upon the hazards of litigation. He may be discouraged not only by the uncertainties of proving his case, but also by the costs involved, both financial and emotional. In addition, in many quarters of society there is a genuine mistrust of legal process.

To overcome some of these difficulties, Parliament in 1968 passed the Trade Descriptions Act whereby persons making certain types of misrepresentation would be subject to criminal sanctions. By s. 1 (1) of the Act it is provided:

> "Any person who, in the course of a trade or business,—
>> (a) applies a false description to any goods; or
>> (b) supplies or offers to supply any goods to which a false description is applied;
>
> shall, subject to the provisions of this Act, be guilty of an offence."

A "trade description" of the type prescribed by the Act is defined in s. 2 as "an indication, direct or indirect, and by whatever means given" of a wide variety of matters relating to goods, e.g. quantity or size; method of manufacture, production, processing or re-conditioning; composition; fitness, performance, accuracy; any other physical characteristics; approval by any person; place or date of manufacture, or name of manufacture; and so on. A false trade description is a trade description that is false to a material degree, which includes a trade description that is misleading; and a false description will be regarded as a false trade description if it appears to be a trade description (s. 3). A trade description can be affixed or annexed to, or incorporated with, goods; or it can be made orally (s. 4); and it can also be included in an advertisement (s. 5).[1] It is also an offence for any person in the course of any trade or business to make a statement which he knows to be false or recklessly to make a false statement about the provision of any services, accommodation or facilities (s. 14).

Unless another penalty is specifically prescribed by the Act, the maximum penalty on summary conviction is a fine not exceeding £400; but on indictment it can be a fine, or imprisonment not exceeding two years, or both (s. 18). A time limit is imposed of the shorter period of three years from the commission of the offence or one year from its discovery (s. 19 (1)), though in the majority of cases which are tried summarily the time limit is twelve months from the commission of the offence (s. 19 (2)). This last provision is in fact an extension of the normal six months limit in magistrates' court proceedings under s. 104 of the Magistrates' Courts Act 1952, but the extension does not apply if the offence arises out of an oral statement or description (s. 19 (4)).[2] The duty to enforce the Act is placed on the local weights and measures authority (s. 26), the officers of which are authorised to make test purchases (s. 27) and, within the limits

---

1 It is also an offence to give any false indication that goods are of a kind supplied to or approved by any member of the Royal Family; or to use without authority and device or emblem signifying, or resembling so as to be likely to deceive, the Queen's Award to Industry (s. 12). It is also prohibited to give a false indication that any goods or services are of a kind supplied to any person (s. 13).

2 This period is far too short, particularly in relation to s. 14 which makes false and misleading statements as to services an offence. If a car is purchased which is orally guaranteed for a period longer than six months, it could be beyond the time limit for prosecution before the buyer discovers the falsity of the seller's claims.

prescribed, to enter premises and to inspect and seize goods and documents (s. 28).[1]

The Act also deals with offences committed by corporations (s. 20), and with the defences available to a party charged with an offence under the Act (s. 24). Both aspects of the legislation were considered by the House of Lords in the case of *Tesco Supermarkets, Ltd.* v. *Nattrass*.[2] S, the appellant company, was running a "special offer" on "Radiant" washing powder at one of its branches. The offer price was 2s. 11d. instead cf the normal price of 3s. 11d.

It was the duty of A, a shop assistant at the store, to put out fresh stocks when supplies of a particular item on the shelves were greatly reduced or had been exhausted. In this case she brought out packets marked with the full price, so that it appeared as if S was claiming that, at 3s. 11d., the packets had "1s. off". A failed to inform M, the branch manager of what she had done, and he, on whom fell the duty of seeing that the correct goods were on sale, failed to notice the error and marked his daily return "All special offers OK". In answer to the charge, S claimed that the commission of the offence had been due to the "act or default of another person" (namely M),[3] and that the company had taken "all reasonable precautions and exercised all due diligence to avoid the commission of such an offence".

It had already been established in an earlier Divisional Court decision,[4] that, because s. 24 (1) (*b*) required the defendant to prove that he had exercised all due diligence to avoid the commission of an offence by "any person under his control", an employee of the defendant, even one employed in a managerial capacity,[5] could be "another person" within the meaning of s. 24 (1) (*a*). However the Divisional Court in the present case was prepared to hold S guilty of an offence under s. 11 because S had delegated the task of overseeing the efficient operation of the system they had devised to M and it was clear that M had failed to ensure the system's efficient functioning.

The conviction was quashed by the House of Lords. Although no attempt was made to challenge the finding that M was "another person", Lord REID

---

1 Where goods seized or purchased are then tested, the procedure to be followed is laid down in s. 30. If the owner of goods seized is not convicted he is entitled to compensation for any loss suffered by the damage or deterioration etc. of the goods (s. 33).

2 [1972] A.C. 153; [1971] 2 All E.R. 127.

3 By s. 24 (2):

"If in any case the defence provided by the last foregoing subsection involves the allegation that the commission of the offence was due to the act or default of another person, the person charged shall not, without leave of the court, be entitled to rely on that defence unless, within seven clear days before the hearing, he has served on the prosecutor a notice in writing giving such information identifying or assisting in the identification of that other person as was then in his possession."

S had, in this case, given the necessary notice, naming M as that "other person".

4 *Beckett* v. *Kingston Bros. (Butchers), Ltd.*, [1970] 1 Q.B. 606; [1970] 1 All E.R. 715.

5 Section 20 (1) does not provide a ground for the prosecution to avoid this defence in relation to an offence committed by a body corporate because that sub-section applies only to "someone in a position of managing the affairs *of the company*", per FISHER, J., in *Tesco, Ltd.* v. *Nattrass*, [1970] 3 All E.R. 357, at p. 364; and see *per* Lord MORRIS, [1972] A.C. 153, at pp. 180–1; [1971] 2 All E.R. 127, at p. 140.

expressed the opinion that the Divisional Court was "plainly right" on this issue.[1] However, that Court (equally clearly in their Lordship's opinion) was wrong in suggesting that, having instituted an effective system, S could be responsible for the failures of that system brought about by the lack of due diligence by its employees.

The drawback to this decision is the ease with which it will enable the proprietor to escape the criminal liability imposed by the Act to remedy, as it were, a defect in the law of contract (in relation to which of course he would clearly be bound by the actions of his agents).[2] Lord REID admitted this possibility, but hinted that the real fault lay with magistrates for too readily accepting "a paper scheme and perfunctory efforts to enforce it" as exercising due diligence.[3] In this case, it is true, the courts seemed most impressed by the rigorous system of inspection operated at all levels by Tesco. Nevertheless, it is believed that the cause of justice would be better served by the approach of the Divisional Court than by that now imposed by the House of Lords. S's "offence" in this case lay not so much in the error of M in failing to notice the situation created by A, but in the nature of S's activities. The fundamental reason why this mistake occurred was because constant price changes are the day to day practice of the grocery trade. Not only do these changes confuse the customer (even if they are not designed deliberately to do so), but they must create the greatest difficulties for the sales staff who have to operate them. In the circumstances, errors are inevitable. The decision in *Tesco* v. *Nattrass* creates a virtual immunity for the company which is primarily responsible for the policy that gives rise to such possibilities of error.[4]

In this type of case, criminal responsibility could be imposed upon the manager of the shop. By s. 6, a person "having goods in his possession for supply" is deemed to offer to supply them, and under the somewhat similar provisions of a number of other Acts it has been possible to hold that a manager of a shop could be "in possession" of the proprietor's goods even though he was only selling them as the latter's agent.[5] And this position is reinforced by s. 23 which provides:

> "Where the commission by any person of an offence under this Act is due to the act or default of some other person that other person shall be guilty of the offence, and a person may be charged with and convicted of the offence by

---

1 [1972] A.C. 153, at p. 169; [1971] 2 All E.R. 127, at p. 130.
2 See above, p. 30.
3 [1972] A.C. 153, at p. 174; [1971] 2 All E.R. 127, at p. 135.
4 Some part of the responsibility must be placed upon manufacturers, who indulge in a variety of stratagems to conceal the true price and value of their goods, e.g. cases of inflated "recommended" prices: packages marked at so-many pence off; and a bewildering number of different sized cartons that makes a comparison of prices difficult. The Act only imposes liability on the person supplying, or selling the goods. Hence it may well be that the seller will be liable under the Act in respect of a description placed on the container by the manufacturer: see *Doble* v. *David Greig, Ltd.*, [1972] 2 All E.R. 195; [1972] 1 W.L.R. 703.
5 See *Melias, Ltd.* v. *Preston*, [1957] 2 Q.B. 380; [1957] 2 All E.R. 449, applying *Hotchins* v. *Hindmarsh*, [1891] 2 Q.B. 181; and see also *Davies* v. *Earys and Earys* (1949) (unreported) cited O'Keefe, *Law Relating to Trade Descriptions*, 29 [1].

virtue of this section whether or not proceedings are taken against the first mentioned person."

However, the wording of this section is not without its own difficulties of interpretation. In the first place it seems to contemplate the existence of a principal offender (i.e. someone who has actually committed an offence), although s. 24 allows such a defendant a special statutory defence where the commission of the offence is due to the act or default etc. of another person. The solution of the conflict appears to be that "when a person first named in s. 23 has no defence to the charge except the statutory defence under s. 24, he or she can properly still be regarded as having committed the offence for the purpose of s. 23".[1]

The second problem may be illustrated by reference to the position of the shop assistant in the *Tesco* case. Presumably in most situations a shop assistant cannot be considered as having goods in her possession for supply,[2] though the words of s. 23 are wide enough to cover her activities, unless she can only be treated as "some other person" for the purpose of s. 23 if specifically named by a defendant under s. 24. This interpretation would seem to be supported by the contention that, even if proceedings do not have to be taken against any one else under s. 23, there should at least be a *prospective* defendant in order for the section to operate. Some limitation upon the ambit of s. 23 (i.e. to persons named by a prospective defendant under s. 24) is clearly desirable. If not, s. 23 would appear to impose liability on any person whose act or default caused the commission of what would otherwise have been an offence by a prospective defendant, but whose act or default did not in itself constitute an offence under the Act.[3]

ii Fair Trading Act 1973

Although the Fair Trading Act has a good deal in common with the Trade Descriptions Act as far as the method of imposing sanctions is concerned, the framework of the legislation and the way in which it is designed to operate are novel. Apart from those of its provisions which deal with monopolies and mergers and restrictive trade practices,[4] a large part of the remainder of the Act, in effect, gives sweeping subordinate legislative powers to the Secretary of State for Consumer Affairs, and striking executive functions to the Director General of Fair Trading.

a *Powers of investigation*

The Director General of Fair Trading (a post established by s. 1 of the Act) is to keep under review commercial activities in the United Kingdom which relate to goods supplied to consumers in this country in order to make himself aware of practices that might adversely effect the economic interests of such consumers

---

1 *Per* Lord WIDGERY, C.J., in *Coupe* v. *Guyett*, [1973] 2 All E.R. 1058, at pp. 1061–2.
2 Though it might be different if she had actual physical possession of the goods (she had them in a basket while she was in the process of stacking them on the shelves) at the time of the "misdescription".
3 A possibility raised but not commented upon by Viscount DILHORNE in *Tesco* v. *Nattrass*; [1972] A.C. 153, at p. 184; [1971] 2 All E.R. 27, at p. 143.
4 See also Part XI of the Act which deals with "Pyramid Selling".

(s. 2 (1) (*a*)). The Director is also to receive and collate evidence with respect to such activities which might affect the interests (whether economic or with respect to health, safety or other matters) of such consumers (s. 2 (1) (*b*)). He is also to act in conjunction with, and in an advisory capacity to, the Secretary of State in the circumstances mentioned in s. 2 (3).

More particularly, when the Director wishes guidance on whether a specific consumer trade practice adversely affects the economic interests of consumers in the United Kingdom, he may refer the question to the Consumer Protection Advisory Committee[1] (s. 14 (1)).[2] By a "consumer trade practice" is meant (s. 13):[3]

> "Any practice which is for the time being carried on in connection with the supply of goods (whether by way of sale or otherwise) to consumers or in connection with the supply of services for consumers and which relates:
>
> (*a*) to the terms of conditions (whether as to price or otherwise) on or subject to which goods or services are or are sought to be supplied, or
>
> (*b*) to the manner in which those terms or conditions are communicated to persons to whom goods are or are sought to be supplied or for whom services are or are sought to be supplied, or
>
> (*c*) to promotion (by advertising, labelling or marking of goods, canvassing or otherwise) of the supply of goods or of the supply of services, or
>
> (*d*) to the methods of salesmanship employed in dealing with consumers, or
>
> (*e*) to the way in which goods are packed or otherwise got up for the purpose of being supplied, or
>
> (*f*) to methods of demanding or securing payment for goods or services supplied."

b *Regulating powers*

The Director has a power to initiate proposals for the making of orders by the Secretary of State prohibiting certain types of conduct. This power is limited in three respects; first as to the circumstances; secondly as to the type of activity to be prescribed; and thirdly as to the procedure to be followed.

1 *Circumstances enabling the Director to act.* By s. 17 (2), when he refers any matter to the Advisory Committee, the Director may include proposals for making recommendations to the Secretary of State in a case where:

> "It appears to the Director that a consumer trade practice has the effect, or is likely to have the effect:
>
> (*a*) of misleading consumers as to, or withholding from them adequate information as to, or an adequate record of, their rights and obligations under relevant consumer transactions, or

---

1 Established by virtue of s. 3.

2 Such a question may also be referred to the Committee by the Secretary of State or any other Minister.

3 Subject to the exception of the services enumerated in Schedule 4 of the Act, which covers a wide range of professional services of a medical, legal or comparable nature (s. 15) and to a more restricted power of reference (i.e. with the consent of the appropriate Minister) in the case of goods and services provided by public corporations operating in the fields of gas and electricity supply (s. 16 and Schedule 5).

 (*b*) of otherwise misleading or confusing consumers with respect to any matter in connection with relevant consumer transactions, or

 (*c*) of subjecting consumers to undue pressure to enter into relevant consumer transactions, or

 (*d*) of causing the terms or conditions, on or subject to which consumers enter into relevant consumer transactions, to be so adverse to them as to be inequitable."

2 *Type of activity that can be prescribed.* Schedule 6 lays down the matters that can fall within the scope of proposals under s. 17 as follows:

"1. Prohibition of specified consumer trade practice either generally or in relation to specified consumer transactions.

2. Prohibition of specified consumer transactions unless carried out at specified times or at a place of a specified description.

3. Prohibition of the inclusion in specified consumer transactions of terms or conditions purporting to exclude or limit the liability of a party to such a transaction in respect of specified matters.

4. A requirement that contracts relating to specified consumer transactions shall include specified terms or conditions.

5. A requirement that contracts or other documents relating to specified consumer transactions shall comply with specified provisions as to lettering (whether as to size, type, colouring or otherwise).

6. A requirement that specified information shall be given to parties to specified consumer transactions."

3 *Procedural requirements.* It is specifically laid down that the Director cannot make recommendations to the Secretary of State for the exercise of the regulatory powers granted by the Act except by way of reference to the Advisory Committee (s. 18). Once a reference is made to which s. 17 applies, the Advisory Committee's Report must be made within three months or such longer period as the Secretary of State may allow after consultation with the Advisory Committee (s. 20).

The Advisory Committee's report must be in the form outlined by s. 21, and more especially it must state whether the Committee:

 "(*a*) agree with the proposals set out in the reference, or

 (*b*) would agree with those proposals if they were modified in a manner specified in the report, or

 (*c*) disagree with the proposals and do not desire to suggest any such modifications" (s. 21 (2))".

In a situation falling within paragraphs (a) or (b), s. 22 empowers the Secretary of State, if he thinks fit, to make an order by statutory instrument giving effect to the proposals in the light of the Advisory Committee's observations. Any such order, or subsequent order varying or revoking it, is to be laid before Parliament and approved by a resolution of each House (s. 22 (4)).

c *Enforcement procedures*

1 *With respect to orders made by the Secretary of State.* This part of the Act is designed to provide against two different types of mischief. The power

granted under ss. 17, 22, etc., is essentially to combat the ingenuity of the salesman and advertisers to invent novel ways of inducing the gullible to buy goods or services, ways that, though perhaps legal under the present law, are of doubtful morality or fairness.

The mechanism provided by the Act will, it is hoped, enable information and advice to be obtained quickly and for remedial action to be taken by means of an order prohibiting the activity in question. Once this step is taken, s. 23 lays down certain penalties for contravention of such an order (to a fine not exceeding £400 on summary conviction; and to a fine or imprisonment for a term not exceeding two years, or both, on conviction on indictment). The prosecution of offences follows the pattern of the Trade Descriptions Act in that it is the duty of the local weights and measures authority to enforce the provisions of any order made under s. 22 (s. 27), and a number of provisions relating to defences (e.g. ss. 24, 25) and the power of the local weights and measures officers (e.g. ss. 28, 29 *et seq.*) are substantially similar to sections of the earlier Act.

However, by s. 26, a contract for the supply of goods or services shall not be void or unenforceable by reason only of a contravention of an order under s. 22. Nor shall the provisions of this Part of the Act be construed as to confer a right of civil action on the basis of a contravention of such an order; nor are the provisions of this Part to derogate from any right of action (whether civil or criminal) in proceedings instituted "otherwise than under this Part of this Act".

2 *Additional functions of the Director.* When the Supply of Goods (Implied Terms) Bill was before Parliament, a number of Members complained that, though the proposed legislation rendered certain types of exemption clause void in consumer sales, there was nothing to prevent traders continuing to employ such terms and trying to rely upon them to persuade customers that they (the traders) were protected thereby against claims in respect of defective goods.[1] Government spokesmen diverted the criticism that the Supply of Goods Bill should have contained provisions making it an offence to continue to include such terms in consumer contracts by referring to the remedy to be provided in the Fair Trading Bill.

By Part III of the Fair Trading Act, the Director is given the power to initiate procedures to prevent persistent conduct that is "detrimental to the interests of consumers", and is also unfair to them. A course of conduct can be detrimental to their economic interests or to their interests in respect of health, safety or other matters (s. 34 (1) (a)). A course of conduct shall be regarded as unfair to consumers:

> "if it consists of contraventions of one or more enactments which impose duties, prohibitions or restrictions enforceable by criminal proceedings" (s. 34 (2)), or
> "if it consists of things done, or omitted to be done, in the course of that business in breach of contract or in breach of a duty (other than a contractual duty) owed to any person by virtue of any enactment or rule of law and enforceable by civil proceedings" (s. 34 (3)).

---

1 See above p. 226.

Once it appears to the Director, from complaints or other sources of information (s. 34 (4)), that a person carrying on business has in the course of that business persisted in a conduct detrimental and unfair to consumers he:

> "shall use his best endeavours, by communication with that person or otherwise, to obtain from him a satisfactory written assurance that he will refrain from continuing that course of conduct and from carrying on any similar course of conduct in the course of that business" (s. 34 (1)).

If the Director is unable to obtain a satisfactory written assurance, or if it appears that the person giving such an assurance has failed to observe it, the Director may bring proceedings before the Restrictive Practices Court (s. 35), or, in appropriate cases (see s. 41), before the County Court. The Court can, if it finds against the trader, either make an order against that person, or accept an undertaking from that person (s. 37). The Act also contains elaborate provisions for dealing with persons consenting to or conniving at conduct detrimental to consumers (ss. 38, 39) and with interconnected bodies corporate (s. 40).

The type of activity, covered by s. 34 (2) and (3), and therefore subject to the Director's powers under Part III, is certainly extensive. However, while it may be a useful procedure for dealing with persistent breaches of a relatively trivial kind by a large organisation to which petty fines or the possibility of small actions for breach of contract would be no deterrent, it is unlikely to be available on a wide enough scale to satisfy the critics of the Supply of Goods (Implied Terms) Act. Isolated complaints about the insertion of void exemption clauses may be evidence of an unfair practice, but a good deal of investigation "on the spot" might be required before it can be shown that the practice has been persistent. Furthermore, in the case of relatively small business concerns, these activities are in any case so limited that the mechanism of Part III seems very much like the sledgehammer in relation to the proverbial nut. It may well be, therefore, that the Director will, in time, be obliged to seek the support of the Advisory Committee for proposals to put to the Secretary of State that will prohibit the continued use of void exemption clauses in consumer sales.

CHAPTER 7

The Buyer's Remedy in Damages

The buyer will have a remedy in damages in two different situations: where the seller has failed to deliver the goods; and where the seller is in breach of some term of the contract. In both situations, the principal rule for the assessment of damages is "the estimated loss directly and naturally resulting, in the ordinary course of events" from the breach.[1] This general principle is of course a statutory endorsement of the so-called first rule in *Hadley* v. *Baxendale*.[2] However, in the case of damages for non-delivery, s. 51 (3) lays down a special rule, or at least a special application of the general rule, in situations where there is an available market in the goods that the seller has not supplied. Accordingly it is necessary to consider the two types of breach that can be committed by the seller under separate headings. In addition there is the problem of assessing damages in a case of late delivery a situation which constitutes something of a hybrid and is not specifically covered in the Act itself.

A. DAMAGES FOR NON-DELIVERY

Section 51 sets out the position with deceptive simplicity:

> "(1) Where the seller wrongfully neglects or refuses to deliver the goods to the buyer, the buyer may maintain an action against the seller for damages for non-delivery.
> (2) The measure of damages is the estimated loss directly and naturally resulting, in the ordinary course of events, from the seller's breach of contract.
> (3) Where there is an available market for the goods in question the measure of damages is *prima facie* to be ascertained by the difference between the contract price and the market or current price of the goods at the time or times when they ought to have been delivered, or, if no time was fixed, then at the time of the refusal to deliver."

i The available market test

If the seller fails to supply the goods, it is reasonable to expect the buyer to obtain replacement goods if such goods are available. Hence the tendency has been for the courts to look to the market price as the standard against which to estimate loss whenever possible. In other words, it is the market price which, when compared with the contract price, demonstrates the "loss directly and

---

1 Section 51 (2)—non-delivery; s. 53 (2)—warranty.
2 (1854) 9 Exch. 341; [1843–60] All E.R. Rep. 461; see further below, p. 274.

naturally resulting" in the context of what has occurred and of the injured party's obligation to mitigate damages.

Unlike the position of a seller who, in a case of default by the buyer, has to find an alternative purchaser for his goods, the concept of a market "available" to the buyer has proved relatively simple to apply. Only rarely will the buyer be able to show that he has no reasonable alternative source of supply. Even if such goods are not immediately available in the United Kingdom, it should be possible to arrange for their shipment to this country.[1] Accordingly, if the buyer does obtain replacement goods at the appropriate time, the likelihood is that the price which he pays will be regarded as providing some guide to what the market price really was at that moment. Similarly, if the seller, instead of supplying the goods to buyer, resells them to a third party, the buyer can clearly, if he so wishes, base his claim on the resale price as representing the market price on the ground that the seller is hardly in a position to argue otherwise.

In *Mouat* v. *Betts Motors, Ltd.*,[2] the import of new cars into New Zealand had been severely restricted and those that were sold were subject to price fixing under government regulations. Thus, when B, a dealer, originally sold a new imported car to S for £1,207, it was subject to a term, required by the regulations, that, if S wished to resell the car within two years of the original purchase, he must first offer it to B at a price of £1,157. In breach of this undertaking S resold to a third party for £1,700. B therefore sued S for non-delivery claiming as damages the £543 difference between the contract price of £1,157 and the "market price" established by the sale for £1,700. S's contention was that, if he had sold the car back to B, B was prohibited by the regulations from selling for more than the fixed new price, so that the most he had lost was profit of up to £50. Influenced by the fact that, by breaking his undertaking, S had made a profit of £543, the Judicial Committee held that, in view of his conduct, S could hardly deny that £1,700 was the market price against which B's loss was to be calculated.

ii Sub-sales as affecting the market price rule

The courts have experienced particular difficulty in dealing with sales by the buyer which are dependent for their performance on the goods to be obtained from the seller. In theory, at any rate, as long as there is an available market in the goods, the buyer can always fulfil his contract to the sub-purchaser by obtaining an alternative consignment. Hence the loss should remain *prima facie* that assessed by reference to the market price.

In *Williams Bros.* v. *Ed. T. Agius, Ltd.*,[3] S agreed to supply B with six cargoes of coal at 16s. 3d. per ton, shipments to be made during 1911. The November shipment was not delivered. At the date of the breach the market price of similar coal was 23s. 6d., although the buyer had earlier contracted to sell coal of the

---

1 See *Hasell* v. *Bagot, Shakes & Lewis* (1911), 13 C.L.R. 374; but cf. *Lesters Leather & Skin Co., Ltd.* v. *Home & Overseas Brokers* (1948), 64 T.L.R. 569.
2 [1959] A.C. 71: [1958] 3 All E.R. 402.
3 [1914] A.C. 510; [1914–15] All E.R. Rep. 97.

same amount and description as that due to be delivered in November at a price of 19s. per ton. The House of Lords held that the existence of the second contract was irrelevant to the rights of the parties under the first. B may have been in breach of his contract to resell the goods, but, as against S, he was clearly entitled to the difference between the contract price and the market price.

However, too strict an adherence to the market price rule can give rise to possible injustice in a number of ways. In a case in which the delivery date is fixed, the market price is also limited to that date. In a volatile market, such a strict principle can give rise to injustice because the buyer could be placed in the position of being obliged to decide what course to adopt in a hurry. Common sense suggests that, particularly in a situation where there is little or no warning of the seller's likely default, the buyer should be allowed a period of time within which to reach some settlement with the seller, and to make enquiries about the current availability of the goods in question. It is a relatively unsophisticated view of the commercial world adopted by the Act that suggests that one can obtain immediate alternative supplies without checking on a wide variety of factors that should influence such a decision.

The buyer's position may be further complicated if his resale contract contains an undertaking to supply the exact goods which the seller is due to deliver, or if the date of delivery on the resale is the same as that under the original contract. From the buyer's point of view there is no available market, but is he able to establish this fact against the seller?

As far as delivery of the self-same goods is concerned, the issue came before the House of Lords in *R. and H. Hall, Ltd.* v. *W. H. Pim (Junior) & Co., Ltd.*[1] B purchased an as yet unascertained cargo of wheat from S at a price of 51s. 9d. per quarter. The contract itself contained provisions relating to sub-sales if B chose to resell. B did resell the cargo before the time of delivery at a price of 56s. 9d. per quarter. The price of similar wheat at the time the goods should have been delivered was 53s. 9d. Their Lordships held that B was entitled to have his loss calculated against the resale price. Although the arbitrators had found that the chances of the buyer retaining the goods or of his reselling them were about equal, it was not unlikely, in the light of the express provisions in the contract, that the means employed would be by resale of the cargo itself as a specific whole.

It is not entirely clear what is the exact *ratio* of this case. As will be discussed shortly, it can certainly be taken as authority for the general proposition that, if there is no available market, a resale can be taken into account if such a resale is probable; and for a thing to be probable "it is enough . . . that there is an even chance of its happening". But how does one exclude the market price on the basis of the resale of the actual goods in question? It may be enough, as in this case, "that the contract contemplated by its terms that he should have the right to do so if he chose".[1] But, presumably this would not exclude the possibility of the buyer showing that the resale of the actual cargo before delivery was in itself a probability.

---

1 (1928), 33 Com. Cas. 324; [1928] All E.R. Rep. 763.
2 33 Com. Cas., at p. 326; [1928] All E.R. Rep., at p. 765, *per* Viscount HALDANE.

iii The two branches of the rule in Hadley v. Baxendale

Where there is no available market in the goods so that the buyer is unable to purchase replacements, the buyer's damages are those naturally arising from the breach (s. 51 (2)) or/and any other loss which ought to have been in the contemplation of the parties as being a consequence of the breach. This latter category arises under the second (branch of the) rule in *Hadley* v. *Baxendale*.[1] Although there is no specific reference to losses in the contemplation of the parties in the Sale of Goods Act, s. 54 is usually taken to have preserved the application of the second rule in contracts of sale. The section reads in part:

> "Nothing in this Act shall affect the right of the buyer or the seller to recover interest or special damages in any case where by law interest or special damages may be recoverable."

The expression special damages, or to be more accurate "special loss", was certainly used to denote the second branch of the *Hadley* v. *Baxendale* rule. In *Hydraulic Engineering Co., Ltd.* v. *McHaffie*,[2] B had agreed to make a pile driver for J to be delivered by the end of August. B then contracted with S that S should make "as soon as possible" the part of the machine called the "gun". S had been aware of the transaction between B and J; indeed it had been J who had made the introductions between B and S. S was unable to complete the gun mechanism in time because of a lack of expert staff and J cancelled his contract with B. S was held liable to B for the loss of profit on the transaction with J, together with the expenditure incurred by B in making other parts of the machine, less the small amount the machinery was worth as scrap.[3] In relation to the loss on the sub-sale, COTTON, L.J. observed:[4]

> "We must follow out the rule that the plaintiffs are only to have the damages which are the ordinary and natural consequences of the breach; but this rule is subject to the limitation that where the breach has occasioned a *special loss*, which was actually in contemplation of the parties at the time of entering into the contract, that special loss happening subsequently to the breach must be taken into account. The plaintiffs had, as the defendants knew, entered into another contract with [J] for the delivery to him of certain machinery within a stipulated time; and the defendants are answerable to the plaintiffs for the loss which the latter have sustained by the refusal of [J] to carry out the contract."

This division between losses naturally arising and additional, or special, losses is also illustrated by reference to the decision in *Victoria Laundry (Windsor), Ltd.* v. *Newman Industries, Ltd.*[5] The plaintiff company, which ran a laundering and dyeing business, ordered a boiler from the defendants. The boiler was delivered late. It was held by the Court of Appeal that, as the defendants knew the general nature of the plaintiff's business, they were liable for some loss of

---

1 (1854), 9 Exch. 341; [1843–60] All E.R. Rep. 461; discussed below.
2 (1878), 4 Q.B.D. 670.
3 In fact S agreed to take the goods off B's hands.
4 At p. 677 (italics supplied).
5 [1949] 2 K.B. 528; [1949] 1 All E.R. 997 (a case on late, not non-delivery, but the principle is of general application).

profit suffered by that company, but that they were not liable for the loss of profits on a number of particularly lucrative dyeing contracts entered into by the company because they were unaware of the existence of these contracts.

Although the division of the award of damages into two categories is so well established as part of the general law of contract that there is little likelihood of any change being adopted, it is not the most satisfactory approach. Particular difficulty seems to have been experienced in relation to sub-sales. It is said that sub-sales should be ignored unless the second branch of the *Hadley* v. *Baxendale* rule applies. But to suggest that losses incurred in relation to sub-sales depend upon special knowledge is to distort the position.

The origins of the "two branches" approach was the statement in *Hadley* v. *Baxendale* that, *"in such a case as the present"* (i.e. a case involving a delay in performing a contract of carriage) the damages "should be such as may fairly and reasonably be considered either arising naturally, i.e. according to the usual course of things, from such breach of contract itself, or such as may reasonably be supposed to have been in the contemplation of both parties, at the time they made the contract, as the probable result of the breach of it".[1] The reason given by the court for distinguishing between the two situations was that it would be unfair upon a carrier to impose such a wide liability for damages unless he was aware of the circumstances in which case he would have an opportunity of imposing special conditions to limit his liability.

In sales of goods, on the other hand, the background knowledge (as opposed to special knowledge) of the parties is likely to be wider, and their relationship closer. To an extent *Hadley* v. *Baxendale* was dependent upon nineteenth century circumstances and attitudes. A small carrier should not be held responsible for a mill's loss of profits unless it was clearly brought home to him the risk he was taking if he failed to deliver in time. Nevertheless, even today, a large haulage contractor might not be as aware of the possible consequences of default as an importer or other supplier of goods. In the words of Lord UPJOHN in *Koufos* v. *Czarnikow*[2] each party "must be taken to understand the ordinary practices and exigencies of the other's trade but it must be remembered when dealing with the case of a carrier of goods ... he is not carrying on the same trade as the consignor of goods and his knowledge of the practices and exigencies of the other's trade may be limited and less than between buyer and seller who probably know far more about one another's business". As a consequence, it is more realistic to admit that, in sales, the two category test of *Hadley* v. *Baxendale* is not always easy to apply with precision.

Where a buyer has purchased 5,000 tons of superphosphates or a cargo of grain, it will be at least an even chance[3] that it is for resale. In addition, the

---

1 (1854), 9 Exch. 341, at p. 354.
2 [1969] 1 A.C. 350, at p. 424; [1967] 3 All E.R. 686, at p. 717; referring to the judgment of Lord WRIGHT in *Monarch Steamship Co., Ltd.* v. *Karlshamns Oljefabriker (A.B.)*, [1949] A.C. 196, at pp. 224–5; [1949] 1 All E.R. 1, at p. 14.
3 The test, quoted above, is from Viscount DUNEDIN's judgment in *R. and H. Hall, Ltd.* v. *W. H. Pim (Junior) & Co.* (1928) 33 Com. Cas. 324, at p. 330; [1928] All E.R. Rep. 763, at p. 767. As a Tasmanian judge pointed out in *Australian Fruit and Produce Co. Ltd.* v. *Terry Pty., Ltd.* (1934), 29 Tas. L.R. 102, at p. 103, the defendants in that case were aware that the plaintiffs did not buy 1,500 cases of apples just to eat them!

likely destination of the goods will become more apparent in the light of the background knowledge of the seller. In *Patrick* v. *Russo-British Grain Export Co., Ltd.*,[1] B purchased a quantity of Russian wheat from S at 56s. 9d. per 480 lbs., and contracted to resell it at 60s. 6d. It was a type of wheat not readily available on the market. When S failed to deliver the wheat, the court held B entitled as damages to the loss of profit on the resale. It was known to S that B, being a merchant and not a miller, was going to resell the wheat so that loss of profit was clearly within the contemplation of the parties as a probable result of non-delivery. SLATER, J.,[2] emphatically placed liability arising from such knowledge under the second branch of the rule in *Hadley* v. *Baxendale*, but this approach tends to be arbitrary without being altogether helpful. As Lord PEARCE pointed out in *Koufos* v. *Czarnikow*[3] even the first branch of the rule depended for its application upon the knowledge of certain basic facts; consequently, how a fact was categorised, as basic knowledge or as a special circumstance, determined whether the case came under the first part of the rule or the second.

In *Victoria Laundry (Windsor), Ltd.* v. *Newman Industries, Ltd.*,[4] the Court of Appeal classified liability to compensate for loss of profits arising from the seller's background knowledge of the nature of the buyer's business as based upon the second branch rather than on the first. Nevertheless it would appear preferable on logical grounds to allow claims in such circumstances under the first branch as damages naturally arising from the seller's breach. Claims based upon basic knowledge and those dependent upon special knowledge do not necessarily present uniform characteristics. Where, from his background knowledge, S is aware of the nature of B's business, the loss naturally resulting from default on S's part would obviously include B's normal loss of profits, whether by using the goods or reselling them, in the course of that business. However, the use of the expression "in the contemplation of the parties" in the second branch of the rule might suggest that something more than knowledge is required.

There is authority to support the proposition that, at least in the case of a carrier,[5] there must be awareness of the special factors together with assent (admittedly this will usually be implied assent) to an assumption of responsibility to see that the consequences, arising from these factors, of a failure to perform the contract are avoided or that compensation will be paid in respect of these consequences if the contract is not duly performed. It would seem logical that,

---

1 [1927] 2 K.B. 535; [1927] All E.R. Rep. 692.
2 [1927] 2 K.B. 535, at p. 538; [1927] All E.R. Rep. 692, at p. 693.
3 [1969] 1 A.C. 350, at p. 416; [1967] 3 All E.R. 686, at p. 712.
4 [1949] 2 K.B. 528; [1949] 1 All E.R. 997.
5 Notably *British Colombia Saw-Mill Co.* v. *Nettleship* (1868) L.R. 3 C.P. 499. Indeed BOVILL, C.J., expressly distinguished between the position of a carrier and that of a manufacturer of goods: "It is to be observed that the defendant is a carrier, and not a manufacturer of goods supplied for a particular purpose. The extent of the carrier's liability is to be governed by the contract he has entered into, and the obligations which the law imposes upon him. He is not to be made liable for damages beyond what may fairly be presumed to have been contemplated by the parties at the time of entering into the contract" (at pp. 505–6); see also at pp. 508–9, *per* WILLES, J.

in contracts of sale, a less stringent test should be applied.[1] Indeed in a variety
of cases the language of the judges has tended towards the use of such expressions
as "natural consequences" even where some basic or special knowledge is
involved.[2] It can also be pointed out in support of this view that Chalmers in
drafting the Act must have regarded the first branch of the rule in *Hadley* v.
Baxendale as of wide and general application to contracts of sale because it was
inserted in ss. 50, 51 and 53. In contrast, the second branch was apparently
regarded of such minor significance that it was relegated to a general provision
covering interest, special damages and the recovery of money paid for a consideration that has totally failed (s. 54).

iv Consequential losses

The point has already been made that the rule that the damages are to be
assessed by reference to the market price of goods at the date when the goods
should have been delivered can place the buyer in a position of some difficulty.
Strictly applied, this rule gives him no time to decide what course to adopt
for the best: he is obliged to make up his mind immediately on whether he
should buy alternative goods. Furthermore, this very question may conceal
an additional problem to that of economic or practical judgment, namely whether
there is a market in goods corresponding sufficiently to those he is to supply to
his own purchaser. Indeed, if the goods are not sufficiently identical he has to
choose between buying goods at a higher cost or perhaps buying goods and
having them rendered suitable for his own purchaser; defaulting on the sub-
sale and compensating his purchaser; and perhaps even defending any legal
action that might be brought against him.

In all cases, provided the buyer acts reasonably, he will be able to recoup his
losses from his seller. In *Hinde* v. *Liddell*,[3] S contracted to supply B with 2,000
pieces of grey shirtings, delivery to be made on October 20. When, shortly
before that date, S informed B that he could not supply the goods in time, B
attempted to obtain the goods elsewhere. As such shirtings were only made to
special order, it was not possible for him to obtain goods of identical quality.
However, B was able to procure 2,000 pieces of a better grade material at a
higher price. It was held that B was entitled to recover the additional expense
which he had incurred. As COCKBURN, C.J., commented, the "course the
plaintiff pursued was right and reasonable; he would have had to pay larger
damages had he not fulfilled his contract"; what he did "was the best for all
parties".[4]

This statement of the law may be amplified by reference to the Australian
case of *Hasell* v. *Bagot, Shakes and Lewis*.[5] The High Court held that B was

---

1 See the deliberate shift from an implied undertaking to pay damages in default to
  liability based upon knowledge in *Hydraulic Engineering Co., Ltd.* v. *McHaffie* (1878),
  4 Q.B.D. 670.
2 *Grébert-Borgnis* v. *Nugent* (1885), 15 Q.B.D. 85, at pp. 90, 93; *Cory* v. *Thames Ironworks Co.* (1868), L.R. 3 Q.B. 181, at pp. 191–2; *Victoria Laundry (Windsor), Ltd.*
  v. *Newman Industries, Ltd.*, [1949] 2 K.B. 528, at p. 539; [1949] 1 All E.R. 997, at p.
  1005.
3 (1875), L.R. 10 Q.B. 265.
4 At p. 268.
5 (1911), 13 C.L.R. 374.

justified in ordering a large amount of superphosphates at a higher price to be delivered to Port Adelaide where there was no market in which he could make up the deficiencies arising from S's default. GRIFFITH, C.J., stated[2] that it was for a court to "ascertain what a reasonable man, acting sensibly on his own behalf and at his own risk, would be willing to pay in order to get the goods at the place and at the time stipulated. The amount is to be ascertained by taking the price at the place of manufacture or other source, together with the cost of carriage and a reasonable sum for the profit of the importer".

The principle illustrated by these cases is equally applicable to situations in which the buyer is obliged, because of the absence of equivalent goods, to purchase more expensive goods to satisfy his own needs rather than the requirements of his own customers. In seeking alternative goods the pressure on the buyer to find them stems from the need to obtain them in time to fulfil his sub-contracts. It is easier therefore for him to show that the more expensive quality was all that was available in the period available. However, the existence of sub-sales is not the only reason that can create for the buyer an immediate need for the goods in question, or at least for some similar to them. If the running of a factory is dependent upon a continuous supply of fuel being available default by a supplier can soon create a position of some urgency in which the buyer may be obliged to choose between opting for a more expensive type of fuel or of shutting down his factory. It would be reasonable in such a situation to decide to purchase the more expensive fuel and to seek redress from the defaulting supplier.

On the basis of what a reasonable and prudent business man might do, the buyer might even be able to persuade a court that the defaulting seller should bear the costs of the buyer setting up his own source of supply. Suppose the main supplier of a dairy decided, in breach of his contract, to discontinue providing the dairy with milk. The dairy is quite unable to obtain alternative sources sufficient to meet the entire shortfall in milk supplies. However, the dairy is able to continue in business by taking such milk as it can obtain from those other sources, and by setting up its own small scale dairy farm. Would the dairy be able to recover its expenses in setting up and operating the dairy farm?

The issue was raised in the difficult case of *Erie County Natural Gas and Fuel Co., Ltd.* v. *Carroll.*[2] B held a number of "leases" which entitled him to sink wells to tap quantities of natural gas. He assigned these leases to S under a contract whereby S undertook to supply B with all the gas he required for working his quarrying and lime works. S later re-assigned the leases to T. T refused to supply B with any gas. The Judicial Committee, having held that S and T were bound in turn to supply B, then went on to consider the assessment of damages. Unable to obtain gas from any alternative source, and with the prospect of litigation continuing to drag on, B had obtained new leases, drilled wells, and established the plant necessary to supply his works. The overall cost had been a little over $58,000. Subsequently B sold his entire business

---

1 At p. 381; citing *O'Hanlan* v. *Great Western Rail. Co.* (1865), 6 B & S. 484.
2 [1911] A.C. 105.

properties in North America for $225,000, $75,000 of which represented the price of his oil wells and plant. The Judicial Committee had no hesitation in accepting that the expenditure of the $58,000 was a reasonable means of obtaining substituted performance: the buyers

> "chose to perform on behalf of the defendants, in a reasonable way, that contract for them and to obtain from an independent source a sufficient quantity of gas, similar as near as might be in character and quality to that which they were entitled to receive. In such cases it is well established that the measure of damages is the cost of procuring the substituted article . . ."[1]

However,

> "if the defendants are to pay for the cost of making those works and of thereby supplying the plaintiffs with the gas the works produced they must get credit for the sum for which these works, after having supplied the gas, were sold . . ."[2]

To an extent one can accept this decision even though it was based upon the over-simplified view that the plaintiffs

> "have got the substituted article, identical in description and quality, have used it, and have failed to show that it has not in the result been obtained by them free of cost".[3]

However, a situation of this type requires more detailed analysis. In order to obtain a commodity to be consumed in his works, B had become involved in capital expenditure and obtained therefore a capital asset. It would seem reasonable that B would only be entitled to recover compensation in respect of the capital he had tied up in the venture to the extent that his overall expenditure exceeded the value of his asset. In this case, clearly the value of his works exceeded his outlay.[4] However, the asset value would seem to be totally irrelevant to the production costs. As B produced gas for use solely in his works, he could clearly recover the amount by which those costs (as representing the price he was paying for the gas from an alternative supplier) exceeded the price provided for in his contract with S. To such an amount B should have been entitled without any question of his having to account for the profit he made when he realised his capital asset.[5] On the facts of the case the Judicial Committee was only correct in awarding nominal damages in so far as B had not shown that he had suffered any loss.

Where B is not able to fulfil his sub-contracts he will be entitled both to loss of profits and to costs incurred in compensating his purchaser. In *Grébert-*

---

1 At p. 117.
2 At p. 119.
3 *Ibid.*
4 It is in any case difficult to estimate how far an asset, the value of which may have increased with inflation, can be regarded as providing a "profit" on resale. Today the position is further complicated by liability to capital gains tax (which also makes no "allowance" for inflation).
5 If one reads too much into the decision a buyer in B's position could increase his entitlement to damages by setting up the gas producing concern as a separate legal entity so that it could then sell the gas to B. If the price was high enough, B would be entitled to recover the difference between this and the contract price.

Borgnis v. *Nugent*,[1] B approached S about some sheepskins which he (B) required to fulfil a contract he was making with a customer in Paris. Subsequently, S and B entered into a contract whereby S agreed to supply 243 black and white skins of a variety of specified sizes. S only supplied 42 skins. As there was no market in which B could acquire alternative skins he defaulted on his contract with his French customer. The latter recovered £28 damages against B in proceedings before a French court. It was held that B was entitled to recover this sum, in addition to his loss of profit, as a reasonable estimate[2] of his liability to his customer.

As long as the buyer acts reasonably, he is under no obligation to defend proceedings that might be taken or threatened against him for failure to perform a sub-sale. In *Elbinger A.-G.* v. *Armstrong*[3], the payment of damages stipulated in the contract was upheld, but even if the damages are agreed after the breach has occurred, providing they are reasonable, the buyer can recover them from his seller. In *Australian Fruit and Produce Co., Ltd.* v. *Terry Pty. Ltd.*,[4] B agreed to purchase all S's Crofton apples grown in the season, an estimated total of 1,500 cases. As S knew, B intended to resell them. S delivered 50 cases, but then refused to deliver the remainder of his crop. B claimed for the loss of profit on the cases S refused to deliver, and the damages of 1s. 6d. per case he had agreed to pay his customer. The Tasmanian court held S liable. In answering the question, should B have resisted the claim of 1s. 6d. per case or have conceded it, CRISP, J., suggested that all depended on the circumstances:

> "When a claim is made by a sub-purchaser, the plaintiffs have to act reasonably: in some cases they should defend, in others, perhaps wisely, not. The test is, in taking the stand they did, whether defending or not, did they act reasonably?"[5]

In this case, B, with his intimate knowledge of the market, was satisfied that the claim was fair and that to litigate it would be to put someone to unnecessary, even considerable, expense.

v Anticipatory breach

a *The general principle*

By s. 51 (3) damages are to be assessed by reference to the "market or current price of the goods at the time or times when they ought to have been delivered, or, if no time was fixed, then at the time of the refusal to deliver". However, this principle is subject to modification in cases of what is termed an "anticipatory breach of contract". This expression is used to described the situation that

---

1 (1885), 15 Q.B.D. 85.
2 A chauvinistic attitude towards a foreign court of competent jurisdiction: it springs in part from the view adopted in *Elbinger A.-G.* v. *Armstrong* (1874), L.R. 9 Q.B. 473, that a penalty incurred, though not recoverable directly by B (see *Borries* v. *Hutchinson* (1865), 18 C.B.N.S. 445), could be accepted as equivalent to a reasonable estimate of the probable liability of B to damages by reason of the breach occasioned by S's default.
3 See above n. 2. The penalties, having been held a reasonable estimate of B's loss, must really be classified as agreed damages.
4 (1934), 29 Tas. L.R. 102.
5 At p. 103, citing *Hammond* v. *Bussey* (1887), 20 Q.B.D. 79.

arises where, before the time of performance, one party notifies the other of his intention not to perform their contract. The party thus notified has the choice between accepting the repudiation there and then, or of accepting it at some later stage before performance is due, or of leaving the contract open until the date for performance.[1] Only if the repudiation is accepted is there an "anticipatory breach".

Immediately the repudiation is accepted, the buyer is entitled to bring his action against the seller (indeed, on occasion, the commencement of proceedings is the evidence that the repudiation has been accepted[2]). In theory, he is entitled to claim as damages the difference between the contract price and the market price at the time when the goods ought to have been delivered. If the latter price is no more, or even less, than the former, then no damages are recoverable.

In *Millett* v. *Van Heeck and Co.*,[3] S and B entered into a number of contracts during 1916 for the export of cotton waste to Holland. In January, 1917, the export of cotton waste was prohibited, but the parties agreed to keep their contracts open until the export ban was removed. In August, 1918, S decided that he no longer wished to be bound by the agreement and notified his intentions to B. In October, 1918, B accepted this repudiation. In mid-January, 1919, the embargo was lifted. At the time when S refused to deliver the goods, there was a substantial difference between the market price and the contract price, but by early 1919, when it finally became possible to perform the contract, the market price had dropped considerably. Hence, the question whether B was entitled to substantial or only to nominal damages depended upon whether they were to be assessed as at August, 1918, or early 1919.

As no time was fixed by the contract, s. 51 (3), on the face of it, laid down the time of refusal to deliver as the appropriate date, i.e. August, 1918, for the calculation of damages. However, the Court of Appeal, affirming the decision of the Divisional Court, held that the section did not apply to cases of anticipatory breach. It was "beyond controversy" that

> "if a contract is made for the sale of goods deliverable in the future by specified instalments at specified dates, and before the time has arrived for performance the contract is repudiated, and the repudiation is accepted, the damages have to be measured in reference to the dates on which the contract ought to have been performed".[4]

And it made no difference to this principle that the contract provided for delivery over a reasonable time as opposed to a specified time. To read s. 51 (3) in this way, ATKIN, L.J., continued,[5]

> "would introduce an anomaly entirely without any kind of principle to justify it. I am satisfied that the code never intended to make that distinction, or to vary what was the rule of law at the time when it was passed ... namely, that the damages are to be fixed in reference to the time for performance".

---

1 For a leading statement of principle, see *Frost* v. *Knight* (1872), L.R. 7 Ex. 111, at pp. 112–3.
2 See *Roth & Co.* v. *Taysen, Townsend & Co. and Grant & Co.* (1895), 73 L.T. 628, dealt with below, p. 322.
3 [1921] 2 K.B. 369; affirming [1920] 3 K.B. 535.
4 [1921] 2 K.B. 369, at pp. 376–7, *per* ATKIN, L.J.
5 [1921] 2 K.B. 369, at p. 377.

b *Mitigation of damages*

While application of this principle appears straightforward enough, in fact the position is rendered more complex by the need on the part of the buyer to mitigate damages. Once he accepts the repudiation so that the breach is established, the buyer cannot sit idly by while the market price of the goods rises: he must go into the market and purchase replacement goods.[1] The hypothesis to be deduced from this situation is that the unfortunate buyer cannot obtain substantial damages for non-delivery unless the market price was higher than the contract price when the repudiation was accepted and remained higher until the date when delivery was due. If the market price of the goods was rising, then the buyer cannot obtain the advantage of the higher price prevailing at the date the goods were to be delivered because of his duty to minimise his losses.

It need hardly be said that, as with the normal breach by non-delivery when the damages are fixed at that date and the buyer thus has to make a quick decision whether to buy or to risk a rise in price, the buyer is placed in a difficult position. Indeed his wisest step is probably not to accept the repudiation until he has a good idea which way the market is going and is also in a position to buy at short notice if necessary. But what if, despite his careful calculations, he buys on what appears to be a rising market, but, before the time for performance, the market falls?

There is no clear authority on this point because the matter has never come up for decision. In *Melachrino* v. *Nickoll and Knight*,[2] the court was dealing with a case in which, on the day when S repudiated and B accepted the repudiation, the market price was above the contract price, but, during the period of expected delivery, the market price was below the contract price. In awarding only nominal damages, BAILHACHE, J., made the point that the damages

> "must be assessed with reference to the market price of the goods at the time when they ought to have been delivered under the contract .... To this rule there is one exception for the benefit of the defaulting seller—namely, that if he can show that the buyer acted unreasonably in not buying against him the date to be taken is the date at which the buyer ought to have gone into the market to mitigate damages".[3]

As a corollary, therefore, as long as the buyer can show he acted reasonably, his claim should succeed.

vi Remedies of the buyer in relation to the goods themselves

In cases of non-delivery, the buyer may have two additional, though rarely used, remedies related to his rights in the goods.

a *Specific performance*

First, he may wish to obtain a decree of specific performance. Although doubt

---

1 Cases illustrating the reverse situation where the buyer is in breach and the seller accepts the repudiation and is therefore obliged to sell as soon as possible in a falling market are dealt with below, p. 322.
2 [1920] 1 K.B. 693; [1918–19] All E.R. Rep. 857.
3 [1920] 1 K.B. 693 at p. 699; [1918–19] All E.R. Rep. 857, at p. 859.

exists as to the continued availability of equitable remedies under the Sale of Goods Act,[1] specific performance is expressly covered by s. 52:

> "If any action for breach of contract to deliver specific or ascertained goods the court may, if it thinks fit, on the application of the plaintiff, by its judgment or decree direct that the contract shall be performed specifically, without giving the defendant the option of retaining the goods on payment of damages. The judgment or decree may be unconditional, or upon such terms and conditions as to damages, payment of the price, and otherwise, as to the court may seem just, and the application by the plaintiff may be made at any time before judgment or decree."

If the goods are unique or of special value to the buyer, or if damages would no be an adequate remedy, an application for specific performance may be successful.

b *Claims in tort*

In cases of non-delivery in which property has passed the buyer may well have an alternative claim in detinue or conversion. The question that must be considered is whether damages may be recoverable in tort that are not recoverable in contract.

The only case directly in point is that of *The Arpad*,[2] in which a shipowner carried 1,000 tons of wheat in such a way that it became intermingled with barley with the result that he was unable to deliver 47 tons at all. In assessing damages, a majority of the Court of Appeal held that, whether the claim was for breach of contract or in tort, the existence of sub-contracts by S, news of which had not been communicated to the carrier, was a factor that should be excluded from consideration.

It is not too easy to assess how far this decision is conclusive, There was a strong dissenting judgment by SCRUTTON, L.J., who was of opinion that[3]

> "the damages in conversion should be the value to the purchaser or goods owner at the time of the conversion. If there is a market in which he can buy, this will fix the value; if there is no market, it may be determined by the goods owners' contract with a solvent purchaser, for that is what he has in fact lost by the conversion".

In addition, there are a number of subsequent developments which create cross-currents that tend to obscure the position. For example, the House of Lords has emphatically stated that, while damages in contract are based upon circumstances within the contemplation of the parties, a tortfeasor may be liable for unusual but foreseeable damage resulting from his wrongful act or omission.[4] On the other hand, there has been an increasing tendency on the part of the courts to allow claims in respect of loss of profit on sub-sales even in the absence of specific knowledge on the part of the seller, and even of the carrier. Indeed the following passage from SCRUTTON, L.J.'s judgment in *The Arpad:*[5]

---

1 See above, p. 260.
2 [1934] P. 189; [1934] All E.R. Rep. 326.
3 [1934] P. 189, at p. 205; [1934] All E.R. Rep. 326, at p. 332.
4 *Koufos* v. *Czarnikow*, [1969] 1 A.C. 350; [1967] 3 All E.R. 686.
5 [1934] P. 189, at p. 203; [1934] All E.R. Rep. 326, at p. 331.

> "In contracts of carriage from wheat-producing districts, it is always so probable that the shipper is sending for re-sale, or for sale to a person who will resell, that the carrier will be liable if there is no market, for the effect on a contract of sale of his conversion or unjustifiable failure to deliver"

was expressly[1] or implicitly[2] approved by the House of Lords in *The Heron II*.

It may be therefore that, even if the damages recoverable in tort are theoretically wider than in contract, in practical terms there is no difference in the case of non-delivery of goods under a contract of sale or carriage. An action in tort would only be of value if it were necessary to proceed against some third party for interfering with the buyer's goods.

vii Money had and received

Section 54, which deals with the right of the parties to recover special damages, also mentions the right "to recover money paid where the consideration for the payment of it has failed". It will be recalled that a buyer of goods to which the seller had no title is entitled to recover the purchase price on this basis.[3] Similarly, if a buyer has paid for goods which the seller fails to deliver, he will be entitled to recover the price paid.

B. DAMAGES FOR BREACH OF CONDITION OR WARRANTY

The remedy for breach of the terms of the contract relating to goods actually delivered and accepted is covered by s. 53 (1):

> "Where there is a breach of warranty by the seller, or where the buyer elects, or is compelled, to treat any breach of a condition on the part of the seller as a breach of warranty, the buyer is not by reason only of such breach of warranty entitled to reject the goods, but he may
>
> (*a*) set up against the seller the breach of warranty in diminution or extinction of the price; or
> (*b*) maintain an action against the seller for damages for the breach of warranty."

As has already been mentioned, s. 53 (2) then goes on to prescribe the first rule in *Hadley* v. *Baxendale*[4] as the primary principle for the assessment of damages:

> "The measure of damages for breach of warranty is the estimated loss directly and naturally resulting, in the ordinary course of events, from the breach of warranty."

i Breach of warranties as to quality, fitness, etc.

However, leaving aside cases of late delivery which form a distinct category,

---

1 *Per* Lord MORRIS, [1969] 1 A.C. 350, at p. 406; [1967] 3 All E.R. 686, at p. 705.
2 In this case it was held that a carrier was liable for loss of profits suffered by an owner of goods through late delivery of a cargo of sugar at Basrah where the carrier knew there was a market in sugar.
3 See above, p. 167.
4 (1854), 9 Exch. 341; [1843–60] All E.R. Rep. 461.

the majority of instances of action for damages in respect of breaches of condition/
warranty relate to the quality, fitness or description of goods. To these cases,
s. 53 (3) applies an additional principle:

> "In the case of breach of warranty of quality such loss is *prima facie* the
> difference betwen the value of the goods at the time of delivery to the buyer
> and the value they would have had if they had answered to the warranty."

a *The value of the goods contracted for*

This division of the value between the goods as they should have been and
the goods as they actually were creates problems of some difficulty for the
courts. Taking the position as it should have been, either party can point
to the contract price as evidence of the value of the goods, but it will by no
means be regarded as conclusive. Much will depend upon the timing. Obviously
the contract price will be of little assistance if it can be shown that the market
has fallen before the time of performance.[1]

b *The value of the goods actually delivered*

Where the greatest problems will usually be experienced will be in estimating
the value of the goods in their defective condition. In *Biggin & Co., Ltd.* v.
Permanite, Ltd.,[2] a manufacturer had prepared a bitumen adhesive for use
with roofing felt. This preparation was transferred under a number of transactions and used in Holland. Within a few months the substance proved unsatisfactory. DEVLIN, J., posed the dilemma as follows:[3]

> "It seems to me that one can very rarely arrive at an accurate figure of unsound
> value. Where the breach is non-delivery, there is often a market price which
> can be quoted, or evidence can be given of the price at which at the relevant
> date similar goods were changing hands, but there is rarely any market price
> for damaged goods, since their value depends on the extent of the damage.
> If the actual damaged goods are sold with all faults, good evidence can be
> obtained of the difference in value, but such a sale is not always possible, and
> a claim for substantial damages cannot be limited to goods which have been
> sold."

In this case, there had been no sale against which to estimate the difference in
value, although a similar Dutch product had been marketed at a much lower
price 18 months later. This price DEVLIN, J., regarded as irrelevant because in
early 1945 the need for such a preparation had been desperate. Indeed, had
the defect been known, the main disadvantage of the preparation could have
been guarded against or reduced in use. Accordingly, these being very abnormal
times, even the defective material could have commanded a "respectable
price".[4]

---

1 *Loder* v. *Kekule* (1857), 3 C.B.N.S. 128.
2 [1951] 1 K.B. 422; [1950] 2 All E.R. 859; rev. on other grounds, [1951] 2 K.B. 314;
  [1951] 2 All E.R. 191.
3 [1951] 1 K.B. 422, at p. 438; [1950] 2 All E.R. 859, at p. 870.
4 [1951] 1 K.B. 422, at p. 439; [1950] 2 All E.R. 859, at p. 871.

Some caution is needed in approaching Devlin, J's reference to a sale of the defective goods as putting a value on them because, as his own subsequent comments about the later price of the similar Dutch preparation demonstrate, all depends upon the circumstances. If the market price alters, this factor should not affect the normal measure of damages to which the buyer is entitled. In *Jones* v. *Just*,[1] the market rose so that B was able to resell inferior hemp for very nearly the invoice price of the goods, though the sale price was only three-quarters of what he would have obtained if he had been selling the higher quality hemp he had bargained for. The Court of Queen's Bench upheld Blackburn, J.'s direction that B was entitled to the difference between the invoice price and the price at which he could have sold the higher quality hemp if he had received the same.

An even more striking development of this principle may be foreshadowed by *Slater* v. *Hoyle and Smith*.[2] S had agreed to supply B with 3,000 pieces of unbleached cotton at a price of nearly 1s. a yard. 1,625 pieces were delivered but B refused to take the remaining 1,375 pieces because of the poor quality of the earlier goods. It was held that B had been entitled to take this step. When it came to assessing damages in respect of the defective 1,625, Greer, J., held that the basis of the calculation was the difference between the contract price of approximately 1s. per yard and his estimate of the worth of the cloth actually delivered, namely $7\frac{1}{2}$d. per yard: no allowance could be made for the fact that B had managed to sell 691 pieces as bleached cotton at $8\frac{1}{2}$d. per yard.

In upholding this decision a majority of the Court of Appeal cast doubt on *Wertheim* v. *Chicoutimi Pulp Co.*,[3] and held that it applied to bring into account a sub-sale, if at all, only when the sale is of the identical article, which was not the case here. But if there is a sub-sale of the identical goods, perhaps with the knowledge of the original seller, can the buyer claim damages when he has achieved what he set out to do, namely satisfied his own sub-contract? To this question, Scrutton, L.J., had an emphatic answer:[4]

> "If the buyer is lucky enough, for reasons with which the seller has nothing to do, to get his goods through on the sub-contract without a claim against him, this on principle cannot affect his claim against the seller."

This dictum is acceptable up to a point, but it would seem that, in the same way as a sub-contract may affect damages for non-delivery where the transaction is based upon the same bill of lading being transferred in a chain of transfers,[5] so the fact that the ultimate buyer in such a chain has accepted the goods in performance of the contract should prevent a previous holder from suing in respect of any defect in the goods. Once that exception is established it may be less easy to assert so categorically that other sub-contracts in the contemplation of the parties are to be disregarded when the sub-purchaser has accepted the

---

1 (1868), L.R. 3 Q.B. 197.
2 [1920] 2 K.B. 11.
3 [1911] A.C. 301; see below, p. 289.
4 [1920] 2 K.B., at p. 23.
5 *Re R. & H. Hall Ltd. & W. H. Pim (jnr.) & Co.'s Arbitration* (1928), 33 Com. Cas. 324; [1928] All E.R. Rep. 763.

goods under a contract in terms substantially the same as those operating between S and B.

If one does exclude in most cases the existence of resales even as evidence of the value of the defective goods, the judges are then obliged to assess the difference as best they can.[1] Similar difficulty was experienced in *Biggin & Co Ltd.* v. *Permanite, Ltd.*[2] as has already been discussed, but in more common situations the commercial court should call in aid whatever professional expertise is available. As DEVLIN, J., said in that case:[3]

> "It is a common practice in the commercial world to deal with this type of case by way of a price allowance, and claims for damaged goods are constantly met to the satisfaction of both parties by the fixing of an allowance by an adjuster or some person skilled in the trade. I think that that is a method which can legitimately be followed by the court where no more precise method of calculation presents itself."

ii Other losses

With regard to consequential losses from defective goods and to damages stemming from breaches other than those relating to conditions/warranties as to quality, fitness, etc. the position falls back on s. 53 (2), subject to any additional losses that may have been within the parties' contemplation under the second branch of *Hadley* v. *Baxendale* preserved by s. 54.

On the whole breaches of other terms than those relating to quality have not occasioned any great difficulty whether the warranty has been implied[4] or express. In *Lloyds and Scottish Finance, Ltd.* v. *Modern Cars and Caravans (Kingston), Ltd.*,[5] S sold a caravan to B not realising that an execution warrant had been issued and a possession order placed on it. B hired out the van under a hire-purchase agreement. When the van was seized by the sheriff, B recovered from S the price of the caravan and the costs incurred. S had been in breach both of the warranties implied by s. 12 and of an express warranty that the caravan was his sole and unencumbered property.

Consequential losses will include the costs and expenses reasonably incurred in testing the likely success of, if not defending, legal proceedings. In the *Lloyds and Scottish Finance* case just mentioned, B was held entitled to recover his solicitor's costs and the various other expenses arising out of the need to ascertain the true position. Similarly, it may be reasonable for the buyer to defend proceedings, though it would not be unreasonable for him to compromise a suit on counsel's advice. In *Biggin & Co., Ltd.* v. *Permanite, Ltd.*, the Dutch government, on whose behalf B had placed the order for the adhesive,

---

1 In *Slater* v. *Hoyle and Smith*, [1920] 2 K.B. 11, at p. 19, SCRUTTON, L.J., referred to GREER, J.'s methods of assessment as "no doubt somewhat rough and conjectural" but that was no basis upon which it could be disturbed if, as it was, it was based on the application of the correct principle.
2 [1951] 1 K.B. 422; [1950] 2 All E.R. 859.
3 [1951] 1 K.B., at p. 439; [1950] 2 All E.R., at p. 871.
4 E.g. the damages awarded for breach of the warranty of quiet enjoyment under s. 12 in *Mason* v. *Burningham* [1949] 2 K.B. 545; [1949] 2 All E.R. 134; see above, p. 171.
5 [1966] 1 Q.B. 764; [1964] 2 All E.R. 732.

had withheld £55,000 because of the unsatisfactory results achieved with it. The matter was referred to arbitration but, on legal advice, B settled on the first day of the hearing. The Court of Appeal,[1] reversing the decision of DEVLIN, J., on this point, held that, although the settlement in this case gave a figure at the upper limit, providing it was reasonable, it should be taken as the measure of damages. It would seem that the onus is upon the buyer to show that the settlement was reasonable. In this case, he was helped by the facts that he acted on legal advice and that the settlement had the effect of reducing the costs of what could have been an expensive and intricate arbitration.

Where there has been a defect in quality the consequential losses can include actual physical damage to the buyer or his possessions. If the seller delivers an animal feed or an ingredient for an animal feed that is toxic, the loss of life to animals or birds is a direct and natural result in the ordinary course of events of the breach.[2] Similarly, if coal is delivered which, when put on the fire, explodes, the seller is liable for the damage to the house and its contents;[3] or, as happened in one Australian case,[4] if a diseased cow is sold, warranted free of defects, S will be liable for consequent losses to B's herd.

C LATE DELIVERY

Where the breach of the contract of sale takes the form of a late delivery, the buyer will often have two choices open to him. He can in most cases reject the goods, because, as was discussed earlier,[5] in most commercial transactions the time of delivery will be regarded as of the essence unless there is evidence from the contract or the circumstances suggesting otherwise. If he does decide to reject, the situation is in effect one of non-delivery. If he accepts delivery, however, the position is more closely akin to a normal case of breach of warranty.

i Application of the rules in Hadley v. Baxendale

In relation to consequential losses, there is not a great deal of difference between the different types of breach all of which are covered by the two branches of the rule in *Hadley* v. *Baxendale*. In fact, *Victoria Laundry (Windsor), Ltd.* v. *Newman Industries, Ltd.*,[6] which was used to illustrate the application of the *Hadley* v. *Baxendale* principles, was itself a case of late delivery.

Similarly, in *Cory* v. *Thames Ironworks and Shipbuilding Co., Ltd.*,[7] S was building the hull of a floating boom derrick for a firm that became insolvent. B agreed to purchase the hull when it was completed; S was allowed to sell

---

1 [1951] 2 K.B. 314; [1951] 2 All E.R. 191 (C.A.), reversing [1951] 1 K.B. 422; [1950] 2 All E.R. 859 (K.B.D.).
2 *Hardwick Game Farm* v. *Suffolk Agricultural and Poultry Producers Association Ltd.*, [1966] 1 All E.R. 309; affirmed in part *sub. nom. Henry Kendall & Sons* v. *William Lillico & Sons, Ltd.*, [1969] 2 A.C. 31; [1968] 2 All E.R. 444; see above, p. 190.
3 *Wilson* v. *Rickett Cockerell & Co., Ltd.*, [1954] 1 Q.B. 598; [1954] 1 All E.R. 868.
4 *Dempster* v. *Simpson* (1904), 7 W.A.L.R. 103.
5 Above, p. 165.
6 [1949] 2 K.B. 528; [1949] 1 All E.R. 997; above p. 273.
7 (1868), L.R. 3 Q.B. 181.

off the lifting equipment already fitted into the hull. S knew that B wanted the hull for use in his business as a coal merchant operating from wharves on the Thames and assumed that B's intention was to use it for storage purposes. In fact B wanted the hull to refit with his own machinery to use for the novel purpose of a floating crane to off-load cargoes from colliers into barges without the need of an intermediate stage of taking the coal ashore. The existing equipment in the hull was so difficult to remove that S was unable to deliver until six months after the stipulated date. As a consequence the machinery for the hull had to be paid for although it could not be fitted, and two additional steam tugs which B had purchased to tow the cranes and the barges were virtually unemployed for the period in question. However, the Court of Queen's Bench held that the loss of profits from the use of the hull as a floating crane and from the underemployment of the tugs were not matters within S's contemplation at the time of the contract. The extent of his liability was limited by the loss arising from the obvious manner in which the hull was to be employed, namely as a storage place for coal.

What this decision left open was what would have been the case had the hull had no obvious use. The Court suggested that, if there had been more than one normal use, B's damages would not necessarily have been limited by the fact that S was contemplating (in the absence of anything in the contract or to be deduced from the circumstances establishing that use rather than the other) the use other than that to which B put the goods. In this case the hull had originally been designed to hold heavy machinery to lift sunken vessels, a novel enough use in itself. B purchased the hull to take different heavy machinery to lift cargoes of coal, an equally novel purpose. If S had not been able to convince the arbitrator that the most obvious use in B's trade of a hull designed to support heavy equipment was that of a coal store, the court would have been faced with the problem of deciding what losses did arise naturally from the late delivery. It may be that, in this exceptional type of situation, where there is no obviously apparent purpose, B's special purpose provides the criterion against which damages are to be assessed.

In short, where the goods have an obvious or apparent purpose, B must make clear to S what his special purpose might be in order to fix S with liability for the additional losses arising. Where there is a range of purposes, or no obvious purpose at all, then B's use of the goods for one of the former purposes, or for a special purpose in the latter situation, will establish the measure of damages. If S is not sure what B intends to do with the goods because no purpose is apparent, then he should enquire further; otherwise B's special purpose might well be regarded as the basis for the assessment of damages naturally arising as a result of the breach. What would not have been recoverable under the second branch of the rule in *Hadley* v. *Baxendale* because of S's lack of knowledge of B's purpose would, in the absence of any obvious or apparent purpose to which S could point, become the basis of an award under the first branch of the rule.

Where there is an available market in the goods then, subject to additional consequential losses, the normal measure of damages will theoretically be the difference between the market price of the goods when they should have been delivered in accordance with the contract, and their market value at the time of actual delivery.[1] In practice, this situation seems rarely to have arisen. It may be that, faced with a possible loss, buyers will tend to reject the goods rather than risking possible difficulty in recouping their losses from their sellers.[2] The principal incentives to the buyer not to reject will be where the market price is comparatively high when the goods are delivered to him, or where he is still able to fulfil existing sub-contracts with the goods.

ii Effect of sub-sales

Because of these practical considerations, late delivery, while having many features in common with non-delivery and breach of warranty cases, may be quite distinctive when it comes to dealing with the effect of sub-sales. A widely held view[3] seems to be that this distinction should not be drawn and that the principal case which supports it is wrongly decided.

In that case, *Wertheim* v. *Chicoutimi Pulp Co.*,[4] S contracted to deliver to B 3,000 tons of moist wood pulp f.o.b. between September 1 and November 1 1900, at a price of approximately 25s. per ton. B's costs in arranging carriage for the goods to Manchester, their ultimate destination,[5] were about 13s. per ton. The price of pulp in Manchester during the expected delivery period was around 70s. per ton, though when the goods were actually delivered, it had fallen to 42s. 6d. per ton. However, B was able to deliver the pulp under a number of sub-contracts, made both before and after the contract with S, at 65s. per ton. The total cost of the goods to B was rightly disregarded. Being a case of actual, though late, delivery B did receive some benefit from having goods worth more than the cost to himself. The vital question was what benefit had he lost as a consequence of the delay. In answering this the Judicial Committee was in agreement with the Quebec Court of King's Bench: the actual loss had clearly been 5s. a ton, i.e. the difference between the market price when the goods should have been delivered and the price B actually obtained for the goods.

The criticism that has been levelled at this decision does not take account of the realities of international trade. The market price rule is essentially based upon the supposition that goods are re-sold when they are physically delivered into the buyer's possession. If he could expect to receive them in January, the price for such goods then must be placed against the price when delivery

---

1 This proposition was certainly taken as the basis of the reasoning of the Judicial Committee in *Wertheim* v. *Chicoutimi Pulp Co.*, [1911] A.C. 301; [1908–10] All E.R. Rep. 707; on the ground that it normally gave effect to the underlying principle that damages should put the party complaining of a breach in the same position as he would have been in had the contract been properly performed.

2 See *Kwei Tek Chao* v. *British Traders and Shippers, Ltd.*, [1954] 2 Q.B. 459, at p. 479, *per* DEVLIN, J.

3 *McGregor on Damages*, 13th Ed., pp. 414–5, para. 580; Treitel, *The Law of Contract*, 3rd Ed., p. 791; *Atiyah, op. cit.*, p. 298; and *per* SCRUTTON, L.J., in *Slater* v. *Hoyle and Smith*, [1920] 2 K.B. 11, at p. 24.

4 [1911] A.C. 301; [1908–10] All E.R. Rep. 707.

5 The reason why Manchester, and not Quebec, was regarded as the place of delivery was commented upon, [1911] A.C., at p. 316.

actually takes place. The existence of a sub-sale at that time should create no problems, because the price will reflect, and be evidence of, the market value at that time. If, after delivery, the buyer retains the goods before reselling, the ultimate resale price is obviously irrelevant because the buyer is accepting the risk of market fluctuations. He cannot impose liability for his losses on the seller, nor can he be made to account to the seller for any profit he might make on the later transaction. The seller's liability can therefore only be fixed by reference to the prevailing market price.

However, in a large number of cases B's "market" will exist prior to the date of actual physical delivery. He may contract with S to cover existing contractual liabilities to other parties; or he may buy from S with a view to contracting, in advance of delivery, with a number of potential customers. In either situation, the concept of a market price, ascertainable at a particular date or during a particular period of expected delivery, is too unsophisticated for establishing a satisfactory test for the estimate of damages. The defect in *Wertheim* v. *Chicoutini Pulp Co.* is that, operating within the confines of the market price at date of delivery rule, the Judicial Committee advanced not altogether convincing reasons for refusing to apply it. For instance, it was pointed out that the market price was taken at the two relevant times because it represented the value of the goods from which the buyer should have benefited at the time of expected delivery; and the value that the buyer presumably received when they were in fact delivered:

> "but if in fact the purchaser, when he obtains possession of the goods, sells them at a price greatly in advance of the then market value, that presumption is rebutted and the real value of the goods to him is proved by the very fact of this sale to be more than market value, and the loss he sustains must be measured by that price".[1]

Given the restricted meaning of the concept of "market price", the Judicial Committee preferred to hold that it was not applicable in the circumstances. To do this, their Lordships called in aid the less acceptable argument that the loss must be measured against the actual selling price unless the buyer is,

> "against all justice, to be permitted to make a profit by the breach of contract, be compensated for a loss he never suffered, and be put, . . . not in the same position in which he would have been if the contract had been performed, but in a much better position".[2]

It cannot be claimed that the damages recoverable by the disappointed buyer have been marked out by the courts with any real precision or that the present position is to be regarded with any great satisfaction. The rules contained in the 1893 Act are primitive in the light of modern needs. They may cover simple transactions reasonably well (though even then the basic notion of defining a market in which to estimate a price can be a source of difficulty[3]), but the more complex world of international trade demonstrates how inadequate these simplistic rules can be.

---

1 At p. 308.
2 *Ibid.*
   See further, below, p. 318.

In cases of non-delivery the courts have recognised that the available market is not the most helpful criterion. If a specific cargo is resold under contracts the possibility of which was at least within the original seller's contemplation, then the buyer's loss can reasonably be calculated against the resale price. Being a specific source, the goods cannot be obtained on the market.[1]

Yet this measure of reality is still dependent upon demonstrating that the market price is not applicable to the transaction in question. The fault of *Wertheim* v. *Chicoutimi* was that the Judicial Committee tried to operate within the existing fixed rules. The same conclusion could have been reached by extending the time factor involved in establishing a market price. Where goods are being shipped, they are more often resold while they are still at sea than they are resold after unloading takes place. In such circumstances it is the "market price" at the moment of physical delivery that is in most cases irrelevant, rather than the buyer's resale price. In cases of late delivery, therefore, if the buyer has effectively resold the goods under contracts that are not affected by the delay, there is much to be said for the decision of the Privy Council, though not of the ultimate reasoning upon which it was based.

---

1 *R. and H. Hall, Ltd.* v. *W. H. Pim (Junior) & Co., Ltd.* (1928), 33 Com. Cas. 324.

CHAPTER 8

The Remedies of the Seller

1 RIGHTS WITH RESPECT TO THE GOODS THEMSELVES

A seller who has not been paid for the goods is naturally concerned to ensure that he does receive payment. Some protection is afforded by s. 28 which provides that, unless otherwise agreed, "delivery of the goods and payment of the price are concurrent conditions". In other words, the seller is entitled to withhold delivery if the price is not tendered, unless of course the terms of the contract provide otherwise. Section 39 of the Act, however, sets out certain specific powers over the goods to which the unpaid seller is entitled "by implication of law". These are:

  (i) a lien for the price while he is in possession of the goods (s. 39 (1) (*a*)), together with a right, if property has not passed, to withhold delivery (s. 39 (2));
 (ii) a right of stoppage *in transitu* once he has parted with possession, provided the buyer is insolvent (s. 39 (1) (*b*), s. 39 (2)); and
(iii) a right of resale (s. 39 (1) (*c*)).

The provisions of Part IV (i.e. ss. 38–48) do not provide a particularly coherent guide to the state of the law. The powers granted entered the common law from the law merchant, but their development during the nineteenth century was inhibited by the emergence of c.i.f. and f.o.b. contracts as the principal vehicles for contracts of sale that involved international carriage. If payment is due against the shipping documents in c.i.f. contracts, or delivery to the carrier under f.o.b. contracts, the ambit of the powers bestowed by s. 39 is necessarily restricted. When the Act was drafted, therefore, the law was still in a state of flux. Since then, the continued development of the methods whereby international trade is conducted, particularly through the widespread use of banker's commercial credits, has decreased the significance of the seller's rights in rem especially the right of stoppage *in transitu*. The reason for this diminution in the importance of the powers granted by Part IV is that they are designed to protect the unpaid seller as defined by s. 38 (1):

"The seller of goods is deemed to be an 'unpaid seller' within the meaning of this act—

  (*a*) When the whole of the price has not been paid or tendered;
  (*b*) When a bill of exchange or other negotiable instrument has been received as conditional payment, and the condition on which it was

292

received has not been fulfilled by reason of the dishonour of the instrument or otherwise."

The object of the system of banker's commercial credits is that the seller should be able to obtain payment from a bank in his own country on presentation of the shipping documents. This credit is made available to the seller on the instructions of an issuing bank instructed by the buyer. The seller can be sure of payment once his documents are accepted, and the paying bank will receive payment in turn on transmitting the documents to the bank which issued the instructions making available the credit facility to the seller. The final link in the chain is then a matter between the buyer and the issuing bank. It is for the latter to decide whether, and on what terms, to release its security over the documents to the buyer. However, in the context of the present discussion, the important point is that the seller's rights are regulated by the terms of credit made available by the bank and there will be no role for his rights in rem against the goods to play because he will rarely be an "unpaid seller".

It should be noticed that Part IV bestows rights not only upon a seller as understood in the rest of the Act, but also on a variety of persons who stand in a position similar to that of a seller. By s. 38 (2):

> "In this Part of this Act the term 'seller' includes any person who is in the position of a seller, as, for instance, an agent of the seller to whom the bill of lading has been endorsed, or a consignor or agent who has himself paid, or is directly responsible for, the price."

The significant factor is that the person concerned should have a personal interest in the payment of the price by the buyer. In a situation where an overseas seller employs a confirming agent in the United Kingdom, that agent is responsible for the price to his foreign principal and therefore, *vis-à-vis* the buyer, stands in the position of seller. On the other hand, in *J. L. Lyons & Co.* v. *May and Baker, Ltd.*[1], it was held that a buyer who had rejected goods was not covered by s. 38 so that he was not entitled to retain the goods against repayment of the price.

A THE SELLER'S LIEN

i The extent of the lien

The definition of an unpaid seller is amplified in two ways by s. 41. According to s. 41 (1):

> "Subject to the provisions of this Act, the unpaid seller of goods who is in possession of them is entitled to retain possession of them until payment or tender of the price in the following cases, namely:—
> (*a*) Where the goods have been sold without any stipulation as to credit;
> (*b*) Where the goods have been sold on credit, but the term of credit has expired;
> (*c*) Where the buyer becomes insolvent."

---

1 [1923] 1 K.B. 685. It was also held that no lien existed in favour of such a person at common law by analogy with the position of the unpaid seller, though it is difficult to see why a buyer who has paid for goods should not be entitled to retain them against repayment if his power of rejection was rightfully exercised.

In the first place, the two clauses, (*a*) and (*b*), bring out the point that a seller is hardly unpaid for the purposes of exercising rights over the goods as against the buyer if payment is not yet due. Once a period of credit is allowed, until that period expires,[1] the seller cannot demand payment, even though he is under an obligation to deliver during the currency of that period. The allowing of a period of credit is of course the parties' agreement that prevents the operation of s. 28.

Secondly, as far as insolvency is concerned, that term is defined by s. 62 (3) as follows:

> "A person is deemed to be insolvent within the meaning of this Act who either has ceased to pay his debts in the ordinary course of business, or cannot pay his debts as they become due, whether he has committed an act of bankruptcy or not."

In so far as a lien is no more than the right to retain goods or other property until a payment due to the person retaining the property is satisfied, it does not add very much to what is implicit in s. 28. Delivery is conditional on payment, and if payment is not forthcoming when the seller tenders the goods he can withhold them until payment is made. The only aspect of s. 41 (1) which strengthens the seller's position is that, if the buyer becomes insolvent, the seller is entitled to retain the goods even during the currency of a period of credit. In the words of BAYLEY, J., in *Bloxam* v. *Sanders*:[2]

> "The seller's right in respect of the price is not a mere lien which he will forfeit if he parts with possession, but grows out of his original ownership and dominion; and payment or a tender of the price is a condition precedent on the buyer's part, but until he makes such payment or tender, he has no right to the possession. If goods are sold upon credit, and nothing is agreed upon as to the time of delivery of the goods, the vendor is immediately entitled to the possession ... But his right of possession is not absolute; it is liable to be defeated if he becomes insolvent before he obtains possession."

In this respect s. 41 (1) does provide for an extension of the seller's rights over and above those to be implied from s. 28, but s. 41 has not otherwise affected the lien's function, e.g. by allowing it to be employed to enforce payment of storage charges.[3]

According to s. 39, the powers granted by Part IV are exercisable "notwithstanding that the property in the goods may have passed to the buyer". In keeping with this provision, s. 41 (2) states that the seller "may exercise his right of lien notwithstanding that he is in possession of the goods as agent or bailee ... for the buyer". This sub-section, however, covers a wider ground than the position where S, having sold goods, remains in possession pending delivery; it also deals with the totally different situation where the nature of S's

---

1 It can "expire" early in the sense that payment by means of a bill of exchange (e.g. a cheque) is conditional on the bill being honoured. If it is dishonoured, the seller's lien revives: *Valpy* v. *Oakeley* (1851), 16 Q.B. 941.
2 (1825), 4 B. & C. 941, at p. 949.
3 *Somes* v. *British Empire Shipping Co.* (1860), 8 H.L.C. 338; though a buyer might still be liable in damages for charges arising after he has failed to take delivery on time: but see Atiyah, *op. cit.*, p. 247.

possession has changed from seller to that of bailee for reward. In *Grice* v. *Richardson*,[1] upon which s. 41 (2) was in part[2] based, S had imported tea which he placed in his own bonded warehouse. Delivery orders had been made out in favour of B who then became insolvent. It was held by the Judicial Committee that S, although he held goods as warehouseman to B's order, still retained a seller's lien over the goods.

ii Termination of the lien

The lien is terminated in the circumstances encompassed by s. 43 (1):[3]

> "The unpaid seller loses his lien . . .
> (a) When he delivers the goods to a carrier or other bailee . . . for the purpose of transmission to the buyer without reserving the right of disposal of the goods;
> (b) When the buyer or his agent lawfully obtains possession of the goods;
> (c) By waiver thereof."

a *Delivery to a carrier or other bailee*

It will be remembered that delivery to a carrier "is *prima facie* deemed to be a delivery of the goods to the buyer" (s. 32 (1)).[4] Hence delivery to a carrier will normally have the effect of terminating the seller's lien under the general rule stated in s. 43 (1) (b). Delivery to a carrier who is the seller's agent does not affect the position because this is in no way a delivery of the goods *vis-à-vis* the buyer. However, even if it is not possible to establish that the carrier is the seller's agent, so that s. 32 (1) applies, the lien will continue if the seller reserves the right of disposal over the goods. This right of disposal is set out at greater length in s. 19, sub-s. (2) of which gives the most obvious example of a retention of the right of disposal:

> "Where goods are shipped, and by the bill of lading the goods are deliverable to the order of the seller or his agent, the seller is *prima facie* deemed to reserve the right of disposal."

b *Where the buyer or his agent lawfully obtains possession*

1 *Meaning of "lawfully"*. There is some controversy over what the expression "lawfully" covers in s. 43 (1) (b). Between buyer and seller it could be given a wide interpretation so that the lien would survive any tortious or criminal conduct on the buyer's part: the seller would still be entitled to retake control over the goods as security for the price.

This interpretation is not irreconcilable with the position that arises on a sub-sale. By s. 47, as will be discussed shortly,[5] the seller's lien is not affected

---

1 (1877), 3 App. Cas. 319; for the position where goods are held by a third party as warehouseman, see below, p. 296.
2 The sub-section was originally drafted to cover the situation which arose in *Grice* v. *Richardson*, namely where B was insolvent; but the draft was amended to its present form at the committee stage.
3 Though not by the seller obtaining a judgment for the price (s. 43 (2)).
4 See above, p. 113.
5 See below, p. 308.

by any sale or other disposition of the goods by the buyer, unless it takes place with the seller's assent. But this section is subject to the provisions of the rest of the Act so that a seller's lien could not affect the rights obtained by a sub-purchaser under s. 25 (2). The only limitation upon the buyer's power to pass title in terms of s. 25 (2) is that he should have obtained possession of the goods he had agreed to buy with the seller's consent. Thus the buyer can pass title in situations in which the consent has been obtained by fraud and to that extent the seller's lien will be defeated once the goods, or a document of title to those goods, are delivered or transferred to a sub-purchaser who has no notice of any lien or other right of the original seller. However, it is possible for a buyer to be in possession with the seller's consent, but for the lien to continue by virtue of the fact that the consent was obtained by fraud so that the possession was not "lawful". If the buyer then disposes of the goods, the lien is defeated, not by virtue of s. 43, but by virtue of s. 25 (2). There certainly seems to be no very good reason for reading the "lawfully obtained possession" in s. 43 as equivalent to "with the consent of the seller".[1]

2 *The meaning of "possession"*. The "possession" referred to here must be physical possession in the sense that either the buyer must take control of the goods, or control must be assumed or acknowledged on his behalf. In a situation where the goods are in the hands of the seller's bailee, the lien terminates when the sale is followed by an attornment, on the seller's instructions, by the bailee to the buyer. It is thus a tripartite arrangement: the seller's lien cannot be defeated by the action of two only of the parties.

In *Poulton & Son* v. *Anglo-American Oil Co., Ltd.*,[2] the plaintiffs, S, had bought some second-hand boilers which remained in O's, the original owner's, premises. S sold the boilers to B who was to pay part of the purchase money before taking possession of them. S informed O of the sale to B. Later B resold the boilers to the defendants. The Court of Appeal held that by s. 29 (3) there could be no delivery by S to B until O, in whose possession the goods were, had acknowledged that he held them on B's behalf. By informing O of the situation, S had not divested himself of his lien as unpaid seller.

c *By waiver*

Only rarely will a waiver occur expressly. In the great majority of cases it will arise by implication from the circumstances.

1 *Where the buyer is given credit*. An obvious example is where the seller allows the buyer credit. Thereupon the buyer is entitled to delivery of the goods without tendering the price. However, providing the seller still has possession of the goods, his power of retaining them against payment of the price will revive once the term of credit expires, or if the buyer becomes insolvent.

The classification of this power of retention is not altogether clear. It is reasonable enough to argue that s. 41 (1) takes precedence over s. 43 (1) (c) in

---

1 For the contrary view, see Atiyah, *op. cit.*, p. 249.
2 (1911), 27 T.L.R. 216.

this respect so that it is the seller's lien which revives. Alternatively it is possible that this situation is covered by the rather ill-defined s. 39 (2):

> "Where the property in goods has not passed to the buyer, the unpaid seller has, in addition to his other remedies, a right of withholding delivery similar to and co-extensive with his rights of lien and stoppage *in transitu* where the property has passed to the buyer."

The explanation of this provision given by Chalmers[1] is that it was necessary "because it would be a contradiction in terms to speak of a man having a lien over his own goods". However, this does not seem to give a complete picture because there is authority[2] to suggest that a lien is lost by the granting of credit, but that if the period of credit expires or the buyer becomes bankrupt, the seller's power of retention over the goods takes some more limited form, i.e. perhaps a mere right of withholding delivery.

2 *Where the buyer gives alternative security.* In principle a lien can be waived if a debtor provides alternative security for the debt. However it is subject to one important limitation which appears to be more relevant to the lien of an innkeeper or banker than to a seller whose claim over the goods relates to the price due for those goods and not to some other debt. The limitation has been expressed thus:[3]

> "It is not the mere taking of a security which discharges the lien, but there must be something in the facts of the case, or in the nature of the security taken, which is inconsistent with the existence of the lien and which is destructive of it."

As long as the seller retains possession of the goods, it will need clear evidence that the security is intended to replace his rights over the goods and to entitle the buyer to obtain delivery without tender of the price. If the seller accepts a cheque or bill of exchange, the circumstances may show the seller's intention to waive his lien although of course it is conditional upon the cheque or bill being honoured, and it will revive upon dishonour if the goods are still in his possession.

3 *Waiver by estoppel.* The waiver can, in appropriate circumstances, take the form of an estoppel which prevents the seller relying upon his lien. In *Knights* v. *Wiffen*,[4] the unpaid seller told his bailee to acknowledge the buyer's delivery order in favour of a sub-purchaser. The bailee therefore dealt with the goods on this basis in relation to the sub-purchaser. Subsequently the buyer became insolvent. It was held that this fact did not assist the seller as the waiver did not take the form of allowing credit. The lien had already been lost: the seller was precluded by his conduct from relying upon it *vis-à-vis* the sub-purchaser.

4 *Breach by the seller.* It is also said that the seller's lien is lost if the seller

---

1 *Op. cit.*, p. 172.
2 See *Griffiths* v. *Perry* (1859), 1 E. & E. 680, considered below, p. 298.
3 *Angus* v. *McLachlan* (1883), 23 Ch.D. 330, at pp. 335–6, *per* KAY, J.; *Bank of Africa* v. *Salisbury Gold Mining Co., Ltd.*, [1892] A.C. 281, at pp. 284–5.
4 (1870), L.R. 5 Q.B. 660; see above, p. 58, n. 3.

himself breaks the contract by some act that is inconsistent with his right to retain possession. In *Gurr* v. *Cuthbert*,[1] B had agreed to buy a stack of hay on S's land for £86. It was to be paid for as removed, the whole to be taken by May 31. B paid for and removed part before that date, but he did not tender the price in respect of the rest until December. In August S had cut up the hay and used it. In an action for trover, S pleaded that, because of his lien, he and not B had the right of possession at the time that he (S) used the hay. This argument was rejected: in the words of PARKE, B.:[2]

> "A lien is a right of possession; but as soon as a party uses the goods in a manner inconsistent with his claim of lien, from that moment his lien ceases, and the right of possession of the other party revives."

While this principle appears well enough established, it is by no means certain how it would be applied in circumstances that are less straightforward than those before the court in *Gurr* v. *Cuthbert*. In *Griffiths* v. *Perry*,[3] S agreed to sell to B two quantities of iron, one of 300 parcels, the other of 100. Delivery was to take place immediately; payment was to be by a bill of exchange at four months' date. The 100 parcels were duly delivered, but, when a delivery order in respect of the 300 parcels was presented, delivery was refused. Subsequently the bill was dishonoured. The view of CROMPTON, J., was that, if there had been no breach by S in refusing delivery, S would have been entitled to stop delivery upon dishonour of the bill or insolvency of the buyer; in his opinion, though, this was not so much the lien which revived, but a form of right of stoppage. In this case, the fact that there had been a breach by S certainly created a right of action in B, i.e. gave B a right of possession, the lien having been terminated by S's breach. However, even although the lien had gone, on dishonour of the bill, S could still withhold delivery against payment and would only be liable in nominal damages for failure to deliver.

The uncertainties of this decision are reflected in the Sale of Goods Act passed more than 30 years later. The question has already been posed of whether it is the lien which revives on insolvency or expiration of the period of credit or some ill defined right simply to retain the goods until tender of the price. However, if the waiver takes the form of a breach, the consequences will depend upon the nature of the breach. A failure by the seller to deliver goods in his possession is in itself not an act sufficiently inconsistent with the lien to destroy it if the circumstances subsequently fall within s. 41 (1). In contrast, if the breach by the unpaid seller takes the form of consumption, or even resale, of the goods, the subsequent insolvency of the buyer can hardly revive the lien as there is nothing for it to attach to, and the seller will be liable in conversion. On the other hand, if the waiver takes the form of an acknowledgment to the buyer's sub-purchaser of the buyer's or the sub-purchaser's rights in the goods, then the sub-purchaser may be protected by an estoppel in much the same way as a sub-sale can create rights under s. 47, which will be considered shortly.

---

1 (1843), 12 L.J. Ex. 309.
2 *Ibid.*
3 (1859), 1 E. & E. 680.

5 *Application to cases of part delivery.* By s. 42:

> "When an unpaid seller has made part delivery of the goods, he may exercise his right of lien or retention on the remainder, unless such part delivery has been made under such circumstances as to show an agreement to waive the lien or right of retention."

The leading explanation in the pre-1893 cases of the principle to be applied in deciding whether a delivery of part amounted to a delivery of the whole so as to deprive the seller of his lien, was that of Lord BLACKBURN in *Kemp* v. *Falk*.[1] However, it must be admitted that his judgment was not entirely consistent. Having first of all made the point that in

> "agreeing for the delivery of goods . . . it may very well be that the delivery of a part of the goods is sufficient to afford strong evidence that it is intended as a delivery of the whole",

his Lordship then cited *Dixon* v. *Yates*[2] and continued:

> "The rule I had always understood, from that time down to the present, to be that the delivery of a part may be a delivery of the whole if it is so intended, but that it is not such a delivery unless it is so intended, and I rather think that the onus[3] is upon those who say that it was so intended."

Nor is the reference to *Dixon* v. *Yates* entirely helpful. In that case, two puncheons of rum from a quantity of forty-six were delivered to sub-purchasers so that they could sample the contents: there was in fact an express refusal on S's part to allow delivery of any others. However, it is clear from the judgment that the important point was that of the parties' intention: did they intend delivery of part to constitute a delivery of the whole,[4] or was there an intentional severance of the part actually delivered?[5]

This principle s. 42 codified in different terms, treating the issue not as one of whether delivery of part was intended to be a delivery of the whole, but of whether delivery of part was made in circumstances that showed an *agreement* to waive the lien. It need hardly be pointed out that a waiver is basically a unilateral act and is not dependent upon "agreement". However, in practice, there would seem to be no difference between the common law and the statutory rule. Under both, *prima facie* the seller is entitled to exercise his lien over the goods still retained. At common law, in effect the party seeking to show that the lien had gone had to show that it was intended by both parties that delivery of part was a delivery of the whole (and therefore a loss of the seller's rights arising out of his physical control over the goods). Under s. 42, the party seeking to show that the seller has waived his lien must point to circumstances showing the parties' agreement that that should be the consequence of their actions.

---

1 (1882), 7 App. Cas. 573, at p. 586.   2 (1883), 5 B. & Ad. 313.
3 Similarly, *per* BRETT, L.J., in *Ex parte Cooper* (1879), 11 Ch.D. 68, at p. 73:
> "a delivery of part, or even of the bulk of a cargo, is not *prima facie* a delivery of the whole; and . . . those who rely upon the part delivery as a constructive delivery of the whole are bound to show that the part delivery took place under such circumstances as to make it a constructive delivery of the whole".

4 *Dixon* v. *Yates*, 5 B. & Ad., at p. 339, per Littledale, J.
5 At p. 341, *per* PARKE, J.; see also *Bunney* v. *Poyntz* (1833), 4 B. & Ad. 568.

Where the contract is severable, that is, where the contract provides for delivery by separate instalments, the seller's right to refuse delivery is limited. In the first place, he would not be entitled to refuse delivery at all, unless the buyer had become insolvent,[1] if payment was not due until delivery of the final instalment. If payment was due in respect of part deliveries, he would certainly be entitled to withhold further deliveries if the buyer was insolvent. In the pre-Act case of *Re Edwards, ex parte Chalmers*,[2] S had agreed to deliver to B 330 tons of bleaching powder at a rate of 30 tons per month from February to December. Payment was to be by cash 14 days after delivery. The November instalment was not paid for. On December 20, B declared himself insolvent. S refused to deliver the final instalment. The Court held that S's action was justified. If a buyer becomes insolvent before the contract of sale has been completely performed, the seller "is entitled to refuse to deliver any more till he is paid the debt due for those already delivered, as well as the price of those still to be delivered".[3]

If the buyer is not insolvent, the position is less clear. As has already been discussed,[4] s. 31 (2) deals with the continued operation of the contract: it provides *inter alia* that where

> "the buyer neglects or refuses to . . . pay for one or more instalments, it is a question . . . depending on the terms of the contract and the circumstances of the case, whether the breach of contract is a repudiation of the whole contract or whether it is a severable breach giving rise to a claim for compensation but not to a right to treat the whole contract as repudiated".

It seems to have been assumed that this section governs the situation even where the point in issue is not the continued existence of the contract,[5] but the seller's right to retain subsequent instalments against payment for past deliveries.

The only case in which the issue appears to have been raised directly on the facts is *Steinberger* v. *Atkinson & Co., Ltd.*[6] B had agreed to buy 2,000 bags of small onions and 1,000 bags of large onions. There was a dispute over the first shipment which was partially defective. A variation in price was agreed upon to take account of the defects. However, for some reason not disclosed in the report, the buyer still had not paid the full amount due as the varied price, in respect of the first instalment. ATKIN, J., held that there had been no such conduct on B's part as would entitle S to repudiate the contract (i.e. the circumstances did not show any intention on B's part to repudiate) so that S was not entitled to

---

1 This would seem to be supported by *Re Edwards, ex parte Chalmers* (1873), 8 Ch. App. 289, in which MELLISH, L.J., giving the principal judgment, answered the question, what are the rights of a seller when the purchaser becomes insolvent before performance, by stating (at p. 291) that the seller, "notwithstanding he may have agreed to allow credit for the goods, is not bound to deliver any more goods under the contract until the price of goods not yet delivered is tendered to him".
2 (1873), 8 Ch. App. 289.
3 At p. 291.
4 Above, p. 161.
5 *Mersey Steel and Iron Co., Ltd.* v. *Naylor, Benzon & Co.* (1884), 9 App Cas. 434, is not directly relevant.
6 (1914), 31 T.L.R. 110.

withhold delivery of the second and third shipments of onions for non-payment of the total price due on the first instalment.

The main issue to be decided in this type of case is the extent to which non-payment will constitute an apparent repudiation of the contract. The refusal to pay for no plausible, rather than valid, reason could well raise the inference that the buyer does not intend to proceed with the contract even though he may be demanding delivery of the subsequent instalments. In theory it could place the seller in an awkward situation if he has to adduce evidence of the buyer's intention to repudiate. It will be particularly difficult if the buyer has in fact paid a substantial part of the payment due on the previous instalment or instalments. In practice, of course, problems of this kind seldom give rise to litigation because retention of subsequent instalments in respect of a debt owing for past instalments can be a most effective remedy whatever may be its legal implications. Certainly a buyer would be reluctant to institute proceedings for non-delivery in circumstances in which the seller could point to his (the buyer's) apparently unjustified failure to pay for previous instalments in full.

B THE RIGHT OF STOPPAGE IN TRANSITU

Once the goods are in transit so that the seller's lien has ended, the law nevertheless recognises a limited power in the seller to prevent delivery to the buyer and thereby to resume his (the seller's) control, and therefore his lien, over the goods. Section 44 states:

> "Subject to the provisions of this Act, when the buyer of goods becomes insolvent, the unpaid seller who has parted with the possession of the goods has the right of stopping them in transitu, that is to say, he may resume possession of the goods as long as they are in course of transit, and may retain them until payment or tender of the price."

i Insolvency of the buyer

The first significant feature is the fact that the power is only exercisable in a case of insolvency. It would not be sufficient for the seller to act on a suspicion that the buyer has stopped paying his debts in the course of business, unless that suspicion was proved correct *before* the time of arrival of the goods. As Sir William Scott said in *The Constantia*:[1]

> "if the insolvency happens before the arrival it would be sufficient . . . to justify what has been done and to entitle the shipper to the benefit of his own provisional caution".

ii Duration of transit

By s. 45 (1):

> "Goods are deemed to be in course of transit from the time when they are delivered to a carrier by land or water, or other bailee for the purpose of transmission to the buyer, until the buyer, or his agent in that behalf, takes delivery of them from such carrier or other bailee."

---

1 (1807), 6 Ch. Rob. 321, at p. 587.

a *Delivery to a carrier*

It will be recalled that, by s. 32 (1), delivery of goods to a carrier is *prima facie* deemed to constitute delivery to the buyer.[1] However, such delivery will always be subject to s. 45 unless the carrier is in fact that buyer's agent, not only to transport the goods, but also to take actual delivery of the goods on his behalf. This distinction may be difficult to draw but in the same way as a carrier may be the seller's agent (so that no right of stoppage is necessary because the seller still has possession of the goods through his agent), so the buyer may also have taken delivery through a carrier appointed by him for that purpose. In most cases, however, the carrier will be an independent contractor, who is deemed to be the buyer's agent for the purpose of the carriage of the goods, but not for their actual receipt on the buyer's behalf. It would seem, therefore, that even if the carrier is nominated,[2] and usually even if a vessel is chartered,[3] by the buyer, the goods will remain in transit until received by the buyer, or his agent to take delivery.

b *Delivery taken by the buyer*

The transit continues, in the wording of s. 45 (1), "until the buyer, or his agent in that behalf, takes delivery" of the goods from the carrier. However, s. 45 lays down a number of special applications of this principle. Hence by s. 45 (2):

> "If the buyer or his agent in that behalf obtains delivery of the goods before their arrival at the appointed destination, the transit is at an end."

This rule is, on the face of it, straightforward enough. It operates as an exception to the general principle that the transit continues, and therefore the right of stoppage subsists, until the goods reach their "appointed destination". It is an exception based upon recognition of the fact that a carrier and consignee can agree to a different destination or means of disposal of the goods than that formerly established by the carrier and the consignor.[4] Furthermore, there is authority[5] suggesting that an agreement between the carrier and consignee is not necessary, and that a wrongful taking of possession by the consignee is sufficient to bring the transit to an end. The main criticism of this proposition is that it is anomalous. It is not in harmony with the requirement that the seller's lien terminates when the buyer "lawfully" obtains possession,[6] nor with the converse

---

1 See above, p. 113.
2 *Bethell* v. *Clark* (1888), 20 Q.B.D. 615; *Lyons* v. *Hoffnung* (1890), 15 App Cas. 391; [1886–90] All E.R. Rep. 1012.
3 *Re Cock; Ex parte Rosevear China Clay Co.* (1879), 11 Ch.D. 560; s. 45 (5) leaves the point open:
> "When goods are delivered to a ship chartered by the buyer it is a question depending on the circumstances of the particular case, whether they are in the possession of the master as a carrier, or as agent of the buyer."

Presumably it would only be in a charter by way of demise in which the charterer was also the buyer that the master could be said to be acting as agent of the charterer to receive delivery on the buyer's behalf.
4 See, for example, *London and North Western Rail. Co.* v. *Bartlett* (1861), 7 H. & N. 400; *Butterworth* v. *Brownlow* (1865), 19 C.B. N.S. 409.
5 *Whitehead* v. *Anderson* (1842), 9 M. & W. 518, at p. 534, *per* PARKE, B.; *Kendal* v. *Marshall Stevens & Co.* (1883), 11 Q.B.D. 356, at p. 369, *per* BOWEN, L.J.
6 Section 43 (1) (*b*), see above, p. 295.

situation[1] in s. 45 (6) which provides:

> "Where the carrier or other bailee . . . wrongfully refuses to deliver the goods to the buyer, or his agent in that behalf, the transit is deemed to be at an end."

On the other hand, it can reasonably be pointed out that s. 45 (2) omits any reference to "lawfully"; indeed it refers to the buyer or his agent *obtaining* delivery of the goods. In addition, it can be argued that if an arrangement between the carrier and consignee is capable of putting an end to the transit, the consignee's act of taking possession of the goods without consent should also be capable of having the same effect because the wrongfulness of the act is *vis-à-vis* the carrier, not the consignor.

c *The destination of the goods*

Where s. 45 (2) is ambiguous is in its reference to "the appointed destination", an expression which also appears in s. 45 (3):

> "If, after the arrival of the goods at the appointed destination, the carrier or other bailee acknowledges to the buyer, or his agent, that he holds the goods on his behalf and continues in possession of them as bailee for the buyer, or his agent, the transit is at an end, and it is immaterial that a further destination for the goods may have been indicated by the buyer."

In order for there to be both an "appointed destination" and a "further destination", the transit must include at least two stages. The simplest way of giving meaning to these terms would be to regard the "appointed destination" as being that envisaged by the contract between seller and carrier, while the "further destination" would relate to any other or subsequent arrangement that the buyer makes or intends to make with the carrier. However, whatever logical attractions such a distinction might have, the courts have accepted the guidance of pre-1893 authorities and have not stopped to consider whether those authorities are accurately reproduced by the distinction between an "appointed" and a "further" destination in the wording of s. 45 (2) and (3).

In *Kemp* v. *Ismay, Imrie & Co.*,[2] B was buying goods on behalf of Australian purchasers, although *vis-à-vis* S he was acting as principal. Having agreed to buy the goods, B then gave S instructions to send the goods, marked NXZ Adelaide, to the defendants at Liverpool for shipment per the *Suevic*. B became insolvent after the ship had sailed with the goods. S therefore purported to exercise his right of stoppage. It was held that his action was effective. The "appointed destination" was Adelaide and not Liverpool. In reaching this conclusion, Lord ALVERSTON, C.J., was guided by a dictum of Lord ESHER in *Bethell* v. *Clark* :[3]

> "Where the transit is a transit which has been caused either by the terms of the contract or *by the directions of the purchaser to the vendor*, the right of stoppage *in transitu* exists: but if the goods are not in the hands of the carrier by reason either of the terms of the contract or of the directions of the purchaser to the vendor, but are *in transitu* afterwards in consequence of fresh instructions

---

1 Based upon the decision in *Bird* v. *Brown* (1850), 4 Exch. 786.
2 (1909), 100 L.T. 996.
3 (1888), 20 Q.B.D. 615, at p. 617.

S.G.—11*

> given by the purchaser for a new transit, then such transit is no part of the
> original transit and the right to stop is gone."

In this case, the instructions had been sufficient to enable the carrier to ship the
goods without further reference to the purchaser.

On the face of it this decision and the dictum from *Bethell* v. *Clark* seem to
support the much wider proposition that the "appointed destination" is the
destination arranged between seller and carrier, to which may be added a
further destination if that is communicated by the buyer to the seller. However,
this subsequent "addition" is qualified, in Lord ESHER'S words, by the question
whether the transit is continuous on the basis of the instructions given by the
seller to the original carrier, or whether the subsequent carrier is in effect the
buyer's agent to receive the goods pending the buyer's orders as to their disposal.

This qualification comes much nearer to the proposition advanced above that
the "appointed destination" is that *envisaged*, though not necessarily expressly
provided for, by the contract between seller and carrier. Certainly, this approach
seems to be supported by a number of decisions, even if the judges have not
spelt out the position with any clarity. In *Lyons* v. *Hoffnung*,[1] B had purchased
a variety of goods from S. At the time he had told three of S's employees that the
goods were for Kimberley and had instructed that the packages should be marked
with his initials (WC) over K (standing for Kimberley) and sent to C's wharf in
Sydney. When the goods were in the course of the voyage from Sydney to
Western Australia, B became insolvent and S retook possession of the goods at
an intermediate port in furtherance of his alleged right of stoppage. It was held
that the goods were still in transit so that the exercise of the right of stoppage
was effective. It was never intended that the goods should pass into the actual
possession of B through the agency of C. C did not hold the goods until such
time as B gave instruction for their ultimate disposal, but took them as carrier
under arrangements, made with S, for transit of the goods.[2]

In contrast, in *Kendal* v. *Marshall Stevens & Co.*,[3] B purchased 55 bales of
cotton-waste from S. B arranged with A that the goods should be sent to A from
S in Bolton and that A should ship the goods from Garston to Rouen. B then
instructed S to send the goods to A at Garston. Accordingly S put the goods in
the hands of the L.N.W.R. at Bolton to be forwarded to A at Garston. In the
meantime B warned A to expect delivery of the goods and confirmed his instructions that they should be sent on to Rouen. S still had not received payment
when he heard of B's insolvency. Having ascertained that the goods were still in
A's hands, S therefore purported to exercise a right of stoppage *in transitu*.
It was held by the Court of Appeal that the right of stoppage had ended once
the goods reached the possession of A: A had no control over the goods except
on B's behalf. The only transit which was relevant was that arranged by S with
the carrier on B's instructions. In other words, Rouen was a "further destination" which had no bearing on the relations between B and S.

---

1 (1890), 15 App. Cas. 391.
2 At p. 397; see also in the Supreme Court of N.S.W. (1888), 9 L.R. N.S.W. (L.) 313,
   at pp. 332–3, *per* WINDEYER, J., with whom FOSTER, J., "entirely" agreed, at p. 354.
3 (1883), 11 Q.B.D. 356.

Once it is clear what is meant by an "appointed destination" and a "further destination", it is easier to see what is meant by the expression in s. 45 (2) about the buyer obtaining delivery of the goods before their arrival at the appointed destination. In *Reddall* v. *Union Castle Mail Steamship Co., Ltd.*,[1] B was buying goods on behalf of a merchant in South Africa, although in the transaction with S he was acting as principal. From other sources S knew of the South African merchant but the only information he received from B was instructions to send the goods by the quickest route to the defendants' vessel, the *Armadale Castle*, at Southampton Docks, and the ultimate destination as Algoa Bay. S arranged for the goods to be sent per these instructions. When they reached Southampton, B wrote ordering the defendants to stop all his shipments on the *Armadale Castle*. The goods were not loaded, and the defendants replied telling B that they were holding the goods to await his instructions. The defendants retained possession, charging B warehouse dues in respect of the goods, until they handed the goods over to S on S's claim to stop *in transitu*. On the facts, it was held that the destination of the goods was Algoa Bay, because S had been able to set the goods on their way without the need for any intermediate instructions. However, B had interrupted the transit by instructing the defendants to hold the goods. As they then held the goods subject to his instructions, the transit was at an end and S's right of stoppage was lost.

This over-all interrelation between s. 45 (2) and (3) along the lines suggested gains support from the following statement of the law by BAIHACHE, J., in *Reddall's* case:[2]

> "Where goods are delivered by the seller or his agent to a carrier, and pass at each successive stage of the transit from the hands of one carrier to another, *without the intervention of a forwarding agent*, to the destination indicated by the buyer to the seller, the transit continues until that destination is reached."

The significance of the reference to the forwarding agent is that the consequence of the buyer's instructions to the seller must be that the goods are set in motion and will be directed to the indicated destination under the arrangements made between seller and carrier without the intervention of any agent acting on the buyer's instructions alone. An indication to the seller of where the buyer is planning to send the goods and on which the seller is not expected to act would clearly not affect the "appointed destination". In *Kendal* v. *Marshall Stevens & Co.*[3] it would not have made any difference to the decision had B told S to send the goods for delivery to A at Garston and added the information that A would be making arrangements for the transit of the goods to Rouen. S would in no sense have been putting the goods in transit for Rouen: between him and C and between him and B, the destination would be Garston even though he was aware of what B intended doing thereafter.

d *Part delivery*

Two other aspects of the transit of goods are covered by s. 45. In the first place, s. 45 (7) deals with the case of a part delivery:

---

1 (1914), 84 L.J.K.B. 360.
2 At p. 361 (emphasis added).   3 (1883), 11 Q.B.D. 356.

> "Where part delivery of the goods has been made to the buyer, or his agent in that behalf, the remainder of the goods may be stopped *in transitu*, unless such part delivery has been made under such circumstances as to show an agreement to give up possession of the whole of the goods."

Although the wording is different from that contained in s. 42, the problem of deciding whether a waiver is equivalent to an agreement to give up possession has already been discussed.[1] Subject to those comments, it is believed that the two provisions are substantially similar in effect.

e *Goods rejected by the buyer*

Secondly, s. 45 (4) deals with the situation where the goods are rejected by the buyer. If the carrier or other bailee

> "continues in possession of them, the transit is not deemed to be at an end, even if the seller has refused to receive them back."

In other words, even if the seller states that he will have nothing more to do with the goods on the ground that the buyer has bought them, and that they are therefore the latter's property, the seller can, on learning of the buyer's insolvency, instruct the carrier to withhold delivery from the buyer's assignee.[2]

iii How effected

According to s. 46 (1) the unpaid seller may exercise his right of stoppage either:

(a) by taking actual possession of the goods (which must include possession taken by his agent in order to complement s. 45 (2)); or
(b) by giving notice of his claim to the carrier or other bailee in whose possession the goods are.

At the time when the Act was passed, if the seller wished to stop the goods by giving notice, he could have been faced with some difficulty with respect to goods at sea. Hence, s. 46 (1) went on to provide:

> "Such notice may be given either to the person in actual possession of the goods or to his principal. In the latter case the notice, to be effectual, must be given at such time and under such circumstances that the principal, by the exercise of reasonable diligence, may communicate it to his servant or agent in time to prevent a delivery to the buyer."

If the notice is given to the person in actual possession, i.e. the master of the ship, no problem can arise, but the usual procedure would be to notify the shipowner. This notice will be effective, whether or not the shipowner succeeds in contacting the master, providing it was reasonably possible for the latter to be contacted before delivery was given to the buyer or his agent.

What is an effective notice will therefore be dependent upon circumstances, although gone are the days when a notice could be ineffective because of the impossibility of contacting a vessel at sea. In the case of *Whitehead* v. *Anderson*,[3] decided in 1842, S attempted to stop a cargo of timber that was on a ship from

---

1 Above, p. 299.
2 *Bolton* v. *Lancashire and Yorkshire Rail. Co.* (1866), L.R. 1 C.P. 431. The carrier can hardly become the buyer's agent without the buyer's approval.
3 (1842), 9 M. & W. 518.

Quebec bound for Fleetwood by giving notice to the shipowner at his address in Montrose. At that time all that could reasonably be done[1] by the shipowner was to send the notice to the master to await his arrival at Fleetwood. It was held that S's notice was not sufficient to constitute an effective stoppage.[2] Presumably similar problems could still arise today, though on a smaller time scale, with respect to land carriage in which a carrier's head office might have difficulty in locating, and stopping the delivery of, goods already in course of transit.

iv Consequences of notice of stoppage

Once notice of stoppage has been given, s. 46 (2) obliges the carrier to

> "redeliver the goods to, or according to the directions of, the seller".

It is thus made clear that, although the seller acts at his peril, the carrier is obliged to give effect to the claim to stop the goods as soon as he can.[3] He may be placed in the difficult position of being liable to the buyer, if the seller's claim proves unfounded, or to the seller if the claim is valid. He should therefore seek an indemnity from the seller against any proceedings that might be instituted by the buyer or anyone entitled through the latter.

If the seller does give notice of stoppage, and directs the carrier to redeliver the goods, s. 46 (2) also lays down that the

> "expenses of such redelivery must be borne by the seller".

However, it is not only the costs incurred once the notice of stoppage is given that must be borne by the seller. If the carrier has not been paid his charges in respect of the carriage of the goods delivery of which has been stopped, he is entitled to a lien over them even as against the unpaid seller. As Lord ATKINSON said in *United States Steel Products Co.* v. *Great Western Rail. Co.*:[4]

> "The vendor's right to stop *in transitu* means not only the right to countermand delivery to the vendee but to order delivery to the vendor. It is subject to the possessory lien of the carrier for the charges due in respect of the carriage of the goods, but is not subject to any general lien which the carrier might have, as against the consignee of the goods, in respect of freight due on other goods."

Furthermore, in *Booth Steamship Co., Ltd.* v. *Cargo Fleet Iron Co., Ltd.*,[5] the Court of Appeal held that the shipowner was entitled to exercise a lien in respect

---

1　It was this decision which firmly established the principal's obligation to use due diligence, and if due diligence was used (as in this case) without the notice getting to the agent, the seller's purported stoppage was ineffectual: *per* PARKE, B., at p. 534, giving the judgment of the court. See also *Kemp* v. *Falk* (1882), 7 App. Cas. 573, esp. at pp. 585–6.

2　In fact, agents of B's assignees got on board before the letter was delivered, and obtained the master's assent to hold the goods on their behalf. Later S's agent served notice of stoppage on the ship's mate in the absence of the master. This was held to be effective on the ground that there had been no positive act by the master signifying that he held the goods on behalf of the assignees.

3　*The Tigress* (1863), 32 L.J. P.N. & A. 97, at p. 101; *Booth Steamship Co., Ltd.* v. *Cargo Fleet Iron Co., Ltd.*, [1916] 2 K.B. 570, at p. 577.

4　[1916] 1 A.C. 189, at p. 203; see also at pp. 195–6, *per* Lord BUCKMASTER, L.C.

5　[1916] 2 K.B. 570; [1916–17] All E.R. Rep. 938.

of freight which had not accrued as a payment due because the voyage had never been completed as a result of the seller's notice of stoppage.

C   EFFECT OF DISPOSITIONS BY THE BUYER

Hitherto the discussion of the seller's lien or right of stoppage has centred upon the relationships between the buyer, the seller and the carrier. But what will be the position if there has been a sub-sale or other disposition of the goods by the buyer? *Prima facie*, of course, as he is not in possession of the goods (so that s. 25 (2) cannot apply), no disposition that he might make will be of any effect *vis-à-vis* the seller or the goods themselves. However, s. 47 creates two exceptions to this principle.

i If the seller has assented

The first paragraph of s. 47 refers to the situation where the seller assents to a disposition:

> "Subject to the provisions of this Act, the unpaid seller's lien or retention or stoppage *in transitu* is not affected by any sale, or other disposition of the goods which the buyer may have made, unless the seller has assented thereto."

The term "assent" has been interpreted to mean not only that the seller knows of the transaction but also that he has in effect agreed to its performance in priority to any rights he might have under his own contract with the buyer.

In *Mordaunt Bros.* v. *British Oil and Cake Mills, Ltd.*,[1] S had regularly sold quantities of oil to B who had resold to X. B had then handed X a delivery order which X would endorse with instructions to hold, or deliver, the goods in question and would then send to S. When B fell into arrears with payments to S, S refused to make further deliveries and returned a number of unexecuted orders to X. It was held that there had been no assent by S to the sub-sales represented by these orders. In giving judgment, PICKFORD, J., advanced this interpretation of "assent" in s. 47:[2]

> ". . . the assent which affects the unpaid seller's right of lien must be such an assent as in the circumstances shows that the seller intends to renounce his rights against the goods. It is not enough to show that the fact of a sub-contract has been brought to his notice and that he has assented to it merely in the sense of acknowledging the receipt of the information. His assent to the sub-contract in that sense would simply mean that he acknowledged the right of the purchaser to have the goods subject to his own paramount right under the contract with his original purchaser to hold the goods until he is paid the purchase-money."

In this case, X had been assured by S that B's delivery orders were "in order", but this acknowledgment in no way amounted to an assent to the sub-sale sufficient to deprive the seller of his lien over the goods in respect of the price.

In contrast, in *D. F. Mount, Ltd.* v. *Jay and Jay (Provisions) Co., Ltd.*,[3]

---

1 [1910] 2 K.B. 502.
2 At p. 507.
3 [1960] 1 Q.B. 159; [1959] 3 All E.R. 307.

S (the defendant company) sold to B (a man called Merrick) a total of 250 cartons containing tins of Australian peaches from a consignment of 4,500 cartons (to 500 of which S was entitled) lying at D's wharf. B made it clear that he would pay for the goods out of the purchase money he received on resale. B resold the goods to X, the plaintiff, but agreed to buy the same cartons back at a small profit to X. X paid B, but when the time came for B to repurchase the goods his cheque in X's favour was dishonoured. S, still being unpaid, purported to cancel his contract with B and instructed D to cancel the delivery orders in B's favour. SALMON, J., held that, in these circumstances, S had assented to the resale of the goods:

> "the defendants . . . knew that [B] could only pay for them out of the money he obtained from his customers against delivery orders in favour of those customers. In my view, the true inference is that the defendants assented to [B] reselling the goods, in the sense that they intended to renounce their rights against the goods and to take the risk of [B]'s honesty."[1]

Although SALMON, J., had no hesitation in accepting PICKFORD, J.'s interpretation of the term "assent", nevertheless it is an approach which creates an air of unreality. If a seller is in possession of goods it is doubtful whether he has any intention "to renounce his rights against the goods". If the seller thought about the matter he would probably take comfort from his control of them and feel that he could always retain them until payment was made.

The application of this exception to the overriding principle in s. 47 depends upon inference. While it may be possible to infer "assent" to something that takes place, it is less easy to infer an intention by the seller to renounce his rights. Indeed, it seems unnecessary to insert an additional factor beyond evidence of positive activity showing approval of the resale. In *Mordaunt Bros.* v. *British Oil and Cake Mills, Ltd.*, the sellers knew of the course of business, but their reaction was neutral, until, of course, they stepped in to preserve their rights as an unpaid seller. In *D. F. Mount, Ltd.* v. *Jay and Jay (Provisions) Co., Ltd.*, on the other hand, it was in the seller's interest that the goods should be resold at once because their payment depended upon such a resale: their assent could readily be inferred.

One aspect of the case commented upon in both decisions was the question whether it made any difference that the goods were unascertained. If, by means of delivery orders, goods are sold, it would not seem to be particularly significant whether those orders are accepted in respect of specific goods or goods still in bulk. However, SALMON, J., did observe that:[2]

> "there is no reason why section 47 should not apply to unascertained goods, although I respectfully agree with PICKFORD, J., that an inference can in some circumstances more readily be drawn against the seller in the case of a sale of specific goods than in the case of a sale of unascertained goods."

And perhaps, one might add, the inference might more readily be drawn in the case of goods that have been ascertained by separation from bulk (which requires

---

1 [1960] 1 Q.B. 159, at p. 167; [1959] 3 All E.R. 307, at p. 310.
2 [1960] 1 Q.B. at pp. 167–168; [1959] 3 All E.R., at p. 310.

a positive act on the seller's part) than in the case of unascertained, or even specific, goods.

ii Transfer of a document of title

By the proviso to s. 47:

> ". . . where a document of title to goods has been lawfully transferred to any person as buyer or owner of the goods, and that person transfers the document to a person who takes the document in good faith and for valuable consideration, then, if such last-mentioned transfer was by way of sale the unpaid seller's right of lien or stoppage *in transitu* is defeated, and if such last-mentioned transfer was by way of pledge or other disposition for value, the unpaid seller's right of lien or retention or stoppage *in transitu* can only be exercised subject to the rights of the transferee."

There is obviously a considerable overlap between this and s. 25 (2) whereby a buyer in possession of the documents of title to goods can, by transfer of documents of title under any sale pledge or other disposition, pass title "to any person receiving the same in good faith and without notice of any lien or other right of the original seller in respect of the goods".[1]

Hence in *Cahn* v. *Pockett's Bristol Channel Steam Packet Co., Ltd.*,[2] S forwarded to B a bill of lading in respect of a shipment of copper together with a draft drawn on B for the price. B transferred the bill of lading to X, but did not accept the draft bill of exchange. X took the bill of lading in good faith. When S heard that B was insolvent he purported to stop the goods *in transitu*. The Court of Appeal had no hesitation in holding that X's position was protected by s. 25 (2) and that this interpretation of the situation was in no way affected by the general principle laid down in s. 47 because the proviso clearly covered just such a case as this.

While s. 25 (2) has its counterpart in s. 9 of the Factors Act,[3] the proviso to s. 47 also preserves the complementary provision of the Factors Act, namely s. 10, which states:

> "Where a document of title to goods has been lawfully transferred to a person as a buyer or owner of the goods, and that person transfers the document to a person who takes the document in good faith and for valuable consideration, the last-mentioned transfer shall have the same effect for defeating any vendor's lien or right of stoppage *in transitu* as the transfer of a bill of lading has for defeating the right of stoppage *in transitu*."

In *Ant. Jurgens Margarinefabrieken* v. *Louis Dreyfus & Co.*,[4] S agreed to sell 2,640 bags of seed from a shipment of 6,400 bags. When the seed was received by S's Hamburg store, S gave B delivery orders in respect of 2,640 bags. Immediately B endorsed the orders and handed them to X. When B's cheque was dishonoured, S instructed his Hamburg branch to withhold delivery. It was

---

1 See above, p. 80 for s. 25 (2).
2 [1899] 1 Q.B. 643.
3 See above, p. 80.
4 [1914] 3 K.B. 40.

held by PICKFORD, J., that X's rights took precedence over S's by virtue of both the Sale of Goods Act, s. 47, and the Factors Act, s. 10.

Some comment has already been made[1] on how s. 47, while applicable to a document of title created by the seller himself (as in the *Dreyfus* case), seems to require that the document in question must be transferred. In *Mount* v. *Jay*, X was able to rely upon S's assent to the sub-sales by B, but if that argument had failed, would he have been able to rely upon the delivery order given to him by B? It was SALMON, J.'s opinion that the proviso to s. 47 would not have availed X because B had not transferred "the document" (i.e. the one transferred to B), but one created by B himself.[2] In contrast, the transaction with X would have been protected by s. 25 (2) which is not so restrictively worded in this respect.[3]

D THE EFFECTS OF EXERCISE OF THE LIEN OR RIGHT OF STOPPAGE

The effect of a seller exercising his right of stoppage is to restore the goods to his possession and therefore to recreate his lien or at least a right to retain the goods against tender of the price. It in no way has the effect of rescinding the contract; as s. 48 (1) states:

> "Subject to the provisions of this section, a contract of sale is not rescinded by the mere exercise by an unpaid seller of his right of lien or retention or stoppage *in transitu*."

The reason behind this provision is obvious enough. Unless the time of payment is a condition precedent to the operation of the contract, a delay in payment does not affect the contract which therefore remains in force.

On the other hand, if the seller is in possession of the goods he can resell by virtue of s. 25 (1).[4] However, if he exercises his lien or right of stoppage, his power of resale is extended and no longer depends upon the limitations contained in s. 25 (1). By s. 48 (2):

> "Where an unpaid seller who has exercised his right of lien or stoppage *in transitu* re-sells the goods, the buyer acquires a good title thereto as against the original buyer."

Hence, while under s. 25 (1) the second sale must be followed by a delivery of the goods or transfer of a document of title to a person "receiving the same in good faith and without notice of the previous sale", under s. 48 (2) all that is required is a "resale".

The reason behind this provision is that, in certain circumstances, the original contract may be regarded as rescinded, and it will not always be possible for the second buyer to know the true situation. Accordingly, as long as the seller has exercised his lien or right of stoppage, the second buyer takes as against the first. The operation of s. 48 (2) does not of course affect the position of the seller and

---

1 Above, p. 90.
2 [1960] 1 Q.B. 159, at p. 168.
3 [1960] 1 Q.B., at p. 169.
4 See above, p. 76.

the first buyer to whom the former may still be liable for breach of the contract and conversion of the goods.

Section 48 itself deals with two situations in which the unpaid seller may resell the goods without breaking his contract with the original buyer. By s. 48(3):

> "Where the goods are of a perishable nature, or where the unpaid seller gives notice to the buyer of his intention to re-sell, and the buyer does not within a reasonable time pay or tender the price, the unpaid seller may re-sell the goods and recover from the original buyer damages for any loss occasioned by his breach of contract."

It will be noticed that this subsection does not expressly state that the resale has the effect of rescinding the original contract, in contrast to s. 48 (4) which makes this point clear:

> "Where the seller expressly reserves a right of resale in case the buyer should make default, and on the buyer making default, re-sells the goods, the original contract of sale is thereby rescinded, but without prejudice to any claim the seller may have for damages."

These two provisions were examined in two cases in an attempt to decide whether a re-sale under sub-s. (3) did by implication have the effect of rescinding the contract.

In *Gallagher* v. *Shilcock*,[1] S sold to B on May 17 a motor-boat for £665, £200 being paid by way of deposit. The sale was "subject to survey". When the surveyor's report proved satisfactory, B warned S that he was having difficulty raising the balance of the price and that he would have to obtain a mortgage on the boat itself. In order for a mortgage to be arranged, the vessel would have to be registered in B's name. B heard nothing more about the matter until July 13 when S's son telephoned B to tell him that the balance must be paid or the deposit would be forfeited, and this was followed on July 16 by a letter from S's solicitors giving B until July 31 to pay. On August 22 B visited S and told him he (B) was ready to complete, but S told him that he (S) had sold the boat for £700. FINNIMORE, J., held that this was a valid exercise of S's power of resale under s. 48 (3) and then went on to consider the consequences of this decision. Under s. 49 (1), had S sued for the price he would have been obliged to give credit for the £200, but what was the position where he relied upon his lien and right of resale? Section 48 (3) was a way of ensuring that the seller got his price:

> "The general principle of English law is that mere lateness or unpunctuality in making payment for the goods does not rescind the contract. It would be a curious thing if, nevertheless, the exercise by the seller of his remedy for delay should rescind the contract. The question, therefore, is whether when the unpaid seller sells the goods, he sells them as a person who, by rescission of the contract, has the full title to the goods revested in him, or sells them in a capacity analogous to that of a pledgee, or in some limited capacity?"[2]

---

1 [1949] 2 K.B. 765; [1949] 1 All E.R. 921.
2 [1949] 2 K.B., at pp. 772-3; [1949] 1 All E.R., at p. 924.

In his opinion, S was selling in a limited capacity and had to bring into account the £200. This impression of the law was fortified by the wording of sub-ss. (3) and (4) which were subject to the primary principle of non-rescission in sub-s. (1). Hence, as only sub-s. (4) provided rescission as a consequence, a resale under sub-s. (3) did not have that effect.

Despite the degree of justice in the decision, its rationale was criticised by the Court of Appeal in *R. V. Ward, Ltd.* v. *Bignall.*[1] B agreed to buy two vehicles from S for £850, and paid a deposit of £25. Later he refused to take delivery and pay for the goods, alleging a misrepresentation as to the age of one of the cars (a Vanguard). He made two alternative suggestions, that he should buy the vehicles for £800, or take just the other vehicle (a Zodiac) for £500, but both offers were rejected. S demanded payment and warned B that if it was not forthcoming he (S) would sell the cars and claim in respect of any loss. As B still would not pay, S resold the Vanguard for £350 and then sued B claiming damages of £497 10s., being the balance of the purchase price (£825), less the £350, plus £22 10s. in respect of advertising costs. Although this claim succeeded in the County Court, it was difficult to see on what grounds the award could be justified. If, as was apparently assumed, property had never passed to B, S remained the owner of the vehicles so he was only entitled to damages in respect of actual loss which the Court of Appeal held to be £25,[2] plus the advertising expenses. The attempt was made by counsel for S to support the award of damages by the County Court by arguing that property had passed to B and that S had exercised a right of resale without rescinding the contract so that, with regard to the Zodiac, S was still entitled to the price. The Court held that *Gallagher* v. *Shilcock* was wrong in suggesting that a resale by the seller left the original contract between seller and buyer intact. In the words of DIPLOCK, L.J.;[3]

> "The purpose of the subsection is to make time of payment of the essence of the contract whenever the goods are of a perishable nature, and to enable an unpaid seller, whatever the nature of the goods, to make payment within a reasonable time after notice of the essence of the contract. As already pointed out, an unpaid seller who resells the goods before the property has passed puts it out of his power to perform his primary obligation to the buyer to transfer the property in the goods to the buyer and, whether or not the property has already passed, to deliver up possession of the goods to the buyer. By making the act of resale one which the unpaid seller is entitled to perform, the subsection empowers the seller by his conduct in doing that act to exercise his right to treat the contract as repudiated by the buyer, that is, as rescinded, with the consequence that the buyer is discharged from any further liability to perform his primary obligation to pay the purchase price, and becomes subject to the secondary obligation to pay damages for non-acceptance of the goods."

---

1 [1967] 1 Q.B. 534; [1967] 2 All E.R. 449.
2 The value of the Zodiac was agreed by the parties to be £450 so that the loss after deduction of the £350 and the £25 deposit from the contract price (£850) was £25.
3 [1967] 1 Q.B., at p. 550; [1967] 2 All E.R., at pp. 456–7.

With all respect, it is not entirely convincing to suggest that s. 48 (3) makes time of payment of the essence of a contract to sell perishable goods because it cannot be said to harmonise with the overriding principle that "a contract of sale is not rescinded by the mere exercise by an unpaid seller of his right of lien or stoppage *in transitu*". Furthermore, it is equally difficult to accept that a resale by the seller following the exercise of his lien or right of stoppage necessarily makes the vital difference. If it does make such a difference why, to pose FINNEMORE, J.'s question, should no reference be made in s. 48 (3) to rescission while it is specifically stated in connection with s. 48 (4)? The answer given by SELLERS, L.J.,[1] was that the express reservation of a right of resale covered by s. 48 (4)

> "would permit the unpaid seller to resell without acting inconsistently or in conflict with his obligations. His conduct would not evidence a rescission by him on the buyer's breach. Nevertheless, subsection (4) makes the resale operate as a rescission and leaves the remedy, if any loss ensues, in damages. That brings it into harmony with subsection (3), which also gives a claim for damages for any loss occasioned by the buyer's original breach of contract. If the unpaid seller resells the goods, he puts it out of his power to perform his obligation under the original contract . . . By the notice to the buyer, the seller . . . requires the buyer to pay the price or tender it within a reasonable time. If he fails to do so, the seller in possession of the goods may treat the bargain as rescinded and resell the goods."

But even this explanation is not entirely convincing. The Sale of Goods Act is not entirely free from situations where a particular principle is spelt out in more than one place even though the principle would probably be implied automatically in a subsequent provision from its inclusion in an earlier section. Hence the omission of rescission in s. 48 (3) is as likely, or even more likely, to be deliberate on the ground that rescission was not an automatic consequence of resale following the exercise of the seller's lien or right of stoppage, as it was likely on the ground that rescission could readily be implied. Indeed the omission may have been deliberate for another reason. If one looks at the common law prior to 1893, it was clear that a resale under a reserved power in the original contract had the effect of rescinding that contract,[2] but far from certain what the position was if the resale followed the exercise of the seller's lien or right of stoppage.[3] Hence it is at least arguable that no reference was made to rescission in s. 48 (3) because the point had not been settled by the courts. If that is the case it is not surprising that inferences are difficult to draw from s. 48 as a whole. The section was intended to be neutral so that the courts should be free to settle the matter one way or the other.

Once it is realised that the relationship between s. 48 (3) and rescission is not an interpretative issue, one can reasonably look to s. 48 for guidance rather than for a definitive solution. The reason for the difference between s. 48 (4) and (3)

---

1 [1967] 1 Q.B. 534, at p. 544.
2 *Lamond* v. *Davall* (1847), 9 Q.B. 1030.
3 It is true that a seller could no longer sue for the price once he had resold because he was not in a position to show that he was ready and able to deliver: see *Chinery* v. *Viall* (1860), 5 H. & N. 288. Under s. 48 (3) the seller is clearly not liable for non-delivery, but it does not follow that the contract is therefore rescinded.

would appear to be that, at common law, an express right of resale made the time of payment a condition of the contract, whereas under the latter type of situation all depended upon the circumstances. Of particular importance seems to have been the conduct of the buyer. A seller was only entitled to rescind if the buyer's conduct amounted to a refusal to comply with, or perform, the contract.[1] If it does amount to such a refusal (i.e. a repudiation of the contract), the seller may elect to treat the contract as at an end and resell the goods. However, even if the buyer's conduct is not such as to amount to a repudiation, s. 48 (3) gives a power of resale. In other words, it is entirely reasonable to conclude that in some situations resale will amount to a rescission, but in others it will not, and what is important is to examine the conduct of the buyer.

In *Gallagher* v. *Shilcock*,[2] the buyer's conduct could scarcely be regarded as a repudiation of the contract. All along he had expressed his intention of paying. He had explained that he was short of cash because he had helped someone who was in some financial difficulty, and that he would have to obtain an advance on the security of the boat. In order to do so, the vessel had to be registered in his name, but it does not appear from the report to have been through any fault of his that this process was delayed. In the circumstances, s. 48 (3) empowered the seller to resell the boat after giving notice of his intention, but this could not be interpreted as an acceptance of any repudiation by the buyer.

On the other hand, in *R. V. Ward, Ltd.* v. *Bignall*,[3] once it was decided that the buyer's complaint about the age of one of the cars was unjustified, his conduct was patently tantamount to a repudiation of the contract: he was not prepared to pay that price for those goods. Hence, the resale was not only permitted by s. 48 (3), but it had the effect of rescinding the contract by accepting the repudiation.

On this basis, both decisions were correct, but for a reason different from any of those advanced by FINNEMORE, J., or by the Court of Appeal. The unfortunate buyer in *Gallagher* v. *Shilcock* would not have lost his £200 because the seller would still have been required to account for it. Nor would the reasonable conclusion reached in *Ward* v. *Bignall* be affected. And the interpretation placed upon s. 48 (3) is entirely in keeping with s. 48 as a whole. As s. 48 (1) states, non-payment by the buyer, even followed by the exercise of his lien or right of stoppage by the seller, does not rescind the contract; nor indeed does the resale, unless payment is a condition of the contract (s. 48 (4)), or unless non-payment in the circumstances amounts to a repudiation by the buyer of the contract.

The chief practical consequence under s. 48 (3) of distinguishing between a seller who resells after the previous contract has been rescinded and one who resells though the previous contract remains in being is that in the latter situation the seller receives any profit he may obtain on the buyer's behalf. This was in effect what occurred in *Gallagher* v. *Shilcock* in which, as the resale price

---

1 See the dicta in *Ogg* v. *Shuter* (1875), 10 C.P. 159, at pp. 163, 165.
2 [1949] 2 K.B. 765; [1949] 1 All E.R. 921.
3 [1967] 1 Q.B. 534; [1967] 2 All E.R. 449.

exceeded the original contract price, the buyer was entitled to recover his deposit in full. No claim had been made in respect of the £35 by which the resale price was higher, but this amount could have been recovered, though presumably less any expenses incurred by the seller in effecting the resale. In cases where the buyer's conduct in not paying amounts to a repudiation of the contract, the seller does not have to account for any profit he makes on the resale, and only has to account for any deposit forfeited by the buyer if he (the seller) is claiming damages for non-performance of the original contract. However, if the reasoning of *Ward* v. *Bignall* is correct, in all cases falling under s. 48 (3), the contract will always be rescinded and the seller will be in the position of not having to account to the buyer for any profit he might make out of the resale.

II THE SELLER'S PERSONAL REMEDIES

A ACTION FOR THE PRICE

The seller's action for the price, although not a right in rem akin to his lien or right of stoppage, has something in common with those rights, namely that it is available only to an unpaid seller. As s. 49 (1) provides:

> "Where, under a contract of sale, the property in the goods has passed to the buyer, and the buyer wrongfully neglects or refuses to pay for the goods according to the terms of the contract, the seller may maintain an action against him for the price of the goods."

The other hallmark of this right of action is that it is almost exclusively dependent upon the property having passed to the buyer. It is the fact that property has passed upon which, subject to any term express or implied in the contract as to the time of payment, the action is based.

In *Colley* v. *Overseas Exporters*,[1] S had agreed to sell to B a quantity of leather belting to be delivered "f.o.b. Liverpool". B duly instructed S to send the goods to agents in Liverpool for shipment on the *ss. Kenuta*. This vessel was, however, withdrawn from service and none of the other vessels named by B took on board the consignment of belting. The goods still remaining unshipped two months later, S commenced this action for the price. It was apparent that, on a strict application of s. 49 (1), S's claim was bound to fail. McCardie, J., was not prepared to recognise the principle that, if one party prevented something occurring, it could, in favour of the other party, be regarded as having been done,[2] as one of general application. It was certainly applicable to a condition subsequent,[3] but it did not have the same effect on a condition precedent. Accordingly the time when property was to pass had not arrived (i.e. the goods had not been loaded), so that the price was not claimable.

---

1 [1921] 3 K.B. 302; [1921] All E.R. Rep. 596.
2 A principle illustrated by *Mackay* v. *Dick* (1881), 6 App. Cas. 251, esp. at pp. 263, 264, *per* Lord Blackburn.
3 In *Mackay* v. *Dick* (above) the buyer was not to pay the price of a digging machine until it had performed certain tests satisfactorily. The tests were not carried out because of the buyer's default. The seller's action for the price succeeded.

The only exception recognised by the Act to the primary rule that property must have passed before the price can be recovered by action is where payment is due on a "day certain". By s. 49 (2):

> "Where, under a contract of sale, the price is payable on a day certain irrespective of delivery, and the buyer wrongfully neglects or refuses to pay such price, the seller may maintain an action for the price, although the property in the goods has not passed, and the goods have not been appropriated to the contract."

The main difficulty with this provision is that of defining a "day certain". If a precise date is given, no problem arises, but can a day become certain by the happening of an event? More particularly, if the price is payable on delivery and tender of shipping documents, is the date of delivery and tender a day certain within s. 49 (2)? This question was answered in the negative by ATKIN, J., in *Stein, Forbes & Co.* v. *County Tailoring Co.*,[1] and such a conclusion would seem logical for otherwise most contracts for the sale of goods would include by inference a day (rendered) certain when the price becomes due.[2]

The seller's real dilemma is, of course, that he may have to choose between suing for the price or seeking damages for non-acceptance. It will often be much to his advantage to recover the price of the goods, a course of action which frees him from any obligation to mitigate damages by reselling the goods. However, it may not always be readily apparent that property has passed and, if it is held by the court that property remains with the seller, he will only be entitled to damages for non-acceptance and even this sum could be inadequate to cover the seller's losses in a falling market. It follows that, although the seller *can* claim alternatively for the price or for damages for non-acceptance, he must at any earlier stage have made decisions on what course of conduct to adopt on the assumption that one claim rather than the other is likely to succeed. Moreover, in some circumstances, on the assumption that property has not passed, he may feel the best course is to sell the goods as part of his duty to mitigate, thus barring his right to sue for the price altogether.

B DAMAGES FOR NON-ACCEPTANCE

By s. 50 (1):

> "Where the buyer wrongfully neglects or refuses to accept and pay for the goods, the seller may maintain an action against him for non-acceptance."

The seller's action in damages for non-acceptance is the counter-part of the buyer's claim in respect of non-delivery, and it raises many of the same issues. For example, the normal measure of damages falls within the first branch of the

---

1 (1916), 86 L.J.K.B. 448; see also *Shell-Mex, Ltd.* v. *Elton Cop Dyeing Co., Ltd.* (1928), 34 Com. Cas. 39.
2 Though it must be admitted that there were some rather inconclusive suggestions in *Workman, Clark & Co., Ltd.* v. *Lloyd Brazileno*, [1908] 1 K.B. 968, that s. 49 (2) can apply to instalments falling due at specific stages in the construction of a ship.

rule in *Hadley* v. *Baxendale*,[1] and is reproduced in s. 50 (2) (which has its counterpart in s. 51 (2) in the case of non-delivery by the seller):

> "The measure of damages is the estimated loss directly and naturally resulting, in the ordinary course of events, from the buyer's breach of contract."

The second branch is not specifically enacted although it is probably covered in general terms by s. 54.[2] However, as in the case of non-delivery, so with non-acceptance, there is a special rule for the measure of damages where there is an available market. By s. 50 (3):

> "Where there is an available market for the goods in question the measure of damages is *prima facie* to be ascertained by the difference between the contract price and the market or current price at the time or times when the goods ought to have been accepted, or, if no time was fixed for acceptance, then at the time of the refusal to accept."

i What is an available market?

Although the existence of an available market is a feature of s. 51 as well as of s. 50, it is in relation to s. 51 that most of the discussion has taken place on what is meant by the expression. Some definition is clearly necessary because it is only when such a market exists that sub-s. (3) takes precedence over sub-s. (2). However, it must be admitted that, of the various attempts made, none seems altogether satisfactory.

In the first place, it is stating the obvious to point out that the "market" in question does not have to be any defined place,[3] although it must be an area that is accessible to the seller. This would not be a question of physical accessibility[4] but rather accessibility in terms of the area within which the seller normally operates. A definition (or rather an "interpretation") that has received a degree of academic approval[5] was the following dictum of UPJOHN, J., in *W. L. Thompson, Ltd.* v. *Robinson (Gunmakers), Ltd.*:[6]

---

1 (1854), 9 Exch. 341.
2 See above, p. 273.
3 "A market for this purpose means more than a particular place. It means also a particular level of trade", *per* DEVLIN, J., in *Heskell* v. *Continental Express, Ltd.*, [1950] 1 All E.R. 1033, at p. 1050; see also *per* BATESON, J., in *The Arpad*, [1934] P. 189, at p. 191; and in *A.B.D. (Metals and Waste), Ltd.* v. *Anglo Chemical and Ore Co., Ltd.*, [1955] 2 Lloyd's Rep. 456, at p. 466, SELLERS, J., said: "It is not necessary to establish a market that it should have a fixed place or building, but that there must be sufficient traders who are in touch with each other to evidence a market."
4 One would seldom, if ever, in the United Kingdom be faced with the situation that arose in the Australian case of *Francis* v. *Lyon* (1907), 4 C.L.R. 1023, in which GRIFFITH, C.J., pointed out, at p. 1036, that, when a flock of sheep is to be delivered to a particular spot in the vast pastoral districts of Western Queensland, it must often happen that the conditions giving rise to an available market simply do not exist.
5 Notably by Atiyah, *op. cit.*, pp. 267–8: Fridman, *Sale of Goods*, p. 292; and Sutton, *op. cit.*, p. 337, are more cautious.
6 [1955] Ch. 177, at p. 187; [1955] 1 All E.R. 154, at pp. 159–60. The curious aspect of this dictum is that UPJOHN, J., was in fact saying that, if he had been free to do so, he would have adopted such a definition, but felt himself precluded from doing so by the Court of Appeal decision in *Dunkirk Colliery Co.* v. *Lever* (1878), 9 Ch.D. 20, at p. 25, in which JAMES, L.J., seemed to limit an available market to "somewhere else" where the sellers could dispose of the goods, just as "they sell corn on he Exchange, or cotton at Liverpool: that is to say, that there was a fair market where they could have found a purchaser". However, this pronouncement was clearly obiter and, in its turn, is open to criticism: see *Charter* v. *Sullivan*, [1957] 2 Q.B. 117, at pp. 128, 133–4.

"An 'available market' merely means that the situation in the particular trade in the particular area was such that the particular goods could freely be sold, and that there was a demand sufficient to absorb readily all the goods that were thrust on it so that if a purchaser defaulted the goods in question could readily be disposed of."

Before commenting on this statement, it must be considered in the context of the facts with which UPJOHN, J., was dealing. B, the defendant company, had agreed to buy a Vanguard motor car from S, the plaintiff dealers, but later refused to accept delivery. B argued that the damages should only be nominal on the ground that there was no difference between the market price and the contract price. This argument was rejected on a number of alternative grounds. In the first place, if one adopted a narrow definition of available market to restrict it to recognised trading places for the goods in question, there was no such market at all for new motor vehicles. Secondly, if UPJOHN, J.'s own definition was employed, it was clear that there was not sufficient demand to absorb all the new cars that were coming onto the market (a position in sharp contrast to that prevailing in the immediate post-war years). But, finally, s. 50 (3) was only a *prima facie* rule that could be dispensed with if, in the circumstances, it appeared unjust to apply it. Whichever way one approached this case, it was "plain beyond argument" that S was entitled to his loss of profit on the transaction: he had sold one less car than he would have done had B completed the purchase.

This case may be contrasted with *Charter* v. *Sullivan*[1] in which B refused to accept a new Hillman Minx motor car which S, the plaintiff dealer, obtained for him. On the evidence it was shown that demand for this particular model exceeded supply so that S could sell every such vehicle he could obtain. The Court of Appeal had no hesitation in holding that S was entitled only to nominal damages as he had suffered no loss. But was s. 50 (3) relevant to this decision? JENKINS, L.J., was emphatically of the opinion that it was not:[2]

"Section 50 (3) seems to me to postulate a market in which there is a market or current price, i.e. a price fixed by supply and demand at which (be it more or less than the contract price) a purchaser can be found. If the only price at which a car can be sold is the fixed retail price and no purchaser can be found at that price, I do not think it can reasonably be said that there is a market or current price or that there is an available market. If the state of the trade were such that the plaintiff could sell at the fixed retail price all the cars he could get, so that the defendant's default did not result in the plaintiff effecting one less sale than he would otherwise have effected, it may well be that the plaintiff could not make out his claim to anything more than nominal damages. I am, however, inclined to think that this would not be on account of the necessary equality of the contract price and the fixed retail price at which alone the car could be sold, ... but because on an application of the general principle laid down by s. 50 (2) the plaintiff would be found to have suffered no damage."

---

1 [1957] 2 Q.B. 117; [1957] 1 All E.R. 809.
2 [1957] 2 Q.B. 117, at pp. 125–6.

As far as the definition advanced by UPJOHN, J., was concerned, his Lordship did not find it "entirely satisfactory" although he did not attempt to improve on it, contenting himself with reiterating the point that s. 50 (3) depended upon the possibility of differences existing between the contract price and the market or current price, a possibility excluded by the existence of a fixed retail price.[1]

Indeed, if one looks at the approach of UPJOHN, J., it can reasonably be said that he was dealing with only one aspect of the concept of an "available market". In other words, what he was saying was that, had not JAMES, L.J., in *Dunkirk Colliery Co.* v. *Lever*[2] imposed such a narrow definition, he would have preferred a wider interpretation of the expression taken in isolation. Thus viewed, the market must enable the seller to dispose of the goods freely. However, one should not look at the expression without reference to the role it is clearly designed to play in s. 50. The market is intended to give rise to a "market or current price", a possibility which is excluded by a fixed price. The existence of such a price rules out the normal play of market forces.[3] Hence, as JENKINS, L.J., pointed out, there is no available market in terms of s. 50 (3) in such circumstances.[4]

ii Where goods are made to order

There is likely to be no available market in goods specifically made to order· If the buyer refuses to accept such goods, the seller is entitled as damages to the cost incurred in making them (if work has already been carried out) and the loss of profit on the transaction. If the goods can by alteration be made saleable in the general market, the seller may be required to do that in accordance with his duty to mitigate damages.

In *Re Vic Mill*,[5] S, a creditor of B, a company in liquidation, had completed a special order of machinery for B. S had expended money in altering the machinery so that he was able to sell it at very little less than the contract price. The district registrar had allowed only the difference between the contract price and the "market price", to which was added the cost of the alterations. NEVILLE, J., and the Court of Appeal held, however, that S was clearly entitled to his loss of profit on the transaction. It was acknowledged on all sides that there was no available market in the goods as they had been made. S was "entitled to recover the damages directly and naturally resulting in the ordinary

---

1 [1957] 2 Q.B. 117, at p. 128.
2 (1878), 9 Ch.D. 20, at p. 25, see above, n. 85.
3 "The rule . . . contemplates a continuous market for a commodity, but always subject to fluctuation according to the rise and fall of the market resulting from the demand of buyers and sellers", *per* MANN, C.J., in *Eclipse Motors* v. *Nixon*, [1940] V.L.R. 49, at p. 54. With the gradual disappearance of resale price maintenance there is of course more room for an "available market" to operate.
4 One aspect of the idea of an available market that has not been considered in any depth is whether the test should be applied in a situation where there is such a glut of goods that the consignment in question would have to be virtually given away. The problem is bound up with the time at which the damages should be assessed. A seller is not normally expected to hold on to the goods until the market improves: see *Campbell Mostyn (Provisions), Ltd.* v. *Barnett Trading Co.*, [1953] 1 Lloyd's Rep. 268, discussed below, p. 321; and see *Dominion Motors, Ltd.* v. *Grieves*, [1936] N.Z.L.R. 766, at p. 771.
5 [1913] Ch. 183, 465.

course of events from the buyer's breach of contract". If the machinery had been sold off as it was or for scrap, the loss would have been far greater. When a new customer made an order for similar machinery, S adopted a reasonable mode of mitigating the damages by making the alterations necessary to convert the machinery made to B's order to make it suitable for the new customer; "but it by no means follows that the damages are confined to the cost, a trivial one, of adapting the machines to the needs of the second customer, and the loss on resale to him . . . The fallacy of that is in supposing that the second customer was a substituted customer and that, had all gone well, the makers would not have had both customers, both orders, and both profits".[1]

iii Time for applying the market price test

If there is an available market, then the time for estimating the difference between the contract price and the market price is the date when the goods should have been accepted. Hence, if the market price is lower than the contract price on that day, the seller is entitled to the difference in damages even though he retains the goods and sells them later at a higher price.

In *Campbell Mostyn (Provisions), Ltd.* v. *Barnett Trading Co.*,[2] S had agreed to sell 500 tons of South African ham to B, the goods to be shipped in instalments. After taking delivery of the first 150 cases, B refused to accept the remaining 350. Negotiations ensued, but on October 24, 1951, S. wrote informing B that he regarded B as in breach of the contract. On that date the market for tinned ham was depressed on account of over-buying earlier in the year. However, soon afterwards the new Conservative government announced controls on imports from the continent and the price of the South African ham rose. Thus, in the second week of November, S was able to resell at a price above the market price on October 24. It was nevertheless held that the damages were to be assessed with reference to the value of the goods on October 24, when S's "loss" was substantial. The Court of Appeal accepted the following statement by Lord WRENBURY giving the advice of the Judicial Committee in *Jamal* v. *Moolla Dawood, Sons & Co.*[3] as applicable equally to sales of goods:

> "If the seller retains the shares after the breach, the speculation as to the way the market will subsequently go is the speculation of the seller, not of the buyer; the seller cannot recover from the buyer the loss below the market price at the date of the breach if the market falls, nor is he liable to the purchaser for the profit if the market rises."

While it may not be much consolation to the buyer whose seller has later resold at a profit to know that he would not have been liable for additional damages had the market continued to fall, it is necessary to keep in mind the fact that the seller's predicament is caused by the buyer's default and that all too often that default will have occurred because the price of such goods had fallen well below the original contract price.

---

1 At p. 473, *per* HAMILTON, L.J. Cf. *Hill & Sons* v. *Edwin Showell & Sons* (1918), 87 L.J.K.B. 1106.
2 [1953] 1 Lloyd's Rep. 268.
3 [1916] 1 A.C. 175, at p. 179.

iv Where there is an anticipatory breach

As will be recalled from the earlier discussion of anticipatory breach,[1] the time for the assessment of damages in relation to the market price depends upon when the other party (in the present context it will be the seller) decides to accept the repudiation. Until he does so the contract remains open, and the buyer can still accept the goods when the goods are tendered.[2]

Whether the repudiation is accepted or not is also decisive in considering the seller's obligation to mitigate damages. As long as there is no acceptance of the repudiation and the contract is thus still in force, the seller owes no duty to mitigate. In *Tredegar Iron and Coal Co., Ltd.* v. *Hawthorn Bros. & Co.*,[3] B had agreed to buy a quantity of coal at 16s. per ton for delivery f.o.b. during February. The ship upon which B intended to ship the coal broke down. B wrote to S informing him that he (B) would no longer require the coal, but B included with his letter a written offer from a third party for the coal at 16s. 3d. per ton. S, however, continued to insist that the contract be performed. When B failed to take delivery by the end of February, S sold the coal at the lower price of 15s. per ton early in March. The Court of Appeal had no doubt that S was entitled to keep the contract open despite the alternative offer that B had procured.[4] The repudiation was of no effect until it was accepted, and until that time no duty to mitigate could arise. S was therefore entitled to recover as damages the 1s. per ton he had lost against the original contract price.

If there is an acceptance of the repudiation, the loss is still *prima facie* the difference between the contract price and the market price at the date when the goods should be accepted, but the seller is under a duty to mitigate his loss as soon as the repudiation is accepted. In *Roth & Co.* v. *Taysen, Townsend & Co.*,[5] B had agreed to purchase a cargo of maize shipped by S from Argentina to the United Kingdom. B repudiated the contract on May 28. If S had resold then the loss would have been £680. On July 24 S commenced the present action. The market for maize was falling and if he had sold on this date his loss would have been £1,557. S sold eventually on September 5 at a loss of £3,870. It was held by the Court of Appeal that, although the measure of damages was *prima facie* the difference between the contract price and the market price at the date when the contract should have been performed, a seller could not, once he had accepted the repudiation, allow the extent of his losses to be increased by a falling market.[6] By commencing proceedings on July 24 S had accepted the

---

1 Above, p. 279.
2 For an authoritative statement of the law, see the principal judgment in *Frost* v. *Knight* (1872), L.R. 7 Exch. 111, at pp. 112–3.
3 (1902), 18 T.L.R. 716.
4 In his contract with S, B had promised to export the coal. The offer from the third party involved its resale in this country, so B could not buy himself and then resell.
5 (1895), 73 L.T. 628.
6 Unless S can show a good reason for not doing so, e.g. if he were trying to negotiate a settlement, which is presumably why the critical date in *Campbell Mostyn (Provisions), Ltd.* v. *Barnett Trading Co.*, [1953] 1 Lloyd's Rep. 268, was much later than the actual delivery dates: see *Burns Philp & Co.* v. *Louis Phillips & Co.* (1913), 13 S.R. (N.S.W.) 461.

repudiation and he was only entitled to recover the loss that he would have incurred if he had sold on that date.

This sharp distinction between the situation where the repudiation is accepted and where it is not gave rise to some injustice in the *Tredegar Iron and Coal Co., Ltd.* case. However, taken to its logical conclusion the doctrine of anticipatory breach can have even more unsatisfactory consequences. In *White and Carter (Councils), Ltd.* v. *McGregor*,[1] X supplied local authorities with litter bins in return for the right to place advertisements on bins. X agreed to advertise Y's business in this way for a period of three years. Y repudiated this arrange-ent later on the same day that it had been made. X nevertheless went ahead, placed the advertisements and, at the end of the period, sued for the sum due under the contract. The House of Lords held that X's claim was entitled to succeed. Potentially this decision is of the widest application, but it seems that it must at least be limited to a situation where the contract provides for a specific sum in return for performance. This principle is not normally applicable to sales of goods where the passing of property, which is usually necessary before the price can be recovered, will require the acceptance of the goods by the buyer.[2] However, as the seller's remedy in damages in such a situation is based upon the situation that exists when the goods should be accepted, there is nothing to prevent the seller refusing to accept the repudiation and continuing to manu-facture the goods in question. Even if the seller cannot sue for the price he is able to recover the difference between the contract price and the price he can eventually get for the goods he makes or obtains quite unhampered by any duty to mitigate.

v The extent of the obligation to mitigate

There is a somewhat hazy borderline between what steps the seller (or buyer) should take to mitigate his losses. It is clear, for example, that he should make alterations to machinery to suit an alternative customer after the original buyer has defaulted,[3] though until such a purchaser comes along he might not be expected to make alterations in the hope of making equipment more saleable. In general the injured party "cannot be called upon to spend money to enable him to minimise the damages".[4] However this statement might have to be treated with caution as it was made in a case in which an investor, induced by fraud to advance money to a company on a debenture, lost a substantial amount of that loan. It was held that he was entitled to recover the full amount of his loss and did not have to account for a profit he subsequently made in buying from the receiver, and then reselling, the assets of the company. A more convincing basis for the decision would appear to be that the subsequent purchase of the company's assets was unrelated, for the purchase of assessing, or mitigating, damages, to the loss the investor had suffered.

In the same way the seller's (or buyer's) decision to stay out of the market for a

---

1 [1962] A.C. 413; [1961] 3 All E.R. 1178.
2 [1962] A.C., at p. 437; [1961] 3 All E.R., at p. 1187, *per* Lord KEITH.
3 *Re Vic Mill, Ltd.* [1913] 1 Ch. 465.
4 *Per* LEWIS, J., in *Jewelowski* v. *Propp*, [1944] 1 K.B. 510, at p. 511.

period after the date for acceptance (or delivery) is *res inter alios acta* if he thereby makes a profit. However, if the subsequent dealing is not an independent or disconnected transaction, that transaction must be taken into account when assessing damages. In *R. Pagnan and Fratelli* v. *Corbisa Industrial Agropacuaria Limitada*,[1] the Court of Appeal held that where, after a buyer had validly rejected goods, he bought the same goods from the seller at a reduced price and as part of a continuous dealing between the parties, account must be taken of the buyer's profit on the subsequent transaction in assessing the damages for breach of the original contract. However, it would seem that this decision is based upon the notion[2] that mitigation occurs when the plaintiff takes some prudent act which has the effect of diminishing his loss even though it is not an act which he was bound to take. It does not follow that it extends the ambit of activities that the seller (or buyer) is *obliged* to take.

vi Antecedent contracts

The expression "antecedent" contract is not a term of art, nor has it any temporal significance, but it is employed to cover a contract by which the seller hopes to procure the goods he is to deliver to the buyer. If the buyer defaults, the seller is still bound by the contract with his supplier. If there is an available market then he is under an obligation to receive the goods and to resell them in order to establish the damages by reference to the difference between the market price and the contract price agreed with his defaulting buyer.[3] If there is no available market, then the best that the seller can do may be to reach some accommodation with his own supplier and recover the additional expense from the buyer under s. 50 (2).[4]

But what is the position where the seller has not yet entered into an antecedent contract to obtain the goods with which to supply the buyer when the buyer repudiates? In the New Zealand case of *Pacific Overseas Corporation, Ltd.* v. *Watkins Browne & Co. (N.Z.), Ltd.*,[5] S had contracted to provide B with plaster casting f.o.b. Melbourne at £10 5s. per ton, but B repudiated before S had finalised arrangements to obtain the order. S established that, under these arrangements, he would have obtained the plaster at a cost to him of £7 15s. f.o.b. Melbourne. He therefore claimed the £2 10s. difference per ton as the basis upon which his damages were to be assessed. If S had in fact ordered the plaster, he clearly would not have been entitled to loss of profit. If there had been an available market, he would have been limited to the difference between the market price and the contract price at the time the goods should have been

---

1 [1971] 1 All E.R. 165; [1970] 1 W.L.R. 1306.
2 Advanced by Viscount HALDANE, L.C., in *British Westinghouse Electric and Manufacturing Co., Ltd.* v. *Underground Electric Rail. Co. of London, Ltd.*, [1912] A.C. 673, at pp. 689–92; [1911–13] All E.R. Rep. 63, at pp. 69–71.
3 Though if *both* transactions are dependent upon the buyer providing a confirmed letter of credit so that the seller is unable to obtain the goods from his supplier, the existence of an available market and a market price higher than the contract price is irrelevant because the seller cannot obtain delivery of the goods: *Trans Trust S.P.R.L.* v. *Danubian Trading Co., Ltd.*, [1952] 2 Q.B. 297; [1952] 1 All E.R. 970.
4 *Whitaker, Ltd.* v. *Bowater, Ltd.* (1918), 35 T.L.R. 114.
5 [1954] N.Z.L.R. 459.

accepted. The court adopted the same approach in the present situation. It had not been shown that there was no available market, and the goods in question were a normal marketable commodity. Hence it was S's duty to minimise his losses by seeking an alternative market for the plaster, and, once a buyer had been found, to take up the quantity that was available to him in Australia. On this basis, the amount of damages was limited to 10s. per ton.

The main doubt to which this case gives rise is whether a seller can be expected to enter into a contract to obtain goods once his buyer has defaulted. If he does so, his profit can be taken into account under the principle laid down in the *British Westinghouse* case,[1] but he should not be expected to go to substantial expense to relieve the buyer of some of the losses that would otherwise arise. The justification for the decision lies in s. 50 (3) which contains a "built-in" rule for the mitigation of the seller's loss. Although it was presumably designed to cover the situation in which the seller actually had the goods in his possession, there is no reason why it should be so limited. However, what the decision fails to take into account is that, where the seller has not yet agreed to obtain the goods in question, there *should* be an additional burden[2] placed upon the buyer to show that the alternative market was so readily available that a prudent businessman would have gone ahead with the purchase of the plaster.

---

1 See above, p. 324, n. 2.
2 The court, rather unsatisfactorily, took the view that the seller had not obtained an alternative market for the plaster because, not being under any obligation to take it from his supplier, there was no pressure on him to find a buyer. As the text points out, however, it should be for the buyer to establish the reasonableness of the course of conduct by showing how readily the plaster could have been resold.

Index